The Last Generation

From Lost to Greatest Again

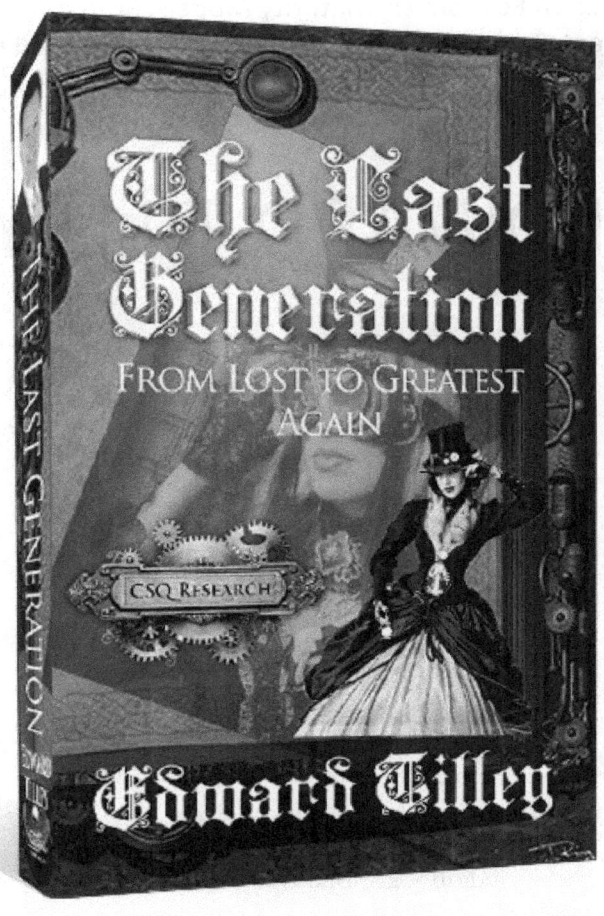

From the Author who wrote the book on Common Sense, Transition Economics, Maturity Models, SUSTAIN Project Management, Teaching Doers, Modern Love and World Peace - The Transition.

EDWARD TILLEY

Copyright © 2017

All rights reserved.

Hardcover ISBN: 978-1-987964-21-9

Book ISBN: 1-987964-20-2

Book ISBN-13: 978-1-987964-20-2

eBook ISBN: 978-1-987964-22-6

AudioBook ISBN: 978-1-987964-23-3

To the Humanity of Parents

CONTENTS

Chapter 1 - The Last Generation 1
    Freedom 10
    Learning from Smaller Economies 17
    Firing on all Cylinders 19
      Transition Economics Automation 23
    The Squeaky Wheel 24

Chapter 2 - Cycles and Phases in Capitalism 27
    Policies Change with each Cycle 30
    Boiled Frogs 37

Chapter 3 – Spring & Summer Phase 41
    Policies in the Spring Phase 42
    Policies in the Summer Phase 43

Chapter 4 – Autumn Phase 45
    Policies in the Autumn Phase 46

Chapter 5 – Winter Phase 49
    Policies in the Winter Phase 58

Chapter 6 - Democracy that Builds Inequity 59

Chapter 7 - Social Collapse 69
    Resetting Collapse Trending Economies is Critical 69
    What does Social Collapse look like? 70
    Correcting Social Collapse 71

- Inequity Increases 75
- Incomes become Scarce 76
- Housing becomes Scarce 77
- Social Problems Increase 77
- Transition Economics Tracker Version 1.0 78
  - Investment in Renewable Automation 79
- Winning Battles and Losing Wars via Policy 80

Chapter 8 – Restarting the Cycle 85

- Transition Economics Problem Solving 85
  - Increases to Interest Rates in Winter Phase: 86
- Stimulus that Builds Equality 87
- Trickle-Down Failures to Households 88
- Trickle-down Failures to Businesses 89
- Small, Mid, and Large-Sized Business Mix 90
- Restarting the Next Economic Cycle 93
  - Logic Roundabouts 93
  - Direct Logic 96
- Inflation versus Markets - Bubblenomics 99
- An End to Usury 103
- What to Correct First, Second, Third… 104
- What is not on the High Priority List 107
- Freedom 109
- The Case for Distributing Wealth Quickly 110

Chapter 9 - Transition Economics Maturity Model 113
Mature vs Immature 114
TE-Maturity and Calculus 115
Economic Trending 117
Collapsing 117
Advancing 117
TE Maturity Math 118
Level 1 – Immature 120
Level 2 – Right Plan 120
Level 3 – Sustain 126
Level 4 – Mature 128
Level 5 – Global Transition 128
TE Maturity List by Country 129
Data Quality 133

Chapter 10 - Automation as a Renewable Resource 135
The Cancer Research Problem 137
Can we really automate everything? 139
What do Sustainability Robots look like? 140
The Necessity of Planning 143
The Engineering Safety Net 144
Algorithms in Rate of Automation Transition 147

Chapter 11 - Guaranteed Incomes 151
Guaranteed Incomes 151

Chapter 12 - Sustaining Equality creates Wealth 157
    Wealth Creation 158
    Wealth Distribution 159
        Patterns in Income Inequality 166
    Setting Targets – Living Wage & Graduated Tax 167
        Wealth 167
        Income 168
        The Lowest Quintile (20%) 168
        Next Lowest Quintile 169
        Middle Quintile 169
        Second Highest Quintile 169
        The Highest Quintile 170
        Wage Stagnation 170
        Minimum Wage 170
        Graduated Tax 171

Chapter 13 - Universal Healthcare, Benefits & Pensions 173
    Pensions 173
    Benefits 176
    Managing Pension Plan Sustainability Risk 177
    Mitigating the loss of Employer Pension Plans 177
    Mini-retirements 178
    Universal Healthcare 181

Chapter 14 - Housing Policy Cycle Controls 185

Economic Controls for Housing Bubbles 186

Housing Bubbles vs Good Lives 191

How to Correct and Reverse Bubbles 191

    Eviction 192

    Anti-Eviction and Suicide 193

    Leadership in Interest Rate Increases 195

Governing the Housing Market 197

Housing Controls Summary 198

Home Ownership & Mortgages 201

Government Land Ownership 202

Can we switch back and forth? 202

Housing Changes from K-Wave Spring to Winter 205

Understanding lending costs 207

What sort of home would I get? 209

What is the right place for you to live? 210

Automation in Housing 212

Housing KPIs (Performance Measures) 215

Chapter 15 - Immigration & Refugee Policy 217

    Refugees 219

    Immigration 224

        Population Increase and Fertility Rates 229

        Gender Equality 230

        Improving Fertility Rates by providing a Good Life 231

  Immigration for Humanitarian Reasons 232

  Immigration for Skilled Labor 232

  Immigration for Unskilled Labor 232

 Protecting Culture 233

Chapter 16 - Energy Policy 235

 CO² is the Foundation of Life on Earth 236

  New Energy Poverty and Legal Recourses 237

 Full-Time Power Generation 238

  Geo-Thermal Electricity 239

  Hydro Electric 244

 Nuclear Fission - Thorium Reactors 244

  Fusion - Cold and Hot 247

  Combustion 249

  Incineration and Plasma – Energy from Waste 250

  Solar Thermal Tower 251

  Nuclear Fission - Rapid Breeder Uranium 253

  ThermoElectric 254

 Part-time Energy Production 255

  Solar Energy Cells 255

  Wind Power 255

  Wave Power 256

 Energy Conversion 256

  Steam Turbine 256

  Gas Turbines 257

Engines - on Earth and in Space 257

Energy Collectors 259

    Rapid Charge Battery Systems 259

    Flywheel Kinetic Energy Management Systems 261

    Super Capacitors and Ultra Capacitors 261

    Nuclear Diamond Batteries 262

Fuels 263

    Clean Fuel & 100-MPG Diesel-Hybrids 264

    Diesel is Very Important 267

    Defending Diesel Vehicles is Very Important Too 268

    Hydrogen Fuels & Vehicles 269

    Fossil Fuel is not needed 269

    Avoid Alcohol Fuels that dissolve in water 269

Pipelines versus producing fuels locally 270

    Alternatives to Pipelines 270

    PROs and CONs of Oil Pipelines 271

    Rail vs Pipeline, the Environment, and Safety 272

    Moving Natural Gas 273

    Fuels Summary 273

Chapter 17 - Reshoring Production & Engineering 275

Chapter 18 - Business, GDP & Taxation 279

    Transition Economics Throttles 279

    GDP Quality 281

    GDP Export 282

Tax Revenue & Tax Increases 283

Tax Laws and Tax Avoidance 284

Chapter 19 - CSR & Sustainable Business 289

Reconciling CSR and Sustainability Metrics 290

Government Controls 291

Good Process Never Takes Longer 292

Revisit Law and Policy Regularly 293

Designing Accountability 294

Business Accountability 295

Corruption 297

    Mitigating Multinational Business Extortion 297

Transition Economic for Business 298

Chapter 20 – Government Thought-Leadership 299

Government must lead Technology 299

Fund Automation in a Focused and Planned Way 300

Citizens want their country to be a World Leader. 302

Build an Engineering Safety Net 303

Engineers must Lead 304

Life's messy, Clean it up 305

Chapter 21 - Democratic Reform 307

Separating Wheat from Chaff 310

The Pitfalls of Managing Proactively 314

Economic Controls - Right and Left 316

- Policy Creation and Policy Committee Reform 317
- Left & Right Must Support Important Policy 319

Chapter 22 - Cost of Divorce in Society 323

Chapter 23 - Failing to Restart a Cycle 329

Chapter 24 - Responsible Transition 335
- TE Throttles and Throttle Rates 337

Chapter 25 - Business Cases 339
- The Transition Economics Business Case 340
- What to look for in a Business Case 340
  - Begin with a Dashboard Summary View 341
  - Inputs 343
  - Outputs 343
- Approvals to Proceed 346
- Contribution, Acknowledgments and Recognition 346
- SUSTAIN Project Management Method 347

Chapter 26 – Voting Better 349
- Think like a Founding Father 356
- The Mayflower Compact 358
- The Importance of Education in Democracy 359
- Voter Comparison Charts 363

Chapter 27 – The #WPProjects Global Right Plan 365
- The Three Teams are: 368
- The Four Steps are: 370

Step 1 & 2 – Social and Technology Projects 370

Each Country is assigned a #WPProject 370

    Automating Production Economies 373

    Step 3 – Manage the Transition 374

The "Worldville" Competitions 377

Science Fiction is just a Technology Project 378

Team Two – Automating our Production Economy 381

Adding World Peace Agenda Projects 381

Building Great Technology 383

The WPProjects List v1.0 384

Chapter 28 – Terror, Race, Gender, Religion or Empathy 395

The Business Case for Empathy 395

Conclusions 399

Lack of Empathy in History 401

Chapter 29 - Values and Sustainability 403

The Golden Rule 403

The Definition of Evil 404

CSR – Corporate Social Responsibility 405

Sustainability Planning 406

Inequity versus Diversity 406

Merit & Reward 407

Revere Thought Leadership 407

Thought Leadership 409

- Individual Contributors 409
- Expert Panels: 411
- For Business, Government and Academia 412
- Freedom 416
- Values 417
- Human Rights 420
  - Respect for Life 421
  - Respect for Equality 422
  - Women's Rights 423
  - Children's Rights 423
  - Respect for Family 423
  - Right to Healthcare 424
  - Free Speech 424
- An End to Terror 425
- Freedom from Fear vs Global Crises in News 426
  - A Global Energy Crisis 427
  - A Global Water Crisis 427
  - Voicing Frustrations versus Solutions 427
- Populism is Revolution 429
- Which Governments manage which Policy? 432

Chapter 30 – Case Studies 435
- Case 1: Albert Einstein 435
- Case 2: A Letter to Country Leads and Innovation Ministers 437
- Case 3: A Letter to your Senator 438

Case 6: Party Policy Reform Letter 444

Chapter 31 - Summary 449

    The Transition Engineering Safety Net 452

    Rollout Worldwide 452

ABOUT THE AUTHOR 455

Bibliography 459

Index 468

ACKNOWLEDGMENTS

Writing prodigious books about worthwhile subjects began as a parenting exercise for me. This is my sixth book and I have researched and learned a lot in the process of writing each one. The Last Generation explains how our society is failing our latest generation – and how we can turn it around.

The more that I researched why were my five kids coming out into over-competitive times, the more that I came to learn that our societies are the natural result of unsustainable policy and laws. Our laws – many from the 1950s and 1960s - were well-intentioned and encouraged freedoms and opportunity successfully when inequity was low, but they also permitted housing bubbles, high-unemployment, a new energy poverty and other scarcities that took away opportunity as inequity grew over time.

Policies that restricted higher education, left society with fewer worthwhile jobs while pensions, incomes and benefits were vanishing or unattainable for a new generation just starting out.

I grew up in Canada, a society that supported freedoms, human rights, Most young people emerging from high school today are not able to start worthwhile lives with homes, families of their own, cars, travel, and higher education right away.

At the same time, 72% of economies globally are trending toward collapse. We had a Good Life, an American Dream, in North America and in many G20 countries; and now most of our nations have lost it.

Manual Economies are Automating – and this is a very good thing, but our governments are not ready with new minimum income policy and planning needed to transition citizens safely to exciting and productive lives that are afforded by that automation.

Failing to support families in economic change causes social collapse that is the underpinning of revolutions and world wars. We live in a mature nuclear era; a world in which world wars are deterred by the threat of global annihilation - so these policy failings are socially irresponsible, even reckless - and they are entirely the doing of us parents.

Our kids didn't build this; rather, their parents did not manage normal growing inequity with civics classes and new policy as we should have. We did not permit "peaceful revolution" as JFK put it.

In this book, we are going to discuss how to reset our societies - with new incomes, new spending-power, and proven sustainable thinking that supports incredible new global tools and freedoms that are supported by our engineers and renewable automations.

We are going to discuss how to make revolution peacefully, insistently, and unlike other revolutions the results of this change will amount to a proper long term plan for a sustainable society that is worth being a part of, and one worth handing down to our children.

Finding a way through complex problems in society can be frustrating, but there can be no more worthwhile goal either.

Chapter 1

-

The Last Generation

Societies throughout time share much in common. In most communities, citizens have the opportunity to live peacefully and comfortably for a period of time - and then inequity and competition take away that opportunity over many years.

Today, rich people earn three million dollars per day. Some, have been earning at that rate for thirty years – and so the second or third job of a poorer person is never going to compensate for quickly widening wealth gaps in society. This is inequity and it is perfectly normal within a Capitalist Cycle.

Inequity is low at the start of an economic cycle and then it becomes high as a natural product of normal successful Capitalism. Big companies consume little companies, profits must grow at increasing rates year after year, and competition for resources and labor creates scarcities, militias and conflicts historically.

Technology has accelerated annual productivity and growth for thousands of years but it leapt forward quickly at the start of the Industrial Era in the early 1900s and it really improved dramatically in the 20th century with the invention and availability of energy, motors, and then tractors and other farming and manufacturing equipment.

In civilization's 4000-year historical record of Capitalist Societies, back to Babylon, Egypt, and I suspect within Bronze Age Britain and Cypress back in 3500 BC as well, economic controls have successfully managed recurring economic and social ups and downs many times.

When the gap between rich and poor is not controlled; when the gap becomes so great that poor people cannot start families nor have meaningful lives, historically – two things happen. Either new Policies; new economic controls, are added into law which permit resource and wealth distribution - or if this is not permitted, a violent revolution or war erupts that restores opportunity.

With renewed opportunity, equality, and incomes, the economic cycle restarts and a boom is enjoyed by all - for a while.

This is the history of our capitalist civilizations in a nutshell; these cycles of opportunity and then inequity, repeat one after in historical record country by country.

But, what if, we could choose a system of controls that sustained incomes, maintained wealth distributions and spending power? What if we could ensure that we monetized our economies at the same time so that the wealth of our country grew too? Then, in theory, there would be rich and poor - but that would be alright because all would have the things they needed including the opportunity to move from one income-level to another based on merit.

I think most agree this is an ideal situation. But it is also a fictitious example, yes? Surely such a state does not now, nor has ever existed?

But, if you think this is true, you are mistaken. I think that it is healthy, for each country to consider themselves "the best"; for each country to cherish their important peaceful culture and history. It is absolutely fool-heart however, to not sit back and never observe the results of your policies as they affect inequity within your country.

You never want to take pride in a policy that is wrong for your present economic cycle timing and is causing pain and suffering today.

There are 180 to 200 countries in the world that track and publish their policies and their GDP statistics online today. Wikipedia and others consolidate this information and make it very easy to find and to view online.

If you look at the economic statistics, the numbers say that some managed capitalism's natural inequality cycle better than others.

You might be surprised to hear that fully 10% of these 180 countries – the ones that adhere to "TE-Mature" Policies - are actually living the American Dream still. Why is this an important thing to measure?

The American Dream was the 1950s term that we used to describe

Aristotle's much earlier definition of a Good Life within a sustainable society. Many of our families here in North America lost the American Dream back in the 1980s and 1990s.

We are going to discuss these 10% (20 to 30) TE-Mature countries quite a bit here in the book because within this group, only around 5% have economies in a "Collapse Trending" today. 5% is not 0%, but it is fourteen-times smaller than the 72% collapse rate that is the norm for all countries measured.

If we remove these American Dream countries from the list, the countries remaining have an 80% chance of being in a Collapse Trending simply because they still employ the same policies that made America great in the 1950s – back when inequity was low.

Housing Policies from the 1950s included owning your own home and almost everyone could. Living Wage Jobs with Pensions and healthcare benefits could be found too, so Interest Rates and Unemployment Policies that "Did nothing" worked well to inspire people to get off their couches and get a job that paid for all of the basics that were needed.

Fast forward sixty years and those jobs, pensions, homes, and benefits are not attainable for a great percentage of the labor force today – but our Policies have not changed with the changes in inequity.

Jobs of insufficient quality that provide incomes of insufficient quantity, alongside Government Safety Nets that don't include healthcare nor incomes sufficient to live a Good Life, equals a society with fewer freedoms and opportunities where family-friendly communities are not available to everyone any longer.

I will discuss run-away Corporate Social Responsibility and Business School Ethics problems and solutions here in the book below.

What has inequity changed that makes 1950 Policy so ineffective? Why have these exact same policies that worked so well, no longer able to sustain a healthy society for all?

Inequity, I have mentioned, is a big problem but education is the cause of it. We never taught our kids about Civics in other nations - nor Democratic Change and Reform.

Sure we taught them about our 1950s Civics, our policies, our democracy, but only by the definitions that we used then and today. Our society was perfect as it was and it worked so well that we taught our students that other systems were not as good.

Worse, we talked about our own neighbors like they were traitors when they wanted to learn about or discuss alternate systems.

Systems like Communist Housing Land Grants, like socialistic healthcare, daycare, and care for the elderly.

McCarthyism in the 1950s vilified those who observed that there were merits to a communist system that made homelessness illegal, provided homes and degreed education to everyone, and made healthcare available to everyone as well. These "traitorous" thinkers were labelled communist sympathizers, un-American, a liberal, or whatever other deprecating absolute that their mob mentality could muster.

Suddenly, being smart, educated and curious was a bad thing. As if somehow freedom was not possible until everyone thought in the exact same way and all other investigations were criminal. As you read this note you might notice that I am actually describing the polar opposite of freedom. A little less obvious is this point: failing to provide the American Dream to all creates its own anarchy and undermines the value and values of democracy too.

In this book I am going to explain: that economies do have scientifically confirmed cycles; that those cycles need for our policies to transition/change at different times in the cycle; and that once we all understand how to responsibly change to and balance policies that are appropriate for the times, we can avoid wars and social hardships sustainably.

When we learn to change government policy in keeping with normal, changing inequity and opportunity imbalances in capitalistic societies, we put an end to a phenomenon that I call the Last Generation.

The Last Generation are young adults that arrive into their twenties unable to buy a home, nor a car; they cannot afford rents with their available wages, are unable to get into academic programs as they wish, unable to start families at a young age if they choose, and unable to pursue careers that are worthwhile or interesting to them.

Lost – as they begin adulthood with the short end of the stick by most reasonable measures of opportunity.

Last – because this is the Generation that creates positive Revolution. This is the generation that arrives into each economic cycle's end unable to make a life easily, until first we see social anxiety and social problems, and then desperation as scarcity continues and societies collapse, and then finally – large groups of people get angry.

At the point that death with a pitchfork in one's hand becomes a preferable alternative to death by starvation or freezing to death in the winter streets, you will have a full-blown revolution by this generation.

Those who make peaceful revolution impossible will make violent revolution inevitable.

John F. Kennedy, 1962

Approximately 80% of the time in historical record, remediation and policy changes ease this suffering and reset us to the next cycle peacefully – and 20% of cycles end in revolution or war.

This Last Generation is also the group that emerges from an Economic Reset to begin a new economic prosperity as well; so they are literally, the Last Lost Generation of a sixty-year Longwave Economics Cycle.

Today's "Last Generation" were born around 1995 and the previous group would have been the young adults of the mid-1930s – born around 1918. We call that group "The Greatest Generation" today because they took society through our last Reset – World War II – and on to economic success in a society filled with opportunity and equality.

We are living in a mature nuclear-weapons era today. Nuclear arsenals are designed to keep the peace – ironically; to deter us from self-annihilation through war – or to ensure our own end should we decide that war is a more desirable alternative to devising thoughtful, peaceful solutions to our problems.

So, is this latest Last Generation going to be the last of the Last Generations as well? They very well could be, but not because of nuclear holocaust; this could be the Last Lost Generation because of Education.

Transition Economics is a brand new science made possible within just the last few years by the incredible work of search companies like Google Research and Wikipedia lists. Never before has there been so much empirical research readily available in easy reach and this has led researchers who are handy with spreadsheets and A.I. to create some incredible discoveries within the data.

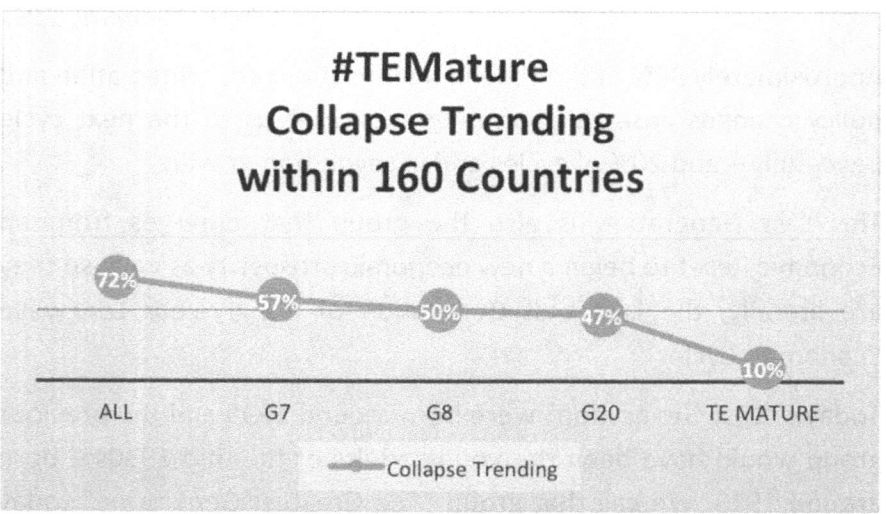

For instance, we can find which policies support an Advancing Economy most consistently by comparing policies country to country side-by-side. This is how TE-Mature Policy tables were created and we will discuss these more in the book.

This could be the last Last Generation because now we know which policies create a sustainable capitalism. By teaching these lessons within our high-school Civics courses, future democratic voters will be able to see through Special Interest sidetracks and emotional leadership pitches, to vote for policy that make cycles of boom and trough a history record only. See "CSQ Common Sense 101" at csq1.org for a High-School course in TE-Mature Policy learning.

The irony in today's housing bubbles, energy poverty, interest rate-driven homelessness, unsustainable monetary policies, etc., is that the policies that protect inequity and start revolutions late in an economic cycle, are actually costing nations hundreds of billions, and even trillions, of dollars annually to maintain.

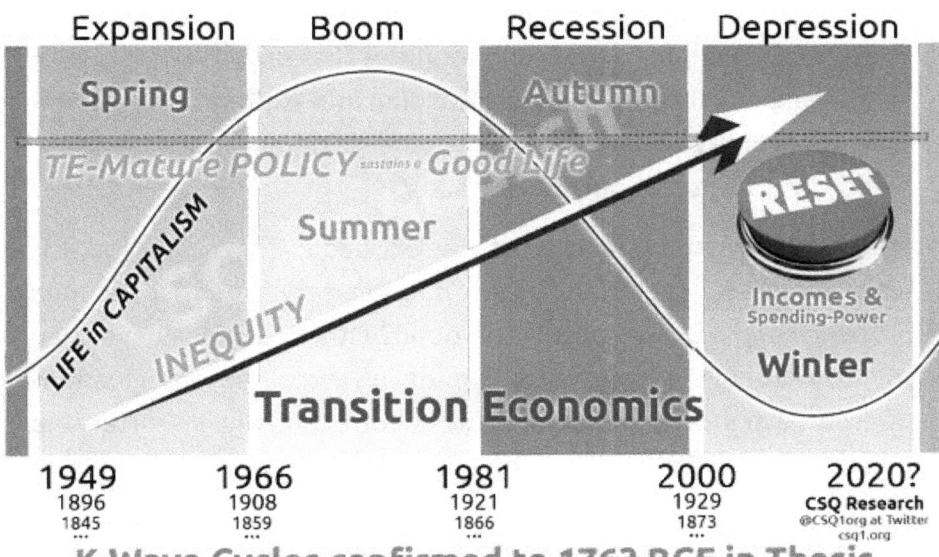

Worldwide statistics show conclusively that countries who ensure a Good Life for everyone, have three-times, six-times and more - per-capita-exports (new wealth per citizen) - because every supported citizens can afford to contribute to their economy; and the stats prove that being productive is the result of this result.

In the U.S., according to the 2010 U.S. Budget, 160 million people (40%) have nothing; no assets, no money, insufficient incomes to start and maintain commercial businesses nor contribute to the growth of the economy in any way. The cost of protecting Inequity here can be estimated credibly at almost $8 trillion per year. In Canada, the U.K. and Australia, which are all countries that are in Collapse Trendings alongside the U.S., an average $700 billion of new export revenues are lost annually per country.

Freedom

Freedom is a twenty-year-old who can choose to start a family in a home of their own; one who can choose a degree education or work as he or she wishes; one whose children and children's children will live in secure family-friendly communities that promise lifetimes of interesting worthwhile projects, learning and exploration; without fear of scarcity in the basics of life including food, energy, healthcare, transport and other needs.

Freedom, is what we, and all of the G8, had in the 1950s and it is what our latest generation has lost due to a very expensive inequity problem today. Do we turn this around? Other societies have tried to "Do nothing" in history and it ends in revolution; other nations offered partial corrections, and these corrections just shorten the benefit of an ordinarily sixty-year cycle of prosperity.

So, we must make corrections now – and clearly there are proven roadmaps already working in other nations around the globe so that we don't have to guess at what might work; and risk failing to reset as needed.

Transition Economics is a teaching and learning framework that recognizes the scientific, proven-in-observation lessons of Cycle Economists, and then it also documents the lessons-learned about what policies lead to a resetting of opportunity once again. For example over the past 300 years, we know that approximately 80% of cycles have restarted peacefully and that 20% have resulted in war or revolution.

War has never been a desirable option for communities touched by it, and this is the true value of democracy too because democratic nations do not maintain wars against other democratic nations.

When our governments provide citizens with incomes and renewed spending-power programs at the end of an economic cycle, our economies reset for another sixty-years of prosperity and opportunity safely and responsibly. When those prudent economic policies also permit easy transition to automation, we can all look forward to more interesting and productive work, lives, learning, and freedoms sustainably.

Why is automation important? Well, for starters no-one starves once food is grown and delivered to our homes robotically - and no-one is homeless when robots build life-cycle-managed homes as needed either. So, chipping away at automation is always a pragmatic investment. Also, robotics in manufacturing, mining, forestry allow us to generate profits from our highest profit exports at the same time that we minimize our reliance on our most expensive imports too.

Automation, once well directed, becomes a brand new financial injector for the economy – just like our work force, just like our pension systems, just like our in-country investments in companies and in the national debt of other nations.

The life-cycle-managed robotics that serve society can be thought of as Renewable Automations and the 250 smart factories that build robots as needed to provide for the needs of everyone are called Worthwhile PLC Projects - or simply #WPProjects.

History documents that when we fail to provide these important supports for individuals and families, we create the underpinnings of Populism, the gentrified name for Revolutions - and even World Wars - and this warning from the past takes on unprecedented urgency within today's mature nuclear era as mentioned.

When cycles of Weaponry, Automation, and Capitalistic Unsustainability collide, as they do today - within a democratic society that is untrained in how to vote in support of policies that protect families during these changes, we find an urgent need for the new science of Transition Economics (TE).

TE leverages a Scientific Method Process that we term "Thought-Leadership". I reference Economic Theory occasionally, but Thought-Leadership Processes will take you through good old-fashioned legwork procedurally with real-world research to arrive at empirical cause-and-effect conclusions. Theory - is not something we teach in Transition Economics – rather we teach process; and that process must lead to observable repeatable results scientifically – just like in engineering and science.

180 countries each run an array of similar policies discussions worldwide and we want to understand what were the measurable GDP costs or benefits of those policy decisions over time.

So if I say that countries with socialistic policies are not the countries that are collapsing, I am not referencing Marx, Keynes, nor Schumpeter's theories on Capitalism versus Socialism. Instead, I am comparing their GDP Exports per Capita (Wealth Creation) and Trade Balances for the Nordic States versus 180 other countries over the past twenty years, to confirm which housing policies, energy policies, social supports, immigration, and other important policies resulted in GDP successes or declines.

Economies that are succeeding are those that are trending in an

Advancing direction; otherwise they are falling and those economies are in a collapse trending – or trending toward collapse.

This empirical and constantly improving approach to supporting policy is an important part of Thought Leadership in Transition Economics - as is Release Management and Version Controls that ensure Policies adjust and update as monitoring mandates. The Policies that result from TE Thought-Leadership Process are called "TE-Mature" or TE-Maturity Modelled Policy.

I am introducing you to a lot of new science and terminology in a hurry, so feel free to look for much more detailed explanations in the reference guide for Transition Economics – The Science of Sustainability; www.Csq1.org is the home base for Transition Economics so get online for more explanations, updates, books, and articles.

Transition Economics mandates Economists to present planning that explains very specifically HOW to provide sustainable next-steps and solutions leveraging best-practices, scientific method, and proven mature and transparent project management processes.

The book that introduced TE to the world first, World Peace – the Transition, dedicated 150-pages of Business Case supporting statistics that explained the financial windfalls of good philosophy and strong social underpinnings in Government Policy – so our solutions; our plans that explain HOW step-by-step, also seek to improve social conditions in pursuit of those revenue injectors that I touched on above and explain through this book.

As Transition Economics does have a problem-solving mandate, students are taught an understanding of best-practice project method drawn from Engineering, Science, Business, Epistemology, and History; all necessary learning is summarized in the TE Reference guide and in the soon to released SUSTAIN Project Management

Method manual. These are also the foundations and building blocks of strong leadership; foundations that are bolstered and improved with strong thought-leadership – and so you will want to look for these skills in the people that you vote for.

Explanations of problems that end without planned, proven next-steps and clear directions - amount to platitudes at best, and they amount to voicings of emotional frustration at worst. There can be no responsible leadership without understanding how to build a communicable plan and so I will explain to readers how to best approach presenting planning for this Last Generation too.

Economists are not engineers and they are not creatives by training either; a generalization might call them statisticians, historians, social scientists, and most will work in the finance industry and in government during their careers outside academia. A poll of dozens of Economists only very rarely draws a consensus of opinion, so it can be said fairly that the faculty insists on few over-arching conventions.

Economics PhD students often explore a very specific area of economic research in great detail. For this purpose, a control group is sought; a situation small enough to understand well; one which can be said to be free of external influence.

The Fibonacci Sequence is the algorithm that accurately predicts plant growth as 1 leaf, then 1, 2, 3, 5, 8; ever-summing the previous two values so that the next numbers are 13, 21, and so on. Named after its discoverer Leonardo Fibonacci in the 12th century, the sequence is easily observable and thereby proven Scientific.

Similar to the Fibonacci sequence, the Economist's research and math are true and provable within the confines of an artificial micro-climate. Once outside that isolation, hundreds of other algorithms – like a forest's processes for precipitation, erosion, competition, sunlight, storms, climate, etc. weigh in to explain a complex forest.

Economies are similar to forests in that they have hundreds and thousands of processes at work at once; and yet, like Geysers in Geology, Economies have predictable Cycles by observable Scientific Method too. Isolating the processes that influence an economy consistently is the object of search in Transition Economics.

"Truth is ever to be found in simplicity, and not in the multiplicity and confusion of things."

Isaac Newton, Physics & Co-Founder of Calculus

Aristotle's systems of thought leadership are perhaps the most famous in all history. He is the founding father of both Scientific Method and also our University Curriculums; and therefore, all of our subordinate school curriculums as well.

According to Aristotle's "Scientific Method", any approach that does not take into consideration real world observation cannot be considered true. Without this constraint, he realized that academically peer-reviewed theory was at risk of becoming theoretical fiction.

Scientific Method insists that measures in science be confirmable both by Calculation and Observation – and, of the two, observation is the more relevant measure. Calculation endeavors to understand a thing more thing fully once observation proves that it is true.

Astrology has become fundamentally important in this past century for this reason. Here on earth we cannot emulate a substance with gravity density so great that it bends light - or even prevents light from passing, but within our universe this phenomenon is readily observable.

Where I think that Economics has failed us in the past, can be explained by individual measures of success for PhD Economics students and papers, which are not always based on observation in the real world. Measures are the Peer-Reviews of other PhDs with similar training in many cases, without burden of explaining real world observations like – If this theory is sound, why are 72% of all economies in decline?

Peer-reviewed research paper arguments and calculations can be considered sound for an isolated topic without regard for the sustainability of the building-block theories upon which they are based. Thesis studies in banking systems, debt and monetary systems that are also built on Keynes Theory are frequent – but Keynes Theories are proven by observation to be unsustainable. And this is a trap fallen into by even the most prestigious economics schools.

When Economic Theory does not insist upon credible tests of observation, success and failure, most scientists will confirm that the conclusions cannot be considered scientifically valid.

The global economy around us in 2016 is widely acknowledged to be in a collapse trending by most observable measures. How else to explain 72% of economies in a collapse trending today after graduating generations of economists from our academic institutions? My engineer and scientist's viewpoint is to think it fair to suggest that the Faculty of Economics continues to learn - and is in need of Scientific Method now; more than other faculties.

Cycle Economics explains why "Reset" (Wealth Distribution and Debt Forgiveness) is a normal requirement of all capitalist economies; and it explains that sustainable, proactive economic controls can prolong equilibrium in capitalist economies too. Transition Economics aspires to be Scientific, and even consistent, by using these cycles to explain **why policies work sometimes, and not at other times**.

TE bases decisions for change on rate-of-change algorithms called TE-Throttles; observable, measurable calculation documented transparently in Business Cases which estimate short, mid and long-term monitored targets for responsible rate of policy change.

An example of changes that would require TE-Throttles and Throttle Rates are Interest Rate Increases or Rate of Guaranteed Incomes required to offset Automation Job-losses. Most changes will require Throttling spending as offset by incomes.

Learning from Smaller Economies

The consequences of socially irresponsible management and policy are not easily correlated in a large economy and population like the United States and China. America's GDP is the largest in the world and the population is twenty times that of many others at 340 million people; China and India populations are almost four times higher than the U.S. again.

Rather than listing Economics studies alphabetically as does Harvard,

Transition Economics suggests a cyclic teaching start. Sometimes a policy works well and sometimes the same policy does not work at all; policies that work well short-term do not always work well long-term too.

Rather than listing Economics studies alphabetically as does Harvard, Transition Economics suggests a cyclic teaching start. Sometimes a policy works well and sometimes the same policy does not work at all; policies that work well short-term do not always work well long-term either.

Transition Economics explains when a policy is appropriate; when is it most likely to move a society forward; and when will it move an economy toward collapse.

In much smaller countries, like the Nordic States – populations are between five and twenty million people – so the impacts of offshoring engineering and creating trade deficits (importing more than exporting), were felt severely within a short few years after policy implementation. Because these populations were small, they could also vote for socialistic policies that were more sustainable more easily too; democratic voters could react to bad policy almost as soon as the impacts were felt – and in this way corrections were made quickly that turned around the problems.

In the U.S., the Federal Reserve's 2010 Budget confirmed that 160 million Americans (40% of the population) had nothing (their wealth totaled just 0.3%) – and these individuals had no vote to effect change because the U.S. has a two-party system where the majority 60% are living well enough to feel they must protect what they have. American's can be legitimately worried to lose their jobs and health benefits after seeing the reality of life for the lowest 40% of income earners, for the unemployed, and for those without health benefits.

Who benefits from Inequality? No-one - is the correct answer.

Firing on all Cylinders

Think of a strong economy as one might think of a combustion engine. The strength of the engine relies on the production, or force, in each of its cylinders as each pushes to move a car forward. There are primary, secondary and tertiary economies that provide incomes to a labor force - but this labor force often comprises less than half of the citizens of any country.

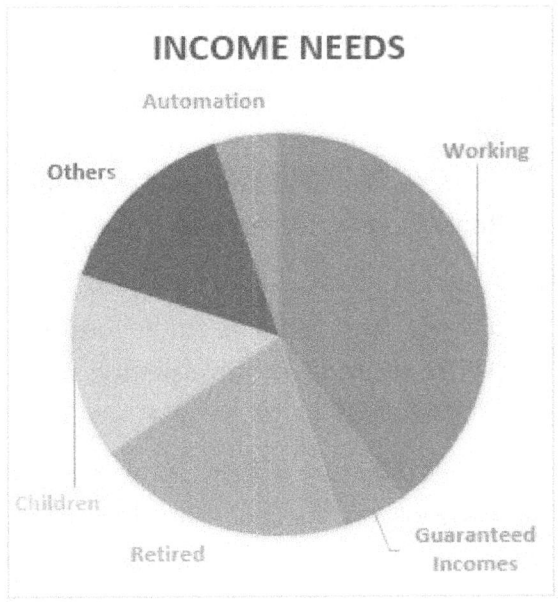

Unemployment is often double the advertised rate and so is commonly 9% to 18%; the retired of most countries are 20%, and the rest of citizenry are children, students and disabled persons.

If you were to rely on the labor force alone, this promises an engine running at 41% to 55% efficiency at best.

Cash rich and strategically minded nations, profit by purchasing government debt from other nations or take ownership stakes in local companies, and this serves as another injector of wealth into the country.

The reason that programs like Guaranteed Living Incomes have such strong business cases is that they ensure that the unemployed, retired, and all others in an economy can contribute through their spending as well.

Finally, Renewable automation can begin to contribute to

productivity and to a country's GDP as well. By targeting high-profit exports and expensive imports for automation first, we invest once and generate revenue many times – even while we sleep.

In our present economy, where automation is transitioning, and economies are transitioning too, an Engineering Safety-Net program permits skilled engineers to continue to develop very specific Renewable Automations.

I discuss throughout this book that many of our Engineers are unemployed or underemployed due to lax offshoring protections which resulted in job scarcity; and other engineers have simply retired but still wish to be productive whenever they choose.

With TE-Mature policies, now our economy is firing on all cylinders; now, we are focused on taking economic productivity from much more that just 40% of our working population.

With Transition Economics policies, our wealth distribution policies become wealth creation strategies. As evidence, I present the Netherlands' citizens who generate almost three-times the export wealth of a Canadian and six-times that of an American by running TE-Mature Policies.

Once incomes are in the hands of all citizens wishing to be productive; and once we restore spending power as well, we reset our economy for a new sixty-year cycle of prosperity in capitalism. This goals are the targets of a maturing Transition Economy.

We didn't teach our children Cycle Economics in high-school as we should have, nor did we teach them about other systems of housing policy, economic controls, etc. We taught our kids only about the systems that were status-quo today - and so now as adults, we have to wonder are these "new" cycle-appropriate Policies something that we should be suspicious of.

If you attempt to use strategies that are status quo in the first part of a Monopoly Game - during the final hotel-round; you will very shortly see that these previously-winning practices, do not work any longer. Why? Because the game has changed. Your relaxed, successful game strategies had to change with the new hyper-competitive, dice-roll-driven luck that is needed to succeed near the end of the game.

The end of a monopoly game can be very frustrating and it takes the resetting of the monopoly game altogether before the game can be enjoyable for all players again.

Similarly, everyone enjoys the start of a Capitalist Economic Cycle because they have incomes, and because those incomes have strong spending-power that is sufficient to buy and have a good life.

The Cycle Economics controls discussed above have managed Capitalism for 4000 years; there is nothing new in these discussions even though you may be hearing these explanations of Cycles for the first time.

And now for the first time in Cycle Economics history, along comes a game-changer in the computer and automation. For the very first time in a global Capitalist cycle, we have automation, smart robotics, and even rudimentary artificial intelligence making our computers easier to automate, faster, safer, and more accurate and useful too.

Why have these automations become important to consider in social policy?

The computer is a game changer for civilization beyond anything that the Industrial Era of the 1800s likely imagined. With computers, we are completely automating our 10,000-year-old manual economies in each of the three Economic Sectors:

Sector 1 are our Resources - farming, mining, fishing, forestry...

Sector 2 Productions - are our manufacturing, baking, packaging...

Sector 3 are our Tertiary-Economy Companies – Insurance, Banking, Credit Cards, Transportation, Retailers...

Automation software has been running our richest Tertiary companies since the 1950s. Automated manufacturing followed soon after when computerized welding robots were first added to the assembly lines at General Motors in Detroit in 1961. Today's robots box one-million bottles an hour and can build the most sophisticated cars in the world without a single human operator required.

A painful void of engineering leadership followed the 1970's post-cold-war's over-arching constraint for profitability globally.

The business environment was so constraining that it took until 2016 for Spread Inc. of Kyoto, Japan, to announce the world's first fully automated farm; a hydroponics-based factory that produces 30,000 head of lettuce daily, sustainably, without a human hand required.

I said painful, and now I will add short-sighted too, because Automation is a powerful mitigation for year-over-year inflation and unsustainable Keynesian Monetary Policy. The automation of our basic needs of food, shelter, energy, transportation, pharmaceuticals, and other essentials makes concerns for income interruptions quite a bit less worrisome. The impacts of lost incomes is dramatically reduced when everything that we need arrives at our doorstep automatically, sustainably, and abundantly - without a human hand required too. These renewable resources could very well have put off this latest economic downturn indefinitely and eased the suffering and death of millions.

As our basic needs of food, shelter, transportation, and energy are automated, the costs of social safety-nets are reduced considerably. Automation, therefore, when responsibly planned and implemented, can clearly protect families from interruptions to their incomes and livelihoods – and that is the reason for having a government too.

Transition Economics Automation

"When you change the way you look at things, the things you look at change."

Max Planck, Quantum Mechanics in Physics

Automation is an important building block for civilization - and for humanity. Aristotle famously observed 2500 years ago that there will ever-be need of slaves until the assembly of the things we need in life are built by themselves.

In 1960, George Jetson's futuristic science-fiction lifestyle featured two-day, three-hour work-weeks of "brutal" button-pushing. This went on while joining their kids and robot-maid on journeys in their anti-gravity car. The Hanna-Barbera TV show "The Jetsons" was set in 1998 - and here in 2016 we still have barely begun to build even the most basic of those automations.

Driverless cars, as with every other technology, was science fiction until an engineer – in this case an engineer with limitless resources - made it work first in 2013 at Google; of course the engineer that I am referring to is Larry Page, Google's then CEO.

In 2017, AirBus is promising to test its autonomous air-taxi design - for short-haul trips beginning in 2021.

In 2015, the World Peace Transition Projects - #WPProjects, explained the 250 Connected Smart Factories needed to automate every economy's basic needs of life – and then it assigned the workload to many hands by assigning one sustainable automation project to every country in an effort to create a profitable new international trade marketplace as well.

Without this sort of planning, automation is simply eliminating jobs at dizzying rates. Automation Job losses are projected by some experts to reach 50% of all jobs by the year 2035. We will talk about these next coming thirty-years of 972 jobs lost monthly, per million population – along with other TE Throttle Rate discussions.

Transition Economics uses TE-Throttles, to explain the responsible rate of change that permits the most effective automation of society - so that we can all see the benefits without unnecessary hardships.

The Squeaky Wheel

Change is an important topic for the Last Generation. How do peaceful calls by voters and public rallies result in real, rapid and meaningful change?

To answer this question, let's compare the AIDS Lobby in Washington in the 1980s versus the Breast Cancer Lobby active at the same time.

AIDs sufferers were dying without access to medicines and having needed researchers and specialists assigned to the problem. Lobbyists campaigned loudly and belligerently; always peaceful but nonetheless loud and in the face of lawmakers. These folks truly were squeaky wheels - and they got results in prompt attention and action.

Thirty Years into the Pink-Ribboned Breast Cancer Lobby's very polite and respectful campaigns however, many resources are still not available to people with cancer today. If anything, Breast Cancer rates appear to have climbed to reach near-epidemic numbers.

Treatments are too expensive for many to afford despite decades of donation and volunteer contributions to research, hospitals and medical universities.

Meaningful and effective change takes a squeaky, up-front, tactical plan - balanced by educated and peaceful civil action.

Chapter 2

-

Cycles and Phases in Capitalism

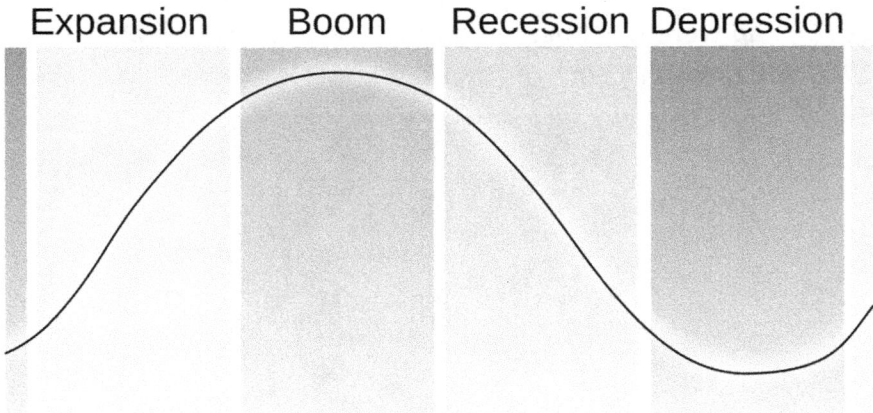

The sixty-minute game of Monopoly is a close approximation of Capitalism's sixty-year cycles. Would you be surprised to hear that there has been a Great Depression in capitalist economies consistently, give or take ten years or so, on record for 4000-years as well? The phases and cycle looks somewhat similar to the line and rectangles on this chart above.

Nikolai Kondratiev was the brilliant Soviet Economics Historian and Researcher who's book "The Long Wave Cycle" first documented this phenomenon in 1925. He divided each economic cycle into four phases of Spring, Summer, Autumn and Winter - similar to the chart at the start of this chapter labelled Expansion, Boom, Recession,

Depression.

I try to provide enough citations so that readers can validate presented facts for themselves. In this case, I encourage you to Google "K-Wave Economics" to confirm this point and I encourage you to read more from the many citations referenced throughout this book.

K-Waves, or Kondratiev Waves or Longwaves, are proven in thesis back to 930 AD China (Snyder, 2014)("William Thompson | Department of Political Science | Indiana University Bloomington," 2016), and were documented on the Code of Hammurabi stone in 1760 BCE through its use of "Jubilees".

The Code of Hammurabi in the Louvre in Paris. (Bartz, 2005)

According to records of historical cycles traced back to 930 AD, we are in a nineteenth Depression today; a Depression is simply a deep and pervasive recession, and we will emerge from this time once our policies permit new incomes and spending-power.

Jeffery Sachs of Columbia University included a discussion of Cycle

Economics in his recent book; William Thompson at Indiana University has published influential papers and books documenting eighteen K-Waves dating back to 930 AD in China's Song Province as well; and I will wrap up this aside with Michael Snyder who wrote "It should be noted that economic cycle theories have enabled some analysts to correctly predict the timing of recessions, stock market peaks and stock market crashes over the past couple of decades." (Snyder, 2014)

And so the cycle has repeated, back through history. Longwave K-Waves are observable, well-documented and repeat regularly in Capitalistic societies. As enough evidence confirms the existence of these phenomena and as this is my third book in Economics that researches them too, I feel comfortable referring to Cycle Economics as not just a theory but a Science. Transition Economics endeavors to be scientific as well and so we will look at Automation and at methods to empirically pinpoint supporting TE-Mature Policy scientifically too.

What happens at the end of a game of monopoly? Does status quo get everyone back on track in the final hotel round? No - unfortunately not. All wealth must be thrown back into the game's bank; the game must Reset, and money and properties redistributed and available to everyone again so that a new game/cycle can restart.

In real life, the equivalent of this game Reset takes smart government policies that permit people to change from our unsustainable housing bubbles, and our hit-and-miss income sources, to new guaranteed incomes and renewed spending-power.

Policies Change with each Cycle

Different phases in Cyclic Economies call for different Policy. Capitalist Economies are cyclic economies; play a game of Monopoly to see this cycle play out from start-to-end within sixty minutes or so.

Incomes and Renewed Spending Power are needed to reset a cycle when Economic Controls have ignored within Autumn Economies and Inequity prevents the poor from contributing to economic production any longer.

Pure Capitalism is unsustainable by itself; a Monopoly Game must Reset every time and so too must Capitalist Economies. ***Socialistic Policy***, and specifically the TE-Mature policies developed in Transition Economics, are proven to increase production outputs similar to per-capita results seen in Nordic States, The Netherlands, Germany, Switzerland and others.

These countries are not in Collapse Trending today; their Economies are Advancing with positive Trade Balances and many of these nations boast Good Lives wherein citizens live the American Dream still.

TE-Mature policies create a Sustainable Capitalism or Socialism that maintains citizen spending-power in housing, energy, healthcare and other needs through pragmatic Economic Controls.

I mentioned in the introduction above that 80% of the time, other compromises were found to enable the wealth distributions needed to begin the next cycle. The Great Depression of 1835 was ended when the California Gold Rush multiplied America's Gold Reserves by ten-times, 1779 & 1893's "Panics" were ended by new Immigration Wealth but both resets were very shallow resets that resulted in Depressions again in 1835 and in 1929.

And so the cycle has repeated, back through history. Longwave K-Waves are observable, well-documented and repeat regularly in Capitalistic societies. As enough evidence confirms the existence of these phenomena and as this is my fifth book in Economics that researches them too, I feel comfortable referring to Cycle Economics as not just a theory but a Science. Transition Economics endeavors to be scientific as well and so we will look at Automation and at methods to empirically pinpoint supporting TE-Mature Policy scientifically too.

What happens at the end of a game of monopoly? Does status quo get everyone back on track in the final hotel round? No - unfortunately not. All wealth must be thrown back into the game's bank; the game must be Reset, and money and properties redistributed an available to everyone again - so that a new game/cycle can restart.

When a Monarch ran the country, back in 1763 BCE Babylon (Egypt), King Hammurabi reset his economy every fifty years proactively - in anticipation of these sixty-year depressions. Universal Debt Forgiveness was called "Jubilee".

Today we are a Democracy – and regrettably, we are a democracy that is untrained in Cycle Economics. I say regrettably, because when we did not get these basic sustainability lessons in our high-school Civics classes, we can now be easily misinformed and misled by special interests that might not like to have their status quo upset.

In the 1930s, Keynesian Economic Theorists distracted governments from wealth-distribution for long enough to create an opportunity for Adolf Hitler to come to power during Germany's 1930 revolution-vote – we call these elections "Populism" today. Brexit and Donald Trump are examples and there are many others in Spain, France and elsewhere following stride.

The democratic vote of Germans too long oppressed by slave-wages and Versailles Treaty oppressions – alongside a flaw in the then German constitution, permitted the forming of a Dictatorship that led to a World War which killed 60-million people.

War, therefore, is an observable result of Keynesian Economics' attempt to extend unsustainable capitalistic monetary policy indefinitely at the end of a K-Wave Economic cycle.

Keynes (pronounced "Canes"), dismissed the consequences of his progressively unsustainable practices by stating very ironically, "And then we are all dead". Let's hope he doesn't get to be right twice.

Financial industries and the rich flocked to Keynes' Theories as these systems protected their wealth by building layer upon layer of evasive and socially irresponsible protection tactics; each one more outlandish than the next - from Borrowing Fiscal Policy to Currency-Devaluing and Inflation-Driving Monetary Policy, to Distributive Justice (borrowing without paying it back), to Debt+Inflation=Prosperity mathematical logic gaps.

In the end, typical Keynesian tactics included government spending designed to stimulate very short-term demand, low tax, and under-investment in government sponsored projects (like automation) and business governance. In layman's terms, Keynes' theories were a study in short-sightedness almost from start-to-end.

Revolution and War are required in just about 20% of K-Wave Cycle restarts historically, and the more pervasive the Wealth Distribution, the longer and more prosperous is the new Cycle that follows it.

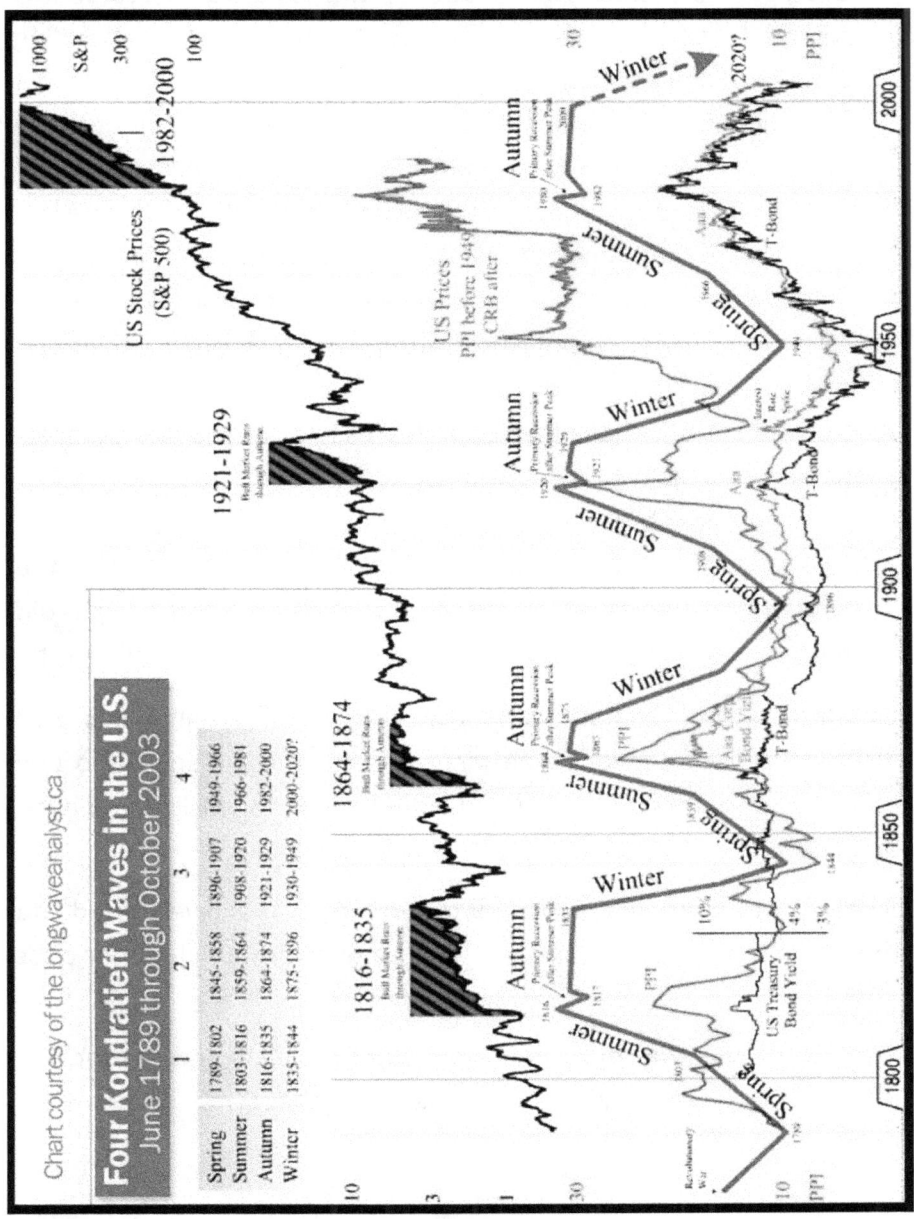

(Gordon, 2009)

Let's look at K-Wave Cycles chronologically to see how wealth distributions have played out in the past:

- 1772's Credit Crisis was ended by the American Revolution's forced debt forgiveness – remember the Boston Tea Party? King George and the British Treasury got stuck with that bill for almost $1 million in 1776 dollars. France's $1.3 billion investment in the American Revolution went on to fuel the French Revolution.
- 1835's Great Depression was ended by the California Gold Rush which multiplied America's Gold Reserves ten-times
- 1883's Panic in the US was ended by new Immigrant Wealth
- 1929's Great Depression distributed wealth through WWII; and of course
- Academic Thesis have tracked K-Waves back to 930 AD in China's Song Province Capitalist Economy
- "Jubilee" distributed wealth every 50 years for 1000+ years as carved on the Code of Hammurabi Stone – now located in the Louvre – ensuring that the misery of routine capitalist troughs did not turn into a revolution again the Kings of Babylon and Egypt.

Our last Spring Economy began around 1950. Wealth was well distributed and everyone had incomes that they needed - to buy homes and to afford a good life. Opportunities to get live and even become successful were readily available to all.

Summer was approximately 1969 to 1982. All was still very good and the boom of the American Dream began to afford a rich upper class now.

Fall, or Autumn, was much more difficult to explain and Winter was more difficult again – and so I will devote a chapter to discuss each individually.

Our most recent cycle is summarized in the following slides. You can follow along and view this slide deck in high-resolution online at: http://ow.ly/OKmj305xto1 (Edward Tilley, 2015).

Many topics in following chapters will make use of this deck as well.

Spring and Summer

Autumn

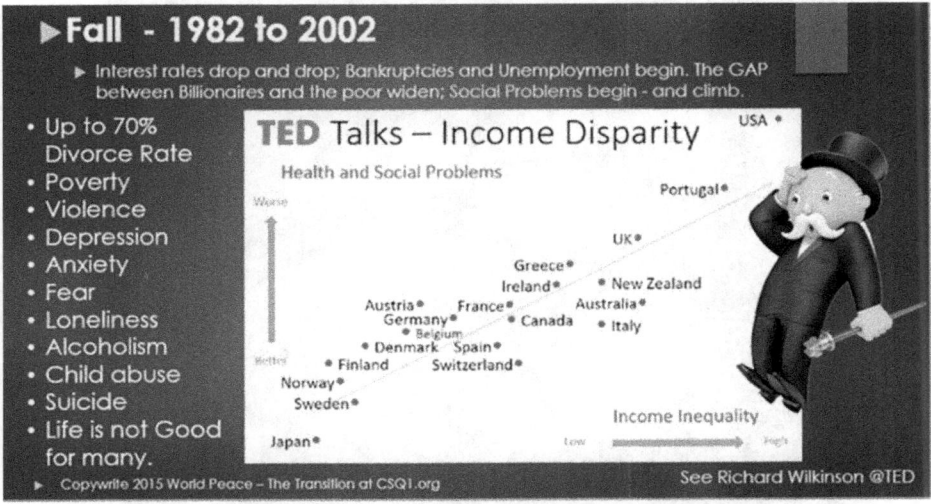

The next and last phase of the cycle is the **Winter** phase – our Great Depressions; the deep and sustained Recessions.

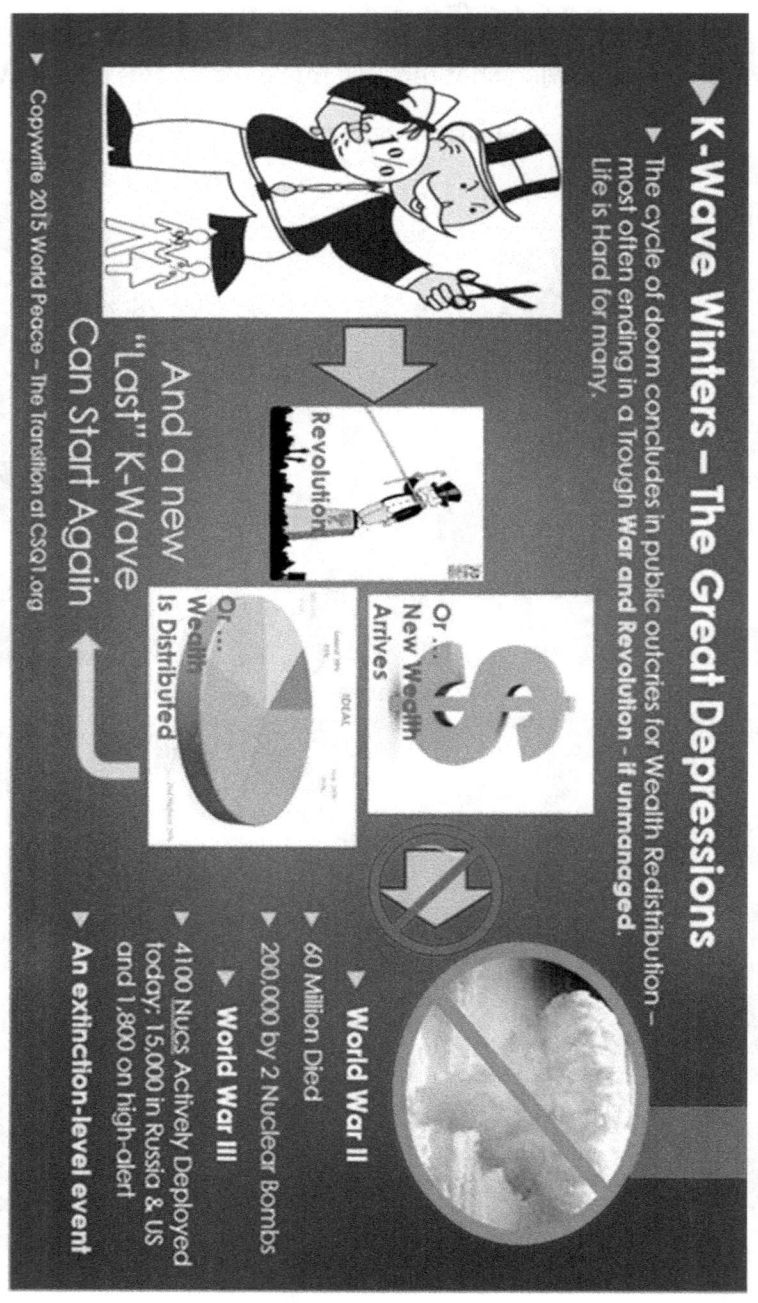

Boiled Frogs

Life feels very competitive in Winter Economies. With quality jobs scarce and affordable housing difficult to find in major cities, many couples are living paycheck to paycheck and cannot be ready to begin a family until well into their 30s and even 40s.

But it wasn't always this way...

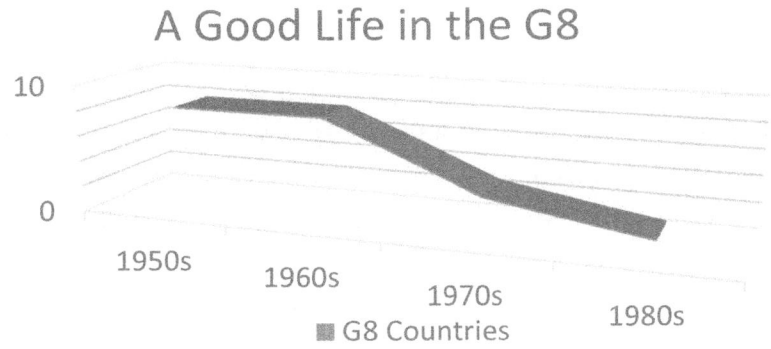

In all of the G8 countries, like the American Dream and Good Life in the USA of the 1950s up until the 1970s, a high-school education was sufficient to find lifelong employment with a full pension, healthcare, benefits, and to buy a home that would be paid free-and-clear its mortgage almost 100% of the time. A young family could begin life at the age of twenty without amassing the lifelong debt that we see today.

So too could Russian families, start a family and home easily until 1986's Perestroika changed their land-grants system to a North-American style open real-estate market.

All of our systems of pensions, benefits, insurance, childcare, education, etc. were built based on this one-job-for-a-lifetime model of benevolent capitalism. Back then there were plenty of jobs that paid retirements, drug and dental benefits, and just one income afforded a comfortable living for most families with educations for family members as needed. Here in Canada, a plumber or steel worker could easily afford a nice cottage with a beach-front as well.

As pensioned, high-paying jobs disappear and gaps in wealth between the rich and the poor become more and more unequal, two-income families emerge as the new norm. Housing bubbles and billionaire-ranks grow alongside many more poor until the bottom 40% of Americas income earners came to own just 0.3% of America's wealth and income in 2010.

Remember that Rich people are making $3 to $5 million per day seven days a week for 30 years and longer now. That much inequity is not going to be overcome by asking workers to take two or even three jobs. Over time the gap just grows and grows naturally.

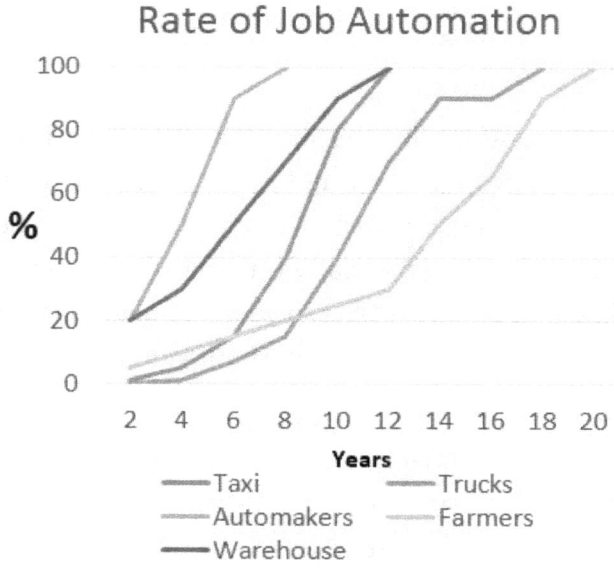

With Automations reducing repetitive jobs by up to 50% over the next twenty years, families will be fortunate to find a single high-paying conventional job. Incomes, not jobs, become the priority.

In a large country like the United States, this represents 160 million people who own nothing and have no vote either. No vote, because 60% routinely vote to continue their status-quo – as per their basic in-class training and political instruction. The result is a modern-day American Revolution manifest in dramatic social problem statistics which include incarceration rates five-times higher than the next G7 country acts of onshore terror in 400 mass-shootings annually.

By applying the much higher GDP Export-per-Capita of socialistic country citizens from the Netherlands and Norway, it is possible to estimate the opportunity cost of keeping 160 million Americans unable to contribute to the economy. This opportunity cost is a staggering – an optimistic $8 trillion dollars annually; and in Canada, Great Britain and Australia where GDP Export per Capita is one-third and one-sixth, the costs of denying socialistic policies an average of $630 billion annually.

This serves as the basis of an estimate for what is the annual cost of protecting inequality in the G7 countries in a K-Wave Winter. I will expand on this discussion further in the book.

Country	GDP Export per Capita	Multiplier to Dutch Export/Cap	Export 2015 (in billions)	Opportunity Cost New Export (in billions)	Collapse or Advance Trending?
Netherlands	$33,652	100%	$477	$0	Advance
Norway	$28,807	117%	$103	$17	Advance
United States	$5,057	665%	$1,510	$8,538	Collapse
Sweden	$18,688	180%	$151	$121	Advance
Germany	$18,316	184%	$1,309	$1,096	Advance
Canada	$13,286	253%	$411	$630	Collapse
United Kingdom	$7,378	456%	$436	$1,553	Collapse
Australia	$10,446	322%	$188	$418	Collapse

Let's take a closer look at each of the four phases of a repeating K-Wave Economic Cycle next.

Chapter 3
—
Spring & Summer Phase

Spring - is the American Dream. Wealth is distributed; everyone has what they need and many have the means to buy some luxury items as well. In our most recent spring economy in the 1950s, a high-school education and single income would afford a home, a car, a cottage, education, healthcare and retirement easily.

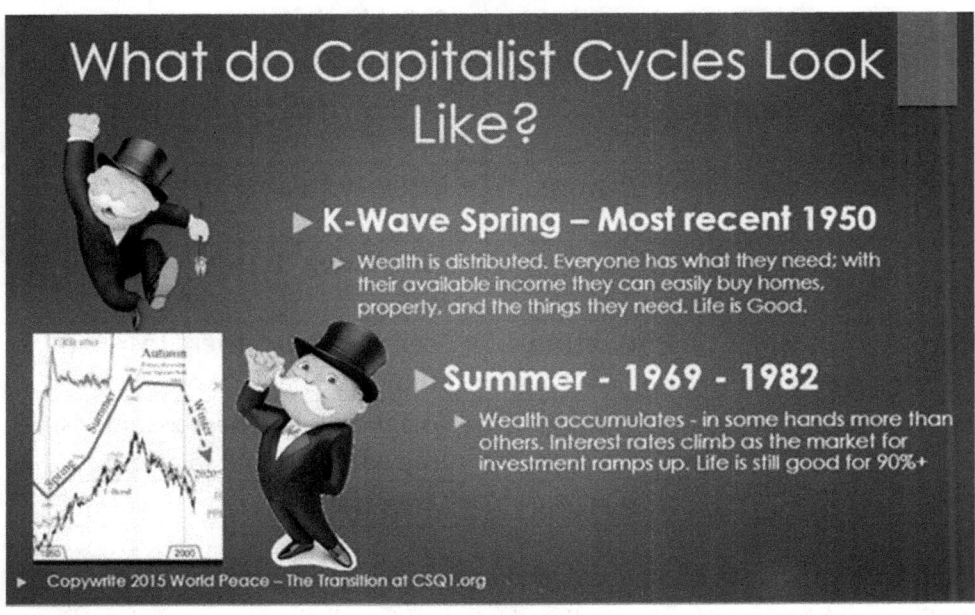

Policies in the Spring Phase

Wealth Creation	Policy	
Capitalistic ☆☆☆☆☆	Housing	• Homes are owned. Bought with Cash or mortgage with high rate of ownership. • Very little Usury (unpayable lending). • Easy to buy cottage and land.
	Education ☆☆	• Free through high-school. University affordable. Smaller % could afford a higher education, a home, family, at the same time. Students with money put ahead of students with ability.
	Incomes	• Reliable via Jobs • Easy, equal access to start business and buy land.
	Healthcare	• Pay – Poor die 13 years sooner
	Pensions	• Easily available from most Jobs
Socialistic China ☆☆☆☆ USSR ☆☆	Housing	• Land Grant System – Homes free
	Education	• Free – salary given to good students as well.
	Incomes	• Assigned Jobs. Most essentials free with minimal salaries too.
	Pensions	• Universal

In Spring, living is good, easy, and even fun – just like in the start of a Game of Monopoly. Capitalism is arguably a little more productive early-on, while Socialism produces a more broadly educated society with arguably better healthcare and longevity.

Policies in the Summer Phase

Wealth Creation	Policy	
Capitalistic ☆☆☆☆☆	Housing	• Homes are owned. Bought with Cash or mortgage with high rate of ownership. • Very little Usury (unpayable lending). • Easy to buy cottage and land.
	Education ☆☆	• Free through high-school. University affordable. Smaller % could afford a higher education, a home, family, at the same time. Students with money put ahead of students with ability.
	Incomes	• Reliable via Jobs • Easy, equal access to start business and buy land.
	Healthcare	• Pay – Poor die 13 years sooner
	Pensions	• Easily available from most Jobs
Socialistic China ☆☆☆☆☆ USSR ☆☆	Housing	• Land Grant System – Homes free
	Education	• Free – salary given to good students as well.
	Incomes	• Assigned Jobs. Most essentials free with minimal salaries too.
	Pensions	• Universal

In Summer, living is still good for 90% of the population; wealth begins to accumulate in some hands more than others. Interest rates will begin to climb near the end of this phase as money comes available to investors and private fortunes begin to amass. Prices for homes were $5000; but now cost $60,000. Single-Income families are the norm still.

It matters less in these early boom phases whether Socialistic or Capitalistic Policies are preferred. It is vitally important, however, that an economy **monetize** by generating strong Export Revenues from their productions.

After the Summer Phase, we begin to see the importance of pragmatically switching to socialistic policies that maintain a Good Life, incomes, and spending-power for everyone within a society. Without these controls, spending-power will now begin to drop away as incomes decrease too.

Chapter 4

—

Autumn Phase

Autumn is where Policies need to begin to change. Capitalism plays out and begins to become unsustainable in this phase. The bigger the economy, the slower will be those citizens to see it. Responsible Economic Controls were put in place by Nordic Nations that preserved a Good Life for their citizens in 1990 but in the G7, they implemented Capitalistic Trickle-down Low-Tax instead and then failed to monitor incomes nor inequity.

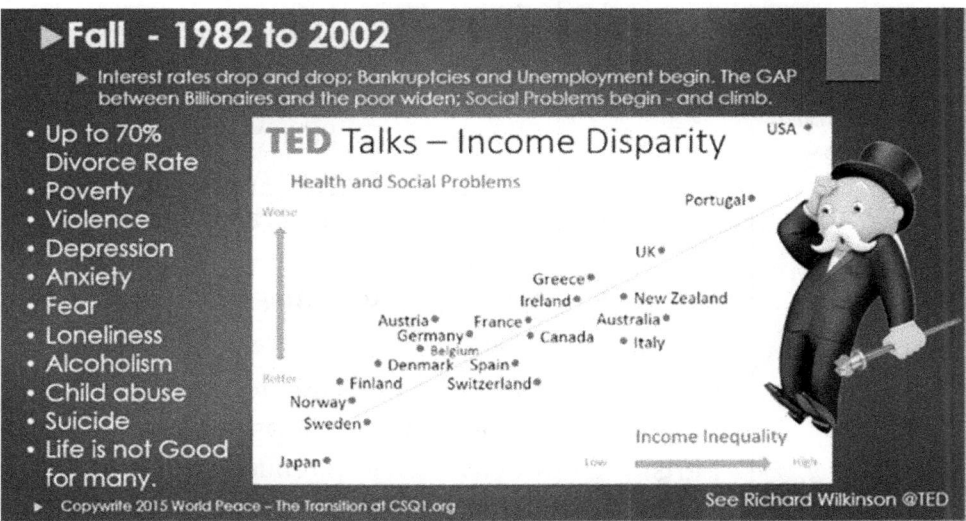

Policies in the Autumn Phase

Wealth Creation	Policy	
Socialistic China ☆☆☆☆☆ *Nordic States* ☆☆☆☆☆	Housing	• Homes are bought but protected from bubbles and foreign investment. Most are mortgaged with high rate of ownership. • No Usury • Cottage and land more difficult but attainable
	Education ☆☆☆☆☆	• Free. A larger % can afford a higher education, a home, family.
	Incomes	• Reliable via Jobs & Strong Safety Nets • Support for hitech and strategic automations; equal access to start businesses and buy land.
	Healthcare	• State funded
	Freedom	• Many can start families in their own homes by 24
	Pensions	• State funded
Capitalistic ☆☆	Housing	• Homes are bought but are 70% owned by the bank. • Usury rising (unrepayable debt)
	Education	• Expensive and few can marriage and student life.
	Incomes	• Jobs begin to getting scarcer
	Healthcare	• Paid – Poor die 13 years sooner
	Freedom	• Fewer can afford to start families before 26 years of age.
	Pensions	• Pensioned jobs reduce

In Autumn, living begins to get hard for many. Billionaires begin to emerge, wealth begins to accumulate in an ever-smaller number of hands. Inequity drives Social Problems and Housing costs soar as Interest rates fall. Prices for homes were $60,000 and are now $250,000. Salaries have not improved and a Good Life, also called "the American Dream", is no-longer supported in the G7.

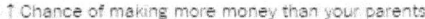

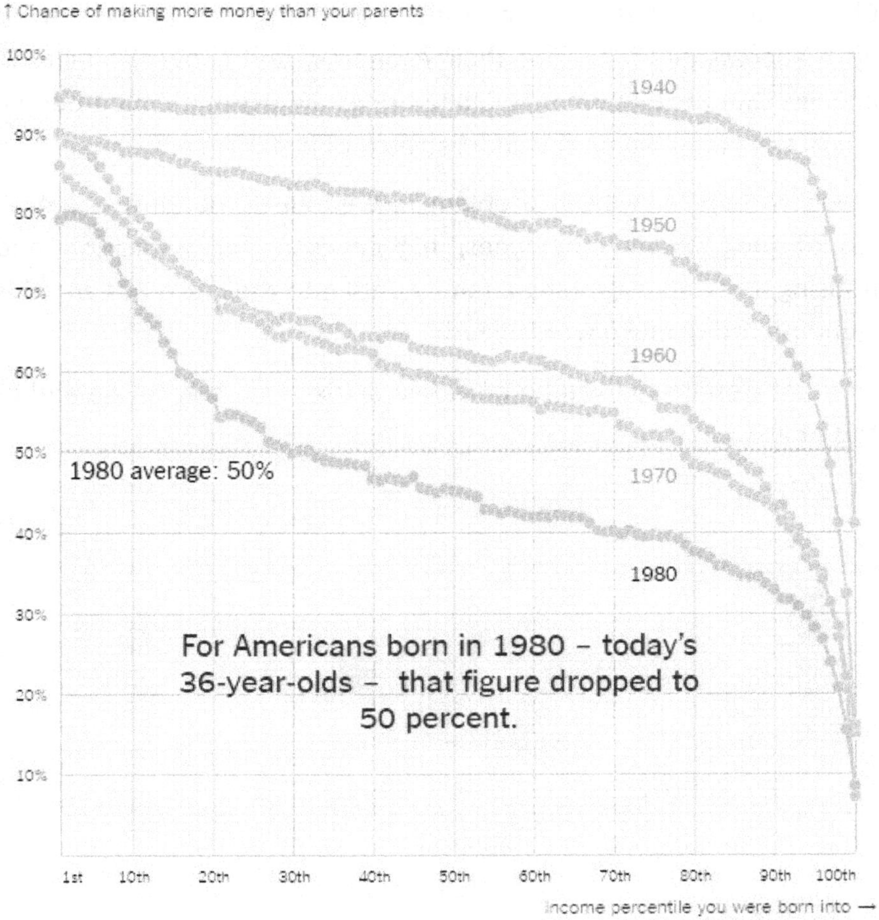

(Leonhardt, 2016)

Two-income families are now 35% of all households and Divorce rates are rising sharply. Socialistic Policies emerge in the Nordic

Nations because they have smaller populations and are able to feel the effects of unsustainable offshoring and foreign investment policy more quickly. Also, they can turn more quickly as they are not such a big ship as the U.S. and as other large-population G7 countries are. Support for their neighbors is a strong value in Nordic Nations too – as is true in most harsh-climate countries.

China pulls ahead as a Communist Nation that clearly knows how to both successfully monetize their economy, and show flexibility in policies that protect growth. China brings almost one-billion people out of the stone-age in the short stretch of just 30 years.

Freedom begins to be a problem in Capitalistic nations as longer work-hours, fewer employees, higher costs for education and housing, prevent beginning a family until into their late 20s and this trend is getting much worse yearly.

The Last Generation will be born five or six years before the end of this phase.

Chapter 5

—

Winter Phase

In antiquity, Winter was one of the easiest phases. This was true because in Babylon, a Monarch would simply follow the Economic Controls carved into the Code of Hammurabi Stone in 1760 BCE. The King would implement "Jubilee"; a time-proven program of nation-wide debt forgiveness policies - and simply Reset his economy.

This directive would begin another fifty-year cycle of Capitalist prosperity and side-step the riots, wars, and suffering that often accompanies the struggles experienced by citizens in Winter phases.

Today we live in Democratic nations where no instructions are given to our high-school students in basic civics and economic controls for Capitalism. This means that the change-over to a new cycle can play out very painfully. In fact, we see today that it has played out painfully in both of our most recent Winter phases.

The notion that Debt is "Forgivable" is not a topic that special interests and Money Lenders in society might wish to discuss. This despite the very public debt-forgiveness that was provided to industries in finance and manufacturing in 2009. Unfortunately these debt-forgiveness initiatives did not go far enough.

Princeton Professor Paul Krugman's 2012 book "End this Depression Now", called for more-extensive stimulus spending citing the military spending that ended our last Great Depression. Then Berkeley Economics Professor Emmanuel Saez released a very important paper in 2013. "Striking it Richer: The Evolution of Top Incomes in the United States" confirmed that 95% of all income earned since 2008 has gone directly to the 1% again as well.

And yet, no pervasive mention of a "Great Depression" is printed in mainstream media nor explained by neither politicians nor financial industry experts either. These omissions in the news can be questioned credibly given the body of evidence in books and scientific observation. The media, financial industries, and politicians too - are special interests after all; each's well-being and personal status-quo is tied to carrying on the unsustainable cycle as it is – for a broad array or reasons. Major news organizations are owned by a different billionaire; Politicians who have no plan for transition, do not want to be seen to have permitted the country to descend into a worse Depression, and Money Lenders at the bank want us to continue to buy into Mortgage-programs-turned-Usury as this creates some jobs and ensures their bonus.

Economists employed by banks and can rarely agree on much either. The only consensuses opinion that I was able to confirm was that these professional have seldom or never heard of Cycle Economics.

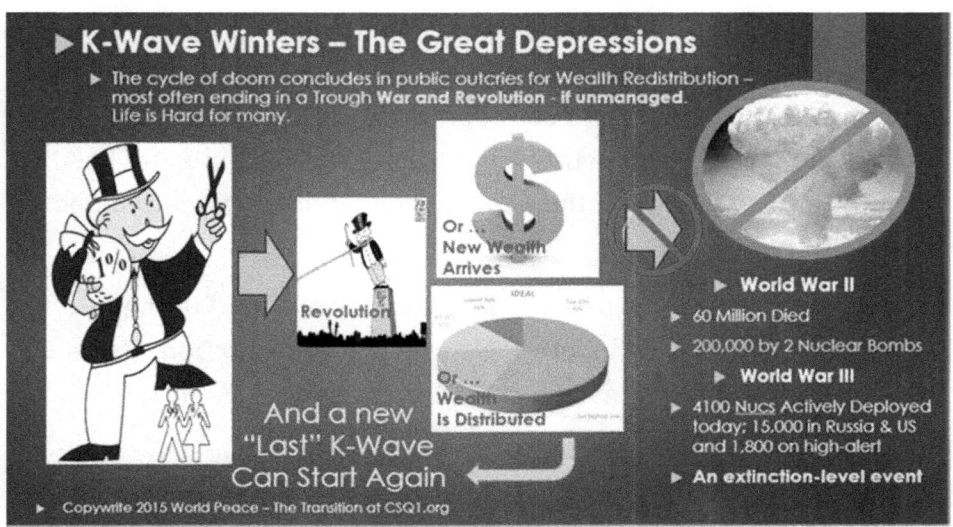

My explanation of these realities might even sound humorous were it not for the fact that there are very real reasons for concern when the reset of a capitalist cycle is delayed.

When Wealth Distributions are delayed in Winter Phase, opportunities for Wars and Revolution emerge – just as they did in 1939's conventional World War II that killed sixty-million people.

A World War in a mature nuclear era, where much of the world's aging arsenal of perhaps 8000 nuclear warheads could plunge us into an extinction-level event within approximately 30-minutes of any day or night, is surely something to avoid with highest priority.

Ironically, this surreal Nuclear Holocaust scenario hovers above us at the very first same time that humanity could be deploying our automation technologies to make money completely unnecessary.

Imagine how foolish history will judge us once we have permitted special interests to safeguard inequity – even at the risk of obliterating all in a nuclear war – at the very same time that humanity could have deployed our renewable automations to make money unnecessary.

If you wonder how is a world without money ever going to be possible, answer this. Does anyone imagine we will starve once food is produced and delivered to our doors automatically? The answer is "No - of course not". Yet, in the 71 years since the computer has been with us, it has taken until this year for the world's first automated farm to be built.

Spread Inc. of Kyoto, Japan hopes to be shipping 30,000 head of lettuce daily sustainably before the end of the 2016. McDonalds was the first to create a fully automated kitchen this year as well.

We have delayed automating food abundance in this way, while 21,000 people starve to death daily on the planet due to avoidable food scarcity (see http://www.poverty.com/). And if something inside you wonders, can the world survive with population-levels, as they are, consider that the Island of Java in Indonesia is about 20% larger than Cuba or the size of the state of Mississippi - and despite its small size, it is home to 138 million people. There can be no reason to want to starve people as our planet can clearly sustain populations in many multiples of today's seven billion.

I love Tom Hanks movies too, but "Inferno", the Dan Brown book and now movie, is a work of fiction with little foundation in hard science. Like Kingsmen, with its similar theme, it's just good entertainment.

Stories of crisis in the press, and even in our schools, often need closer examination too. I live immediately beside one of North America's Great Lakes. My response to my kid's insistence that we must conserve water - per the lessons that they had been drilled on in school that week - was not complementary of their school curriculum.

In Toronto, water is treated and returned to the lake in a closed system that will never run dry of its own volition for a thousand years. Elsewhere, water can be cleaned or desalinated through electrolysis with energy – which is the reason that Saudi Arabia and Aruba, both nuclear countries, have no limits to their fresh water supplies.

That we don't have an automated society already – is only the result of shortcomings in global and country engineering leadership.

Fortunately, perfectly feasible alternatives exist to solve both the nuclear obliteration and scarcity scenarios as well. First, a solution exists in TE-Mature Economic Controls for responsible Wealth Distributions for every country – and second, there is a detail engineering plan of Connected Smart Factories that abundantly feed and shelter the planet sustainably.

Worthwhile PLC Transition Projects, #WPProjects, is a list of the 250 automation projects that build the connected smart factories that provide for all of our basic human rights of food, energy, transportation, shelter, and more. Each country is assigned just one of these projects in order to encourage shared contribution and a new global robotics trade.

Aristotle called this planning a "Right Plan" and #WPProjects is a Global Right Plan as well. Responsible Country Right Plans need their own smaller subset plans.

Perhaps Mr. Hanks might consider making his next movie about WP Projects?

Responsible Economic Controls were put in place by Nordic Nations that have preserved a Good Life for their citizens since 1990. The G7 implemented Low-tax and Trickle-down Economics practices - and then they did not monitor inequity either. As you continue to read, you will shortly come to recognize these were rookie mistakes.

By the 2010's, we had very serious inequity. Scarcity of incomes drives social problems like racism, gender inequality, religious extremism, and terrorism. (Edward Tilley, 2016a)

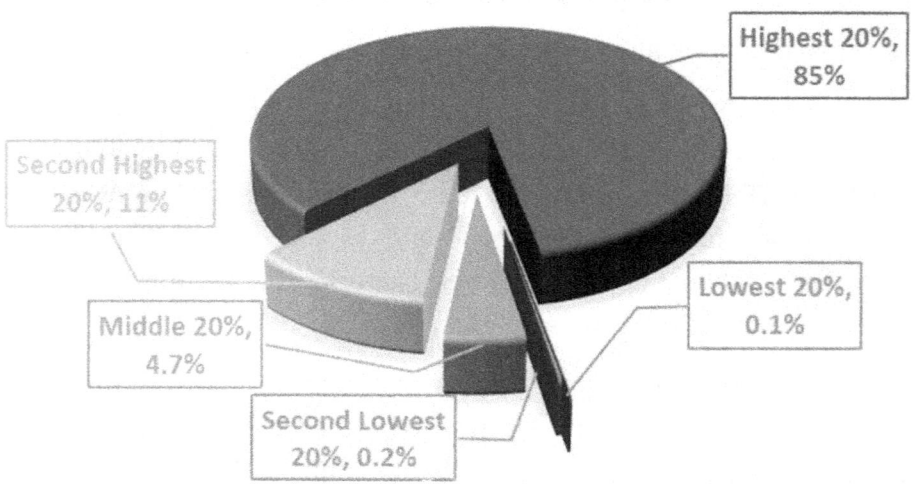

See Richard Wilkenson's Ted Talk and YouTube Video at
https://www.ted.com/talks/richard_wilkinson

Inequity is pervasive now and personal hardships can grow pronounced without incomes due to job scarcities as well.

"Research by economists at the IMF suggests that income inequality slows growth, causes financial crises and weakens demand... A survey for the World Economic Forum meeting at Davos pointed to inequality as the most pressing problem of the coming decade (alongside fiscal imbalances). In all sections of society, there is growing agreement that the world is becoming more unequal, and that today's disparities and their likely trajectory are dangerous."

Zanny Minton Beddoes, 2012

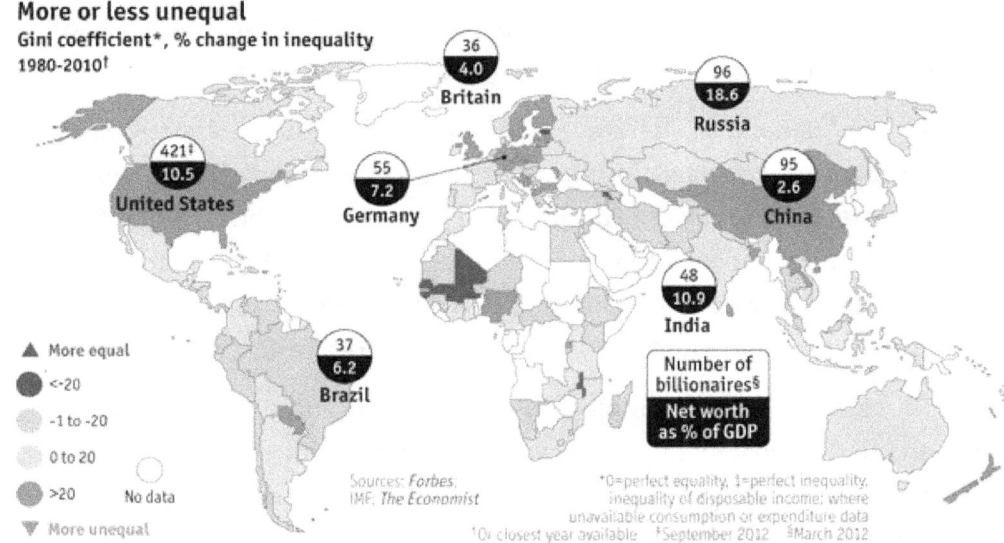

("For richer, for poorer | The Economist," 2012)

Economic hardships drive Social Problems and Housing costs soar as Interest rates fall to levels that cannot be reduced any further.

Bank rates (Country Interest rates) are at all-time lows, and can go no lower, nor can go no higher either because speculators, foreign investors, public investment funds, and families just trying to live, have leveraged cheap money to drive up the price of homes to thirteen-times inflation. In Oakville, Ontario. Canada in the summer of 2016 were bidding up $300,000 to $600,000 over the asking price by ten bidders - all foreign buyers; and all using undisclosed income sources (simply declaring payment by "cash").

Mortgages for New Homes and also Rentals are driven up, rents are up 50% to 100% in the past three years, as people who cannot buy homes drive competition for available rentals. If Interest Rates increase just 2% or 3%, the sheriff will begin evicting paycheck-to-paycheck working families into the street. If Canada was forced to defend inflation or its currency, by lifting interest rates by 3% to 5% - perhaps 50% of all new home owners would lose their homes because incomes are not going to increase at the same rates needed.

So, in Canada - where February brings -20 degree Celsius temperatures for two months, citizens cannot find shelter. Public homeless shelters were routinely full last winter in the GTA and they are already reporting that conditions will be worse this winter. Safety Nets fund one-seventh the cost-of-living and personal possessions are not protected if income cannot afford storage costs.

These are the underpinnings of desperation and revolution within one of the most income-rich cities; within one of the most resourced and educated countries in the world. And yet, here in Canada, as anywhere, the way in which government manages country policy can mean success or Collapse in a K-Wave Winter Phase.

In K-Wave Winter, living is hard for many. As families struggle to afford the price of homes that were $250,000 at the start of Winter, and are now $1,250,000. Salaries have not improved and a Good Life is no-longer supported in the G7. Two income families are now 71% of all households and Divorce rates and costs have risen sharply. Anti-eviction and Populist Political Parties and Leaders are rising out of no-where to win major elections internationally.

72% of all Economies are in a Collapse Trending and only those nations with Socialistic Policy and strong planning are Advancing.

Smart Policies for Change are needed and cannot responsibly be delayed any longer in Capitalistic nations. Incomes are needed whether they come from safety-nets, jobs, job creation programs, or even guaranteed income programs, and policies to reset spending power – in housing, energy, cost of living, childcare, education, and more are now critical.

In the closing five years of the Winter phase, the Last Generation are sure to feel most Lost as well.

Policies in the Winter Phase

Wealth Creation	Policy	
Socialistic China ☆☆☆☆☆ Nordic States ☆☆☆☆☆	Housing	• Homes are bought but protected from bubbles and foreign investment. Most are mortgaged with high rate of ownership. • No Usury • Cottage and land more difficult but attainable
	Education ☆☆☆☆☆	• Free. A larger % can afford a higher education, a home, family.
	Incomes	• Reliable via Jobs & Strong Safety Nets • Support for Hitech and strategic automations; equal access to start businesses and buy land.
	Healthcare	• State funded
	Freedom	• Many can start families in their own homes by 24
	Pensions	• State funded
Capitalistic ☆☆	Housing	• Homes are bought but are 70% owned by the bank. • Usury rising (unpayable loans)
	Education	• Expensive and few can marriage and student life.
	Incomes	• Jobs begin to getting scarcer
	Healthcare	• Paid – Poor die 13 years sooner
	Freedom	• Fewer can afford to start families before 26 years of age.
	Pensions	• Pensioned jobs reduce

Chapter 6

-

Democracy that Builds Inequity

Democracy is very important to humanity because nations that democratically vote on wars, do not sustain war upon other democratic nations. However, like any system, democracy can suffer from corruption – and it can suffer from shortcomings in strategic direction too. "Status-quo" is generally preferred in Democracies, even to the historically well-documented end-result of collapse within that society too.

Poland was the world's longest running democracy - running for 400 years beginning in the year 1600 CE. Between then and now, despite one of the greatest education systems and mathematicians in history, the country shrank to one-sixth its original size without an active army until 20% of its pre-war 25-million population became the victims of war and genocide at the hands of the Russians and the Germans in World War II.

By the end of that war, 400 years of deal-making and selfish, self-interested Polish land-owner alliances had all but obliterated the country and 20% of its people.

Like any system, democracy can suffer from corruptions forced through manipulations by special interests – and it can suffer from complacence.

Other models of government, like the French Constitution of 1791, employed a hybrid Republic and Democracy where a trained Monarch contributed expert leadership in Economic Policy but could not declare war. The English Monarchy too was hemmed in; although English Monarchs could declare war, they relied upon the finances of their House of Commons and so it became prudent for Kings to rely upon a vote before deciding the issue.

Rarely have systems in government been left unchanged for very long stretches in time historically. Public education in Democratic Reforms and Process goes a long way toward shaping a sustainable democracy

Socialistic Policies emerged in the Nordic Nations twenty-five years ago because they have smaller populations and are able to feel the effects of unsustainable offshoring and foreign investment policy more quickly. Also, they can turn more quickly as they are not such a big ship as the U.S. and as other large-population G7 countries are. Support for their neighbors is a strong value in Nordic Nations too – as is true in most harsh-climate countries.

China pulls ahead as a Communist Nation that clearly knows how to both successfully monetize their economy, and also knows how to show flexibility in policies that protect economic growth. China brought almost one-billion people out of a stone-age of extreme poverty in the short stretch of just this past 30 years.

The United States Electoral College was setup as a decidedly non-pure democratic system early-on (in its constitution) realizing that in pure democracies, larger states often ignored the needs of smaller states. In the Electoral College system, even the smallest states are still important and can't be ignored.

Similarly, if a perfect governance structure ever were to exist for society, perhaps it might look like a Monarchy, or Economic Policy Governance Committee perhaps, that is well-trained in Economic Cycle Management and then mandated with authority to meet growth targets.

This group could assume responsibility for management of Business and Engineering Programs contributions to society while Democratic Voters retain the decision-making authority for Wars and matters relating to their own standard of living and communities – in keeping with cultural values. I will explain more why I think there is a definite need for expert-only economic policy controls throughout this book.

Monarchies for millennia were believed to be the more stable form of leadership. The reason for this is that in a perfect scenario, Monarchs were after all, incorruptible in-so-far as the children of a king or queen, and their children's children as well, were protected for life. This left a dutiful, eminently well-trained Monarch with no incentive to make decisions that profited him or her personally. Socially irresponsible behavior would leave a smudge on their legacy, good family name and reputation in history. The Mad King – King George the 3rd of England is a great example of an unqualified King with a legacy that no Monarch would wish for. A Monarch's duty was to the people.

Remember that common citizens were quite a bit more-lowly educated in past centuries as well. Today our citizens are better educated, although we are educated almost not at all in alternate options in housing, monetary systems, banking, democracy, responsible government reforms, nor economic controls – and this is really very unfortunate.

Without formal training in K-Wave Economics and Economic Sustainability Controls like the Policies that we discuss here Transition Economics, voters rely instead on their emotions, media reports, or other anecdotal checklists to support their democratic voting decisions.

Most messages and policy presented by political party marketing people have much more to do with what people want to hear than what is needed to avoid social Collapse today. Polls confirm emotional pain-points among the electorate – which is good; but not so good are solutions that give you what you think you want – and not what is needed to avert Collapse. This sounds onerous and even Orwellian but every parent and guardian has had to consider this balancing act based on what they know to be safe and healthy for inexperienced family within their care too.

Sometimes policy is needed that might be unpopular or unfamiliar, but responsible economic controls that are proven to turn around a collapsing economy, create incomes, and renew spending power are vital.

Voters, therefore, must also learn to recognize what are the policies that sustain a society.

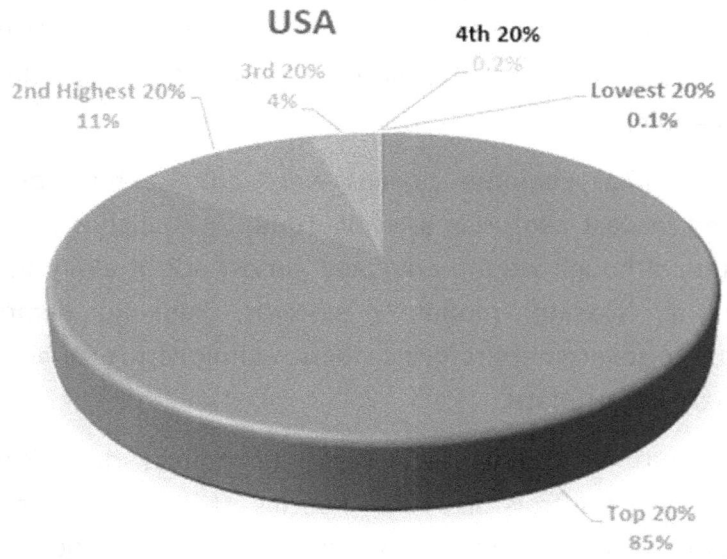

It can be said that the U.S. actively, albeit inadvertently, maintains a dividing line of people who have nothing at around 40% (according to the 2010 Fed Reserve). 40% equals 160 million people in that country. The chart above was taken directly from Wikipedia in 2015 as it reported the 2010 Federal Reserve Budget Report Statistics.

Notice that this dividing line is not at 51%. Why is it only 40%? The answer is because that small shift from 40% to 51% would create a change in the status-quo; because at that point, the majority of voters – who have nothing today, will insist on change through their vote. Media calls these Populist votes today.

Populist votes happen routinely in Economic Winters – revolutionary votes that voice frustration - such as Brexit, Trump, and even Justin Trudeau's election in Canada are examples. The policies that correct inequity are surprisingly little-understood by both voters and political party leaders and so these populist elections have had inconsistent success in turning around economies through history.

If I draw from similar populist election winners, there was Hitler, Mussolini, Stalin and Castro; and sometimes their changes worked well. Hitler did great things for the German economy initially; and Castro had an outward reputation as a benevolent dictator. There was also a dictatorship created and a World War that killed tens of millions.

Canada has packed on record fiscal spending debt in its populist government's first year, while its trade deficit, unemployment rate, and housing crisis have spiraled to rates never seen before. Canada's populist election appears to have accelerated Canada's Collapse Trending greatly. Brexit results and Mr. Trump's government record will be next to monitor.

Clearly, resorting to populist votes out of frustration are not circumstances that one plans for strategically; living conditions have to get pretty bad - and stay that way for too long. Had economies been responsibly managed to begin with, you would not see this frustration in voters. I think you will agree.

There are no populist elections in the Netherlands – except for issues created by E.U. Policies like refugees, immigration, and so on. If there was a problem in a socialistic nation, we often hear about it quickly because Special Interests groups here are quick to confirm any hint that socialistic policies can't possibly work well in the Media. Success in Socialistic nations is usually simply unreported in North America.

How does a "dividing line" of inequity become established? How is it maintained? Inequity is created by politicians who work with large staffs diligently to ensure that $100 million or 1,000 jobs, makes it into specific communities (of voters) whenever it's needed – and in doing this, the line of inequity is carefully preserved under the guise of "winning the election".

This is no exaggeration; you have seen politicians in the news recently making big funding amounts appear on a short notice and these almost always media-covered. Loyal and arguably well-purchased supporters are at the podium to speak to how this or that politician are terrific.

Here we see yet another project for Democratic Reform. Benjamin Franklin noted that 'When the people find that they can vote themselves money, that will herald the end of the republic.' Today, we see that the 1% of rich clearly have this power to vote themselves money; they are not choosing to self-govern and self-correct as well, and so now democratic reforms are needed.

Our electoral systems and economic policies are influenced by special interests – but we stick with these systems because we don't know anything else – this is our "Status-quo"; it is the only system ever taught to us and that sad shortcoming is overdue a reform.

Why change status-quo? Because – elsewhere in the world, the average Netherlands citizen, living in a country full of citizens that still enjoy the American Dream, generates 300% more wealth (measured in GDP Export per Capita) than a Canadian or a Britain, and generates six-times more than an American. Why is this true?

Because all of their citizens – 100% – can participate in the economy. They have affordable housing, childcare, healthcare, retirements, and guaranteed incomes – all of them – and so naturally their per capita export income stats will be higher.

What is really incredible, is how much more productive are these socialistic policy counties. If the United States citizens realized the same Export per Capita, it would export $500 billion additional to its present $1.2 trillion annual exports; Canada the U.K and Australia would add $60 billion to its current $31 billion – and these programs amount to small tax increases that I will discuss in more detail in coming chapters.

The Netherlands ranks #5 on the CMI; the United States is #80, Canada #100. Others can be viewed at The CMI at CSQ1.org.

In the chapter for Democratic Reforms below, we discuss the Transition Economics tactics that adjust Democracy as could better be taught to our students.

Immigration: A 20% increase in Canada's population over the past 20 years has added six million new citizens and has given Canada the largest immigration rate of the G7; a rate 35% higher than the next G7. Many immigrant families are required to bring with them $250,000 each, so if 1.5 million families had four members on average, approximately $375 billion in new immigration wealth entered Canada annually in this way – in theory.

The strategy of boosting new immigration had a historic track record of improving economies 100-years ago. New immigration was observed to relieve great depressions in 1883 and in 1779; however today's offshore banking and online trade networks seem to be negating a positive economic benefit as business and employee benefits are not shared within Canadian communities.

With no immigration controls nor monitoring of their final settlement communities, nor immigrant investment once they were in the country, the financial benefit and cultural impacts of immigration here were empirically negative in keeping with Canada's disappointingly negative economic performance in the same time period. The same is true for other high-immigration countries, while low immigration countries count among the strongest economies during the same 20-year period.

Interest Rates: Interest rates can go no-where – up nor down, Canada has a safety-net that provides one-seventh of the Cost of Living in major centers, there are serious housing bubbles that have doubled rents in the past three years and steadfastly blocked young people from starting families, 30 degree winters kill homeless people, and both unemployment, and unreported unemployment, are at record-highs in 2016 alongside record trade deficits.

Education: Schools in Canada, and in many countries, do not teach multiple policies in housing, democracy, and economic controls from around the world; voters are taught the status-quo for their country in school only and this is a failing that the parents of sustainable societies should be concerned about.

High School Students are not asking for Business Cases and they are not taught to measure the success of suggested policies in other countries either. By comparing the economic GDP benefits of the same policies over time in other countries, voters could be taking away a clear picture of policy benefits and costs. Instead voters are left with the best guesses of political marketing teams who are searching for policies that can get them elected; with no long term plans nor understanding of long-term economic impacts.

Good Management: Canada rates at #100 on The CMI Country Management Index while politicians here seek to publish whichever statistic that will call them #1 for presentation in their press and to their voting public. I mention this because "bluster" often wants to trump substance in any society that marginalizes intelligent and intelligence in their citizenry. Instead of thought leadership, election campaigns seek to maximize emotional discussions that are deemed important according to voter demographics. Examples of demographics are middle-class, female, male, retired, working, immigrants and so on.

Planning: I subscribe to the simple logic that "failing to plan is planning to fail". If you do as well, one can easily raise concern for the long-term well-being of many G7 economies – as most G7 nations do not actively maintain bipartisan Strategic Long Term Plans today.

Canadian political parties, for one, laud a system of policy creation where anyone has an equal vote at the policy decision table regardless of career experience nor training. Because policy ends up being so emotionally charged, marketers change whichever policy they like with impunity at elections - and at any other times as felt necessary.

Parties do not collaborate on long term planning and this is important when one party will be replaced by another party in fairly predictable routine. This results in an absence of strategic planning and long term investment safeguards.

Democratic Reforms: are important to revisit ongoing and would help North American systems elect qualified individuals to senior offices. Consideration should also be given to empowering citizens with the ability to vote for policy directly too.

In Canada, **Unemployment**: is the fifth highest of the G7 and offshoring of jobs and profits are perhaps higher here than in any other country due to a complete absence of offshore employment protections. Gallop, and other journals, have started to report "unreported" unemployment figures that are double the reported rates in the U.S. and the same is true in most of the G7 countries.

Unreported unemployment is the result of government administrator's playing with the definition of what is an unemployed person. A person might be unemployed and looking, but because they have not applied for or perhaps have exceeded their unemployment insurance – they are no longer included in the official count.

I am using the polite Irish tactic of picking on one's self first, but these are examples of irresponsible management and education practices that have clearly impacted countries both economically and socially throughout the G20 just the same.

Chapter 7

-

Social Collapse

Social Collapse takes a little time to happen, but unflinching adherence to poor social policies such as Low Tax and Liberte in Capitalism is the time-honored road to Collapse.

Any discussion of managing cycles in society must surely touch on the symptoms and failings of control that permit Social Collapse. This is as true for the Romans, as it was for Germany at the start 1930s, as it is for Venezuela, Greece, Spain, and us all today.

Resetting Collapse Trending Economies is Critical

This topic is important to discuss and resolve as carefully and well as we possibly can. Our past 20-year period of increasingly competitive workplaces, have spawned management teams that led 72% of all nations' globally to report a collapse trending today. The Socio-economic impacts of Collapse include Recessions, Depressions, Populism, Racism, Social Problems, Religious Intolerance, high incarceration rates, military spending, terrorism, increasing cost of living, lower standard of living and human rights - on and on. Young people cannot start lives in family-friendly communities without stable homes suitable for young children.

Turning around economies requires that decision makers of policy are not be bureaucrats nor politicians – but SMEs (Subject Matter Experts). SMEs are twenty-year experienced thought-leaders, engineers, authors, experts, and major project builders with experiece from many countries and corporate settings – and not career admins nor generalists.

We really cannot afford to not look at policies that reset economies actively now.

Countries that correct these problems and successfully reset their economies, keep their heads above water - even in difficult economic times. Statistics confirm that they position themselves for prosperity sustainably.

The countries that are good examples of sustainable policy making today include The Netherlands, Japan, China, Germany (except in Energy), Russia, Italy, Norway, and twenty others discussed in the Transition Economics Maturity Modeling discussions that follow.

What does Social Collapse look like?

1. Inequity increases, salary incomes drop to subsistence-wages, or people have no spending power with their incomes due to hyperinflation and housing bubbles
2. Incomes become scarce, job loss and homelessness increases
3. Incarceration rates increase, divorce increases, fertility rates decrease
4. Trickle-down income distribution is a proven failure due to business ethics shortcomings and no business accountability regulations.
5. Reliance on immigration revenue increases but burdens the economy's resources further

6. One of the final steps in any collapse is the failure to provide food. This was true for the demise of the Roman capitals 2000 years ago as it is for Venezuela today.
7. Revolutions and war follow miserable, unproductive lives as society continues to collapse.

Correcting Social Collapse

Throughout this book, I encourage Transition Economists to apply the lessons of Cycle Economics that recognize when it is appropriate to make policy changes proven to reverse social collapse.

The ability to change has ever been a strong benefit of the Monarchy model of government; that governance team can turn quickly and easily and it is for this reason that every military organization is run by this model.

The challenge in the Monarchy system, is that educated citizens will be affected by change and will want to retain a Good Life for their family and for their community. An educated society wants to be given the opportunity to understand the business case and social merits of a plan - and then adjust to the change.

Democracy is very important. However we do not train our children in democratic reforms nor in the economic policy changes appropriate for changing economic cycles – as we absolutely should.

In modern democracies, instead of business cases and social merit, a very large number of citizens vote for relationship managers who tell them what they expect or want to hear. Hard planning is scarce, difficult but socially responsible decisions are avoided, and emotional buzzwords are plentiful – words like gender inequality, immigration, middle class, transparency, making this country great again – add your own limerick here - as these were just the few that came to me as wrote this.

And we vote for relationship managers and salespeople because we are not knowledgeable enough to be comfortable with making a change in policy. We need to know to ask ... Will it work. Has it worked before? Where, When? There are 200 countries whose policy decisions and GDP results provide lessons-learned for other nations.

Jared Diamond's fifth interconnected cause in his 2005 foundation-stone book "Collapse: How Societies choose to fail or succeed" is inappropriate attitudes to change.

Life is messy, clean it up ... sounds like terrific and easy advice, but change is seldom easy for democratic voters who are bombarded with misdirection far more often than responsible advice. We all want Good Lives for our families the same, and yet 1-in-20 recommend courses of action (policies) are based on confirmable track records that could stand up to a credible Business Case and due-diligence review.

We do not realize that we need to demand a business case with enough decision support information to vote responsibly. Instead, we hear - emotion; I will work for you, I feel that the best thing is – You know; and I know; and I feel it strongly! Rubbish.

A car speeding for a cliff does not benefit by slowing, nor does it avert disaster by status-quo's changing nothing; "Do nothing". Status-quo strategies from the start of a Monopoly Game does not work near the end of the game.

Ronald Reagan was a wonderful individual and genuinely motivated by wanting the best for everyone. His incredible influencing skills, however, also walked the world straight into another unmanaged Great Depression. Even ten years after he left office; his popularity was still relied upon to win elections - and Reaganomics, is Trickle-down Economics. The lesson here is that we don't benefit from unsustainable policy no matter how wonderful is the leader.

When change is needed, democratic voters must be trained to understand – what are the next steps - and insist upon it at election time.

As there is a World War and species-ending-event scenario that pops-up whenever we fail to protect society from collapse today, a solution to timely and accurate democratic change becomes a matter that is imperative to get right.

I make every effort in my books, to keep solutions absolutely reasonable and even conventional, partly in an effort to avoid the lazy barbs of "don't-rock-the-boat-type" academic peer-reviewers. My book "Teaching Doers" discusses how Einstein, Turing, Pons and Fleishman, to name just a few geniuses, have all felt these barbs dramatically so, bolstered by the fact that I am in good company, I will suggest a conventional, modern solution and I will suggest an interesting albeit unconventional option – called Jubilee.

Jubilee would take place in Economic Winter just once every fifty years. A Monarch - a role that has often been defined as an elected leader with impunity, historical accountability, over-arching Economic Policy control, but no power to commence or sustain wars. This individual could be asked to govern redistribution projects in a model to implement the new cycle safely and peacefully country-by-country.

Once the two-year Cycle Restart program is complete, a return to today's model of democracy is restored. I suggest it here because this really sounds to me like a charming blend of proven lessons in history, smart culture, and progressive democratic self-governance at the same time.

A modern, conventional method would be accomplished by training high-school teens, and every immigrant and voter, in Transition Economics - see the course CSQ Common Sense 101 for one such example Civics Course. Our trained democracy would then vote for policies and leaders that are trained to arrive at a similar result. My concern for this method is in the lower probability of a deep reset and no-one would be accountability in the change either by this model. Romantically perhaps, I lament a lost opportunity to celebrate history and culture too.

If there are two good solutions to implementing the cycle change-over safely, I see that a traditional solution is more elegant than the more modern and conventional alternative – in this case.

To the question, "Is - do nothing - an option?" Unfortunately No, historically, capitalism is only sustainable when explained in the context that every sixty years or so, it needs to reset.

The last time that we failed to reset responsibly, disgruntled democratic voters endorsed leadership that led to a world war that killed sixty-million people.

Leaders did such a poor job of resetting Capitalism during the Panic of 1883 that World War I, and revolutions in Italy, Austria-Hungary, Bulgaria, Greece, Turkey and Russia, were likely consequences of unsustainable inequity in an abbreviated K-Wave cycle that lasted just forty years.

The Great Depression of 1835 was ended by enormous new wealth as the California Gold Rush multiplied America's Gold Reserves ten-times. The wealth redistribution after this great depression was deep but it was also local to North America and so it fueled only a fifty-year cycle of new prosperity. Europe did not fare as well.

Nikolai Kondratiev is sometimes referred to as the patron Saint of Economics because upon his concluding that Capitalism was sustainable by in this way, Stalin had him imprisoned and put to death (Quigley, 2012). In the 1940s, Harvard University Professor Joseph Schumpeter lauded Kondratiev's discovery and renamed these Cyclic Economic phenomena Kondratiev-Waves or K-Waves in his honor. William Thompson of Indiana University later confirmed sixty-year K-Wave cycles back as far as 930 AD in China (Snyder, 2014) ("William Thompson | Department of Political Science | Indiana University Bloomington," 2016).

My own contribution is to suggest that King Hammurabi's fifty-year Jubilees, Debt Forgiveness - explained on the Code of Hammurabi in 1763 BCE, is perhaps the first confirmation of the existence of Longwave Economic Cycles in Capitalistic Societies, which would make the Code the first proactive economic controls for these cycles as well.

Inequity Increases

We can reverse Inequity with Graduated Tax, guaranteed income and other programs that provide incomes and restore spending-power - in housing and similar. The society of the United States in the 1940s and 1950s boomed at a time when the highest income earners paid 92% tax so there is no business case that supports the argument that graduated tax hobbles an economy.

The Trickle-down approach, a theory where low tax gives money to business so that they can create jobs and distribute wealth, is a proven failure - so if your worthwhile goal is to build a sustainable society Business Accountability measures must also be insisted upon.

Business Accountability solutions for Governments include:
- On-shoring controls for:
  - Ownership
  - Manufacturing
  - Engineering
- Deny Tax Evaders and Offshoring groups Access to Markets and growth

- Monitor and Control Foreign Investment
- Residential Homes are Shelter; monitor for bubbles and penalize investment that makes supply scarce.
- Business Storefronts are transient (they will not be required as technology improves) but desirable for recreation centers.

Incomes become Scarce

Maintaining incomes across 100% of the population is essential for an advancing economy. For the active workforce (approximately 50%), Income Scarcity must be countered with Guaranteed Incomes that meet Cost of Living – in part, so that pension savings can be maintained.

The Non-workforce of any country often exceed 50% of the population; retired people over sixty-five-years of age are often 20% +- 5% so it is critical that protections for pensions permit retired individuals to continue to contribute to the economy - and to be self-sufficient.

Failing to mitigate income scarcity leads to dramatically lower wealth creation per citizen. Export-per-Capita is a readily searched GDP statistic that can also be considered a warning indicator of collapse when it is compared alongside trade deficits, fiscal balances in deficit, and Cost of Living.

Cost of living is a statistic that can be greatly reduced long-term through sustainability in automation too – so there is an added Opportunity Cost when countries do not have strategic planning in place to incorporate Renewable Automations that provide food, shelter, energy and transportation automatically.

Housing becomes Scarce

Scarcity in housing occurs when normal Supply and Demand are prevented. For example, if too many people immigrate and are forced to move into a small region to find incomes where new housing construction projects cannot accommodate them, scarcity drives housing bubbles.

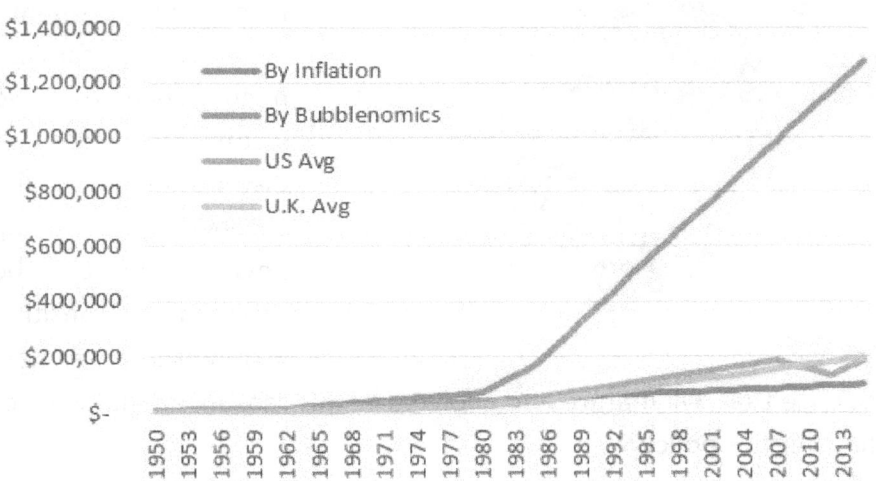

Average Home Prices in Toronto vs Inflation

When housing becomes too expensive to afford with available incomes, people lose the ability to own a home; then, as demand for rentals increase, rentals become unaffordable too until whole families can be forced to become homeless. High housing costs and unaffordable rental housing, creates housing scarcity too.

Social Problems Increase

Social problems correct themselves in communities that enjoy a Good Life within a strong economy. As sustainable social and economic policies, and renewable automations, are adopted locally and even worldwide, tensions inside and between communities ease. Culture is very important too so patience and tolerance are in much greater supply once everyone has what they need. The reverse is true when economies are collapsing.

Transition Economics Tracker Version 1.0

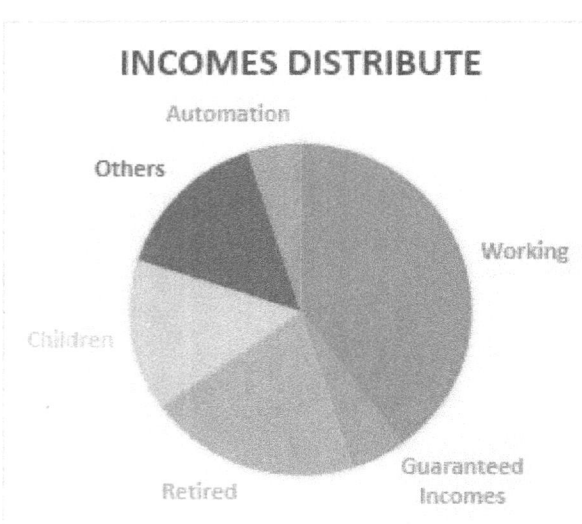

Initially we have two sets of requirements that must be met to reset an economic cycle. First, families need incomes; so incomes must be distributed; and second, spending power must be restored. Transition Economics is a new science that will mature and evolve. For this reason, an initial list of housing policy change methods are suggested and version controlled. So what follows is a v1.0 list to begin with.

Similarly, the rates of change in society will have to happen responsibly and

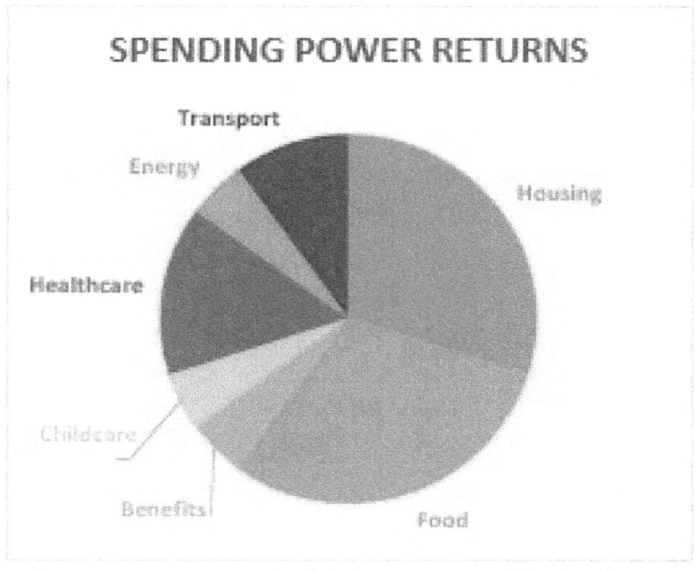

this means pilot projects and algorithms that throttle change at rates that do not jeopardize safety and standard of living. We will discuss algorithms and throttles throughout this book.

As we step through detail explanations of Transition Economics solutions, these tracking charts will serve to reference how the discussion serves this purpose.

Setting and meeting social policies and targets for automations increases your country's RAI – Renewable Automation Index and Transition Economics Maturity (see csq1.org for both measures) are an obvious mitigation to the risk of collapse.

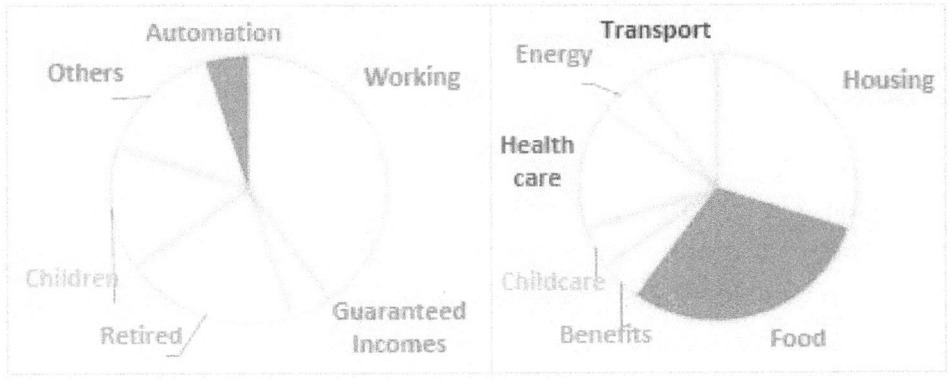

Investment in Renewable Automation

Not all technology creates renewable and resalable resources, and so it is important to learn to and invest heavily in automations that create our basic needs of food, shelter, transportation, infrastructure, energy, goods and services.

Technology investment that does not support renewable automation amounts to a distraction from a sustainable society and therefore, are not worthwhile projects nor investment.

This speaks to most investment in Innovation today. The leaders of the last wave of technology thirty-years ago – companies like

Hewlett-Packard, Xerox, IBM, Cisco, Microsoft, Oracle and similar are marketing big-data, fintech, regtech, cloud and social media companies that do not also build renewable automation. As such they can be considered less worthwhile in keeping today.

Countries too offer Innovation Strategies comprised of nothing but unsustainable non-renewable technologies. Companies are missing this boat altogether and this is true of Canada – a country without a transition plan of any kind, like Britain, Australia, Spain and others.

Coordinating Renewable Automation projects internationally creates new trade wealth, distributes cost, improves quality and mitigates the risk of monetary distribution shortcomings and social collapse.

Winning Battles and Losing Wars via Policy

Inequity is the natural result of Capitalism; and inequity is also capitalism's highest Opportunity Cost. Opportunity Costs are the potential incomes lost from other alternatives; and often these loses are recoverable by enacting a few smart policy changes too.

Cherry-picking of statistics, and logic-gaps in the conclusions that facts within GDP statistics reveal, are frequent in media and in the economics articles printed in our major news publications. One always hopes that each country's management team and economic performance are well protected once highly paid PhDs coach economic best-practice to their body politic. And yet, we do arrive poorer for it. Collapse Trending is a verifiably valid observation; so Science demands we rethink current best-practices.

In this book, I will cite statistics for 180 countries. The G7 countries include France, America, Germany, Canada, Italy, Japan, and the United Kingdom. The G8 adds Russia. The G20 adds Turkey, Saudi Arabia, Mexico, China, Indonesia, India, Brazil, Australia, Argentina, South Africa and South Korea (there are just nineteen countries in the G20 at present). The Nordic States include the three Scandinavian Kingdoms of Denmark, Norway, and Sweden plus Finland, Greenland, Aland Islands, and the Faroe Islands.

Consider that the costs of inequity are at least two-fold initially. First, in the United States there is a constant revolution where welfare, military and incarceration spending is roughly five-times more per capita than the next-highest G7 nation (the U.K. is second in incarceration rates). Second, the Opportunity Cost of having 160 million people who are unable to contribute to the productivity of the country's Gross Domestic Product (GDP) is tremendous. The U.S. has an Export-per-Capita of just $5,000 where TE-Mature nations like the Netherlands are six times higher at $33,000.

In Chapter 11 we will compare GDP Export-per-Capita statistics to a socialistic-policy nation like the Netherlands, to explain how to calculate the costs of inequality ("Exports per Capita," n.d.). For the United States, inequity costs a staggering $8 trillion in lost productivity and new export wealth annually.

Canada, the U.K., and Australia each bypass approximately $600 billion annually by protecting inequality; by not providing socialistic support systems for their citizens like Guaranteed Incomes, Engineering Safety Nets, Day Care and Higher Education. Complaints that Canadians raise too few children are used to permit the diluting of its own world-famous culture through the highest immigration rate in the G7 - with little or no governance protecting quality of life impacts here.

Germany, and recently France and Switzerland, have been shoring up their socialistic policy quite a bit; Germany enjoys the strongest per capital GDP of the G7 in large part due to socially responsible reforms.

Pre-Perestroika - before the U.S.S.R changed to a Capitalist model in

1986, Moscow citizens were the last of the G8 to lose the American Dream. By "American Dream", I mean to say that all Muscovites had an exemplary definition of freedom; modest apartments were provided to young people when they wanted to move out after age sixteen; at nineteen they could marry and started a family in a larger assigned home; and all families were assigned a family cottage (Dacha) outside the city if requested. 21-year-old women were often the oldest among their friends if their first child had not arrived already, and both parents could continue university degrees and post-graduate studies while raising their children at home. If their marks were high, the couple's student salaries were increased as well - so that they could afford a car for the family.

Little money was a constant complaint, quality and variety of goods could have been better too, and yet basic needs were provided. Homelessness was illegal in the U.S.S.R. states and many are uncomfortable with the new situation today where 3.5% of the population are homelessness in Russia. There are between 30,000 and 50,000 homeless people in St Petersburg alone. They are called Bomzhi - having no fixed abode - the official status of those who lack the Propiska; a stamp in the internal passport verifying an official place of residence. Without a residence permit, the homeless are deprived of employment, medical services and social welfare, and can be sent to prison for up to two years for "vagrancy, begging or leading a parasitic life." ("Homeless in Russia: A visit with Valery Sokolov, by Jan Spence, Share International Archives," 1997)

Unlike China, Russia failed to monetize their productions while operating as a communist government; this means that they failed to sell their watches, machinery, jets, and automobiles to other countries in sufficient quantity. These freedoms came to an end when Mikhail Gorbachev changed to the Capitalistic Policies suggested by U.S. President Reagan and other major trading partners at the time.

Most would agree that China is an economic powerhouse and even a force-of-nature, but how did they get there? In the west, students are taught that Communism (communistic or socialistic policies) are policies that result in a terrible financial failure – the U.S.S.R.'s challenges in monetizing their Communist economy is usually brought forward as an example. But what of Communist China's undeniable success?

The Chinese not only own 10% of U.S. Debt, but they also own extensive property holdings that can be counted among the most prestigious real estate in the United States, Canada and the United Kingdom too. Why invade another country if you can just buy the bits that are worth having – and leave the headache of managing lower-class indigenous people to local governments?

This is what brilliant planning and responsible management looks like; North Americans and European leaders might actually like to play a move or two of this strong planning chess game in their own defense once in a while.

The Netherlands managed better economically as a direct result of its adopting Socialistic Policies 25-years ago. At #5 on The CMI, the Netherlands guarantees living wages and incomes, maintains a trade surplus, has universal daycare, retirements; they implement graduated tax, offshoring protections, and housing controls that ensure that young families can get started. Dutch citizens earn three-times export per capita (new wealth) than a Canadian. Why? Because they can; their citizens are not forced to sit idly without the means to begin commercial businesses that make them productive.

Socialistic Policies are not the only solution for all phases of Economic Cycles, nor for all population-level countries, but you will come to understand why TE-Mature Socialistic Policy are the only choice in

Autumn and Winter phases. Socialistic Policies are probably the only option that works in all economic phases for countries with populations of less than twenty million as well.

Like the Roosevelts and Bushes, I am the descendant of the 400-year Puritan family that originally helped to build Harvard University; my name is on the Mayflower Compact, and so it does not surprise that my own values prefer sustainable equality very much. I like them for both their business performance and obvious humanism.

The Netherlands, Norway, etc. make use of the productivity of 100% of their population through social supports - in keeping with their national values just the same.

Liking or nor liking something does not enter into research and observation, a socialistic policy may make a better business case – or it may not. Often I research a conclusion that I might like to prove correct only to find no support or that the opposite is even true.

To the question "Does Socialism make people lazy?" The answer is verifiable in GDP Export statistics as Absolutely Not. Inequity's Special Interest lobbyists jump quickly to cite negative examples in sub-communities – Canadian Indians are perhaps one example.

Based on GDP stats, and easily noticeable in CSQ Research's CMI Country Management Index, giving citizens the tools and means to be productive, is proven to make countries advance economically.

In Transition Economics, I offer many supporting examples of TE-Mature Countries Advancing their economies consistently and I will present a formal Business Case for Empathy as well - in Chapter 28.

Chapter 8

—

Restarting the Cycle

The number one priority of a Winter Phase Economy like the one that we live in globally in 2016, is the restarting of the next Economic Cycle as quickly and as constructively as possible.

Capitalist Economic Cycles run for sixty years. In Ancient Egypt and Babylon, King Hammurabi, his sons and forefathers too – reset these Cycles every fifty years in a practice called "Jubilee" - Universal Debt forgiveness and Wealth Distribution.

At the end of a Monopoly Game, how do you restart a new Cycle? You turn in everything and start again; with money in your pocket from the bank, regular incomes, and fresh spending power in an economy of affordable homes and businesses that can be purchased and developed.

Capitalism restarts in just this exact same way.

Transition Economics Problem Solving

At each phase of an economic cycle, policies must solve problems unique-to and routine-within that phase.

Increases to Interest Rates in Winter Phase:

Economies defend their currency valuation and national debt load by increasing interest rates. The upside of a lift is that this problem is now solved; however, there is a real downside in that as interest rates rise, mortgage payments also rise; first for variable mortgages and then for fixed mortgages. Housing Bubbles have forced many mortgage holders and real estate speculators to take on enormous mortgages that are many multiples of their salaries. As interest rates rise and owners cannot pay their mortgages, owners dip into retirement savings and then, if they cannot sell their homes, they lose their homes to the mortgage provider.

Evicted families turn next to an overstressed rental market and will often hold an overpriced rental without hope of returning to a home ownership position.

If homeowners lose their income as well, or cannot find income due to automation job-loss, high divorce rates, or high-unemployment, a large percentage of evicted home-owners will become homeless and 5% of homeless will commit suicide.

Regrettably, the status-quo answer in most capitalist countries today is to "do nothing" about this problem.

Now, Transition Economics are needed to save lives. See the Housing Policy Chapter below to see that many anti-eviction options, real estate bubble controls, and other proven, researched policies are available to balance the Interest Rate Increase.

What are other Problem Solving examples?

Automation: tests poorly with voters due to concerns for job-loss – and yet Automation is a direct economic production booster at the same time that it mitigates concerns of collapse entirely.

Consider also that no-one starves once food is automatically grown and delivered autonomously to everyone's door; and no-one goes without shelter once robots build serviced homes where and when needed too.

Guaranteed Incomes, Retraining, Engineering Safety Nets and perhaps even Corporate Automation Taxes, solve the job-loss problems at the same time they are proven to increase exports per capita (economic wealth creation) dramatically.

The needs of society to sustain families who no longer send someone to commute to office cubicles in order to sustain an income is now addressed. People can retrain, or begin worthwhile careers in fields that they love as opposed to repetitive labors.

For business, the savings from automation are substantial – consider that an automated shop floor has no need of night shift workers; can run 7/24 using equipment engineered to run for years at a time; and there is no need for even overhead factory lights in many cases.

For just two examples where Transition Economics save lives while building sustainable societies.

We discuss policy problem solving in much more detail in the Chapters ahead.

Stimulus that Builds Equality

We have discussed how stimulus spending in government was suggested in the 1930s' Depression years by Keynesian Economics to create demand to get the economy going before World War II.

Intuitively – the theory and practice seems sound in short spurts; if you fill the ordering queues of businesses, those businesses will start producing not only your order, but also they might fill additional inventory in anticipation of new demand as well. This kicks off ordering queues upstream - with all of their sourcing and processing of raw materials, and downstream businesses get busy with their work of packaging, transport, banking, and insurance.

If, however, you leave order queues empty - not only are factories not manufacturing to meet your order, but there can be no anticipation of new orders and this means that no inventories will be created here, upstream nor downstream either.

It seems sound as I say, but why does this approach not work in to restart a new economic cycle in practice in 2008?

Recall that I mentioned that only Wealth Distribution restarts a new Capitalist Cycle. If trickle-downs were working perfectly well, these new orders would create profits and then new incomes would then be commuted to all employees working in that company.

Trickle-Down Failures to Households

But I also mentioned that trickle-down was confirmed to be a failed approach according to the U.S. Federal Reserve record back in the 1990s. Visible here in this chart below, the split from the profit of companies - and the profit of households – is clearly evident in statistics.

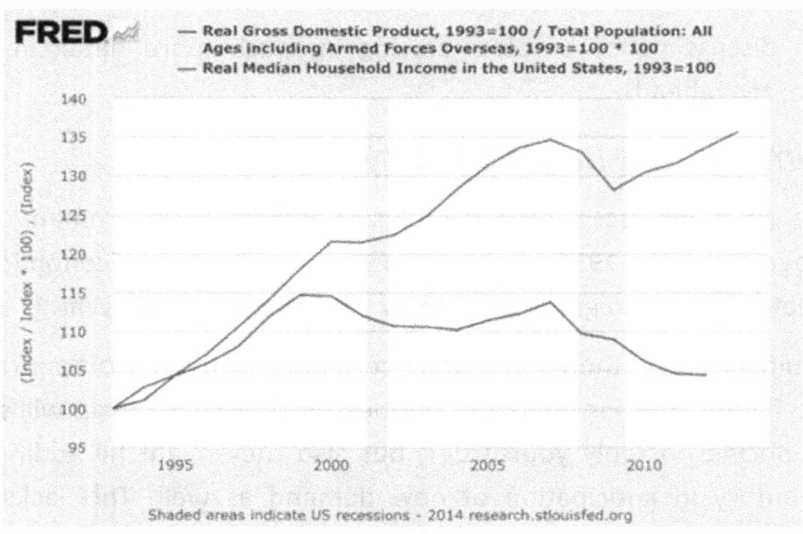

Salaries too, peaked in the 1970s, then dropped throughout the 1980s and 90s. Salaries have never recovered.

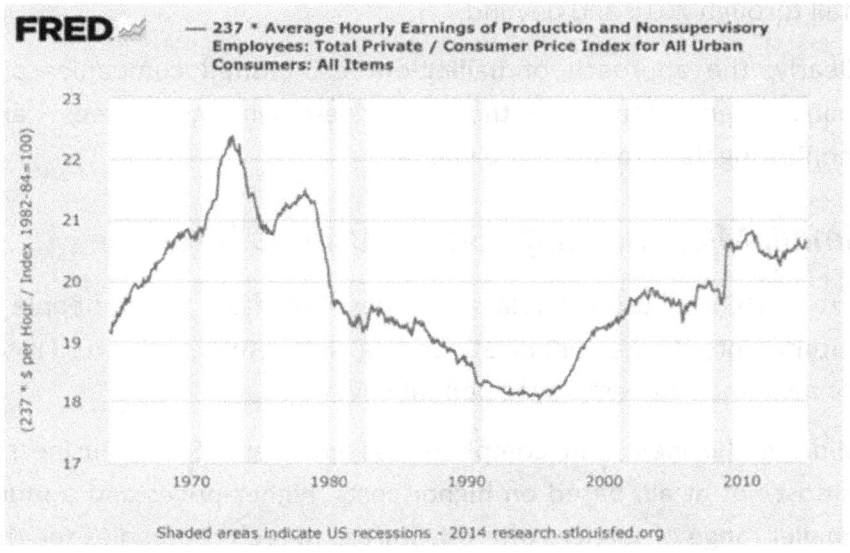

Trickle-down Failures to Businesses

Businesses too could have their profit redirected away; a contract-winning company or division could be purchased by a losing business and have profits redirected back to the purchasing company. In this way, new wealth distributions are prevented.

Procurement competitions in private and public organizations assisted these failed trickle-downs whenever they did not monitor the behavior of their winning supplier companies. When trickle-down misses accumulated year after year, this form of stimulus spending became an unsustainable and ineffective approach.

The same was true of companies who had their debts forgiven in 2008 and 2009. As mentioned above, Berkeley Economics Professor Emmanuel Saez's paper "Striking it Richer: The Evolution of Top Incomes in the United States" confirmed that 95% of all income earned since 2008 has gone directly back to the 1% (of rich) again.

Without wealth distribution, and without the return of buying power again, the Economic Cycle cannot restart and we with continue to stall through 2016 and beyond.

Clearly, the approach of bailing-out established companies and management teams without trickle-down guarantees and monitoring, fails to distribute wealth.

Small, Mid, and Large-Sized Business Mix

Size matters in business. A large business can afford to hire people to optimize processes, minimize spending, and demand preferred rates for insurance and employee benefit coverages.

Mid-Size Business can complete less well, and Small Businesses almost not at all, based on higher-costs, higher-prices and a much smaller range of services offered. Startup hi-tech companies see this when dealing with large fund managers who prefer to one-stop-shop at companies that can offer larger funding deals. It takes $30 million to make a hi-tech startup company a multi-billion dollar success – even the ones that offer a game-changing beneficial technology.

Small Business requires considerable support to keep running and thriving. Accounting fees cost $400 per month, insurance for liability and an employee-shared pick-up truck is $2000 per month, office rentals are $3000 per month and up - on and on. Tax Revenue Agencies who have been unable to make a dent in the $100 billion tax avoidance tactics of big businesses, can only turn to small business operators who cannot afford to defend themselves properly.

When too many families are forced to turn to their own small businesses for incomes, hyper-competition sets in until there are too many plumbing stores, tire shops, tile stores, etc. to support a decent living for any of them. There are 3,000 Realtors registered in Oakville,

Ontario. Canada – a small city of 170,000; 80% do not earn more than they spend on fees, ads, vehicle, and other costs – these become zero and negative-income small businesses.

The expenses for small businesses are high and support for failed businesses and employees has to be there as well. Risk taking small business men and women face not just bankruptcy, but they also stand to be turned into the streets as homeless, to lose all worldly possessions entirely, if their business fails and they exhaust savings. In Canada, where no anti-evictions laws exist and homeless shelters turn away people in February's -20 temperatures, small business owners risk not just livelihoods, they risk their lives too in fact.

Fifty Men between the age of forty and sixty commit suicide every week in Canada, and this is in no small part due to the experience of not being able to re-enter the job market once released from employment without sufficient income supports. Poor coping skills can falter quickly as divorce, loss of family, loss of status and unemployment, loss of income and homelessness descend quickly in winters that are not well suited to depression. Imagine losing everything, being unable to communicate or participate in activities with friends, to own a car, to go to the gym, to sky, to do the things you enjoy, to find a mate and to only look forward to homeless shelters that clearly cannot accommodate you easily – and this situation can carry on despite your best efforts to find work for more than a year and then two years.

The bill collectors call daily, revenue agencies take you to court, you cannot defend yourself nor declare bankruptcy as that costs $1,500. Without family support, anyone will be hard pressed to endure it. Many pensioning parents find themselves supporting children and grand-children at a time in their life when they are least able to do so - and this depletes pension incomes' positive impacts for the economy.

The descent for small-businesses people without income supports in society is steep and severe.

Diversity programs work against small businesses too as now neither working husband nor working wife has time to shop at small stores. As a result, spending becomes entirely focused on one-stop-shopping at big-box stores and large businesses. As a voter, you should recognize that Diversity Programs are usually vote grabs that deny families' pensions, create dual-income traps, and mean women cannot look after family, should they wish it - and worse, diversity is often used as distractions designed to deflect attention from far more important anti-Inequity priorities. Harvard University might laud their Diversity for example, because it deflects attention from that fact that their 99% are from money. See Chapter 29's section on Inequity vs Diversity for more.

As incomes decrease, Dollar Stores & 99p Shops become the last refuge of an insufficiently incomed population within an unsustainable economy. There are no dollar stores in Germany and Germany imports little from China – for precisely this reason. Instead, people go to work to produce things that are needed by others; their neighbors can afford to purchase these goods because they are working and generating an income as well. In this way businesses are supported; imports decline; self-sufficiency increases; prices rise a little but are also afforded.

Policies that call for more reliance on unsupported small businesses, low prices, no reshoring and no self-sufficiency, are policies of a collapsing to be certain. In short, emulate Germany and the Netherlands and do the opposite of every policy that collapsing Canada and the U.K. hold to (in 2016) – basically. One caveat is that Germany suffers from energy poverty as a result of their world leadership in part-time wind and solar energy; so avoid that problem and look instead to energy policies recommended in Chapter 16.

Restarting the Next Economic Cycle

Status quo and do-nothing policy, fails to distribute wealth and then keep it distributed in a Winter Phase. So, how then can our governments, and we citizens, spend in a way that stimulates the economy so that first, wealth is actually distributed and second; so that incomes regain the buying power needed to recover a Good Life; a life complete with all of the things that we need?

On the first point, we cannot assign stimulus spending contracts to companies and thereafter ask them to trickle-down nicely; rich companies will simply buy the new contract-winners and Status-quo will fall back into the hands of the 1% again almost immediately.

Clearly there is a failing in our Business Schools and Accountability Governance that permits, and even encourages this socially irresponsible behavior, and so we need to address Corporate Social Responsibility immediately as well.

Logic Roundabouts

On the point of stimulating a new Economic Cycle restart, we really need to train ourselves to ignore a lifetime of Roundabout and Sideways logic now. What is Roundabout Logic? Roundabouts are non-direct attempts to give people incomes. Instead of simply directly giving incomes through guaranteed income programs and engineering safety nets. Instead of direct solutions, we give incentive funding to employers in hopes they will give it to employees via trickle-down, but we don't confirm that the money makes it to employees. Or, we give grants to re-train unemployed coal miners to be programmers, welders, trades people, and so on, but we don't always ensure that this retraining results in incomes by initiating engineering reshoring controls, and other checks that ensure that new incomes are created. Trickle-down and unmonitored retraining programs are good examples of Roundabout Logic proven not to work.

No incomes means no economy. So if we guaranteed that the programmers could use their new skills to create automation, with Engineering Safety Nets that paid their bills as they produced food, shelter, and the things we needed automatically; and robotically - those trainees who were not swept up by businesses as employed workers anyway, we would realize two benefits with our retraining spending.

What of prisoners? Repurposed to build society's automation needs, what better way to repay their debt to society, than to retrain them to be useful in society upon release, and – automations can greatly reduce or the costs of their incarceration as well. This is a terrific example of Direct Logic that promises to greatly reduce prison populations by creating productive, engaged, and employable citizens - as we automate.

A sustainable society that affords a Good Life for all will greatly reduce incarceration rates and military spending generally. Inequity – a lack of access to incomes that can afford Good Lives - is the reason that the U.S. incarceration rate is five-times that of the next G7 country, the U.K.

Without shelter and incomes, the homeless live worse lives than prisoners. Retrained and repurposed, building automation and new human rights standards; the statistics say that we would see life spans increase, fertility rates become self-sustaining; benefits upon benefits basically. The business case is compelling; which is probably why all of your Sunday Schools drilled you on care for the needy in the first place.

Ignoring great Philosopher's lessons-learned, as they explain a time-tested sustainability model, makes poor business sense too. The

Golden Rule and Ten Commandments appear in every religion and throughout philosophy; and they are not simply a nice nor unrealistic moral sentiment. Others countries make it work and they are not collapsing - as are half of the G20.

Most of the philanthropic organizations of our major companies fall into this roundabout logic trap today. Cisco Networks, for one example, supports charities that make available micro loans (credit) to women in developing countries. This permits a handful of local women to buy and sell, but does not protect their profits from being stolen easily by others around them who are also in need. There is short-term benefit for a handful, but no sustainable benefit as any benefit ends as soon as credit is removed. There is also the very real risk of human subjugation of these women by others who would steal from them. The program is not without merit, there are simply better and more sustainable alternative and more direct approaches.

Here are other examples:

1. **Stimulus Spending** – Military, Government, and similar spending - **without** trickle-down monitors. The way that we implement stimulus spending today is unsustainable. The evidence against trickle-down today is well weighed & measured. History shows us that this approach plays out negatively time and time again.
2. In 2008 we tried to implement **Debt-Forgiveness**, but we implemented it as trickle-down roundabout stimulus spending to major companies and so it did not result in a positive change for the economy.
3. **Infrastructure Spending** – Infrastructure spending will not restart a next Economic Cycle by itself. You must add trickle-down guarantees that put incomes into households directly – and with other spending-power renewals and automations, it can work well and also very sustainably as well.

Infrastructure spending without a minimum 10% percent budget assigned to build automation deliverables will leave you with no efficiencies for building the things you need year-after-year; like roads, train tracks, bridges, and so on. Look to Automation projects examples at CSQ Science Magazine at CSQ1.org/mag.

Buckminster Fuller, the inventor of the Geodesic Dome, referred to Government spending on automation as investing in "Livingry" instead of Weaponry. These investments in Renewable Automation would we sustainable and therefore desirable and preferred.

4. **Government Hiring & Military Spending** – closer, because now you are putting incomes directly into people's hands, but there are few less-productive places on this earth than in a government cubicle. Being a person who is not "built" for a cubicle, nor office politics, nor academic peer-reviewed environments - is not a bad thing. Creatives and engineering geniuses will not function in this setting easily, so you are always wise to rely on the GDP Export (Wealth) stats and give these folks a funded outlet where they can be creative and productive either alone or in teams. See Engineering Nets in the next illustration's lower-right corner ...

Direct Logic

Instead, to distribute wealth most efficiently and quickly - go "direct". Bypass the logic roundabouts and middlemen altogether, and assign citizens a guaranteed income that leaves them capable of participating in commerce.

This sounds easy right? We could begin to implement Cost of Living based Income Guarantees, Engineer Safety-Nets, and we could do this in a week as well. But would this be enough to restart the next financial cycle?

Guaranteed Incomes go a long way toward distributing wealth quickly, but providing guaranteed incomes to citizens alone does not mean they can buy important things with this money. A few more steps are required to ensure that money flows broadly and does not simply cascade back into the same small handful of purses again.

Remember that goods and services, pharmaceuticals, insurance, banking fees, and everything else has increased in cost year-over-year - in keeping with inflation or in keeping with a bubble or open market rate. The largest expenses among these spending-power corrections is usually going to be rent, housing, and energy costs.

As an interesting side note in theory, another way that we could have kept things affordable was to increase salaries in keeping with housing bubbles and other rapidly incrementing costs of living.

Assuming low unemployment rates, these salary increases would have protected us from inflation and communities would not have lost their Good Life - in perpetuity in theory.

Instead, prices rose in keeping with a market-driven demand – and more. In theory, if demand for a home is supplied easily; if there is no scarcity, then prices should not rise. However, when a real or imagined scarcity, competition, or even investor speculation is introduced – and there are no housing controls in place to dissuade these behaviors, prices rise sharply. These are the conditions that explain housing bubbles.

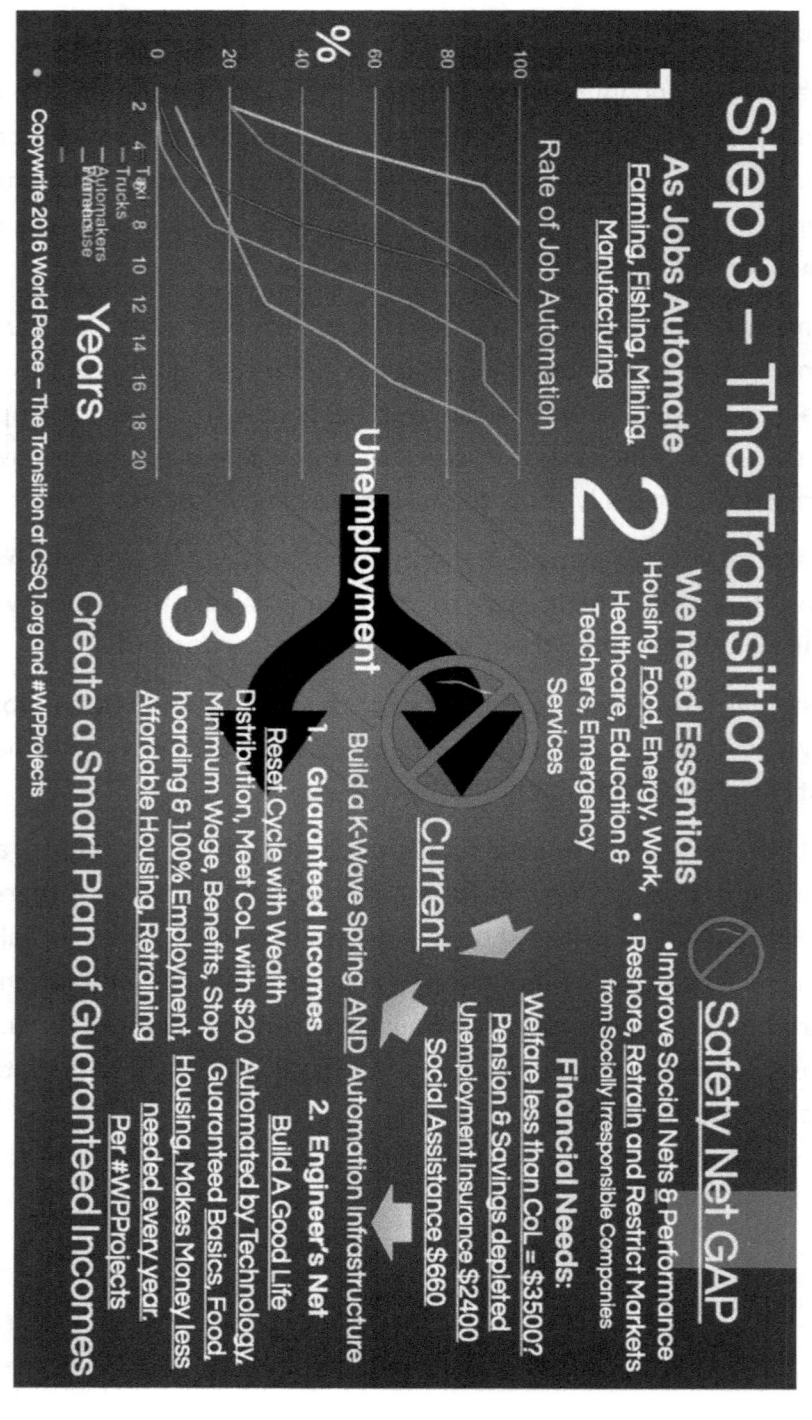

Let's look at Inflation in isolation first. Inflation is a value measured as the Consumer Price Index – The CPI; a list/index of staples whose prices are monitored monthly and yearly by governments in most countries. In this next chart, we see that Canada is fortunate to have not seen rates of inflation higher than 12% since the 1950s.

During collapses of hyperinflation, or monetary devaluation, as you saw most famously in Germany after World War I, prices doubled every two days reaching as much as 30,000% per month. People used wheel barrows to carry enough currency to be able to buy bread. The worst case ever hit Hungary after World War II – and you see a similar situation in Venezuela today where money is weighed instead of counted and a dozen eggs costs $150.

If housing increases were based on Inflation alone, a house that cost $10,000 in 1950 would today cost $102,000 in 2015 65-years later. That's an average value increase of $1,415 annually on average or a 3.65% inflation rate compounded annually.

Inflation versus Markets - Bubblenomics

- Housing bubbles, also called Real Estate "Bubblenomics", have been much in the news in recent years. (Aldrick, 2015).

In his Telegraph article Housing Bubbles from November 2015, Philip Aldrick notes, "What's remarkable about this bubble is it has inflated without a recovery. *Markets have become completely detached from economic reality.*"

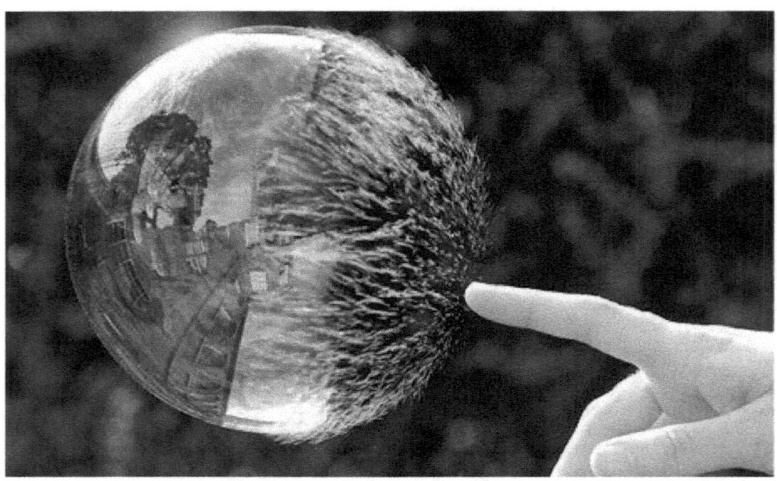

Near every major city in every major country including New York, Vancouver, Paris, London, Tokyo, Hong Kong, have all turned basic housing into private and publicly-traded Investment speculations, businesses, from both foreign and domestic investors. Housing has become a very profitable business that has outperformed conventional financial markets since 1980 - and most noticeably in this past 10 to 15 years.

Indeed the line between: What is an investment, and - what is an essential - is blurred quite a bit in housing bubbles. Is Housing an investment commodity - or is housing an essential shelter? Clearly it must be the later first - no matter what else it might like to become.

Toronto is a city that experiences -20 degree Celsius winter nights for as much as a month each year. The U.N. has been openly critical of Canada's "persistent housing crisis" and has pointed to social assistance not being in line with housing costs specifically. ("UN critical of Canada's record on housing, homelessness - Business - CBC News," 2016)

The reality is that people die in these temperatures and a civilized society's values have to stand for the basic human right of shelter as a minimum here. In the U.S., one could argue that homeless citizens might make it to Florida or California - to survive the winter, but this isn't an option in Canada really.

For those viewing this chart below in black-and-white, the Bubblenomics market-driven price line for an average home in Toronto is the logarithmically-increasing line stretching seven-times farther above other housing market norms – which are shown here for the United States and for the United Kingdom. The lowest line is simple Inflation.

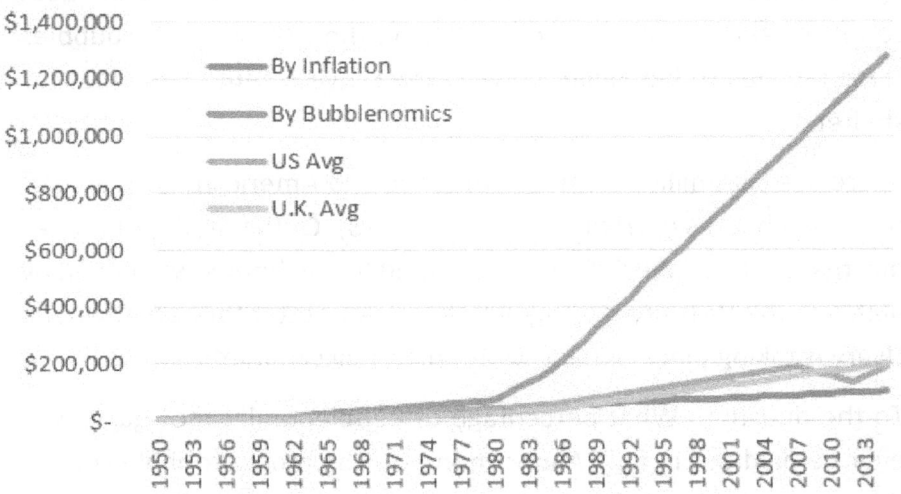

Toronto's average home price is thirteen-times higher than Inflation over the same 65-year time period.

Recall that Capitalism is a 60-year Cycle - more or less. Note also that I have discounted Condo sales here – which take down the average Toronto household price to $750,000. The reason for this is that condos are not the norm in other markets nor eras here in North America - nor in Great Britain. As such, the inclusion of Condo sales could be seen as a misrepresentation of the true cost of Bubbles within major centers.

Stats for market-driven, Bubblenomics-affected Toronto are markedly different from costs run up through regular cost of living Inflation. A house that cost $10,000 in 1950, today costs $1,280,000 65-years later. That's an average value increase of $19,538 annually every year or 7.75% interest compounded annually; more than double compound-interest due to inflation.

The impact on citizen's freedoms; nor the legal and ethical implications of this change cannot be understated. Usury is the condition that occurs whenever a debtor is lured or forced into loan agreements they can never exit. The practice is illegal in most countries and yet, usury is obviously on the rise wherever bubbles force families to bid against much larger investment companies for shelter.

There are 130 million homes in America and Americans own 30% of their own homes outright (CBC News, 2013). Of those 70% of homes mortgaged, less than 50% are not owned by the homeowner even by half, and the stats are getting worse and not better for homeowners. Usury is taking place outside of Bubblenomics markets as well.

To the question: What percentage of Bubblenomics mortgages will ever be paid out in full? Almost none - is the most probable correct answer - and the statistic "percentage of mortgages that are-not paid off" is not tracked publicly - but it clearly should be.

An End to Usury

Clearly a forced Usury-based Mortgage Lending system – one that is mandatory for any young family starting out, is an important social problem to be corrected actively.

The opportunity to control housing prices proactively was taken on by the Nordic States fifteen years ago and houses remain affordable there still (Delmendo, 2016).

In Holland, a maximum $245k mortgage is insurable and interest is tax deductible on their primary residence. I have even heard second-hand that Switzerland requires new home owners to have $500,000 down before they are permitted to enter into a mortgage - as an assurance that they will be able to pay off the mortgage reliably. By way of comparison, in the U.S. a 3% down payment will get you into a mortgage with "easy, low-interest rates" once again. Sound familiar?

Rental Markets in Toronto are no better than the vastly over-priced housing market; with rents jumping 50% in just the last 3-years as families become ever-more desperate for shelter and take whatever they can get within a market where ten bids from Chinese investors increase homes $300,000 to $600,000 over asking routinely now. Many new foreign investors will never live in these houses themselves and most foreign investors never disclose their source of financing; they simply declare a Cash Sale. In the Netherlands, properties can be purchased by foreign investors but they must be financed by Holland Banks. Taxes, legal, and financial requirements are very onerous for foreign investors compared to Canada with no controls almost whatsoever. ("Investing in Dutch property," 2016)

92% of Netherlands rentals are Rent Controlled to a maximum of €710 (euro dollars) and renters have a 30% flat-tax on rental yields with no tax write-offs for investment property. 8% are designated free-rentals. In this way, rental buyers are dissuaded from driving up the price of homes.

In summary, Market-driven Housing and Essentials have to be corrected as well.

What to Correct First, Second, Third...

Here is a list in weighted-priority ordering. This ordering is sequenced somewhat but one task does not need to complete before the next can begin. All of these solutions intend to ensure that Wealth Distribution and Spending Power is returned as follows.

- **Priority A - Guaranteed Incomes & Engineering Supports are first.**
    - 1. Get Cost of Living money into the hands of the people that are going to restart the economy.
    - 2. Calling on every CEO of every major company and telling them to hire more actively, and perhaps even monitoring hiring and pension health per company, costs little and monitors a countries corporate well-being.
    - 3. Support Engineers and Builders. We have left career "builders" unsupported too long. See Guaranteed Incomes in Chapter 11 below.
- **Priority A – Housing**. Who wins in every Monopoly Game? It's not usually the businesses owners – but rather the multi-property and rental-property land owners. So, top on the list of things to correct, is Housing.

For housing, we need to correct bubbles – through public housing and an option to switch between a home-ownership system and land-grant system as needed. Anti-eviction laws should protect society as we work toward a zero homeless solution now too. Housing Speculation needs put to an end with controls similar to those in the Netherlands where there are no bubbles and 35% public housing.

- **Priority A - Business Accountability** – Taxes and Penalties for failed trickle-downers, tax evaders, and so forth. And also, by the way, that CEO won't last a week after having every product pulled from the shelves country-wide in your market, so insist on manufacturing sites locally.

  Trading partners have played victim to one another because they haven't supported one another; closing a Plant in Canada or the U.S. to open a Plant in Mexico – and vice-versa – would be better be greeted with insistence on manufacturing plants in all three countries.

  There is no message of getting tough with business here. Those that profit fairly and supportively within the societies that support them are welcome; and the pariahs who are of benefit to no-one but themselves less so. Smart companies will shine with Accountability checks and balances - and lesser management teams will leverage, influence, bargain, and collude their way to unemployment lines if this is done well.

- **Priority A – Robotic Automation of Production, Essentials, Exports, Imports**. The last generation of technology leaders put the computer's capability to use by consolidate knowledge into all of our hands; the next wave will give us robotic automation and Connected Smart Factories. See the #WPProjects Chapter below. Take profit from automation directly now.

Robotic automation of our society puts an end to much of the money-related shortcomings in society today. We might actually start seeing Cancer Cures, smart Democratic Elections & Policy, and Abundance, instead of Scarcity, thinking. Rewards should be commensurate with Social Merit, and there are many important social improvements that only equality of opportunity will provide.

- **Priority A – Pricing protections for Essentials.** Giving a dollar back its spending power means rolling back and then controlling inflation of all of our essentials. These include pharmaceuticals, energy, construction materials, housing, daycare, education, healthcare, vehicles and service. All of these have exceeded inflation at the same time that salaries have decreased in Winter.

- **Priority A – Deliver Sustainable Projects and Policy.** The definition of sustainable is little understood in today's world. For example, "feed a man a fish, and he eats for a day" is not a sustainable solution. If you give him the tools and knowledge he needs to fish for a lifetime, he can sustain himself and his family perhaps. Rome had this; and yet they fell and so this is not sustainable either. To create sustainable solutions, you must combine the Golden Rule, and build a solution for all of this man's neighbors at the same time.

Sustainable Projects, therefore, are only those projects where abundance is automated and repeatable for all.

Are the U.N.'s Global Goals sustainable? No, unfortunately not at all at this time. The UNDP hire financial donation administrators and not a single engineer in support of sustainable automation projects. This specific definition of sustainability - is not a Global Goal of the U.N. either.

Building sustainably is Good Engineering and Innovation Leadership; unsustainable policy are suitable as they are Tactical solutions only and should be improved upon with good planning at first chance.

Investing in unsustainable projects counts for 99% of Charitable Foundation work too; so always keep eyes open to support sustainable options ahead of other charities and initiatives.

The best way to ensure that projects are run and built sustainably, is to insist that they adhere to **SUSTAIN Project Management Method**. SUSTAIN is discussed further along in the book in Chapter 25.

What is not on the High Priority List

Socially irresponsible policy is the norm in North American politics today...

- **Infrastructure Spending** without Trickle-down targets, monitoring and Guarantees. Never spend on Infrastructure without a percentage spending designated to Automation Livingry – Renewable Automation.
- **Transit-Spending**
    - **Buses** – must take into consideration driverless cars. Drivers and buses are coming to an abrupt end very soon so do not invest twenty-five year money in today's model of transit.
    - **Subways (Raised or Subterranean)** – are fine projects as long as they are future-ready, driverless-transit compatible, and building Engineering teams locally that can be remarketed internationally too.
- **High Executive Salaries** – 92% Graduated Tax is probably appropriate here again as it was in the 1940s and 1950s when

the economy boomed. Many boards are approving salaries for friends and co-workers that could hardly be called competitive as well.

- **Tertiary & Financial Industries - non-producing.** This includes Legal Tax Avoidance and Offshored Engineering

- **Investment Bankers and Hedge-Fund Managers** - Unsustainable, Socially Irresponsible and even Offensive

- **Immigration** - without melting-pot-like "mixing" rules, protections for culture, and requirements for keeping business ownership local while keeping profit and employment within country. Immigrants who run Manilla to U.S. export sweatshops can do so from somewhere else as it benefits our economy and citizenry not at all.

- **Low Tax** costs Canadians, Britain's, and Australians $630 billion in Exports annually on average; Americans lose somewhere in the neighborhood of $5 trillion annually. Read Chapter 11 - Guaranteed Incomes - below.

- **Foreign Real Estate Investment** – that creates artificial bubbles in housing which makes finding family homes difficult or impossible.

- **Political Charitable Foundations** – The Clinton's family members benefit directly from contributions made to the Clinton Charitable Foundation, while Hillary Clinton sat in office these past several years. Justin Trudeau followed suit recently and has accepted constituent contributions while sitting as Prime Minister as well. Instead, create an official Charity for all politicians per country and legislate contributions are made there transparently.

- **Gender Inequality** – In developing nations, and wherever it does not exist, Women's Rights are crucial. As a vote-grab in North America, the implementation is socially irresponsible when it insists on equal numbers of women and men in the workplace. Misunderstanding of the point of Gender Inequality gives irresponsible businesses a false reason with which to lay off twenty-year workers and thereby deny family pensions worth $1.2 to $1.8 million; it can never shame women into not raising their own children should they wish; and it can never force families into a dual-income trap. (Edward Tilley, 2016b)

Freedom

Planning Solutions for the restart of the next Economic Cycle requires lessons from other countries, lessons from history, and careful throttling of Transition Economics researched Policy corrections explained here in the book.

After you have completed a plan of corrections, begin the effort and work immediately. I discuss throttling a fair bit because important change cannot happen too slowly, but it also cannot happen so quickly that people are left without their basic needs of food, shelter, and security. Transition Economics is largely about enacting sustainable policy and then transitioning to that policy responsibly.

Discussions can tend to wander a bit but can never aim away from pragmatic, monitored, and confirmed progress toward the goal of income distributions and renewed spending power needed for of a Good Life and tremendous individual Freedom. What is Freedom?

Freedom is a twenty-year-old who can choose to start a family; one who can choose an education or work as he or she wishes; one whose children and children's children will live in family-friendly communities that promise lifetimes of interesting worthwhile projects, learning and exploration.

Is this freedom possible? More than possible, it was also the norm in the G7 until the early 1970s; just as it was the norm for 40 million in Moscow right up until 1986 as well. By comparison, G7 Capitalist countries struggled to support higher-education while young families were required to afford the purchase of their own homes too. Between the two, Russia had the better model because the G7 lagged behind in education due to the fact that young adults could not easily support a home, family and university degree studies at the same time.

The G8 made this definition of freedom work with only farm equipment, basic trucks, and very little automation of food, transportation and shelter. Automations, however, are going to be available to us in just the next short handful of years, which can sustain us entirely.

Does anyone imagine that we will starve once food arrives from an automated farm to our doorsteps without a human's effort required? Does anyone doubt that a home will be available once homes are built immediately upon demand and maintained automatically by robotic machines? No – of course not.

We simply haven't built the connected smart factories that provide this yet – and that fact is a leadership problem because there is nothing beyond a decent engineer's capabilities here.

The Case for Distributing Wealth Quickly

Assuming that this redistribution of incomes and automation projects were to happen quickly enough, we would probably all be busy and productive enough to allow us to skip right past any fear of World War III's obliterating the planet.

A WWIII discussion is thought provoking and as such, is worth bringing up now. A World War III would be an extinction-level event, on the eve of our retiring the scarcities that have historically driven wars for millennia. In this context, Wealth Distribution and Abundance through Renewable Automations is the "ounce of prevention that creates a pound of cure" for humanity.

We are probably one single coordinated push away from making money much less important and perhaps even irrelevant within twenty years. Arguably the best thing about an automation transition strategy is there is no need to change monetary use overnight; no surprises nor hardships – just augmentation of our needs as quickly as we can build the technology.

Isolationists love over-population scares, but there is no foundation for it; just as there are no foundation for terrorist fear mongering in our media. We have abundance in energy, lebensraum (living space), and resources – and all we have to do is choose to build it.

By way of one final higher-validation, all of the great thinkers – Plato, Aristotle, Socrates, Elizabeth I, Buddha, etc. without exception spent lifetimes confirming and articulating that selfishness is unsustainable; that only the greater good, with the guidance of a Right Plan and action could attain a self-sustaining community and society.

As a young man coming of age in the 1980s, I thought this sort of discussion sounded too religious but it seems to me now that religions merely came to adopt these lessons and truths over time. It is clear to me now that Transition Economics is simply a reversal of short-sighted, unsustainable thinking.

Aristotle said that to build a right plan, you had to be a Greek, a man, and more then forty years of age. In those times, this was the only resume possible for a person who had run a household and made provisions for the launching of his children into advanced education and into families and households of their own as well. Today, women take on this role as often as men of course.

Maturity, experience, and a lot of research, have taught me to agree with this contemporized explanation of Aristotle's sustainable thinking. It took more than just a few of my own grey hairs before I fully comprehended the need to provide for the next generation of families too. For me, the five kids that I raised brought this message home very clearly.

Aristotle simply wanted to take a moment to impart forty years of life-wisdom - as I suppose anyone would.

Chapter 9

Transition Economics Maturity Model

Maturity Models are standardized measuring charts that help direct the services offered by any group within a subject area. These Models are commonly seen in Construction, Technology, and Transformation Project Management Offices and serve us well here too.

Maturity Models often discuss five or six major steps, which are usually just a series of building block projects that must be implemented to take a group from Immaturity — as a reactive fire-fighting organization; to Maturity — a proactive, professional and transparent problem solver. The high-level maturity groups transcend their cost-center beginnings by offering products and solutions that make them a profit generator and a strategic differentiator; a business-enabling force for their company – or for their country.

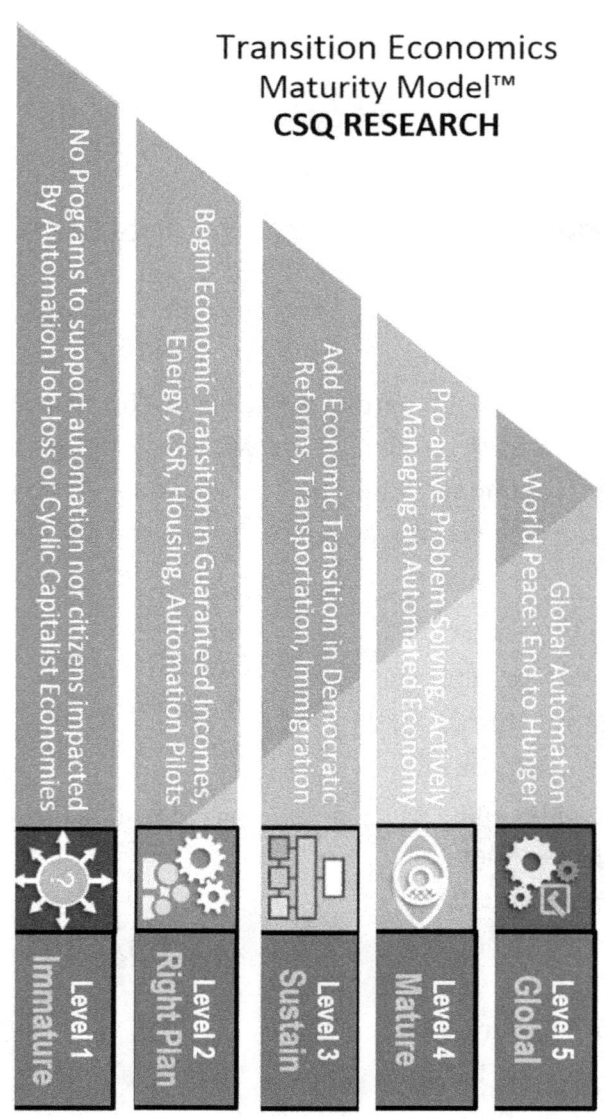

Mature vs Immature

What would a mature Transition Economy look like? Surely it would be running the strongest policies that their business cases and ongoing monitoring confirm that they are sustaining a healthy, advancing economy. GDP reports would confirm that citizens have incomes and renewed spending power; and more than this, the most mature countries will have the time and best practices to help other countries achieve maturity the same.

A TE-Immature Country will be using policy inappropriate for this phase of our current economic cycle.

TE-Maturity and Calculus

Isaac Newton and Gottfried Leibniz solved the timeless problem of how to determine Instantaneous Velocity by inventing limits (called infinitesimals back then) and derivatives in Calculus. Leibniz went on to develop differential and integral Calculus as well, and both men could be easily regarded as giant contributors to science who made enormous advances in not only modern mathematics, but physics, science, philosophy, and economics.

Calculus is also an advanced mathematics, which is based on a very, very simple solution that allows us to calculate rise-over-run slope at point so small that there is no delta; at an instant.

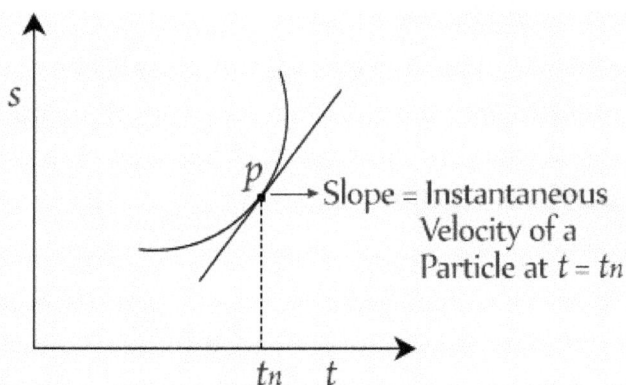

Similarly, the measure of Aggregate Performance for the many policies deployed within one country's economy, is suggested to be determined by TE-Maturity. We accomplish this measure by normalizing an arbitrary definition for Trending and then establish a baseline called "Collapse Trending".

Consider that Transition Economics policies are driven and monitored by a business case empirically, measurably; this means that the many and varied ways of implementing any single policy are defined and can be controlled so that differences between one *housing* policy and another, for example, can be easily compared. If the policy aligns with TE Maturity policy, we can assign a statistical value reliably like 1 or 0, "Yes" or "No", Like or Not Like, etc.

Draft Version .9 Country	Collapse (C) / Advancing (A)	TE Maturity Model Estimate	GDP Export Per Capita	Wealth Distribution	Minimum Wage Targets	Graduated Tax (High Tax on Rich)	Guaranteed Incomes	Housing & Usury Law	End Tax Evation	Social Programs - DayCare	Social - Free Higher Education	Social - Universal Healthcare	Onshore Engineering	Wealth Creation	Quality Exports	Reduce Imports	Manufacture Locally	Local Profit	Transition Economics Maturity	Automation Project Safety Nets	Increase Spending Power	Renewable Automation #WPProjects
Afghanistan	C	1	$ 122	N	N	N	N	N	N	N	N	N	N	N	N	N	Y	Y	N	N	N	N

Non-Binary weightings and percentages can also be used, especially in artificial intelligence and analytic "deep-dives", but initially we want to prove that our method has value in simplest terms.

Each Country has sixteen policies as discussed here in this book initially. Countries with more TE Maturity-aligned policies, earn the assignment of a value greater than "1" – Immature Maturity. A more readable list of these policies is also in the Level 3 Maturity chart a few pages below.

The very detail-oriented among us will want to automate the assignment of maturity values as needed to build decision-support tools from models; and this will surely happen with TE Maturity Model adoption. Much can be learned about housing, and all other policies, from comparing collapsing and advancing groupings.

TE Maturity is not Calculus yet, but it is at the start of a wave of development as was when Newton and Leibniz began.

At this time there are just two countries that are deemed to be at a Level 3 and other maturing nations are Level 2. Maturity levels are defined in the next few pages.

Economic Trending

Collapsing

Collapsing (C) – In K-Wave Winter (which is where we are today), when policies are not proven to create incomes AND are not targeting renewed spending power policies AND a trade deficit exists, countries can be said to be trending in a Collapsing direction.

If that country is also in Fiscal Deficit that exceeds a year of GDP Exports (Incomes), one can say something about the rate of collapse as well, but for now we will simply state that the economy is in a Collapsing Trend.

Advancing

Advancing (A) – A country's economy is said to be advancing if its Trade Balance is in Surplus (GDP Exports minus GDP Imports GT 0) and is greater than 5% of GDP Exports. Get online at Wikipedia to find lists of GDP Imports and Exports listed for every country annually.

Growth of GDP alone is not considered an indicator of an advancing economy. Although the number is easily track-able, GDP cannot be easily correlated back to our ultimate goal of creating a sustainable Good Life. An increasing-GDP country with high levels of inequity could as easily be said to be headed for high social-problem spending and could be unsustainable or even unstable and moving toward revolution. Not to say that this is happening; rather simply GDP in itself tells us little.

GDP Export per Capita, alternatively, often shows a correlation with the GINI wealth distribution Index and with the United Nations HDI – Human Development Index, which are qualitative measures of the lives of citizens as well.

TE Maturity Math

By summarizing a list of 180 countries in this way (see the Charts below), we can make a number of important conclusions.

First, we can determine what percentage of countries have Collapsing or Advancing trends.

Changing the definition of Collapse Trending will change the resulting value but by drawing a best-effort line in the sand, we build a basis to start with. Recall that our goal here is find which combination of policies lead to reliably Advancing Economies.

Trade Deficit	Trade Surplus	**Collapsing**	Advancing
132	54	114	45
71%	29%	72%	28%
11	8	9	10
58%	42%	47%	53%
4	4	4	4
50%	50%	50%	50%

Second, now that we know that some number (72%) of all nations measured are in Collapse Trending, with this control group - and baseline number, we can determine was our assumption about higher-TE-Maturity nations correct.

If our TE-Maturity Policy assumptions are correct, we should expect to see that a smaller percentage of TE Maturing countries are in a Collapse Trending; and if we are incorrect, we should see that our TE Maturing countries have a similar or worse Collapse Trending.

On reviewing our simple initial list, just one or perhaps two of the twenty TE-Maturing nations (nations with a TE-Maturity of 2, 3, 4 or 5), exhibit Collapse Trending initially. By this comparison, TE-Maturing countries show collapse rates from 5% to 10% compared-to much higher rates for G8 (50%), G20 (47%), and 72% Collapse Trending for all countries.

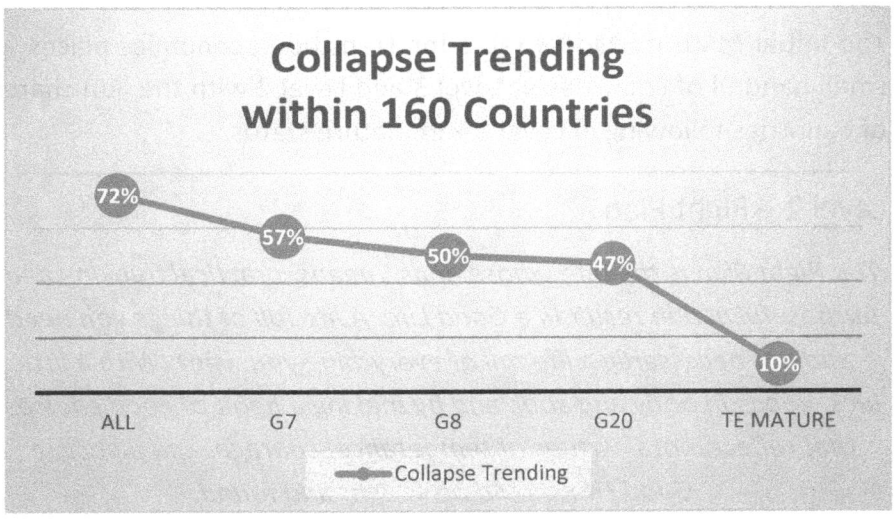

Many adjustments can be made in policies and data collection accuracy is important too. Fine-tuning and optimizing country policies until the best economic and social results are measured is the point and value of this exercise. At the end of the day, TE Maturity permits all countries to make policy decisions that arrive at a predictable, measurably sustainable, and economically advancing society.

Which countries are trending towards Collapse? In the G8 - Canada, France, United Kingdom and United States; G20 nations also include Australia, India, Mexico, South Africa, and Turkey.

Let's consider TE-Maturity Level definitions next.

Level 1 – Immature

Immature – Indicates that a country has insufficient Transition Economic Policies & Programs to support incomes, a return of spending power, nor support of automation and automation-driven job-losses. A look at the Trending chart below shows what you might expect within our Current Global Depression; correcting these trends takes policies with GDP-proven results.

The initial Maturity Model table for Transition Economics places a small handful of countries at Level 3 and Level 2 with the lion share of countries following in Level 1 – Immature status.

Level 2 – Right Plan

The Right Plan is the one whose ends, means, practical thinking and purposeful action result in a Good Life. A life full of things you need – and not necessarily a life full of everything you want. With a little luck, goods in body and soul, and by making a habit of good choices that reflect moral virtues of temperance, courage, and justice, a Good Life should be sought and found.

Abridged from Politics 322 BCE (Messerly, 2013)

A ***Right Plan*** for transitioning our world and country, is a plan of well-researched, worthwhile Goals, Proven & Transparent Process, the Right People, Great Vision and business-case-driven projects.

WHAT DOES IT TAKE?
TO BUILD A RIGHT PLAN

- Worthwhile Goals
- Simple Steps
- Proven Process
- Right People
- Clear Directions
- Great Vision

A Country Right Plan:

- Ensures Incomes:

INCOMES DISTRIBUTE (pie chart: Automation, Others, Working, Guaranteed Incomes, Retired, Children)	**Transition Economics Mature Policy** 5% to 10% in Collapse	**Collapse Policy** 72% of All Countries are in Collapse
Working Families & Individuals	Graduated Tax, Big-Business Tax Avoidance Crackdown, Inequity targets, Local Business Ownership, Local Govmt Business Ownership	Low Tax, Trickle-down, Middle-Class Focus, Diversity, Cheap Imports, Immigration, Small Business w/o support
Unemployed	Guaranteed Cost of Living Incomes, Business Automation Revenue Sharing	No benefits for underemployed nor all unemployed
Retirement	Employee & Pension Fund Protections, Cost of Living minimums, CSR & Business Accountability	Offshoring, Misuse of female diversity rules, ignoring pensions
Children	Free Mastery-based Education & Transition Economics Voter Education	Failure to support 20-year-olds starting families, High Divorce Rates
Others	Cost of Living Benefits for Disabled	Insufficient Support, High Debt Servicing Costs
Automation	Engineering Safety Nets, #WPProjects & Renewable Automation Support, Multi-Party Long Term Strategic Planning	Innovation programs that fail to support Renewable Automations and Trade & Selling Needs

- Returns spending power to citizens

SPENDING POWER RETURNS	**Transition Economics Mature Policy** 5% to 10% in Collapse	**Collapse Policy** 72% of All Countries are in Collapse
Healthcare & Benefits	Universal Healthcare, Employee Benefit Plans to Revenue Neutral Business Case targets	Private Plans, Patents that externalize Government R&D
Childcare	Universal Daycare & Free Education incl. University	Unaffordable Childcare
Housing	Public Housing (30%) Controlled to Inflation, Land Grants, Anti-Eviction, and Foreign Ownership Taxes	Energy Poverty, Housing Bubbles created by lax controls
Food & Goods	License Renewable Automation, Local Harvesting, Driverless Transport & Distribution, Local Self-Sufficiency & Abundance	Insufficient Farm Compensations, Failure to develop automation, Dollar & 99p Stores, Cheap Imports, Austerity Measures
Energy	Abundant Geo-Thermal, Hydro, Cold-Fusion, Thorium Nuclear, Zero-Pollution Fuels	Part-time Wind & Solar, Fossil Fuel Oil Pipelines, Energy Poverty
Transport	Driverless-cars & Automated Goods Delivery, Auto Road & Rail Construction	Infrastructure w/o Automation & Trickle-down Protection, Transit

Run-away Housing Bubbles Ownerships Cost and Rents

Average Home Prices in Toronto vs Inflation

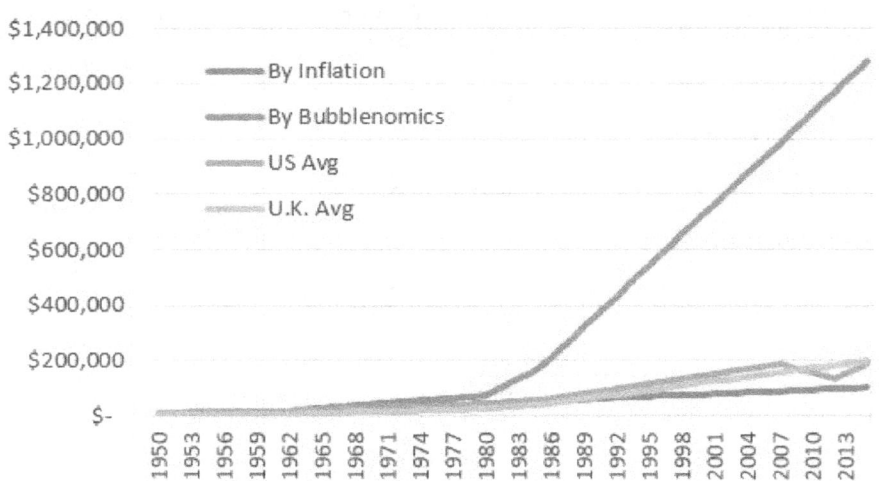

New Energy Poverty

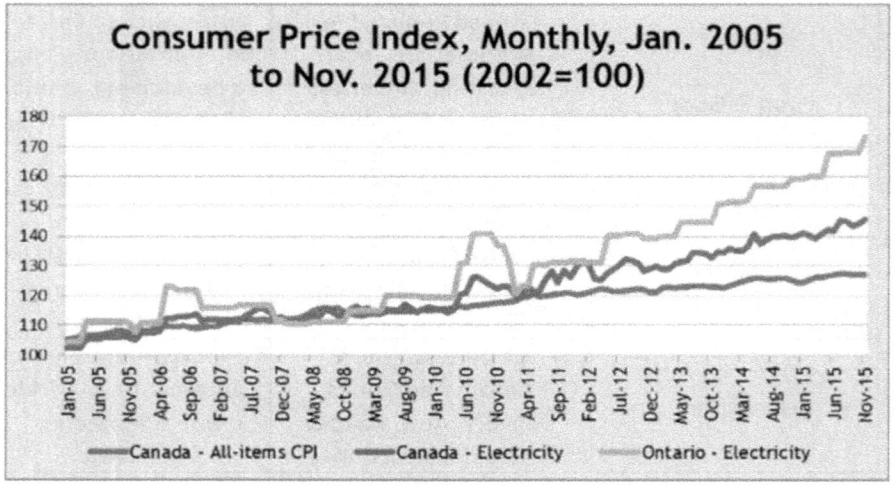

- Affords Engineering Safety Nets and the re-shoring of Engineering
- Balance tax & revenue-neutral solutions that add living wage income supports
- CSR – Corporate Social Responsibility and Business Ethics

retraining programs

- Support and Planning for Pilot Automations in Energy, Housing, Food, Clean Water & Transportation

I have stressed that Economic Controls alone are sufficient to sustain a Good Life and economy for any country. In order to take advantage of the benefits of automation too, #WPProjects is an example Global Right Plan of Connected Smart Factories and supporting social Policy, that was introduced in my last book World Peace – The Transition.

That #WPProjects Right Plan assigned 250 initial social and automation projects to 200 countries as needed to provide for the basic needs of food, water, top pharmaceuticals, furnishings, shelter, roads, automatic delivery and transportation, and so on.

The Right Plan needed for your country requires just a subset of these projects.

For most countries, just one automation project is typically required to build a new international trade network in hi-tech robotics and to spread the workload and expense of the automation project work. And what better way to leverage international expertise, experience, and also to include everyone as well?

The list of #WPProjects Connected Smart Factories can be viewed online at http://csq1.org/world-peace-transition-projects-faq/

Level 3 – Sustain

The Projects needed to achieve this next level of maturity include wide Transition Economics training and adoption, Reversal of Housing Bubbles, Engineering On-Shoring, Safety-Nets, Immigration Policy, and advances in Renewable Automation Programs.

This example Voting Chart is a summary list of policies proven to create profitable Social Program Business Cases with positive economic results. This book will spend time in explanation of every policy and point in the Chapters to come.

To create a chart like this for your country, simply replace Political Parties along the top of the chart and fill it in per the policies of each group running election-by-election. Elections for Housing are typically regional or municipal; Energy is often a State or Provincial Election issue; Tax Avoidance, Exports & Immigration are Federal.

The Chart below is an aid to help democratic voters and politicians stay focused on sustainable policies that improve your Country's Transition Economics Maturity and economies ongoing.

#	A+ Priority Social Policy	Canada			
		Cons	Lib	NDP	Grn
1	Long Term Right Planning	No	No	No	Yes
2	Bench Strength of MPs for Project Execution	Maybe	No	No	No
Wealth Distribution					
3	Pension Controls				
4	Minimum Wage Targets	No	Maybe	Yes	Yes
5	Graduated Tax	No	No	No	Yes
6	Guaranteed Incomes	No	No	Yes	Yes
7	Housing & Usury Controls	No	No	No	No
8	End Tax Avoidance	No	No	No	No
9	Daycare, Healthcare, Higher Education	No	Maybe	Yes	No
10	Onshore Engineering	No	No	Yes	No
Wealth Creation					
11	Increase & Automate Quality Exports	No	No	No	No
12	Reduce Imports	No	Yes	Yes	Yes
13	Sellers Automate Manufacture Locally	No	No	Yes	Maybe
14	Local Profit becomes Investment & Tax Revs	No	No	Yes	Maybe
Transition Economics Maturity					
15	Engineering Project Safety Nets	No	No	No	Yes
16	Increase Spending Power & Opportunity	No	No	No	No
17	Renewable Automation #WPProjects	No	No	No	No
18	TE Maturity Model	No	No	No	No
	If Yes=2, Maybe=1, No=0	3%	13%	47%	53%
	Leaning	Right	Left	Left	Left

Level 4 – Mature

Countries with a Mature Transition Economics plans are now actively monitoring and Release-Controlling improvements to their automated infrastructure. If the United Nations and member countries adopted projects similar to #WPProjects tomorrow, they could all be living sustainably within as little as five years.

The positive impact on equality and human rights should be tremendous for the first countries to reach Levels 4 and 5. Rewards will also be higher for early adopters - as would risk in development investment. This risk is addressed by revision control, automated upgrades and life cycle management supports in each project.

Transition Economics sets reasonable goals that exceed U.N. Global Goals with timings perhaps eight years sooner than Global Goals' 2030 targets. The reason for the productivity improvement can be found in the planning and in the SUSTAIN Project Planning Processes introduced later in the book.

Level 5 – Global Transition

These are the Strategic Differentiators and Game Changing Countries that build their local needs and then carry on to assist Global teams with consulting, thought leadership and best practice.

With a Good Life well on its way to being rolled out locally, Level 5 countries can now contribute to ensuring that these solutions are rolled out and running well with partners and global communities as needed. Our sustainable automations were designed to scale to this level quickly, and by now we are at release 2.0 and release 3.0 levels of technology maturity so that systems are reliable, renewable, and even elegant.

TE Maturity List by Country

All aforementioned Maturity measures are scored on the chart for every country based on the sixteen policy areas listed above; Healthcare, Guaranteed Incomes, and the other policy measures as discussed in the chapters that follow. At present, maturity levels are evaluated one country at a time and each country can request an assessment of how close or distant are they to their next maturity milestone.

As mentioned above, Right Plans are suggested to detail the projects needed to advance one's policies and country through these five levels of maturity. The transparency of this process will improve so that anyone has the ability to grade their own country more fairly than we have graded them here in isolated research.

The v1.0 initial list follows; see CSQ1.org online for the latest updates to the Transition Economics Maturity Model charts countries are welcome to update their data on this list by sending an email to info@csq1.org.

Draft Version .9

Country	Collapsing - C / Advancing - A	TE Maturity Model Estimate	GDP Export Per Capita	Wealth Distribution	Minimum Wage Targets	Graduated Tax (High Tax on Rich)	Guaranteed Incomes	Housing & Usury Law	End Tax Evation	Social Programs - DayCare	Social - Free Higher Education	Social - Universal Healthcare	Onshore Engineering	Wealth Creation	Quality Exports	Reduce Imports	Manufacture Locally	Local Profit	Transition Economics Maturity	Automation Project Safety Nets	Increase Spending Power	Renewable Automation #WPProjects
Afghanistan	C	1	$ 122	N	N	N	N	N	N	N	N	N		N	N	Y	Y		N	N	N
Albania	C	1	$ 3,481	N	N	N	N	N	N	N	N	N		N	N	Y	Y		N	N	N
Algeria	C	1	$ 4,414	N	Y	N	N	N	N	N	N	N		N	N	Y	Y		N	N	N
Angola	A	1	$ 4,315	N	Y	N	N	N	N	N	N	N		N	N	Y	Y		N	N	N
Antigua and Barbuda	C	1	$ 9,269	Y	Y	Y	Y	N	N	N	Y	Y		Y	Y	Y	Y		N	Y	N
Argentina	A	1	$ 1,969	N	N	N	N	N	N	N	N	N		N	N	Y	Y		N	N	N
Armenia	C	1	$ 2,099	N	N	N	N	N	N	N	N	N		N	N	Y	Y		N	N	N
Australia	C	1	$ 8,728	Y	Y	Y	Y	N	N	N	Y	Y		Y	Y	Y	Y		N	Y	N
Austria	C	1	$ 26,517	Y	Y	Y	Y	N	N	Y	Y	Y		Y	Y	Y	Y		N	Y	N
Azerbaijan	A	1	$ 8,352	Y	Y	Y	Y	N	N	N	Y	Y		Y	Y	Y	Y		Y	Y	N
Bahrain	A	1	$ 9,216	Y	Y	Y	Y	N	N	N	Y	Y		Y	Y	Y	Y		N	Y	N
Bangladesh	C	1	$ 576	N	N	N	N	N	N	N	N	N		N	N	Y	Y		N	N	N
Barbados	C	1	$ 6,616	Y	Y	Y	Y	N	N	N	N	Y		Y	Y	Y	Y		N	N	N
Belarus	C	1	$ 10,780	Y	Y	Y	Y	N	N	N	Y	Y		Y	Y	Y	Y		N	Y	N
Belgium	A	2	$ 35,359	Y	Y	Y	N	N	Y	Y	Y	Y		Y	Y	Y	Y		N	Y	N
Belize	C	1	$ 5,164	Y	Y	Y	Y	N	N	Y	Y	Y		Y	Y	Y	Y		N	Y	N
Benin	C	1	$ 327	N	N	N	N	N	N	N	N	N		N	N	Y	Y		N	N	N
Bhutan	C	1	$ 3,025	N	N	N	N	N	N	N	N	N		N	N	Y	Y		N	N	N
Bolivia	C	1	$ 2,709	N	N	N	N	N	N	N	N	N		N	N	Y	Y		N	N	N
Bosnia & Herzegovina		1	$ 3,048	N	N	N	N	N	N	N	N	N		N	N	Y	Y		N	N	N
Botswana	A	1	$ 8,683	Y	Y	Y	Y	N	N	N	Y	Y		Y	Y	Y	Y		N	Y	N
Brazil	A	1	$ 1,887	N	N	N	N	N	N	N	N	N		N	N	Y	Y		N	N	N
Brunei	A	2	$ 57,652	Y	Y	Y	N	Y	Y	Y	Y	Y		Y	Y	Y	Y		N	N	N
Bulgaria	C	1	$ 10,759	Y	Y	Y	Y	N	N	Y	Y	Y		Y	Y	Y	Y		N	N	N
Burkina Faso	C	1	$ 463	N	N	N	N	N	N	N	N	N		N	N	Y	Y		N	N	N
Burundi	C	1	$ 57	N	N	N	N	N	N	N	N	N		N	N	Y	Y		N	N	N
Cambodia	C	1	$ 1,999	N	N	N	N	N	N	N	N	N		N	N	Y	Y		N	N	N
Cameroon	C	1	$ 585	N	N	N	N	N	N	N	N	N		N	N	Y	Y		N	N	N
Canada	C	1	$ 13,262	N	N	N	N	N	N	N	Y	N		N	N	N	N		N	N	N
Cape Verde	C	1	$ 2,240	N	N	N	N	N	N	N	N	N		N	N	Y	Y		N	N	N
Central African Rep.		1	$ 70	N	N	N	N	N	N	N	N	N		N	N	Y	Y		N	N	N
Chad	A	1	$ 672	N	N	N	N	N	N	N	N	N		N	N	Y	Y		N	N	N
Chile	A	1	$ 7,144	Y	Y	Y	Y	N	N	N	N	Y		Y	Y	Y	Y		N	Y	N
China	A	2	$ 3,489	Y	N	N	N	Y	N	Y	Y	Y		Y	Y	Y	Y		N	N	N
Colombia	C	1	$ 2,215	N	N	N	N	N	N	N	N	N		N	N	Y	Y		N	N	N
Comoros	C	1	$ 237	N	N	N	N	N	N	N	N	N		N	N	Y	Y		N	N	N
Costa Rica	C	1	$ 4,876	N	Y	N	N	N	N	N	N	N		N	N	Y	Y		N	N	N
Croatia	C	1	$ 9,168	Y	Y	Y	Y	N	N	N	Y	Y		Y	Y	Y	Y		N	Y	N
Cuba	C	1	$ 3,752	N	N	N	N	N	N	N	N	N		N	N	Y	Y		N	N	N
Cyprus	C	1	$ 11,321	Y	Y	Y	Y	N	N	Y	Y	Y		Y	Y	Y	Y		N	Y	N
Czech Republic	A	1	$ 22,402	Y	Y	Y	Y	N	Y	Y	Y	Y		Y	Y	Y	Y		N	Y	N
Denmark	A	2	$ 24,347	Y	Y	Y	N	Y	Y	Y	Y	Y		Y	Y	Y	Y		N	Y	N
Djibouti	C	1	$ 1,712	N	N	N	N	N	N	N	N	N		N	N	Y	Y		N	N	N
Dominica		1	$ 3,396	N	N	N	N	N	N	N	N	N		N	N	Y	Y		N	N	N
Dominican Republic	C	1	$ 3,110	N	N	N	N	N	N	N	N	N		N	N	Y	Y		N	N	N

Country																		
Ecuador	C	1	$	3,178	N	N	N	N	N	N	N	N	N	N	Y	Y	N	N	N
Egypt	C	1	$	1,954	N	N	N	N	N	N	N	N	N	N	Y	Y	N	N	N
El Salvador	C	1	$	2,049	N	N	N	N	N	N	N	N	N	N	Y	Y	N	N	N
Equatorial Guinea	A	1	$	28,543	Y	Y	Y	Y	N	N	N	Y	Y	Y	Y	Y	Y	N	Y	N
Eritrea	C	1	$	234	N	N	N	N	N	N	N	N	N	N	Y	Y	N	N	N
Estonia	C	1	$	22,228	Y	Y	Y	Y	N	Y	Y	Y	Y	Y	Y	Y	Y	N	Y	N
Ethiopia	C	1	$	172	N	N	N	N	N	N	N	N	N	N	Y	Y	N	N	N
Fiji	C	1	$	4,556	N	N	N	N	N	N	N	N	N	N	Y	Y	N	N	N
Finland	C	1	$	15,178	Y	Y	N	Y	Y	Y	Y	Y	Y	Y	Y	Y	N	Y	N
France	C	1	$	10,987	Y	Y	Y	Y	N	N	Y	Y	Y	Y	Y	Y	N	Y	N
Gabon	A	1	$	11,312	Y	Y	Y	Y	N	N	Y	Y	Y	Y	Y	Y	N	Y	N
Georgia	C	1	$	3,200	N	N	N	N	N	N	N	N	N	N	Y	Y	N	N	N
Germany	A	3	$	23,113	Y	Y	Y	Y	Y	Y	Y	Y	Y	Y	Y	Y	Y	Y	N
Ghana	C	1	$	1,683	N	N	N	N	N	N	N	N	N	N	Y	Y	N	N	N
Greece	C	1	$	7,759	Y	Y	Y	Y	N	N	Y	Y	Y	Y	Y	Y	N	Y	N
Grenada		1	$	2,923	N	N	N	N	N	N	N	N	N	N	Y	Y	N	N	N
Guatemala	C	1	$	1,726	N	N	N	N	N	N	N	N	N	N	Y	Y	N	N	N
Guinea	C	1	$	357	N	N	N	N	N	N	N	N	N	N	Y	Y	N	N	N
Guinea-Bissau		1	$	244	N	N	N	N	N	N	N	N	N	N	Y	Y	N	N	N
Guyana	C	1	$	5,539	Y	Y	Y	Y	N	N	N	Y	Y	Y	Y	Y	N	Y	N
Haiti	C	1	$	311	N	N	N	N	N	N	N	N	N	N	Y	Y	N	N	N
Honduras	C	1	$	2,201	N	N	N	N	N	N	N	N	N	N	Y	Y	N	N	N
Hong Kong		2	$	126,467	Y	Y	Y	Y	N	N	N	Y	Y	Y	Y	Y	N	Y	N
Hungary	A	1	$	20,711	Y	Y	Y	Y	N	N	N	Y	Y	Y	Y	Y	Y	Y	N
Iceland		2	$	24,183	Y	Y	Y	Y	N	Y	Y	Y	Y	Y	Y	Y	N	Y	N
India	C	1	$	1,345	N	N	N	N	N	N	N	N	N	N	Y	Y	N	N	N
Indonesia	A	1	$	2,270	N	N	N	N	N	N	N	N	N	N	Y	Y	N	N	N
Iran	A	1	$	5,017	Y	Y	Y	Y	N	N	Y	Y	Y	Y	Y	Y	N	Y	N
Iraq	A	1	$	2,892	N	N	N	N	N	N	N	N	N	N	Y	Y	N	N	N
Ireland	A	3	$	50,338	Y	Y	Y	Y	N	Y	Y	Y	Y	Y	Y	Y	N	Y	N
Israel	C	1	$	10,887	Y	Y	Y	Y	N	N	Y	Y	Y	Y	Y	Y	N	Y	N
Italy	A	1	$	9,927	Y	Y	Y	Y	N	N	Y	Y	Y	Y	Y	Y	N	Y	N
Jamaica	C	1	$	2,706	N	N	N	N	N	N	N	N	N	N	Y	Y	N	N	N
Japan	A	3	$	5,366	Y	Y	Y	Y	Y	Y	Y	Y	Y	Y	Y	Y	N	Y	Y
Jordan	C	1	$	5,004	Y	Y	Y	Y	N	N	Y	Y	Y	Y	Y	Y	N	Y	N
Kazakhstan	A	1	$	8,879	Y	Y	Y	Y	N	N	Y	Y	Y	Y	Y	Y	N	Y	N
Kenya	C	1	$	496	N	N	N	N	N	N	N	N	N	N	Y	Y	N	N	N
Kiribati		1	$	195	N	N	N	N	N	N	N	N	N	N	Y	Y	N	N	N
Kosovo	C	1	$	1,547	N	N	N	N	N	N	N	N	N	N	Y	Y	N	N	N
Kuwait	A	2	$	58,696	Y	Y	Y	Y	N	N	Y	Y	Y	Y	Y	Y	N	Y	N
Kyrgyzstan	C	1	$	1,516	N	N	N	N	N	N	N	N	N	N	Y	Y	N	N	N
Laos	C	1	$	1,795	N	N	N	N	N	N	N	N	N	N	Y	Y	N	N	N
Latvia	C	1	$	13,280	Y	Y	Y	Y	N	N	Y	Y	Y	Y	Y	Y	N	Y	N
Lebanon	C	1	$	10,742	Y	Y	Y	Y	N	N	Y	Y	Y	Y	Y	Y	N	Y	N
Lesotho	C	1	$	1,159	N	N	N	N	N	N	N	N	N	N	Y	Y	N	N	N
Liberia	C	1	$	284	N	N	N	N	N	N	N	N	N	N	Y	Y	N	N	N
Libya	C	1	$	14,181	Y	Y	Y	Y	N	N	N	Y	Y	Y	Y	Y	Y	Y	N
Lithuania	C	1	$	19,633	Y	Y	Y	Y	N	N	Y	Y	Y	Y	Y	Y	N	Y	N
Luxembourg	C	2	$	185,119	Y	Y	Y	Y	N	N	N	Y	Y	Y	Y	Y	N	Y	N
Macedonia	C	1	$	6,258	Y	Y	Y	Y	N	N	N	Y	Y	Y	Y	Y	N	Y	N
Madagascar	C	1	$	425	N	N	N	N	N	N	N	N	N	N	Y	Y	N	N	N
Malawi	C	1	$	361	N	N	N	N	N	N	N	N	N	N	Y	Y	N	N	N
Malaysia	A	1	$	19,062	Y	Y	Y	Y	N	N	Y	Y	Y	Y	Y	Y	N	Y	N
Maldives	C	1	$	12,977	Y	Y	Y	Y	N	N	Y	Y	Y	Y	Y	Y	N	Y	N
Mali	C	1	$	513	N	N	N	N	N	N	N	N	N	N	Y	Y	N	N	N
Malta	C	1	$	27,266	Y	Y	Y	Y	N	N	Y	Y	Y	Y	Y	Y	Y	Y	N
Mauritania	C	1	$	2,030	N	N	N	N	N	N	N	N	N	N	Y	Y	N	N	N

Country																			
Mauritius	C	1	$	9,620	Y	Y	Y	Y	N	N	Y	Y	Y	Y	Y	Y	Y	N	Y	N
Mexico	C	1	$	5,197	Y	Y	Y	Y	N	N	N	Y	Y	Y	Y	Y	Y	N	Y	N
Moldova	C	1	$	2,061	N	N	N	N	N	N	N	N	N	N	N	Y	N	N	N	N
Monaco	C	1	$	23,204	Y	Y	Y	Y	N	Y	Y	Y	Y	Y	Y	Y	Y	N	Y	N
Mongolia	A	1	$	4,259	N	Y	N	N	N	N	N	N	N	N	N	Y	Y	N	N	N
Montenegro	C	1	$	5,904	Y	Y	Y	Y	N	N	N	Y	Y	Y	Y	Y	Y	N	Y	N
Morocco	C	1	$	2,422	N	N	N	N	N	N	N	N	N	N	N	Y	Y	N	N	N
Mozambique	C	1	$	333	N	N	N	N	N	N	N	N	N	N	N	Y	Y	N	N	N
Namibia	C	1	$	4,122	N	N	N	N	N	N	N	N	N	N	N	Y	Y	N	N	N
Netherlands	A	3	$	39,090	Y	Y	Y	Y	Y	Y	Y	Y	Y	Y	Y	Y	Y	Y	Y	N
New Zealand	C	1	$	10,442	Y	Y	Y	Y	N	N	N	Y	Y	Y	Y	Y	Y	N	Y	N
Nicaragua	C	1	$	1,881	N	N	N	N	N	N	N	N	N	N	N	Y	Y	N	N	N
Niger	C	1	$	214	N	N	N	N	N	N	N	N	N	N	N	Y	Y	N	N	N
Nigeria	C	1	$	1,011	N	N	N	N	N	N	N	N	N	N	N	Y	Y	N	N	N
Norway	A	2	$	25,230	Y	Y	Y	Y	Y	Y	Y	Y	Y	Y	Y	Y	Y	N	Y	N
Oman	C	1	$	27,035	Y	Y	Y	Y	N	N	N	Y	Y	Y	Y	Y	Y	N	Y	N
Pakistan	C	1	$	608	N	N	N	N	N	N	N	N	N	N	N	Y	N	N	N	N
Panama	C	1	$	13,787	Y	Y	Y	Y	N	N	N	Y	Y	Y	Y	Y	Y	Y	Y	N
Papua New Guinea	A	1	$	1,348	N	N	N	N	N	N	N	N	N	N	N	Y	Y	N	N	N
Paraguay	C	1	$	3,996	N	N	N	N	N	N	N	N	N	N	N	Y	Y	N	N	N
Peru	A	1	$	2,795	N	N	N	N	N	N	N	N	N	N	N	Y	Y	N	N	N
Philippines	C	1	$	1,824	N	N	N	N	N	N	N	N	N	N	N	Y	Y	N	N	N
Poland	C	1	$	11,324	Y	Y	Y	Y	N	N	Y	Y	Y	Y	Y	Y	Y	N	Y	N
Portugal	C	1	$	10,916	Y	Y	Y	Y	N	Y	N	Y	Y	Y	Y	Y	Y	N	Y	N
Qatar	A	2	$	105,868	Y	Y	Y	Y	N	Y	Y	Y	Y	Y	Y	Y	Y	N	Y	N
Romania	C	1	$	7,965	Y	Y	Y	Y	N	N	N	Y	Y	Y	Y	Y	Y	N	Y	N
Russia	A	2	$	7,163	Y	Y	Y	Y	Y	N	Y	Y	Y	Y	Y	Y	Y	N	Y	N
Rwanda	C	1	$	212	N	N	N	N	N	N	N	N	N	N	N	Y	Y	N	N	N
Saint Kitts and Nevis		1	$	7,328	Y	Y	Y	Y	N	N	Y	Y	Y	Y	Y	Y	Y	N	Y	N
Saint Lucia		1	$	4,823	N	Y	N	N	N	N	N	N	N	N	N	Y	Y	N	N	N
Saint Vincent and the Grenadines		1	$	2,869	N	N	N	N	N	N	N	N	N	N	N	Y	Y	N	N	N
Samoa		1	$	1,768	N	N	N	N	N	N	N	N	N	N	N	Y	Y	N	N	N
Saudi Arabia	A	1	$	28,280	Y	Y	Y	Y	N	N	N	Y	Y	Y	Y	Y	Y	N	Y	N
Senegal	C	1	$	587	N	N	N	N	N	N	N	N	N	N	N	Y	Y	N	N	N
Serbia	C	1	$	5,306	Y	Y	Y	Y	N	N	N	Y	Y	Y	Y	Y	Y	N	Y	N
Seychelles	C	1	$	18,766	Y	Y	Y	Y	N	Y	Y	Y	Y	Y	Y	Y	Y	N	Y	N
Sierra Leone	C	1	$	820	N	N	N	N	N	N	N	N	N	N	N	Y	Y	N	N	N
Singapore	A	3	$	157,680	Y	Y	Y	Y	N	N	Y	Y	Y	Y	Y	Y	Y	Y	Y	N
Slovenia	C	1	$	21,555	Y	Y	Y	Y	N	N	N	Y	Y	Y	Y	Y	Y	N	Y	N
Solomon Islands		1	$	1,128	N	N	N	N	N	N	N	N	N	N	N	Y	Y	N	N	N
South Africa	C	1	$	4,007	N	N	N	N	N	N	N	N	N	N	N	Y	Y	N	N	N
South Korea	A	1	$	18,525	Y	Y	Y	Y	N	N	N	Y	Y	Y	Y	Y	Y	Y	Y	N
South Sudan	C	1	$	369	N	N	N	N	N	N	N	N	N	N	N	Y	Y	N	N	N
Spain	C	1	$	10,656	Y	Y	Y	Y	N	N	N	Y	Y	Y	Y	Y	Y	N	Y	N
Sri Lanka	C	1	$	2,188	N	N	N	N	N	N	N	N	N	N	N	Y	Y	N	N	N
Sudan	C	1	$	323	N	N	N	N	N	N	N	N	N	N	N	Y	N	N	N	N
Suriname	A	1	$	9,427	Y	Y	Y	Y	N	Y	Y	Y	Y	Y	Y	Y	Y	N	Y	N
Swaziland	A	1	$	3,697	N	N	N	N	N	N	N	N	N	N	N	Y	Y	N	N	N
Sweden	A	2	$	19,768	Y	Y	Y	Y	N	N	N	Y	Y	Y	Y	Y	Y	N	Y	N
Switzerland	A	2	$	41,527	Y	Y	Y	Y	N	Y	Y	Y	Y	Y	Y	Y	Y	N	Y	N
Tajikistan	C	1	$	482	N	N	N	N	N	N	N	N	N	N	N	Y	Y	N	N	N
Tanzania	C	1	$	604	N	N	N	N	N	N	N	N	N	N	N	Y	Y	N	N	N
Thailand	A	1	$	10,590	Y	Y	Y	Y	N	N	N	Y	Y	Y	Y	Y	Y	Y	Y	N
Togo	C	1	$	548	N	N	N	N	N	N	N	N	N	N	N	Y	Y	N	N	N
Tonga		1	$	945	N	N	N	N	N	N	N	N	N	N	N	Y	Y	N	N	N

Country																		
Trinidad and Tobago	A	1	$ 19,227	Y	Y	Y	Y	N	N	Y	Y	Y	Y	Y	Y	Y	N	Y	N
Tunisia	C	1	$ 5,228	Y	Y	Y	Y	N	N	N	Y	Y	Y	Y	Y	Y	Y	Y	N
Turkey	C	1	$ 4,818	N	Y	N	N	N	N	N	N	N	N	N	Y	Y	N	N	N
Turkmenistan	A	1	$ 10,259	Y	Y	Y	Y	N	N	Y	Y	Y	Y	Y	Y	Y	N	Y	N
Uganda	C	1	$ 397	N	N	N	N	N	N	N	N	N	N	N	Y	Y	N	N	N
Ukraine	C	1	$ 4,120	N	Y	N	N	N	N	N	Y	N	N	N	Y	Y	N	N	N
United Arab Emirates	A	2	$ 60,417	Y	Y	Y	Y	N	N	Y	Y	Y	Y	Y	Y	Y	N	Y	N
United Kingdom	C	1	$ 15,432	N	Y	N	N	Y	N	N	N	Y	Y	Y	Y	Y	N	Y	N
United States	C	1	$ 25,670	Y	Y	Y	Y	N	N	Y	Y	Y	Y	Y	Y	Y	N	Y	N
Uruguay	C	1	$ 4,703	N	Y	N	N	N	N	N	N	N	N	N	Y	Y	N	N	N
Uzbekistan	A	1	$ 1,429	N	N	N	N	N	N	N	N	N	N	N	Y	Y	N	N	N
Vanuatu		1	$ 1,430	N	N	N	N	N	N	N	N	N	N	N	Y	Y	N	N	N
Venezuela	C	1	$ 4,762	N	Y	N	N	N	N	N	N	N	N	N	Y	Y	N	N	N
Vietnam	C	1	$ 4,441	N	Y	N	N	N	N	N	N	N	N	N	Y	Y	N	N	N
Yemen	C	1	$ 1,207	N	N	N	N	N	N	N	N	N	N	N	Y	Y	N	N	N
Zambia	C	1	$ 1,644	N	N	N	N	N	N	N	N	N	N	N	Y	Y	N	N	N
Zimbabwe	C	1	$ 540	N	N	N	N	N	N	N	N	N	N	N	Y	Y	N	N	N

Data Quality

Note that TE-Maturing nations (Nations greater-than GT > 1) appear at a much lower 5% to 10% collapse trending rate initially.

Although statistically significant, we recognize that much is dependent on quality of research data and we continue to improve data collection. We will keep an update of this list on the Transition Economics Maturity Model page at csq1.org.

Chapter 10

-

Automation as a Renewable Resource

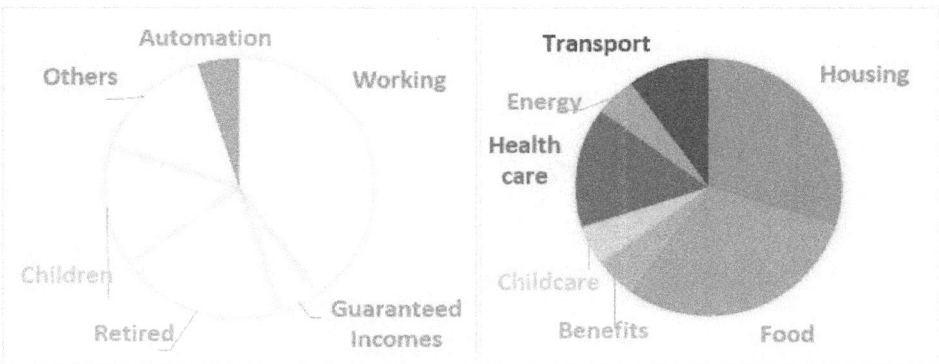

Automation is mankind's most important evolution since manual economies and civilization began 10,000 years ago. Well-planned projects in Automation have the power to create a renewable, sustainable infrastructure that provides for the basic needs of a Good Life reliably, scalably, and flexibly.

Progress has been slow in creating this Renewable Automation due to an absence of central planning, and still Automation is widely acknowledged to be proceeding well on its way toward outmoding as many as 50% of today's jobs within the next twenty to thirty years.

Politicians and Government staff alike will admit openly that Automation does not "test well" in populations worried about unemployment. How do we fix this?

Jobs that can be better accomplished by Automation are important to automate, but the incomes lost to these changes must be maintained too. Losing jobs in a Winter Economic Phase is a normal event historically; and both unemployment and automation both force governments to shift focus to Income distribution policies, and not simply focus on trickle-downs to middle class via unsustainable Job creation; middle class usually have incomes already as well.

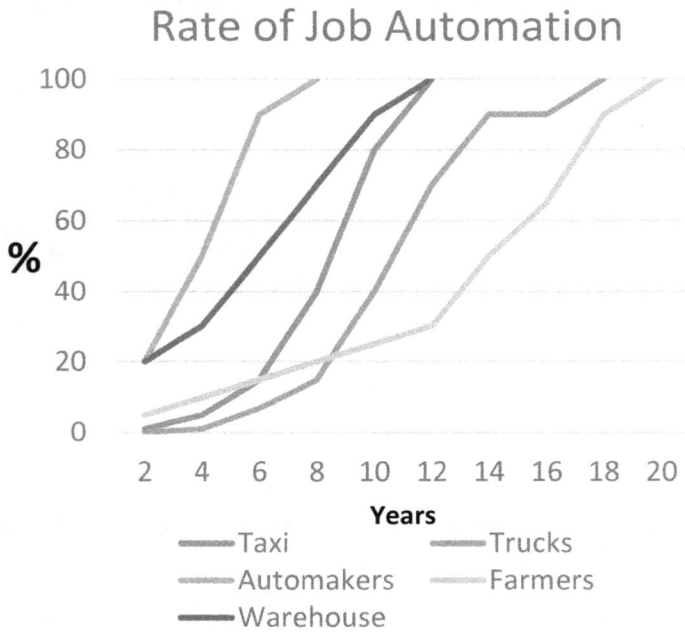

Guaranteed Living Wages and Incomes are the surest method of directly distributing wealth as needed to permit beneficial Job Automation and to begin a new Economic Cycle. Engineering Safety Nets on top of these minimum incomes, support Renewable Automations and give governments who coordinate both of these activities, benefits many times.

Renewable Automation is a new industry and now is the time that Governments will want to establish rules to either have, share, or control communal ownership of their food supply, public housing, transportation and energy.

The Cancer Research Problem

The last thing that should be permitted is a repeat of what happened with Cancer Research. Billions were given to Cancer Research over 30-years – by Governments and by Charities. In this time, Cancer:

- Has reached epidemic proportion – society is suffering; people are dying.
- Has a handful of companies that profit exorbitantly from their pharmaceutical treatments - which were discovered leveraging the research R&D and Scientific Education spending mentioned
- Has very few approved treatments; fewer cures; and …
- Healthcare and Insurance systems are fighting an unsustainable battle to afford the pharmaceuticals developed by all of this thirty-years of R&D investment.
- Those with no medical coverages are ignored and left to die – despite Charity and Government investment for a generation.

How did rich pharma companies run away with all the profits while externalizing all of this R&D cost? The answer is in very poor government sustainability planning and controls.

Governments want to encourage renewable automation, which means assisting or paying for R&D; and heavily supporting rapid development. Society should take the time now to ready laws and patent rules that ensure this automation will be used to eradicate homelessness, hunger, energy poverty, alongside improving the human rights of all - in healthcare, education and support for the young and elderly - sustainably.

This time, governments want to license the financial rewards of

Renewable Automation - to Business; ensuring that services are available for all, and ensuring that we can recover our investments in R&D and guaranteed incomes and Engineering Safety Nets. Perhaps governments should look to own or part-own all renewable automation smart factory patents in law too.

Consider in all of these discussions that anything less works against a sustainable society, leaves us with the unworkable Cancer industry model above, and therefore has to be considered poor planning that is in no-one's best interest.

In 2015, #WPProjects - the World Peace Transition Projects, explained step-by-step what are the 250 initial Connected Smart Factory projects needed to automate our economy's basic needs of life — and then this planning assigned the enormous workload needed to many hands as well. The work-packages in these automation projects are large by themselves, and so assigning one sustainable #WPProjects automation project to every country on the planet creates inclusiveness, a profitable new global trade market, and important social needs like automated food delivery, energy, shelter, transport and more.

As our economies become ever more unsustainable here in the Winter Phase, the automation of our essential needs reduce our reliance on money too.

Does anyone believe they will starve once food delivery to their door is automated - as ordered and as needed? No, of course not. Will anyone go without a home for his or her family once life-cycle-managed shelter is automated? Will elderly or school-children be unable to get to their doctor's appointments and schools once transportation is automated? And finally, will we freeze or go without clean water once clean abundant energy is available for everyone automatically? No.

Can we really automate everything?

A driverless car, as with every other technology, was science fiction until an engineer – in this case the engineer was someone with unlimited resources - made it work for the first time in 2013. That engineer was none other than Larry Page, Google's CEO.

Singapore was the first city to launch driverless taxi services in September 2016. Now ask yourself honestly; if you had not seen a driverless car working in real life five years ago, would you ever believe such a sophisticated automation would ever be possible?

Many of us might think it was impossible in our lifetime; most people would think that this technology was just too advanced.

The reality is very different: the Driverless Car took just two years of development to get to Alpha - and then Beta tests. The car's testing was so successful that Ford has committed to mass-producing autonomous passenger automobiles within five years. Driverless trucks are driving on our roads in automated testing today as well - and have been for most of the past year.

This explanation is as true for Leonardo da Vinci's Helicopter – which was a 4-Year Project that was realized in 1939 by Ukrainian-American Igor Sikorsky. His Armored Tank was a 2-year project realized in 1916 by the British Army. It was the same for Jules Verne's Nautilus submarine; Nautilus was two 3-year Projects of the U.S. Government; the first launched a diesel submarine in 1930 and then a nuclear submarine followed in 1954. Mr. Verne's Trip to the Moon was a seven-year Project accomplished by the U.S. Government & NASA.

These example technologies were all a fanciful science fiction for hundreds of years, but today we look back at these machines that are obviously viable and proven. Often we even forget that they were once science fiction.

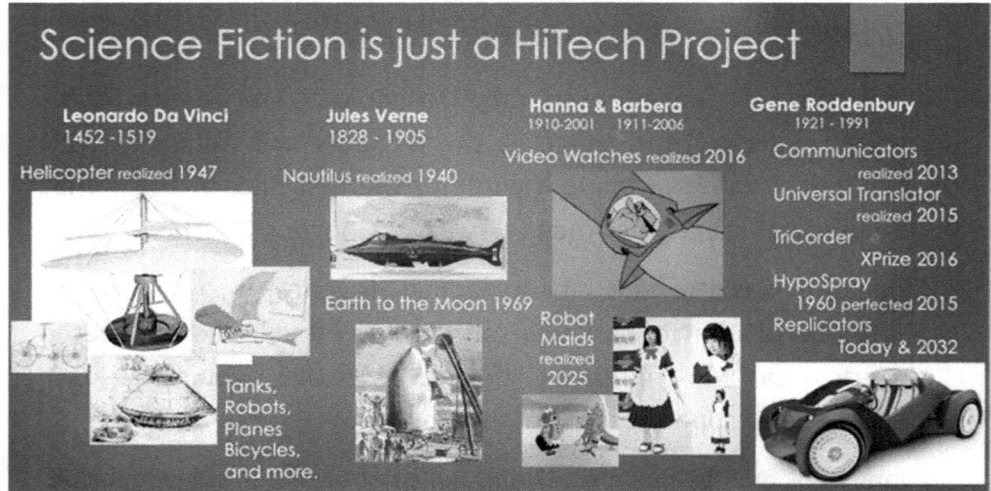

Spread Limited of Kyoto, Japan, looks as though it may become the first company to build a completely automated farm once it begins delivery of 30,000 heads of lettuce daily in operations scheduled to start late in 2016. Automated Lettuce - is not sexy – but it is an important first and now automated farms are no-longer science fiction.

Are the automated Mushrooms (assigned to El Salvador), Cabbage (Angola), Bananas (Ecuador), and 100 other top-100 grocery store sales items on the #WPProjects' list any different? These projects are the same. And there is no science fiction in these automation projects either because everything needed is already working today. These projects simply have not been integrated together because no central plan has recognized the importance yet.

In any recession, infrastructure spending - like road construction - is often recommended - and all that this plan is changing is that now we are building automated road builders - instead of simply roads.

What do Sustainability Robots look like?

Many of us think of robots as mimics of humanoid workers; we can watch robots perform as a human might in his or her factory work – in a YouTube video easily. A Star Trek "Replicator" - if you never saw the show - was a machine that converted energy to matter and produced a wide variety of goods based on a user's voice command. WP Projects emulates this - by taking your request - for food, a car, a TV, an appliance, etc. - on a phone app or a Call Center Operator. Each order starts a sub-routine that automatically assembles, distributes and ships the ordered product to your door - automatically.

Very shortly, Audi Automotive will be building some of the finest driverless automobiles in the world, on assembly lines that are completely automated and require almost no human workers on the shop floor at all. In this example, it is the Assembly Line that is the sustainability robot; and the autonomous cars are their automated, robotic products.

Each self-driving automatically-built car is a sophisticated robot unto itself, but again - it is the sustainability robot that we are more interested in creating; again and again, in order to ensure repeatable scalability and abundance worldwide.

In the example of Spread's automated lettuce farm, the assembly line that pieces together its hydroponic components, complete with robotic farm-attendants, is the sustainable robot that we want to build.

Self-driving taxis, delivery vans, fuel trucks, GPS-driven tractors, trains, drone cargo planes, mining equipment, fishing trawlers, even emergency vehicles - will soon be entirely automated in this way.

Once designed and tested, these completed Sustainability Robot/ Assembly Lines for each product will be rolled out to produce many farms throughout many countries, and many regions, in sizes and configurations as needed by the local communities.

Robotic assembly lines add limitless and easy scalability that creates abundance - as opposed to our current scarcity-based financially limited systems today.

These services will eventually install and life-cycle-manage your appliances, homes, etc.; and most of the things we need can be delivered in just 250 projects. Each of these projects could deliver a v1.0 product within just one or two years as well. These projects can all start at once, so the entire program of products could complete within just two years too.

These are big automation projects, but 90% or more are entirely pilot-able within just a year. In some more complex examples, pilots might have to happen within two or three years at maximum.

House-building Sustainability Robots build robots that travel to building sites and assemble homes; and not just the same home, but multiple models and floor-plans for apartments, townhomes, semi-detached, and single family dwellings whose designs are enhanced year over year. If a third or fourth child surprises you, a granny suite and bedroom can be added to some of these home automatically upon request and need. One can only be limited by a failing of imagination really.

Having variety in home layouts, finishing, rooflines, furnishings, etc. adds needed practical utility and also adds charm and visual appeal to our neighborhoods. Renovations or upgrades can be planned in; appliances can be installable in an automated and as needed way as well.

Energy Robots build the automated robots that create Power Plants, and then repeat that construction again and again, until power is abundant and reliable. Road building robots, train and train-track building robots, mining and metal processing, ships and shipbuilding robots – are all a part of the plan.

As I said, difficult – but far from impossible, and this complexity is the reason that automation projects must be distributed to many countries with a consistent and sophisticated SUSTAIN Project Management Method.

The Necessity of Planning

Without planning, automation will have the simpler effect of eliminating jobs at dizzying rates and few governments appear to have a clear direction on how to prepare their citizens for this kind of change.

It is socially irresponsible for governments to not prepare for automation, and clearly today there can be no excuse to say they did not realize this was coming either.

The safe and responsible transition to an automated economy and prosperous new economic cycle lies entirely in good planning. I discuss Guaranteed Incomes in the next Chapter.

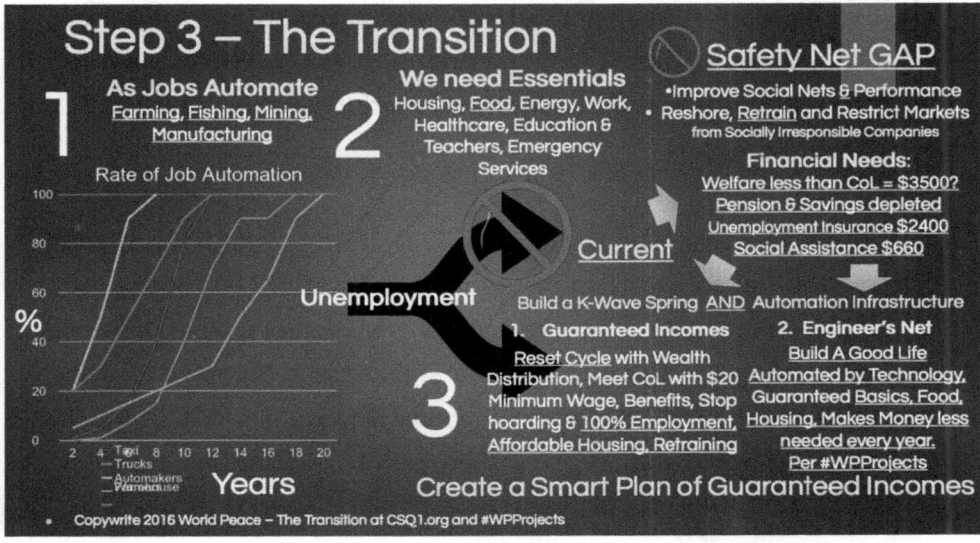

The Engineering Safety Net

#WPProjects' 250 automation projects plug together in a plan that creates a direct economic benefit – a Renewable Automated assembly line of monetizable products and sustainable products that are needed by society every day. These projects are professionally managed and tracked, so that the funding of Engineers who might wish to participate in Automation Construction Programs, can share learning and progress. These supports should well afford their salaries as needed to pay the bills for a home and family life.

Engineering Safety Net workers are much more than productive tinkerers. The work is worthwhile and profitable and warrants funding at the rate of an "IT Architect", Engineer, or "Senior Project Manager". Engineers need to afford the computers and internet access required at a minimum, and then any further funding and space must be made available within automation labs as needed to support their work both remotely and in group facilities – perhaps even within educational institutions. Easy access to free education, project knowledge-bases, benefits programs for healthcare, dental, and medications are also needed to be productive and are essential.

Engineering Leadership

The "Tail can never Wag the Dog" in Transition Economics projects. This means that concerns for insurance, legal, patent, and accounting must take distant second importance to the primary goal of progress in society. Progress and building to a Right Plan is our primary goal, so concerns presented by "the tail" cannot be a weak-link in the chain and so these professionals are tasked with correcting the problems and overcoming any obstacles – just as are engineers.

The sentences "We cannot" or "the law will not permit" are the words of the wrong resource for the job. Everything needs considered and everything needs resolved as best can so that people can eat and have the basics of shelter that they must be afforded.

Progress as a society means that legal obstacles, software and other broad patents, special interest lobby groups, licenses or material price gouging; anything - that forces obstacles in the way of completing automation work with minimal frustration, needs to be understood as a second priority by all levels of government and our legal systems as well. The way must be made clear of these obvious frustrations and obstacles and they cannot become show-stoppers.

Our current slow rate of automation is surely evidence that these obstacles have already dramatically deterred advances over these past forty-five years.

Other spending for automation include educational programs that contribute to #WPProjects. This is a very good optimization of Education Spending because this spending is not only educational, but it is also productive and it engages the next generation of beneficiaries directly too.

Return-on-Investment Business Case calculations for the *Engineering*

Safety Net should include patent and other financial proceeds accumulated during this work. Obviously each engineer's work generates tangible value and also products that promise to return a financial reward. These revenues should be take full advantage of.

Intellectual Property and Patent Ownership

When Engineers enter into Engineering Safety Net programs with a lot of their own propriety information to begin with, ownership of that proprietary knowledge should remain with the engineer as owner and patent holder. In this case, perhaps the government can assist patent development with provisos that profits and employment for these patents stay within the country - or similar simple but fair and effective ownership strategies can be discussed.

When Engineers enter into Safety Net programs with only their own time and "sweat equity" contribution; with very little or no proprietary work in advance, they are remunerated with a salary and worthwhile project work. In this case, ownership for discoveries might stay with the project team and with the country that paid for the work. To promote performance and acknowledgement of contribution, perhaps a profit sharing and awards/rewards formula can be arrived with engineers as well.

Personal incomes from Engineer Safety Net supported projects, from all sources, should be capped (perhaps at a $4 million per year maximum for example) and the rest taxed and poured back into automation project development.

Balancing contribution and investment, acknowledges the promise that society had to make in advance to support everyone's success. This is true for most businesses and these programs can easily be considered Conservative Investments. This message of Balance should be reinforced in Business Accountability rework discussions and Business Ethics courses immediately too.

Algorithms in Rate of Automation Transition

Projects can begin more easily once Automation initiatives are afforded by Income Safety Nets in society. These programs should not be seen as a dependency however; Automation can also happen at a rate that our other GDP incomes can absorb responsibly and many countries will begin without these safety nets in place at the start. Planning is always best and Guaranteed Incomes are a smart planning building-block.

Business Plan for Renewable Automation (ROI-RA)

Consider that the country that plans a business & revenue return on its investment (ROI) in renewable automation infrastructure, probably has a bright future ahead. Even slippery-slope (impossibly worst-case) discussions regarding automation investment, can hold little merit in a country that will shortly receive groceries and other basic needs door-to-door automatically. No-one need starve nor suffer even if money were to be removed completely from the equation; and money would never need to be removed as long as there is benefit in keeping it - in reality.

A famous American slippery slope argument from the 1930s was the introduction of the speed limit on its highways. Detractors made slippery-slope arguments to say that once these freedoms were limited, that eventually we would all be driving five miles per hour.

Once an economy has been automated, the attention of this country's citizens can turn to the monetization of their production economy - if it wishes. This sort of planning is very similar to Chinese Financial Plans that began 25 years ago. China has had a far higher economic success rate over every other country during this time period – and so observation confirms this is a valid approach by scientific method.

The Netherlands' #5 CMI position and leading GDP Export per Citizen, is proof of the economic value of providing citizens with their basic needs. In addition to financial planning improvement, other plans for research, discovery, science and engineering, which are now properly supported, can be expected to skyrocket.

Alternatively, a country that finds itself spending itself into debt without making headway in sustainable self-sufficient automation in infrastructure, has a much harder recovery road ahead and is far less well-positioned for success too.

Money is a non-renewable resource; but sustainable automation of our basic production, can be considered renewable and it is a self-renewing asset that yields a continuing annual benefit, productivity, and revenue stream as well.

The RAI – Renewable Automation Index

The CSQ **Renewable Automation Index – *The RAI*,** is the most recent addition to CSQ Research's Online Database. The RAI measures indexed companies that develop and invest in Renewable Automation. Technology companies, and technologies that do not plug-in nor assist renewable, sustainable projects are counted lower on the Index.

Countries that invest in and encourage Transition Economics Maturity policies increase their Maturity levels. Presently, there is just one TE Maturing country (Luxemburg) that is in a collapsing trend – so there is a data-correlation between TE Maturity and Sustainability.

Companies and educational institutions that build LIDAR sensors permit driverless vehicles to see/recognize people or avoid human injury while they work, will score high on the RAI. So too will warehousing systems that automate manufacturing and order delivery. Fin-tech or Big-Data hi-tech companies that set out to improve marketing campaigns or receivables performance, will score much lower and companies with predatory, bubble-building real estate investment, or socially irresponsible debt marketing practices, score very low.

The RAI - Country Index is updated online and the **RAI - Companies Index** is made available to governments exclusively for their procurement needs.

The RAI tracks each country's automations in Healthcare, Energy, Computing, Manufacturing, 3D Printing, Technologies, Transportation Logistics, Agriculture, Construction, Robots, Sensors, Artificial Intelligence and Consumer Goods Automation.

The Goal of the RAI Country Index is to recognize Countries that invest in Renewable Automation and also recognize the wisdom of the management teams there to move their home infrastructures and business forward in this way.

The Goal of the RAI Company Index is to support Renewable Automation companies both financially and with higher-priority than technology investment that simply improves unsustainable, non-renewable short-term profit.

I might be overthinking this a bit, but acknowledging that status-quo investors will struggle to understand their role in a changing socially responsible, sustainably-profitable investment landscape – is probably a good forethought. The change may take a bit of time, training and even governance protections. For this reason, the Companies Index is licensed to companies only with provisos and penalties that protect against intentionally harmful short-selling injury; we saw some of this behavior targeting the 3D Printing Industry two years ago.

Short-selling behaviors can target any company at any time for any number of reasons of course, we all want to be over-cautious to "not cause harm" to startup renewables is all. In reality, it might be that these technology companies are the ones that are "too large to fail".

The RAI seeks to recognize and reward our Leading Renewable Automation Countries. For Companies wishing to market their compliance with Sustainable and Renewable Technology Targets, CSQ Corporate Social Responsibility Certifications are available. These programs are there to help both consumers and investors make wiser decisions so look for the CSQ logo on your company, customer, and country website.

Chapter 11

-

Guaranteed Incomes

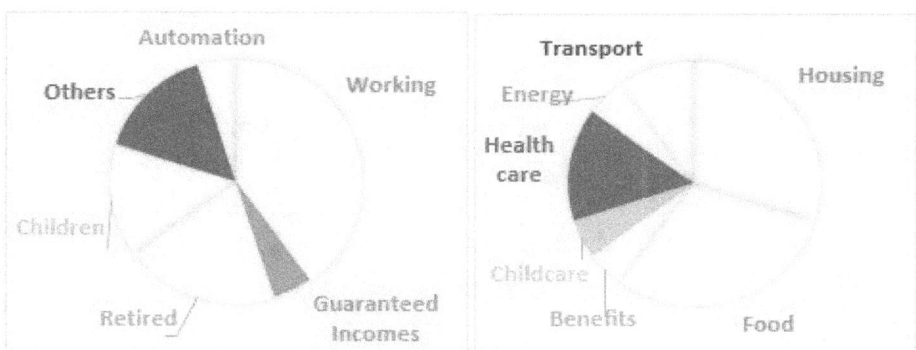

Social projects are sufficient by themselves to build a Good Life in just about any country that is not presently considered a developing nation. Policy selection alone dictates which countries will prosper and which will collapse - and so transition must constantly work to carefully balance tax-neutral targets so that citizen impacts are minimal. Balancing equations are often referred to throughout this books as "throttles".

Guaranteed Incomes

According to the CMI – The Country Management Index, one of the leading countries for GDP Export per Capita is presently held by #5 The Netherlands at $33,652. Ireland does a little better and other micro-economies like Hong Kong and Singapore dwarf these stats, but the Netherlands is a good start for us here for several reasons.

Country	GDP Export per Capita	Multiplier to Dutch Export/Cap	GINI Wealth Equality	HDI	Leaning	American Dream?	Population (In Millions)	Export Quality
Netherlands	$33,652	100%	31	0.915	Socialistic	Yes	17	High
Norway	$28,807	117%	25	0.944	Socialistic	Yes	5	High
United States	$5,057	665%	45	0.914	Capitalistic	No	324	Very High
Sweden	$18,688	180%	23	0.911	Socialistic	Yes	10	Mid
Germany	$18,316	184%	27	0.911	Socialistic	Almost	80	Very High
Canada	$13,286	253%	32	0.902	Capitalistic	No	36	Low
United Kingdom	$7,378	456%	32	0.907	Capitalistic	No	65	Mid
Australia	$10,446	322%	30	0.935	Capitalistic	No	24	Low

Compare the Exports and per Capita Exports of your Country to understand how much revenue your country is failing to earn every year by not engaging every citizen in wealth generating export commerce:

Country	GDP Export per Capita	Multiplier to Dutch Export/Cap	Export 2015 (in billions)	Opportunity Cost New Export (in billions)	Collapse or Advance Trending?
Netherlands	$33,652	100%	$477	$0	Advance
Norway	$28,807	117%	$103	$17	Advance
United States	$5,057	665%	$1,510	$8,538	Collapse
Sweden	$18,688	180%	$151	$121	Advance
Germany	$18,316	184%	$1,309	$1,096	Advance
Canada	$13,286	253%	$411	$630	Collapse
United Kingdom	$7,378	456%	$436	$1,553	Collapse
Australia	$10,446	322%	$188	$418	Collapse

Enabling the success of The Netherlands' citizens, are some of the strongest policies and economic controls in the world. The Netherland government controls protect spending power, employment, housing, and foreign investment and business ownership. Education at all levels is free, daycare, healthcare, guaranteed incomes and even retirements are all paid for through a graduated tax structure that permits all citizens to participate in businesses and other commercial work.

Taxes are higher here than in G7 countries presently, but these differences can be considered tax and revenue-neutral in that they cover healthcare, retirements, and other living costs that other countries do not call "taxes". We discuss historical taxation next chapter as well.

The Export per Capita statistics of Holland prove conclusively that citizens do take advantage of social benefits to improve both their productivity and the standard of living for their communities as well.

High-income earners who are not instructed in the big-picture business and personal benefits of socialistic policies, might look at higher taxes with frustration. At the same time, the standard of living for all of their workers, executive, and owners is sustainable and uninterrupted with this approach. A strong social infrastructure gives the high income earners a place to live in which they are appreciated and even revered in a family-friendly society that they can proudly call home too. This luxury is not afforded to high income earners in other countries where opportunistic capitalist policy creates a very different life.

The cost of Guaranteed Income programs vary based on metrics like Cost of Living, CPI (Inflation as measured by the Consumer Price Index), Rent Controls, housing costs, and so on.

For guaranteed income Calculations, generally the following formula holds true, and the chart that follows calculates the tax increase needed to afford these benefits country-wide in the U.S., U.K., Canada, Australia and Germany.

Labour Pool * (Unemployment Rate x 2) + Cost of Living * CPI

With a little more calculation, we can easily arrive at a crude **Return on Investment (ROI)** estimate for our Business Case for providing Guaranteed Incomes to Labor Force workers.

Country	Cost of Living/mth	Population	Unemployment	Guaranteed Income	Tax Increase
America	$2500	155 mill	5%	$233 bill	1.34%
Germany	$3000	44 mill	4.5%	$60 bill	1.57%
Canada	$3000	19 mill	6.8%	$40 bill	2.2%
U.K	$3500	31 mill	5%	$64 bill	2.2%
Australia	$3000	12 mill	6.8%	$30 bill	2.1%

Return on Investment (ROI) for Guaranteed Incomes

Country	America	Germany	Canada	U.K	Australia
Export Per Capita	$5,057	$18,316	$13,286	$7,378	$10,446
Exports ($bill)	$1,510	$1,309	$411	$436	$188
Export Increase	665%	184%	253%	456%	322%
Opportunity Cost ($bill)	$8,538	$1,096	$630	$1,553	$418
Cost of Living	$2,500	$3,000	$3,000	$3,500	$3,000
Population (million)	324	82	36.5	65	24.2
Labor force (million)	155.4	44.2	19	30.8	12.4
Unemployment	5.0%	4.5%	6.8%	5.0%	6.8%
Current Benefits		15%	14%		
Total Cost ($bill)	$233	$60	$40	$64.6	$30
GDP ($bill)	$17,348	$3,868	$1,785	$2,989	$1,472
Tax Inc vs GDP	26.9%	40.6%	32.0%	39.0%	25.8%
Total Tax Revenues ($bill)	$4,666	$1,570	$571	$1,166	$379
New Tax ($bill)	$3,618	$1,466	$516	$997	$347
Tax Increase	-22.45%	-6.59%	-9.53%	-14.45%	-8.5%
Tax Rev New Export (15%) $bill	$1,280	$164	$516	$233	$62
ROI	**3663%**	**1801%**	**1574%**	**2405%**	**1374%**

If I use Canada as an example, the math says that Canada would generate $630 billion in new export revenue annually via Guaranteed

Incomes. The program would cost $40 billion offset by new export tax revenue – estimated here at a maybe-generous $571 billion based on my imperfect understanding of current tax rates. So, a worst-case drop in tax by approx 10% could result if the Guaranteed Incomes have the planned effect within its workforce. This gives Guaranteed Incomes in Canada a planned Return-on-Investment of 15-times or 1574%. This is the true power of laser-focused attention on improving GDP Export Revenues.

These are very positive returns (ROIs) that encourage the adoption of this important Wealth Distribution Program – and these numbers are worst-case numbers presented before any discussion of optimization nor tax graduation have been considered.

Social benefits from Guaranteed Incomes include:

1. Considerable building industry Automation productivity & Hitech industry boosts
2. Reliance on Immigration for population falls
3. Inequity starts correcting toward 1960s levels
4. Homelessness can be almost wiped out
5. Other programs in housing & onshoring are supported
6. Incarceration, Unemployment, and other Social Problems are reduced.

Chapter 12

-

Sustaining Equality creates Wealth

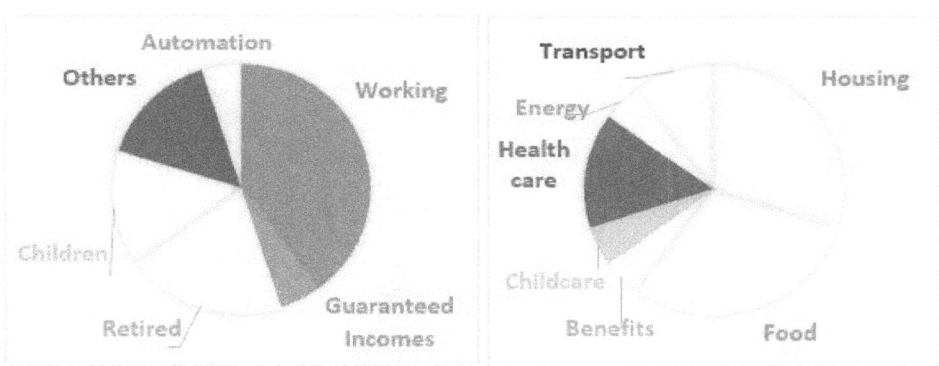

Social projects are sufficient by themselves to build a Good Life in just about any country that is not considered a developing nation. Once the hurdle of surpassing the production and wealth of a developing nation is accomplished, emphasis turns to Wealth Creation and finally to Wealth Distribution.

Wealth Distribution is critical to enabling citizens to participate in wealth building export and Gross Domestic Production taxable production.

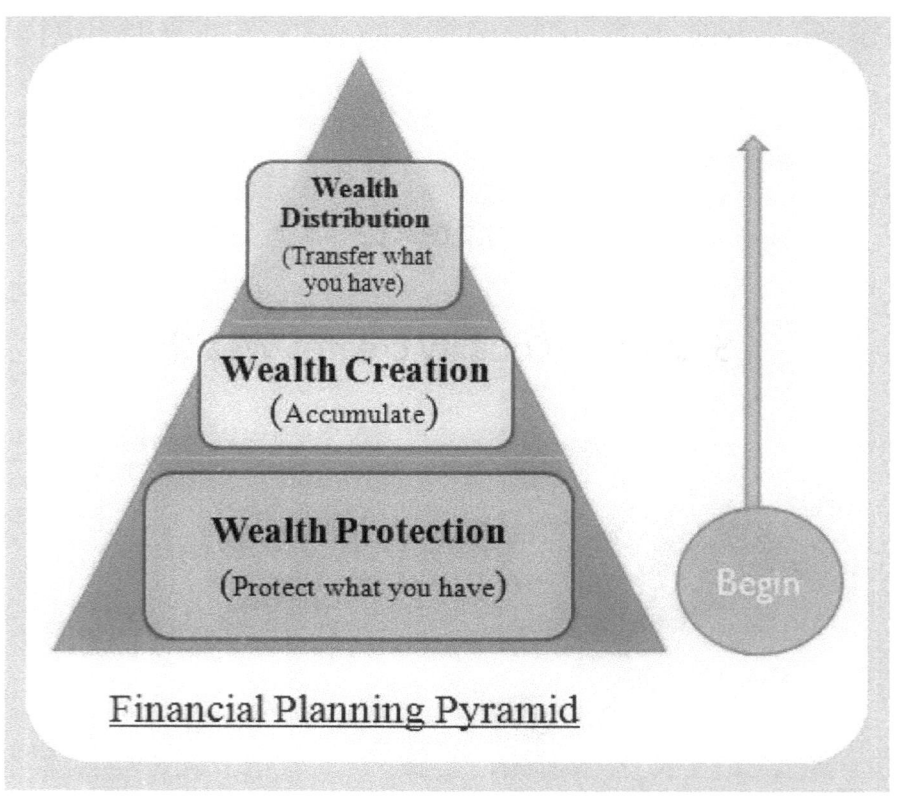

Wealth Creation

The surest way for a country to generate wealth is to take their raw earth, and things that grow on it, and monetize those resources by selling high-quality productized resources and manufactured goods in trade for currency from other nations.

Sales economies do not create this sort of shared economic wealth and benefit because a running shoe, for example, purchased for $1 from the Orient and then sold in North America for $100, has no up nor down-stream industry incomes for the hundreds of local workers who would ordinarily benefit from production all along the supply chain of that product's manufacture. Sales economy profits tend to benefit a handful only and these profits are easier to offshore and avoid tax with at present as well.

Wealth Distribution

Wealth Distribution policy are tax and social benefit programs which include minimum living wages, guaranteed incomes, graduated tax, tax avoidance cleanups, childcare, universal health, child daycare, and retirement social programs.

In the Netherlands, young citizens between the ages of infancy to graduation are invited to take as much education as they want without cost. All dental and medical costs are covered as are massages and other wellness treatments as needed. Retirement age is 60 and all medical, dental, and income needs are met by employers and by the government for the rest of their lives.

The Netherlands' government manages taxes very well and the productivity of Dutch citizens, who are supported by socialistic policy, is almost six-times higher than U.S. citizens per capita by GDP Export.

For the productive working years of its citizens, from ages 22 to 60, the Netherlands takes tax in the area of 55% of earned income; similar to tax rates in the U.S. for most of the past 100 years. See the next chart.

In the next chart, the top line is Top Tax Rate and Red line below is Bottom Tax Rate. I have included US Presidents to give a view to taxation policies and parties in the U.S. over time as well. It was Ronald Reagan's administration that set the stage for our most recent inequity in the 1980s. Before that, low tax for the rich was initiated in 1916 and in 1925 by president's William Taft and Calvin Coolidge.

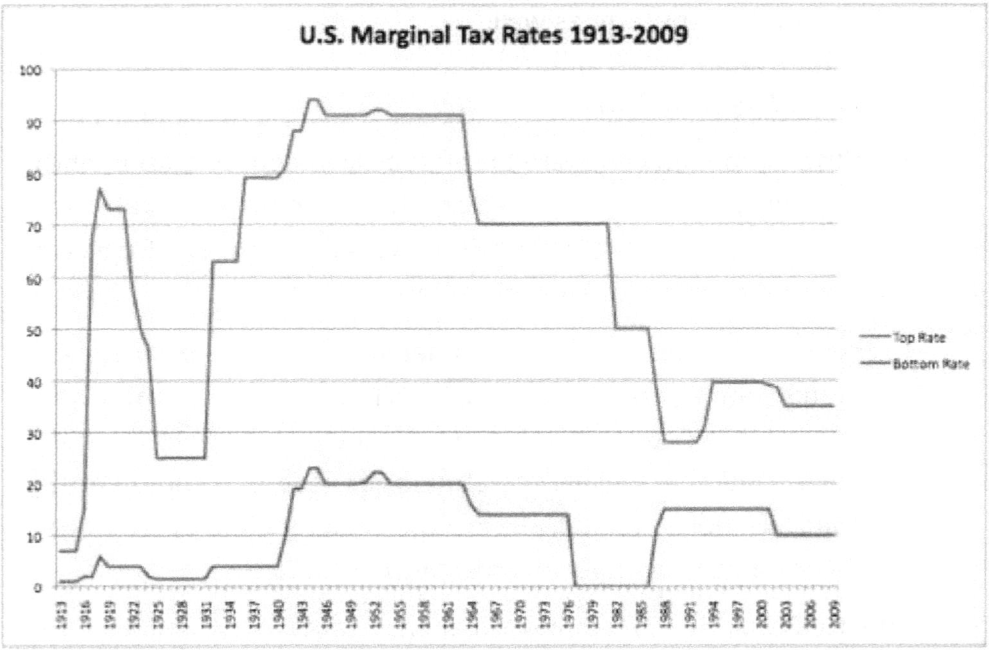

Roosevelt '33-45 | Truman '45-53 | Eisenhower '53-61 | Kennedy '61-63 | Johnson '63-69 | Nixon '69-74 | Ford '74-77 | Carter '77-81 | Reagan '81-89 | Bush '89-93

Dem Dem Rep Dem Dem Rep Rep Dem Rep Rep

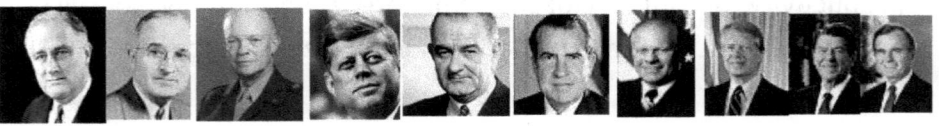

The following chart shows lifespans and earning years is based on average lifespans of 89 years of age, and retirement at 65, which is the norm in France and the Netherlands. This results in a ratio of 50:50 Labor Force Years to Non-Labor Force Years. North Americans have average lifespans of 82 years which means that their ratio is 56:44 .

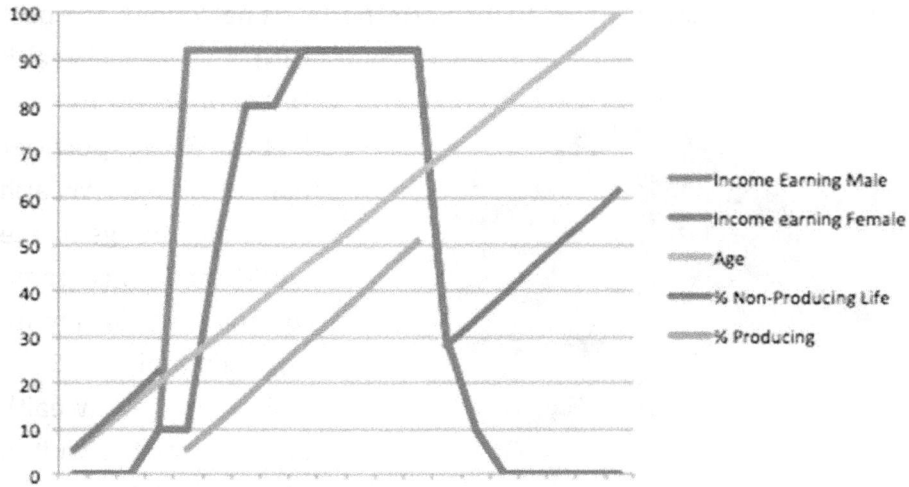

We are all human, we all have childhoods and if we are lucky, we are going to get old and retire as well. With an average life expectancy of 90 years in the Sweden, working to pay your way for 100% of your life costs during the less than 50% of your productive years, both recognizes reality and has a very humanistic fairness to it as well.

Pure Capitalist systems simply ignore the reality of our lifespans and this results in lower quality of life and lower longevity for the 99% majority of non-wealthy society members.

Finland took on a Pilot Project of Universal Basic Incomes in December 2015 to see if the program would help build a Good Life within its population of 5.4 million.

Many of us in Capitalist countries aspire to find work that sets us for life; one among thousands of us finds an income that sets our children's trust funds for life as well. These projects in wealth distribution realize just this goal for everyone in society reliably.

We discussed last chapter that the Netherlands has one of the best GINI (Wealth Distribution Rating) and highest GDP Export per Capita (Wealth Creation) ratings in the world and this same formula would create approximately $500 billion in new wealth annually for the United States all by itself.

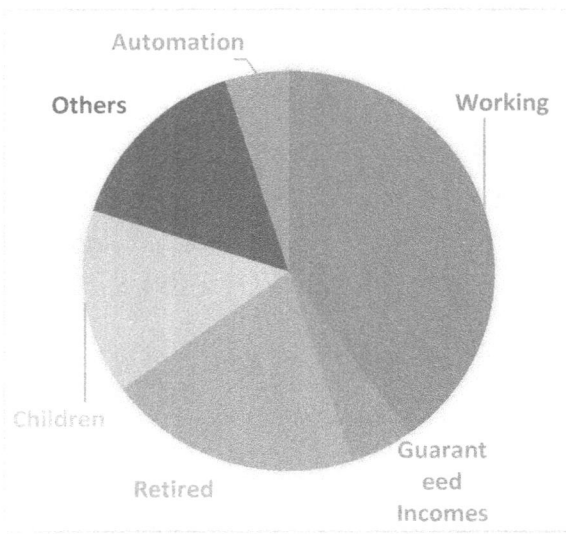

The key to maximizing productivity from citizens is ensuring that all ages and income earners in every income level, benefit group and age group - can participate in the economy. The analogy of an engine firing on all cylinders comes to mind; you want to ensure that all have the opportunity to push the engine forward.

Once your economy supports production in all five income quintiles – including the bottom 40%; and in all age groups - including retired and unemployed. At this point your citizens have the income supports needed to engage in production and in generating taxable wealth.

The leading cause of wage stagnation between 1995 and 2013 included globalization (offshoring and imports) and the decline of labor unions and other forms of group bargaining power that could keep income and benefits onshore.

By 2010, inequity is so extreme in the U.S. that the poor have just 0.3% of the wealth in the United States. That's 160 million people struggling for no stake in the wealth whatsoever.

Much worse than this, according to "Robert Reich: Income inequality the defining issue for U.S.", **95% of all gains since 2009's supposed recovery have gone to the top 1%** as well. *The Denver Post*, January 26, 2014; see also (Wolf, 2015).

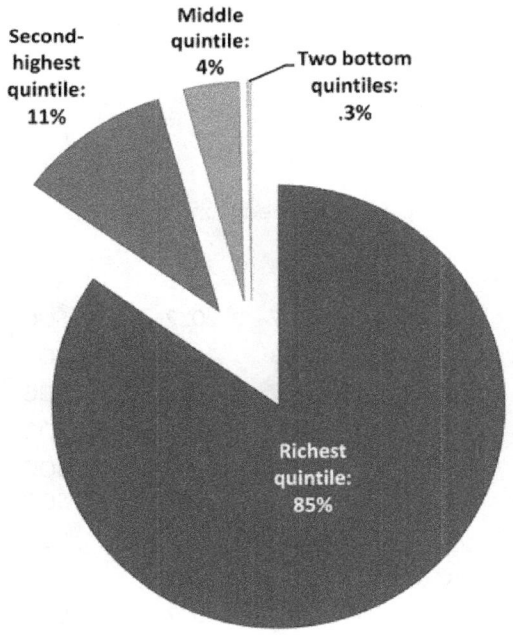

Chart 2: Distribution of wealth in the US by quintile, 2010

Source: Adapted from Norton & Airely, 2012, http://ppd.sagepub.com/

Remember that wealth and income are two very different measures of economic prosperity, and that high income does not necessarily correlate to mean high wealth or "worth". Net Worth is the sum of all assets, including the market value of real-estate, like a home, minus all liabilities.

How do other nations stack up in measures of Income Distribution? The GINI Coefficient Index, named after its statistician inventor Corrado Gini, is one measure of income inequality depicted here globally.

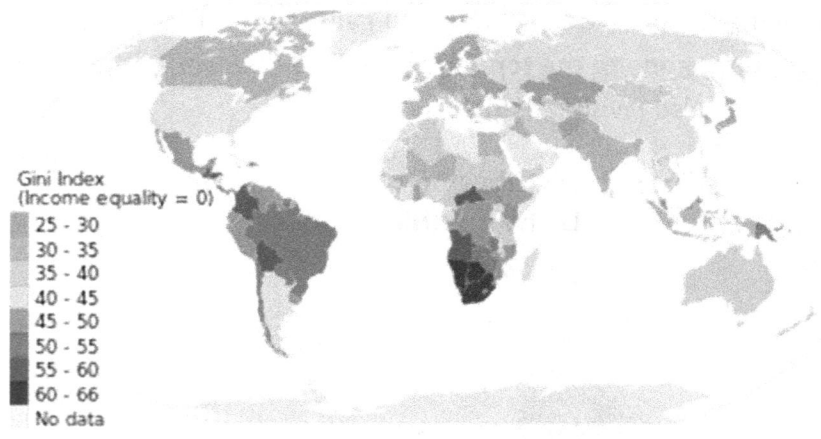

Online at https://en.wikipedia.org/wiki/Gini_coefficient

Country	GINI	Year	Source	
Sweden	23	2005	SOC	CM
Slovenia	23.7	2012	SOC	REP
Montenegro	24.3	2010	SOC	REP
Hungary	24.7	2009	SOC	DEM
Denmark	24.8	2011 est.	SOC	CM
Czech	24.9	2012	SOC	DEM
Norway	25	2008	SOC	CM
Slovakia	26	2005	SOC	DEM
Luxembourg	26	2005	SOC	CM
Austria	26.3	2007	SOC	REP
Finland	26.8	2008	SOC	REP
Germany	27	2006	CAP	REP
Belarus	27.2	2008	SOC	REP
Ukraine	28.2	2009	SOC	REP
Switzerland	28.7	2012 est.	SOC	REP
Kazakhstan	28.9	2011	AUT	REP
Kosovo	30	FY05/06	SOC	REP
Australia	30.3	2008	CAP	DEM

Pakistan	30.6	FY07/08	CAP	REP
European Union	30.6	2012 est.	CAP	HYB
France	30.6	2011	SOC	REP
Netherlands	30.9	2007	SOC	CM
Armenia	30.9	2008	SOC	REP
Cyprus	31	2012 est.	CAP	REP
Korea, South	31.1	2011 est.	CAP	REP
Estonia	31.3	2010	SOC	REP
Italy	31.9	2012 est.	CAP	REP
Spain	32	2005	CAP	PM
Croatia	32	2010	CAP	DEM
Canada	32.1	2005	SOC	CM
Bangladesh	32.1	2010	CAP	DEM
United Kingdom	32.3	2012	CAP	CM
Ireland	33.9	2010	CAP	REP
Poland	34.1	2009	CAP	REP
Taiwan	34.2	2011	CAP	DEM
Greece	34.3	2012 est.	CAP	REP
New Zealand	36.2	1997	CAP	DEM
Indonesia	36.8	2009	CAP	REP
India	36.8	2004	CAP	REP
Israel	37.6	2012	CAP	DEM
Japan	37.6	2008	CAP	CM
Venezuela	39	2011	SOC	REP
Russia	42	2012	SOC	REP
Philippines	44.8	2009	SOC	REP
United States	45	2007	CAP	REP
Malaysia	46.2	2009	CAP	CM
Singapore	46.3	2013	CAP	REP
China	47.3	2013	CAP	COM
Mexico	48.3	2008	CAP	REP
Hong Kong	53.7	2011	CAP	DEM

Legend: From Most Equal to Least Equal

Categories: SOC=Socialist, CAP=Capitalist, AUT=Authoritarian

Types: CM=Constitutional Monarchy, PM=Parliamentary Monarchy, REP=Republican, DEM=Democracy, HYB=Hybrid, COM=Communist

Patterns in Income Inequality

Looking at the Cat - Category of Government in that table above, the top ten GINI countries are acknowledged to favor socialistic policies, regardless of their Government types, be they Constitutional Monarchy, Republic, or Democracy.

Germany, at 12th position, is the first G8 country to appear and then France at 25th. Italy 33rd, Canada is 36th, UK 38th, Japan 66th, Russia 92nd, and the U.S. is at position # 101. All G8 countries shrink from being called Socialist, not wanting to defend a derogatory agenda, and most G8s have predominantly Capitalist policies with Republic or Constitutional Monarchy Government Types.

Germany and France own to a great number of socialistic policies. Germany, for example, has high taxes, universal healthcare, universal college education, great infrastructure and government control of the banks. Germans do it all; they do not buy from China; Dollar stores are non-existent; German workers elect boards of companies. It has the largest ownership of its production economy in Europe giving it a competitive advantage because profit and new investment can be wrapped back into the company rather than going to shareholders and it stays in Germany. Germany owns Deutsche Bahn, Hapag-Lloyd, Airbus, Landesbank, Sparkassen, 20% of Volkswagen, 32% of T-Mobile, KfW Bank, 25% Deutsche Post, Hypo Real Estate, Federal Print Office, and many States own businesses within Germany as well.

Theirs is a socialistic capitalist model open to the free market and non-government ownership within the production economy. Government monitors cell phones, TVs, just as does Canada's CRTC.

Germany is growing strongly where other G8s are not.

The GINI Top-twelve here boast at least seven of the most successful countries, on a per capita basis, in the world today.

Setting Targets – Living Wage & Graduated Tax

The goal of managing Wealth Distribution is not to ensure that everyone has the same income, rather the goal is to ensure that all income levels are able to be productive and contribute to the economy. The setting of minimum wage so that is affords cost of living within communities – is also called a living wage.

Plug your own country's numbers into the formulas here to come up with Quintile income and wealth distribution targets for your country. I used the 2010 budget U.S. Federal Reserve stats here because they were readily validatible at several online sites.

Wealth

> **Available Assets** – per page 199 of the 2010 U.S. Budget containing the following wealth and income statistics for 2008.
> $ 10.2 trillion - in publicly owned assets
> $ 54.2 trillion – in privately owned assets
> $ 57.2 trillion - in education capital
> $ 3.9 trillion – R&D capital
> $ 118.1 trillion in total after assets claimed by foreign interests

> 1995 Assets were about half these numbers at $ 54.1 trillion.

> The Reader's Country Total Assets _____

Debts

> $ 18.15 Trillion – up from 16.1 in 2012 when it was 108% of GDP

Debt was presented by the Federal Government Debt Clock at usgovernmentdebt.us on October 15, 2015

Debt to Asset Ratio

18 trillion debt / 118 trillion in assets = 15%

With $118 trillion in assets, this makes one wonder why the U.S. carry debt at all. The current debt load appears to be within any mortgage lender's serviceable range – which is often 34% of assets.

Income

$12.95 trillion annual (2012 – U.S. Bureau of Economic Analysis)

The reader's Country Total Income

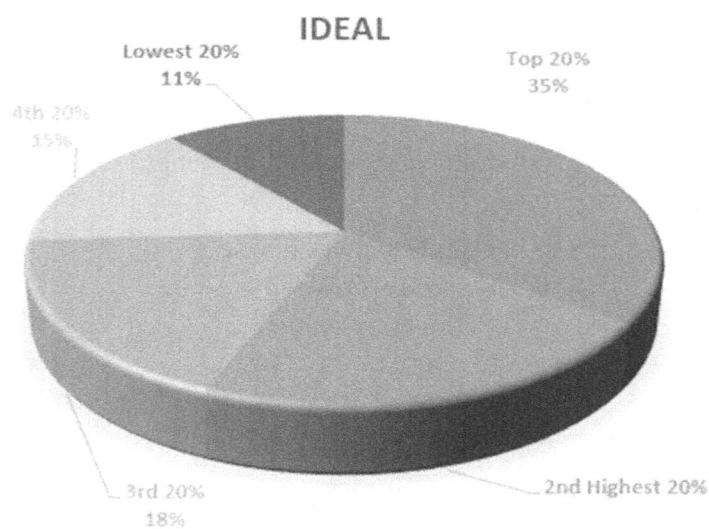

The Lowest Quintile (20%)

To adjust all citizens to wealth and income levels suggested in the IDEAL Income Distribution Chart above, 11% wealth is the target for the bottom 20% of wage earners. This means that wealth within the bottom group of 80 million U.S. income earners, would have to rise to approximately $74,387.

That's 11% of $54.1 trillion of assets (U.S. wealth in 2003) divided among 80 million. Also, these 80 million people would then need to take home incomes of $30,000 as minimum. This income is more than double the current U.S. household income levels today. See Census.gov at the link here (US Census Bureau, 2015) in Bibliography.

To achieve a **zero-tax income** of $30,000 per year would require 100% employment, or equivalent income, with a minimum wage of approximately $18 per hour plus health coverage benefits (allowing for 4% vacation pay).

Next Lowest Quintile

By the "Ideal" targets in the income distribution chart above, 15% of total wealth is assumed for the second lowest Quintile. 15% of $54.1 Trillion divided among 80 million calculates to wealth per individual of $101,438 and family incomes of $60,000 annually or a minimum hourly wage of $34 per hour with benefits after tax.

Middle Quintile

The Middle 20 Percentile targets wealth of 18%. 18% equates to wealth per individual of $121,725 and family incomes of $90,000 annually or a minimum hourly wage of $49 per hour with benefits after tax.

Second Highest Quintile

21% amounts to a wealth of $142,012 and family income of $120,000, or a minimum wage of $65 per hour with benefits after tax.

The Highest Quintile

35% average wealth of $236,687 with an income of $150,000 annually, or a minimum wage of $82 per hour plus benefits after tax.

Wage Stagnation

In this next Federal Reserve chart, household income is the red line beneath GDP (Gross Domestic Product) in blue above it. Leading causes of wage stagnation between 1995 and 2013 include technological change, the decline of labor unions and more specifically, their joint bargaining powers, and globalization.

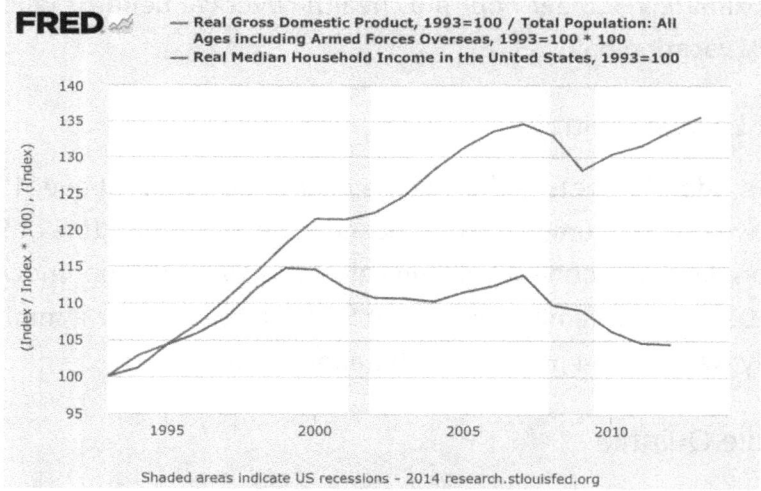

Minimum Wage

By taking this opportunity to target national goals of wealth distribution and employment, governments put an end to "Starvation Wages", ensure a Cost-of-Living affording Living Wage, and reduce the many and varied costs of Social Problems created by Wealth Inequity.

Your policy should ensure that these minimums are regularly reviewed and kept current. Over time, this will not guarantee perfect distribution, but it will go a long way to protect the Good Lives of everyone while permitting movement between the Quintiles for High Performers members of each level.

Graduated Tax

Implementing Graduated Tax structures ensures that wealth distribution meets national targets for sustainable equality. In a graduated system of tax, both large businesses and rich individuals pay a larger percentage of the total costs of running the country and must also be held accountable to keep others employed, salaried, and pensioned as well. The alternative is to jump to the same conclusion that Holland has and host pensions centrally in government.

Haven't we all heard the scenario where asking the Rich pay high tax is bad for society? I have, and yet nothing could be further from the truth. In fact throughout the 1940s through 60s, the rich paid up to 92% in tax and a maximum of $2 million of income per year was permitted as well. Society boomed during these times and it wasn't until the "Low-Tax" Trickle-down policies that wealth-inequity became really extreme in America; as is normal in a Winter K-Wave Economy as well.

As discussed above, there are often five quintiles used to represent the population of a country. This model might be too simple for very large countries, but it serves as a starting point that can be used to monitor the success of graduated tax programs actively over time.

Once wealth creation increases as a result of strong wealth distribution supports, only then can Governments be said to have managed their country's finances very well.

Chapter 13

Universal Healthcare, Benefits & Pensions

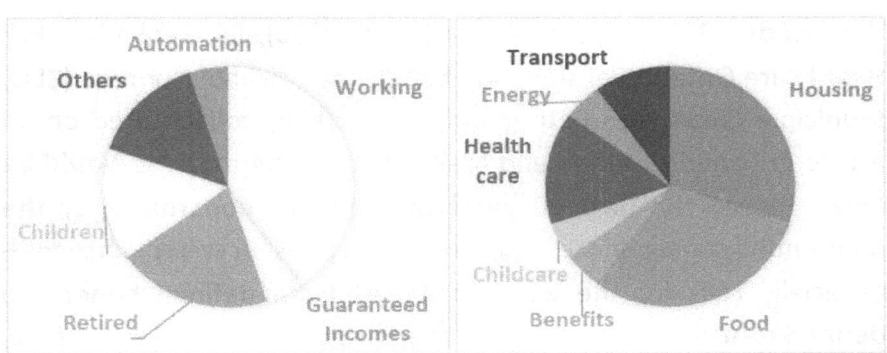

I have mentioned above that it is critical for retired individuals to continue to be able to contribute to the economy based upon their retirement incomes.

Pensions

A disturbing trend in business these past seven years, has been the wholesale release of 20-year or more employees; often layoffs come just immediately prior to pension commitment milestones.

Economic fluctuations, automation, globalization, outsourcing and gender equality have all taken turns as excuses for why these layoffs occurred, but surely the fact that pension plan costs advance logarithmically factors into these decisions.

Some fortunate workers belong to employer-sponsored defined

benefit pension plans which offer a secure, definite, adequate, inflation-indexed monthly pension for life, but these pensions are the first to go and eroding quickly in our societies today.

I am going to leave a number of article links visible here to permit the reader's easy review online at your leisure because there is much more level-setting information available than can be easily and concisely summarized here.

In 2013, Jim Leech (CEO, Ontario Teacher's Fund - #20 Pension fund Worldwide), Bill Hatanaka (CEO, OpTrust #250), Jim Keohane (CEO, Healthcare Ontario Pension Plan #192), and Michael Nobrega (CEO, Municiple Employees Retirement System #56) collaborated on an article in Canada's Globe and Mail, commenting that: "**It would be tragic to see the past 30 years of progress jeopardized by the** unintended consequences of ill-conceived pension system changes – especially calls for the **wholesale shift from defined benefit to defined contribution plans**." (Hatanaka, Keohane, Leech, & Nobrega, 2013)

Good private pension arrangements are eroding fast. Just four in ten workers still belong to a workplace pension plan (based on this 2011 report), and one in four of them belong to defined contribution plans which provide a variable lump sum rather than a defined pension benefit. Defined benefit plans do pay a pension for life, but most do not offer full indexation to inflation. **Six in 10 workers have no workplace pension at all**, but are forced to rely on RRSPs and other forms of individual savings. (Jackson, 2011)

There are two types of Employee Plans: employee retirement savings plans and employee benefit plans. Defined Benefit Plans offer a level of retirement income based on a calculation that typically factors in years of service to the employer and salary earned.

Defined contribution pension plans, group registered retirement savings plans, employee share purchase plans, deferred profit-sharing plans, and group tax-free savings account plans are all examples of defined contribution schemes. Defined Benefit Plans return funds based on the performance of the Pension Plan's investments and therefore protect the employer from the investment risk inherent in Defined Benefit Plans.

Many employers match employee pension savings so choosing not to join can be like saying no to free money; and retirement savings plans force you to set money aside for the future in a disciplined way without the temptation to interrupt your savings.

Defined contribution plans benefit from dollar cost averaging when markets are down, so by investing a set amount on a regular basis, you're able to buy more when prices are lower and this can often be a benefit in the long run.

Workplace pensions and savings plans are less expensive as well offering lower (less than 1% or no) fees as opposed to 2.4% mutual fund fees.

Employers often make contributions to both defined benefit and defined contribution plans.

Pension funds are most often provided by plan administration providers, investment managers, life insurance companies, trust companies and consultants. (Press, 2015)

Just as Guaranteed Income programs ensure that the workforce remains productive and contributing to any economy, so too does defined-benefit pension funds ensure that a retirement income system can offer a national competitive advantage by permitting Pensioners to continue to be a key driver of prosperity in communities large and small. A strong Pension fund are a cornerstone of any national economy.

Benefits

What kinds of benefit plans are there?

Employers can sponsor group life insurance, accidental death and dismemberment insurance, extended health care, dental care and disability benefit plans. It's important to note that when you make a claim, it will be paid based on your employer-sponsored plan's specific coverage.

Group **life insurance** provides for the plan member's (i.e., employee's) family if he or she dies while a member of the plan. The benefit is typically based on a multiple of the plan member's earnings. Sometimes it's a flat amount, sometimes it's a mix of the two. Employers may also sponsor optional and dependent life insurance, which provide additional coverage.

Accidental death and dismemberment insurance provides additional benefits to a plan member's family if he or she dies accidentally. Should the member become paralyzed, lose a limb, or lose his or her hearing, eyesight or speech in an accident, benefits will be paid to the plan member and his or her family.

Extended health care coverage reimburses eligible medical expenses not covered by the plan member's provincial plan. That can include prescription drugs, vision care, hospital care, medical services and equipment, paramedical services and assistance with out-of-province emergency travel.

Dental care coverage is exactly what you think it is. It covers preventive and diagnostic dental treatments.

Disability benefits are designed to replace a portion of a plan member's income if he or she becomes ill or injured and can't work. Employers typically sponsor a combination of short- and long-term disability coverage to assist their members. (Kevin Press, n.d.)

Managing Pension Plan Sustainability Risk

According to Professor Peter Forsythe, a Professor in Computational Risk at the University of Waterloo in Canada, "You're seeing more and more pension funds taking on greater risk in the past 15 years".

Pressure to maintain ever-increasing incomes year-over-year have required some of the World's largest retirement funds to increase the risks they take. In unregulated countries (where investment choices and risk are not monitored), like Canada, a collapse in world real estate markets would result in a very real exposure to retirement pension plans.

Other governments, like the Netherlands', take an active governance role to protect their citizens from risks. These funds grow more slowly but would be affected by global financial calamity to a far lesser degree.

When things are going well, funds and their managers are highly praised.

Mitigating the loss of Employer Pension Plans

Directing High Risk financial rewards into mid-term risk-mitigating Renewable Automation projects, seems an obvious strategic pairing.

Concerns for not being able to afford the basics of life in retirement are mitigated fully by a mature infrastructure of automations that deliver food, shelter, energy and transport automatically.

Monitoring and Enforcement of pension plan minimum obligations by companies operating and profiting from the consumer marketplace in your country is warranted now as outstanding pension needs will surely fall back upon the country.

This is a big part of the reason why the Netherlands administers its own pensions and requires all companies to have local ownership and to pay local tax as well.

Mini-retirements

I mentioned above that an economy is like a six or eight cylinder engine. When only one or two sectors of the population are contributing, it fires on one or two cylinders only and things get bumpy and uncomfortable for most. For optimal performance, you really want to have incomes spending in all "cylinders" - pushing you forward. So, not just working labor force, but you want spending by the unemployed, retired, men, women, disabled, and even military and incarcerated prisoners.

Money sitting in offshore tax haven accounts detriments an economy twice – once by taking money out of circulation, and a second time by not furnishing taxes required to support the infrastructure that enabled those funds to be collected. The importance of hoarding is only reinforced whenever the lowest income and asset individuals in society are being evicted, are starving and homeless. When the lowest levels of society live well, albeit basically, with a roof over their heads, you will tend to see less of this hoarding behavior and more charitable behaviors too.

Mini- Retirements are a healthy approach for over-fifty year olds, and even younger citizens who might like to retire for a few years, live from their pensions, and then go back to work. Some might like to retrain, change careers, and do something different; others might like to work on projects that their career employer never gave them a chance to work on.

Building twenty Facebook apps is of little value to society, but building robotic farms, discovering better medicines, better imaging solutions, caring for the elderly and young; teaching languages, there are hundreds and hundreds of worthwhile projects that mini-retirees could be contributing to while they improve cerebral plasticity and social interactions with others – well into their seventies, nineties and beyond.

Sitting in front of a TV alone all day every day without the funds needed to live well nor contribute, waiting to die basically, makes little good sense and yet this story is seen literally millions of times in every country.

People are living longer, staying in shape, eating better, and want to do worthwhile work and stay connected with others too.

Engineering Safety-Nets are funds set aside for engineers to work based on interests and expertise so that they can work and contribute productively as tinkerers or in teams.

There are a lot of good engineers and resources sitting unproductively without this support and this failing in our society also goes a long way toward explaining mental illness and high suicide rates in forty to sixty year old men during Winter economies. Winter months in Winter economies are the worse combination for despair and suicide at the same time that these are some of the most productive seasons for busy businesses and governments who are engaged in worthwhile change.

Mini-retirements, retraining and Engineering Safety-Nets solve a phenomenon in capitalistic cultures that has been noted in countless texts; Joseph Schumpeter wrote about this as well; Capitalism, he said drives away intellectuals, as rewards in these societies are too often given for non-socially beneficial behavior and menial, repetitive, unchallenging or not-worthwhile work.

In Canada, fifty men between the ages of forty and sixty take their lives through suicide every week; so, similar to anti-eviction discussions, this issue is as much a mental-health discussion as it is a discussion of the basic needs of everyone to live within a fulfilling and worthwhile life; the same conditions that statistics show are the most successful, highest Export per Capita and non-Collapsing nations as well.

CANADA'S TOP 15 PENSION FUNDS

Public fund managers sit in the first nine spots

BASED ON NET PENSION ASSETS UNDER MANAGEMENT*

	Rank in Canada	Global rank
Canada Pension Plan Investment Board	1	8
Caisse de dépôt et placement du Québec	2	14
Ontario Teachers' Pension Plan	3	20
PSP Investments	4	28
British Columbia Investment Management Corp.	5	35
Ontario Municipal Employees Retirement System	6	56
Healthcare of Ontario Pension Plan	7	69
Alberta Investment Management Corp.	8	84
Ontario Pension Board	9	192
Canada Post	10	205
Hydro Québec	11	208
Bell	12	220
Canadian National Railway	13	240
OPTrust	14	250
Air Canada	15	265

* Dec. 31, 2014 for all funds except for CPPIB, bcIMC and PSP Investments (March 31, 2015).

SOURCE: THE BOSTON CONSULTING GROUP INC.   NATIONAL POST

http://business.financialpost.com/news/fp-street/inside-the-risky-strategy-that-made-canadas-biggest-pension-plans-the-new-masters-of-the-universe (Tedesco & Shecter, 2016)

Universal Healthcare

Of the G20 nations, only the United States and India remain without Universal Healthcare. Most developed nations support a Universal Healthcare program as well.

Statistics in the U.S. show that poor citizens die an average of 13-years sooner than wealthy citizens. The chances of dying of very manageable diseases like diabetes, at even the age of 40 or 50, is a very real and even high probability among the lower income earners in these countries.

Almost every other country in the world finds it hard to relate to these stories - and to this policy approach, but these are the facts of countries unwilling to afford a universal healthcare system too.

India is working toward a Universal Healthcare solution and in the United States, the Affordable Care Act – often derisively dubbed "Obama Care" is a struggling program with mixed and even hesitant, widely-gapping coverage.

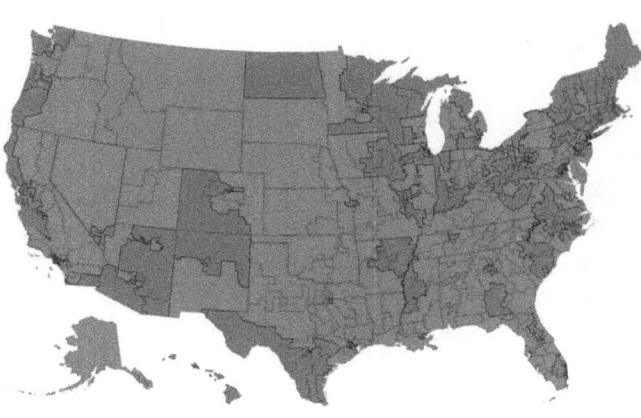

To give an idea of how engrained is resistance to Universal Healthcare in the U.S., the map above indicates House of Representative voting for and against healthcare reforms. Green indicates Yes.

U.S. Longevity Stats are provided by Barry Bosworth of the Wall Street Journal and reported by the Atlantic.

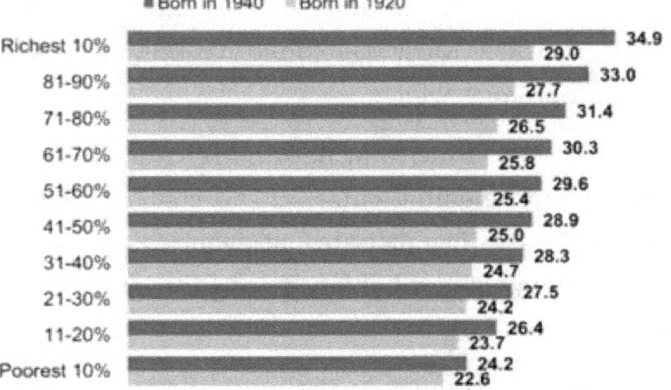

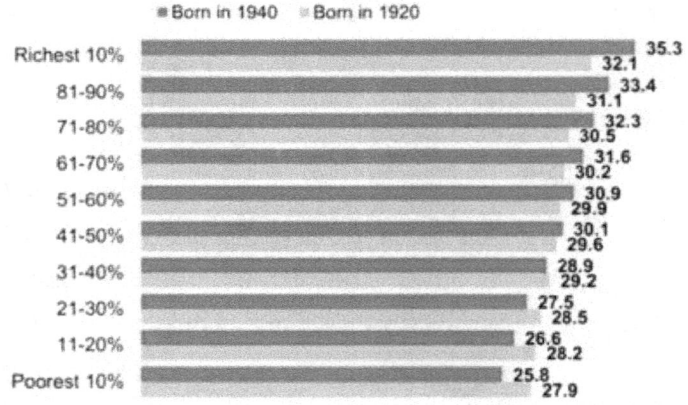

(Thompson, 2014).

In writing a definitive guide to Economics, I have made every effort to leave pejorative or judgmental opinion out of the discussion. Certainly this healthcare is a violation of the Mayflower Compact; a document that a related Edward Tilley signed back in 1620.

Citing a little insight from philosophy here: Poverty is not a sin - most especially where opportunities are limited, and yet the penalty here would suggest that the poor should perish as a Capitalistic ideal somehow. My East-Coast-Sensibility calls to mind the expression "Cutting off your nose to save your face".

But what I find most compelling about this specific gross example of fiercely safeguarded inequity is that there is no business case for it.

A $1.7 trillion dollar cost will be offset easily by new GDP Exports – see Chapter 11 - and then there are $1 trillion in direct costs recovered as well. Why would anyone in a developed nation not choose to manage healthcare?

As these objections appear to come from some of the most religious, and one would hope "moral" parts of the country therefore as well, clearly education in basic philosophy, morality, simple business case assessment, and even transition economics policy - has to play a part in building any sustainable solution for society.

Citizens must have access to supports of the basics – to incomes and those incomes must have spending-power to build a good life.

Chapter 14

Housing Policy Cycle Controls

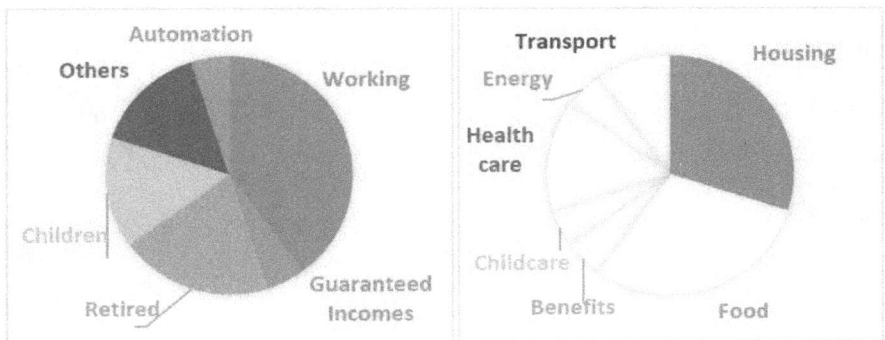

When left uncontrolled, the influence of foreign and local Real Estate speculators is to turn residential housing into an investment marketplace. We call this phenomenon Bubblenomics; a situation where a basic need of life - shelter, is converted into a wealth generation tool through scarcity. Artificial scarcity of this sort denies a market of the natural supply & demand rules to consumers, by those who can afford to control the buying and selling.

Bubbles, however, are not a norm for countries that implement responsible housing controls. The Netherlands have no housing bubbles for one example, and this is by plan and not by luck either.

Economic Controls for Housing Bubbles

Economists can ever be counted upon to fall back on basic Economic lessons of Supply and Demand. If Supply is small, demand will rise and with it – prices also rise, and the opposite is true as well.

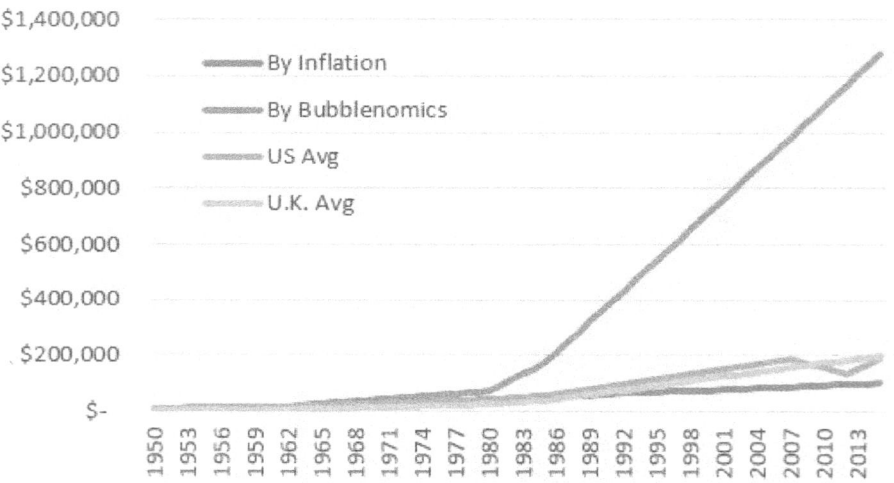

Average Home Prices in Toronto vs Inflation

It is for just this reason that marketing people use scarcity to extol higher prices for goods that could otherwise be supplied readily and at fair market rates.

This is the approach that has created ghost cities in China and other major countries - where housing supply is readily available, but is artificially withheld with high prices – as required for "exclusive" or "luxury" condominiums. As China's economy slows now, it will struggle to transition from "investment-led growth" to a "consumer growth" model under its current housing policies.

At the point where scarcity is planned and controlled, the free-market of pure Supply and Demand can be said to no longer exist.

The Ghost Cities of China

The Netherlands has no housing bubble. The reason for this is that the citizens of the Netherlands relied heavily upon the 92% of controlled rental properties for housing until just this past 10-years or so. Although not perfect in every location, their foreign investment tax structures protected citizens from bubbles and because Economic Controls protected housing costs from soaring, young people can still purchase homes and start a family here today.

This means that when families do decide to purchase a home, they can do so with a high probability of paying off their mortgage as well.

The first rule of home ownership is to avoid paying rent, don't pay condo fees, and pay off your mortgage as soon as possible.

Paying off one's mortgage has become a very great improbability in recent years for many uncontrolled cities; and this is even true in the larger U.S. housing market of 130 million homes where 35% appear to live in expanding mortgage poverty where they will never be able to stop paying a mortgage.

This situation is also the actual definition of Usury; a financial lending practice that is exploitive and a criminal act in most countries. Whenever someone is forced to take on a loan they can never repay, even if the interest rate might appear reasonable, these individuals are victims of Usury.

Usury is preferable nomenclature to equally appropriate historical references to Indentured Servitude and Slavery on the Code of Hammurabi stone. In the historical case of Indentured Servitude, these commitments had to end after just seven years by law.

In uncontrolled centers, the definition of Usury has been altered in law to say that this is the practice where interest rates are set above some threshold that is deemed too high – 35% interest annually might be an example. I jokingly refer to this telling as a "Boiled Frog" definition of Usury; housing markets charge thirteen-time inflation, which amounts to the same result as would exploitive interest rates.

The Greater Toronto Area (GTA) in Ontario, Canada is a good example of a bubble – and not the most extreme example either as Vancouver's, Hong Kong and London's bubbles were quite a bit more extreme.

In Hamilton, just on the outskirts of the GTA, a 1982 house cost $32,000 - with interest at 22% - an all-time high rate. Within five years, interest rates dropped to 12%, and houses skyrocketed to $90,000. The same house has climbed to $500,000 today, increasing steadily as rates dropped to 1%. In Toronto, average home prices climbed to a $1.28 million.

Clearly, falling interest rates encouraged speculation far more than housing costs, because elsewhere, outside of bubble areas, the housing costs were also influenced by markets, but they only ran two or three times the Rate of Inflation.

Annual Inflation Rates are based on the Consumer Price Index (CPI). The CPI is a list of important consumer items that are tracked by governments to confirm that prices for basic goods are either changing or staying the same, and at what rate in %/Year.

A $1.28 million average home's cost is almost thirteen-times the cost of Inflation over the 65-year period running up to 2016. To calculate this, I took a $10,000 GTA house in North York in 1950 and added Inflation year-over-year to arrive at an Inflation Cost of $102,000. The Average U.S. and U.K. home are $188,000 U.S. and £212,000 respectively. As average homes in 1950 were $5000 and £3000, I would say that they have generally increased by three to four-times the Inflation rate as well.

Housing prices become unsustainable beginning with bidding wars over scarce resources (like housing inventories), so when Canada began to add six-million immigrants in the 1990s, and an overwhelming majority of these new immigrants and foreign investors, focused on the GTA and Vancouver – prices climbed with demand. With insufficient controls, scarcity drives bidding wars that bear little resemblance to the underpinning value of an investment - and highest-bidders-won irrespective of all other factors every time, until a bubble was firmly established.

Canada turned away from rent controls in commercial spaces altogether too and there were no controls for new Residential Rental contracts – which have permitted them to grow to double the rental rates asked for just three years ago.

The colors and underlines in the chart below indicate wealth distribution targets being met from the previous chapters. The "Absolute Min. Salary in Bubbles" calculation shows how Bubbles work dramatically against Wealth Distribution targets and a Good Life; observe how higher tax rates now apply to bubble rent-payers as well.

By adding a few assumptions - like a 35% household rent maximum (this number is used in mortgage applications but 25% should be considered conservative), 3 weeks per year vacation, tax rates (Canadian rates are used in this example), and $1000 per month minimum fixed cost estimate per a third-party report (Erin Davis,

2015), we can arrive at a Housing-driven Minimum Wage calculation.

Rent	Monthly Wage b4 Tax	Fixed Cost min. Met?	Pretax Income Needed	Cdn Tax Rate	Minimum Wage /Hr @Tax	Absolute Min Salary in Bubbles
$ 400	$ 1,176	No	$ 14,118	20%	$ 9.53	$ 20,168
$ 600	$ 1,765	Yes	$ 21,176	20%	$ 14.30	$ 23,050
$ 800	$ 2,353	Yes	$ 28,235	20%	$ 19.07	$ 25,931
$ 1,000	$ 2,941	Yes	$ 35,294	20%	$ 23.84	$ 28,812
$ 1,200	$ 3,529	Yes	$ 42,353	24%	$ 29.58	$ 32,776
$ 1,400	$ 4,118	Yes	$ 49,412	30%	$ 36.04	$ 37,339
$ 1,600	$ 4,706	Yes	$ 56,471	30%	$ 41.19	$ 40,451
$ 1,800	$ 5,294	Yes	$ 63,529	30%	$ 46.34	$ 43,562
$ 2,000	$ 5,882	Yes	$ 70,588	30%	$ 51.49	$ 46,674
$ 2,200	$ 6,471	Yes	$ 77,647	31%	$ 57.43	$ 50,488
$ 2,400	$ 7,059	Yes	$ 84,706	34%	$ 63.80	$ 54,627
$ 2,600	$ 7,647	Yes	$ 91,765	43%	$ 74.04	$ 61,953
$ 2,800	$ 8,235	Yes	$ 98,824	43%	$ 79.73	$ 65,395
$ 3,000	$ 8,824	Yes	$ 105,882	43%	$ 85.43	$ 68,837
$ 3,200	$ 9,412	Yes	$ 112,941	43%	$ 91.12	$ 72,279

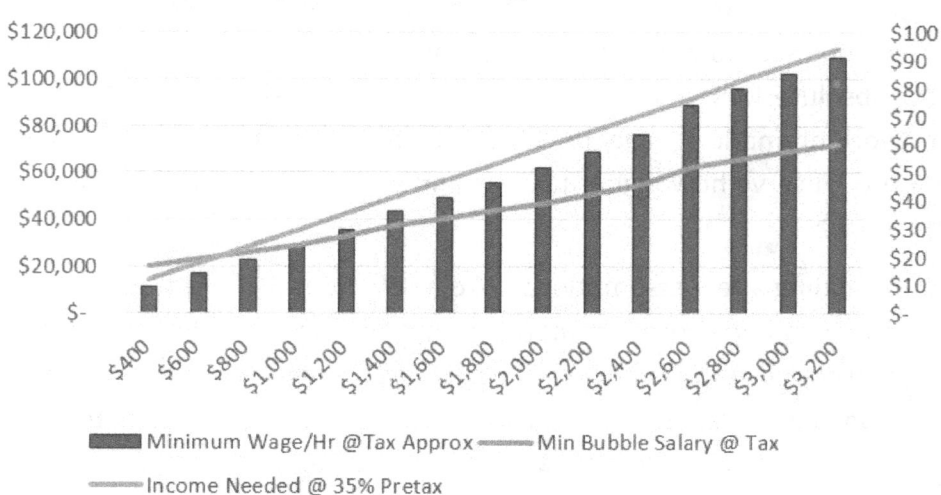

Hourly Minimum Wage vs Rent Costs

With no housing bubbles, the Netherlands can control rents at €710 ($773 U.S or $1030 Can) per month which means that guaranteed income programs can also work well and be affordable at the same time as well.

Elsewhere, rent controls have been in place in New York City; are in the Netherlands too; in Paris, France - where "En Viager" contracts were established, to protected seniors from these market-speculation-based bubbles and other Cost of Living up-swings (American Press, 1995). Housing market controls and comparison from country-to-country could comprise its own book and so these paragraphs introduce and provide enough information to build throttles as needed.

Housing Bubbles vs Good Lives

People need homes to be able to start families and if those children are going to be able to stay close to their parents when they begin their own families, costs of living in the community must be maintained relative to Inflation and salaries. If Inflation has only amounted to one-third housing costs nationally – as discussed; and is one-thirteenth housing costs in bubbles; but salaries and jobs have decrease over the same time period (from the 1970s on), clearly Bubbles work in an opposite direction to that of a sustainable society. Let's fix this...

How to Correct and Reverse Bubbles

So how do we correct Housing Bubbles and restart the unsustainable Winter Cycle into an affordable and sustainable Spring Phase and new Cycle?

Consider that with Central Bank interest rates at 1% for much of 2015 and 2016 - and no-way for interest rates to go up-nor-down easily, a very great number of new homeowners are steadfastly against any policy that requires an interest rate increase.

Put simply, few homeowners have the salaries to permit this interest rate increases on half-million dollar mortgages. An increase of just 2% would cause many families who are living from paycheck to paycheck now, to 1) lose their home (once savings deplete), 2) to be evicted by the Sheriff, and 3) be forced into an uncontrolled, overpriced and under-supplied rental market.

Eviction

When 2008 started their Great Depression, Housing Policies in Spain stuck to their status quo rules in a good example of what not to do. Job-losses progressed steadily to today's 23.8% unemployment rate and high eviction rates was seen in many countries and major U.S. cities like Detroit, Michigan, and San Francisco. These are epicenters of the subprime and foreclosure crisis and now anti-eviction groups like Occupy Detroit and the Eviction Defense Collaborative also.

Eviction groups cited that they are victims "of mass unemployment and mortgage banking fraud." (Noor, 2013) (Garrett, 2015)

Spain is a country with no housing controls and debt is unreleasable for life. There, even after eviction you still must pay principal plus interest charges, and bankruptcy does not release you from this debt either. Authorities evicted 100 homes a day in 2014 through 2015 and conditions got so extreme that Amnesty International interceded for the first time ever by launching an Anti-Eviction Campaign in 2015. ("Amnesty launches Spain anti-eviction campaign - The Local," 2015)

Anti-Eviction and Suicide

Spain's Anti-austerity party Podemos looks poised to win a federal election after beginning just two years ago and who could blame the citizens of Spain in the face of obvious incompetent management of the basic need of shelter. (Babcock, 2015)

Suicides related to Eviction in Spain are reported at five to twenty per week and are now the leading cause of unnatural death; double deaths by automobile accidents. A common slogan among anti-eviction protestors is the chant *"It's not eviction, it's murder."* ("4 commit suicide in Spain over evictions as EU struggles with unemployment — RT News," 2013)(Govan, 2016)

I live in the statistically wealthiest city in Canada, Oakville, Ontario, and suicides at the rail crossing right near the local homeless shelter, which has to turn away homeless people in February due to overcrowding, is a regular occurrence - although incidents seldom reach our newspaper.

The U.N. chastised Canada for failing to see to the needs of its homeless citizens in March of 2016 and with winter fast approaching again, I am unable to update this writing with any report of improvements made. The point I am making is simply that this is an important issue in any housing discussion that is as universally true for wealthy countries and wealthy cities as it is for poorer places today, and this influences any discussion of shelter as a Human Right.

In Spain, just one percent of housing is devoted to public housing compared to 35% in Netherlands and 18 percent in Britain. There are 3.4 million empty homes in Spain and 11 million in all Europe of Europe; 1.8 million in Germany and 700,000 in Britain. There are enough empty homes in Europe to house the homeless twice over. (Neate, 2014)

Canada's rent and housing problems are headed in a collapsing direction as well. Canada has the highest immigration rate of the G7 by a wide margin - 20% per capita where the next largest G7 immigration rate is 14%. Although many new condos were built during the past 20 years, relatively few rental accommodation units were built. Bubbles and immigrant demand too, create high rental demand with low supply which has led to sharp rental increases. Canada has no new-rental increase controls and this demand has permitted landlords to lift their rental rates. This has forced up rents by 50% and more in just 3 or 4 years in major centers of Toronto and Vancouver.

This means that if you are unable to buy a home at bubble prices you are going to be forced to pay greatly inflated rents or condo fees. Condo fees too, can be surprisingly large – at $700 to $1,100 per month and more – a second mortgage basically.

As we begin a discussion of making corrections in housing, I will preface by saying that options for home-owners and renters, need to be well thought through. Too often, administrators force forward rules that don't work; with rules that force people into the street, or that squander personal possessions, and there can be none of those shortsighted calls enforced here.

Leadership in Interest Rate Increases

Interest Rate increases within Bubbles; in regions where Usury has been permitted to artificially run up the cost of housing many times beyond inflation, is proven to lead to a high rate of suicide consistently whenever evictions take place. Giving the statistical facts in evidence, a case for negligent manslaughter can be made because the result of increasing rates without eviction or homelessness mitigations, are well understood.

Economic Policies become life and death decisions within societies where there is increased unemployment and no income guarantees. If your leadership make no mention, acknowledgement nor accommodation via responsible mitigations for this fact, as they adjust interest rates, they are either exhibiting sociopathic behavior or they are not qualified to occupy a leadership or decision-making role.

For too long citizens have been disappointed by uninvested civil servants and police enforcement that do not always have common sense solutions available to them either - when addressing real problems. That track-record must come to an end.

If housing admins are ousting people into the street, they are either not intelligent enough to find solutions – or they are not empowered enough to insist on solutions from their administrators; solutions that actually work to keep people sheltered.

Fearing the loss of your full-time job and benefits in countries with no safety-nets, like Canada, is a non-starter; no positive result can come to pass of these unworkable solutions. The first step in initiating a change is to give housing administrators impunity to spend as needed to protect lives without risking civil servant livelihoods; to curb sheriff's orders that would turn people into the streets in -20 Celsius weather conditions – or even in conditions where countless homes sit unoccupied.

Read the case study on Gander, Newfoundland's handling of the 911 traveler emergency to see what a thinking community is absolutely capable of coordinating.

When people can no longer afford monthly mortgage payments, another program must keep them in their homes. When people lose six or ten rental units that afforded their incomes, an income guarantee must be there for them as their investment properties become homes again.

If interest rates went up by 3% to 5%, this change would probably force out the past 15-years of leveraged low-interest mortgage holders and condo rental speculators. If we then gave an option to defaulting homeowners to continue living in their homes via either a Land Grant system - or via an inflation-controlled Rental Agreement, we would find that we could in fact be able to return to a more affordable housing market and lifestyle safely and with minimal disruption.

Flushing out the investors who have accumulated multiple properties is an important change. The ideal result of any policy is to return Housing to its original purpose - as that of shelter - and not an investment and wealth management strategy. We have stock markets for this investment purpose. Look upon every investor flushed from uncontrolled existing real estate as a victory and ensure that all have citizens have incomes and homes.

We will talk about Housing changeover in detail next, but before we do, let's talk about the controls needed to govern buyer entry into the housing market so that we avoid recreating many of the social problems that led to a wide-open market approach in the first.

Governing the Housing Market

The buyer-entry solution could include restrictions on who can offer to buy property so that new home buyers, previous homebuyers, and local investors – can bid first based on an Inflation-Controlled maximum price. If local bidders make no offer, then bids can be opened to refugees, immigrants, foreign investment, and so on.

In Toronto and Vancouver, 6 million immigrants descended on two major uncontrolled centers with cash-in-hand, pushing out citizens and pushing up prices so that their children could not or would resettle here. Overloaded schools and overloaded road systems resulted.

Large immigrant communities moved together, established beachheads that voted together, did not inter-marry, nor did they invest locally nor do business in their new host country in many cases. Requests to change Canadian culture and political correctness were frequent and many challenges were also found to be staged to permit lawsuits or other illicit financial gain.

All manner of small businesses were swamped with competition from households with twenty immigrants living under one roof – which is a decidedly non-Canadian standard of living. Corporate employment failed to keep up with job demand – or did not hire the newcomers. As a result, wherever three tire-shops stood before, twenty more sprung up - until no small businesses could make a decent living.

There was new home construction, but the housing-suppliers increased prices and pricing bubbles maintained the benefits of ever-higher investments through flipping and renting. As commercial investors turned to housing, and interest rates continued to drop and stay low year-after-year, prices took on a life of their own – similar to a stock market.

New homeowners in Toronto's suburbs buy direct from China in bidding wars for property that often ends up selling for $300,000 to $600,000 over asking – with 10 Chinese buyers vying for the home. Once the sellers exit their home, they are "out of that market" because neither they nor their children can rebuy easily. Only their own Chinese Real Estate agents are invited to handle the sale initially, and at a later time of sale as well, until local realtors realize that they are a few years from collapse as well.

Housing Controls Summary

The setting in place of housing entry controls protects the cost of houses from bubbles so that young people have a chance to begin productive lives in the neighborhoods in which they grew up in. These are desirable goals in many countries where citizens think to the future.

A discussion of Housing Controls from Cycle to Cycle, therefore, must mitigate several risks:

- Beginning in late K-Wave Summer phase, **Interest Rates** may want to run up, and if they do, they cannot then drop below an agreed minimum that dissuades savings or responsible foreign investment – a 6% to 8% rate perhaps.

  Interest Rates cannot be permitted to rise in high-Usury regions without Anti-Eviction and other housing alternatives in working order and in affect in Law and in the hands of trained government staff. Treat this need as importantly as you protect against as laws governing manslaughter because the notion that there is a difference is not based in fact; nor in statistically proven reality nor science.

- A **per-Square-Foot Price-Increase Cap** that would prevent rapid increases in housing prices. Perhaps Caps could be tied to Inflation (CPI) or perhaps tied to an immigration benefit of some sort?
- For **First-time Homeowners** – Locally-born Citizens could have three avenues to find a home nearby their parents' homes, and the option to stay in school while raising a young family.
    - **Rent-controlled access to a home suitable for children** – for married couples by age 19. Rents should be affordable via guaranteed incomes if parents elect to stay in university while raising young families.
    - **Land Grants** - A home is assigned and is there for the family to use as they need until remote work moves them - or their kids leave home to their own homes. The average person lives in seven homes in a lifetime, so moves are permitted as needed.
    - Access to **Zero-down-payment Homes** with mortgage payments that fit into guaranteed income payments for university/post-secondary students low debt-to-income ratios, low unemployment, and high minimum wage are required to service a mortgage. One home is permitted only. Higher salaries to high-performance students.
- **First time Homeowners – Non-Locally-born Citizens**
    - Rent controlled access to a home suitable for children – for married couples by age 19. Rents should be affordable via incomes that their parents should maintain allowing them to stay in university while raising young families. Marriage to a Locally-born Citizen is encouraged when an option.

- **For Existing Owners**

    Existing Owners trade up if they own property and use the equity of that property to also purchase another property
    - **Purchasing Trade Up** – Residents must use the equity in an existing property while trading up, down or other.
    - **Land Grant**
    - **Rent-controlled** - Higher down-payments for existing owners with preference to owners that grew up in or live in the area presently.
- **Merit** – The idea that some roles in society afford a higher Merit than others; and then High Performers too may be a consideration in deciding who gets more desirable water-front locations, etc. Examples used above compared the value of a Cancer or Burn Care Worker to a Financial Worker with a track-record of socially irresponsible decisions. Although difficult to implement and manage fairly without corruption, this is worth considering as a performance incentive.
- **Investment Properties**, similar to rules implemented in Holland, Investment Properties are possible with higher-down-payment percentages than owners, and taxing of gains. Controls should encourage investment and productivity while discouraging non-productivity.
- **Offshore Investment** – Should housing be considered an investment before all have shelter? If you see from my observations above that this question should be answered "No", then you might also agree that offshore investment in private homes should be discouraged through heavy tax and rules that permit heavily protected rental-properties only perhaps.

- **Foreign investment** brings the Real Estate Bubbles and problems of other communities to your country. Perhaps these bidders could be permitted to compete only after local bidders are not interested at mandated pricing. In this way housing costs stay reasonable and new home construction is encouraged.
- **Monitoring** is required to ensure rental properties are not soaring in monthly costs.

Clearly, our present systems for managing housing are not brilliant. Current rules and systems are flawed, so my advice is to not blindly protect any status-quo that has played-out as can be expected in a Winter Cycle. Enact corrections as needed.

Nothing is too big to fail and nothing is too important that it cannot be adjusted in pursuit of Human Rights and a Good Life – once a system of protections have been put in place.

Home Ownership & Mortgages

This is the system that most of us in the G7 grew up with. Many in our society are never taught that there are any other systems. Mortgage borrowing is stressful, it reduces our quality of life and even longevity, and as with most non-production-generating financial services, it advances society negatively when not controlled. Uncontrolled ownership bubbles make properties exponentially more expensive, our children cannot begin lives in their hometown within bubbles, many feel forced to take on debt beyond their means and reasonable debt loads, and home ownership encourages investors to live on the production of those forced to rent in unregulated bubbles.

In Mesopotamia, borrowers had to become the indentured slaves of moneylenders when they could not repay their obligations; and then, every seven years, these servants were released from their debt entirely by law. In many ways, the majority of today's mortgage borrowers and forced renters are committed to a similar form of indentured servitude – but for a lifetime and not just seven years – in Usury scenarios.

Government Land Ownership

Ownership of homes is the norm in most G8 countries but, in our national parks, 100-year leases are granted only.

So – what was wrong with a government system that handed out homes as needed in the soviet system? Opponents might like to argue that this is a socialistic or communistic policy. The point remains that this is another system of land assignment that is widely used throughout G8 and G20 countries today. It is also a tried and true option for getting the next cycle started.

When we have an unlimited number of homes to give to citizens, land grants seem a natural option. Where we start seeing inequities is when land grants award estates, or prime waterfront locations, giving preference to some individuals above others. This becomes a Merit and Reward discussion.

This happens all the time today of course because families have been protected by class laws within a capitalist system, just the same as were Royals or Races in other class-based societies.

Can we switch back and forth?

I mentioned that in K-Wave Spring, Property Ownership works well enough, and then I mentioned that in K-Wave Winter, switching to Government Ownership works better. Remember that the important objective here is ensure that everyone has what they need and to ensure a Good Life for everyone. Can we switch from "Government

Owned" to "Self-Owned Housing"?

Yes, absolutely; why ever not? When the Soviet Union converted all of its states into Republics in 1986, all land grants were simply switched from a land grant model to an ownership model.

Since then, these same apartments in central parts of Moscow jumped up to cost millions of dollars. Nothing changed in the homes; residents simply became victims of their own housing bubble. This example, and China's ghost cities also, showcase that Land Grants are a far more sustainable system than uncontrolled home ownership.

Will landowners want to give their property to the state?

Yes and no. I suspect there are four groups of decision makers and preferences as follows:

1) Free and Clear Home Owners - 30% currently

Those who own their homes free-and-clear might prefer to retain ownership of their home. If swapped for a land grant arrangement, a low percentage of their incomes would go toward tax. These owners would maintain their properties themselves - until robotic maintenance arrives, so that taxes would be lower again.

2) Mortgage Owners – 70% currently

Owners with a short time left on their mortgage, and no concerns for employment incomes, may elect to continue paying for and buying their home. Lower taxes would be levied in this scenario because homeowners are assuming all costs and upkeep.

Other homeowners with low-percentage ownership may decide to sign their properties over to government in the same way that the Russian Government did for its citizens. Higher Taxes or rents would be needed to offset government admin costs - perhaps.

Residents might prefer to be responsible for upkeep – until robotic maintenance projects complete. These folks would pay lower rents or tax.

3) Renters

Renters might prefer to request land grants, assigned homes, or to be able to secure quality rental homes at a controlled rate in keeping with the financial capabilities of society. A higher tax rate and resident upkeep would be required.

4) Landlords

Landlords too, either own their properties or work with high mortgage costs; some Landlords have a single or several rental units, and some will have 500 or even 5000 units. High Tax on rental homes and perhaps even higher rates over a certain number of units, perhaps 20 units, in addition to higher interest rates, will distribute this wealth in a way that doesn't hurt the landlord's ability to make a personal livelihood, but one that does discourage the rent and housing price bubbles created by rental landlord "dynasties".

The objective of wealth distribution is not to have everyone in society earning a similar amount, there will be high and low income earners in every economy and Cycle, the objective is to avoid thousands of hundred-million dollar offshore accounts that do nothing and benefit society not at all.

Transition Economics would have to dictate the rate of change that could be accepted in a housing system switchover. In democratic countries, 51% might like have to vote for these changes as well. These options would not be accepted easily until a high percentage of the population are disadvantaged or stranded outside the housing bubble – as in a K-Wave winter.

Recall also that our technology will shortly permit us to live anywhere we like, to build anywhere we like, without reliance on a power grid, or a daily commute into an office, nor a drive to a nearby mall to buy groceries or clothing. What difference will it make if the land is handed to us from our community's pool of available land – or if we go out and purchase it ourselves? Is our right to grind our way through a mortgage really so important to us?

Like any privilege, failure to maintain or upkeep assigned property before maintenance bots come onto the scene, could result in penalties financial or other.

As our automation projects make money less important, the residual value of an estate handed down to our children, also becomes less important.

Housing Changes from K-Wave Spring to Winter

Russian Dachas are cottages that were assigned to families living in the major cities pre-Perestroika in 1986. Even the poorest Moscow citizen owned one so that children, grandparents, and families could get away and enjoy the countryside, plant gardens, and change pace from a busy urban life during the summer months.

Trains connect the major urban centers to cottage country where dachas could be reached easily, often on foot by walking for just a mile or two.

Most North Americans aspire from a young age to own their homes, and then we work toward paying off a mortgage for much of our adult lives too. This is Capitalistic Housing Policy and Home Ownership. We host Communistic Housing Policies as well, an example is when the State leases cottage property only in its Parks.

Many people who were able to purchase their homes before the housing bubbles of the 1980s, were able to pay off their home and cottages easily given the availability and relatively high wages of full-time salaries then compared to today.

In 1963, you could purchase three acres of Muskoka waterfront property, one of the most beautiful cottage areas in the world, for about $250. At the same time, salaries for steel workers was $300 to $450 per month, and this meant that most Canadians could easily afford a cottage.

When my 71-year-old best-friend-Tom's father was 17, back in 1965, he was a teenager working a student summer job. With his savings he had the choice of buying either a used car or two acres of waterfront property in Burlington, Ontario. Today that property would sell for millions of dollars and his summer income be probably less than $100 per week

In 1982, incomes were up to $5,000 per month, and the average home price for a modest detached dwelling was approximately

$35,000. That house would rocket up in price by approximately three times over the next three years and would never come down.

My parents told me from a young age to buy a home and pay it off as quickly as possible – and that made a lot of sense because mortgages could be paid off completely with five or ten years of concentrated effort. Today, only 29% of homes in the U.S. are owned free-and-clear, and the rest are paid off only 50% on average. Falling interest rates had to go so low to stave off depression in 2008 that raising them even a few percentage points would force the foreclosure of tens of millions of homes in North America.

Needless to say, countries that do not implement Transition Economics Maturity Model controls, tend to find themselves Collapse Trending in Winter Economic Cycles.

Understanding lending costs

Usury is the practice of making unethical or immoral monetary loans intended to enrich the lender unfairly. Many countries enact Usury Laws that govern maximum interest rates, maximum monthly payments, and maximum debt load as a ratio to income.

Banking laws in Canada presently permit Canadian Lenders to extend $26 for every $1 on deposit. This means that for the average detached home in Toronto which costs $1 million dollars financed at 5%, the bank will ask you to pay $5,816 per month; $1,613 will be the principle and $4,203 will be the interest payments. Borrowers will pay $50,436 in payments annually for the next 25 years, to return to the lender the $38,461 that they originally had to have on account. That is a working lifetime of steep payments in exchange for $38,461.

If at any time during that 25 year period, the homeowner is unable to continue payments, the bank can foreclose and sell the property to repay the full value of the mortgage commitment. Your forces your family to find shelter in a marketplace where rental rates increased 50% to 75% in response to the rising demand. There will be many additional monies wasted on moving and storage costs, and you might spend many years worrying about financial pressures as well.

No-one imagines that they will not be able to meet payments when they first apply for a mortgage, but the statistics show that most mortgage takers will have to refinance, downsize, or suffer foreclosure. 70% of all mortgages in the U.S. are never paid off by the original borrower.

My point in mentioning this example is that owning property is great, but it is terrific only when your system of government and economy supports it. The G8 economies supported home ownership in K-Wave Spring, Summer, and early Autumn, until around 1995, but that was 20 years ago. Today in K-Wave Winter, the statistics say that our economies and housing markets do not support home ownership.

At this time in a capitalist cycle, soliciting low-interest, low-down-payment mortgages, ceases to be beneficial to society and becomes Usury. The availability of easy financing creates bidding wars and pricing bubbles, and mortgages that statistics say will never be paid off. Most countries enact laws to protect its citizens against this form of Usury as well.

China and other countries that support land ownership are in the same situation where land ownership forces a very hard life for the great majority of its citizens.

Low-interest rates with just 3% down-payments are being offered in the United States again this year as people who lost their homes in 2008 become eligible to buy again. Does this sound like the beginning of just another bubble?

What sort of home would I get?

This is a discussion of options and not recommendations. Discussion of a change in land ownership is going to shake any community to its core. I know myself that the notion of a government administrator deciding my lot in life – would worry me deeply.

Our robotic or manual home-building capabilities determine the quality and size of granted homes, as does current government incomes, available consigned properties, economy wealth, wealth distribution, and individual incomes.

If you are a brilliant engineer who builds hi-tech businesses, technology, and writes books that improve mankind's well-being, would, or should, your contributions be recognized with a larger and better parcel of land or home?

Our society rewards these considerations almost not at all today.

Would a Trust Fund Manager who earns $50 million per year by squandering 100,000 jobs to other countries - be rewarded with a larger parcel of land?

Our present capitalist system *does* reward this behavior today – with bigger houses, nicer cars, private schools, on and on. If you buy finished sneakers for a dollar and sell them for $100, we throw in a very handsome fleet of yachts as well. The net benefit to the planet is just about zero in this last example, as the value is delivered by the shoemaker and transportation can be automated right to the wearer's doorway. The same situation holds true for coffee growers who barely recover costs for their work and equipment while sales organizations reap enormous profits.

Consider that as money becomes irrelevant with new technology, are skills like "driving financial efficiencies" – especially the ones without regard for social well-being, important, desirable, or necessary? The answer is probably - less-and-less.

Would a cancer-care nurse who dedicated his or her life to attending to the needs of the suffering and dying be granted a more comfortable lake view and a nice home to come back to?

Today, our system rewards in-hospital nurses modestly and nursing home attendants are almost paid as minimum wage workers.

Through these examples, I am introducing a merit measuring discussion that focuses on using different measures to trigger social rewards. What contribution does this person bring to society? What is their performance? In the case of a Mother Theresa – this person is a leader as well? Does he or she inspire others by example to do amazing work for society with little regard for personal recognition? If yes, then a very nice lot would make a lot of sense. Just don't get me started about pro-sports salaries.

Whether you like the idea or hate it, this is just another very implementable change that makes a lot of sense and only takes a well-managed project and operation to achieve.

What is the right place for you to live?

Should people live alone? Should they live in Dorms? Do they live in apartments? Do they live beside lakes? Do they live on boats? Should special requests be considered?

I love these questions because there are many correct answers. When I was very young, the answer to this question was that I needed to live in a home with my family – ideally in my own room, with a yard for my dog, close to my friends and school. That was house number One.

When I headed off to degree studies at seventeen, some of the best times of my life were lived in a dorm room with other students my own age; that was House Two.

When I had almost finished degree studies, I took a two bedroom bachelor flat with a buddy; House Three, and when I started working and wanted to start a family at twenty-five, I took a small three bedroom house with a big mature yard, on a quiet cul-de-sac, that needed a lot of weekend projects. House Four.

The woman of my dreams came along and our family grew to need a four-bedroom home with a pool within two years. A cottage would have been too much work so we owned a motorhome for a year or two until the kids convinced us that it was all about a pool for them.

Half of our neighborhood's kids agreed that our pool was the best on the block and so my wife and I had to camp poolside at House Five to watch bathers for eight hours a day - some days. That went on for ten years until kids were eleven or twelve – and then the pool was very rarely used and we could have done without the extra maintenance work and energy cost as well.

Divorce came when the kids were thirteen and seventeen and we needed two homes temporarily. My kids headed off to University and a friend and mine; a woman who was in a similar situation to my own, shared a three bedroom condo. Home Six. Our parents were getting older and we wanted to bring them closer to live with us, so a three bedroom bungalow with a nanny apartment or two, would have been ideal; House Seven.

As we get older, our needs will change too - until our kids either take us in to live with them, or until we decide to live with other seniors within supervised apartments; House Eight. Like everyone, we will need 90% of our lifetime's healthcare within our last 5% of days most likely, and we hope to look back on a full life with grandchildren and maybe even a great-grandchild or two if we are lucky.

Everyone is important; some individuals represent a greater utility to society than others - and this must be recognized and rewarded. If we all keep two or three children families, it is entirely likely that a sustainable flow from home to home might actually work very well throughout our lives.

Automation in Housing

Automations are on the cusp of making exciting innovations in housing. The #WPProjects chapter below introduces automatically built and serviced towns called "Worldvilles"; Worldville is, of course, a temporary name given until a proper town-name can be assigned.

Where online games like MineCraft and WarCraft encourage young builders to design virtual buildings and neighborhoods today, online Worldville software tools will likely enable these same people to compete for Best Real-World Community Design competitions. Simply hitting the Enter button will build the approved winning design in real life; and this will happen surprisingly quickly and soon too.

Building these computer-assembled real-world homes are an array of new large-scale 3D-Printers, assembly robots and connected smart factories, and of course, new ideas about what are efficient and interesting homes.

China has been 3D-Printing six-story buildings and luxury homes for four years now. Automated bricklaying and other sophisticated construction robots are becoming mature and affordable but lack integration with one another. Pre-fabricated home factories build homes that either simply pop-up once they are towed to their lot -

ready for occupancy – see https://www.youtube.com/watch?v=gTGVqZX4o0w for an example.

Micro-homes too are providing inexpensive, energy-efficient housing in both rural and intercity settings where low costs and rapid construction make these small, cute and practical homes better solutions for the elderly and the homeless.

#WPProjects assigns home automation projects to Serbia and Uzbekistan initially with component plumbing, heating, electrical, windows & doors, and servicing etc. assigned to other countries.

As to why we have been able to put a man on the moon by not build an automated house, of course the answer is one of direction and leadership only.

Instead of building sustainable communities, we are instead leaving companies to churn out gadgets and building materials as simply and cheaply as possible - without regard for sustainability. A robotic assembly line that builds homes is a sophisticated engineering project and not one that can capitalistic business can be counted on to build without direction – obviously.

Milton Friedman was a very well-funded Economist in the early 1980s, famous for consistently defining Greed over the Greater Good and defending that the most important innovations in time were created by capitalist needs and corporations. His six appearances on the Donahue Show are interviews available still on YouTube at https://www.youtube.com/watch?v=MQ0-cDKMS5M.

The facts in reality, however, clearly show that Milton was a misinformed and socially irresponsible individual forwarding a message by special interests. It was government who lead almost all great advances in civilization – and this was especially true throughout the cold-war technological era when engineers were in charge of projects as well. I explained in the TED Slide show of World Peace – The Transition, that mankind's incredible technological leaps and strides of the 20th century only came about at the direction of government funding and programs – from computers, to nuclear energy and drive systems, to jet and pressurized aircraft, to a moon launch, strides in space and ever cities on the water as in nuclear aircraft carriers.

After the cold-war; after 1975 or so, all that capitalism created were profitable refinements on the same technologies. Advances in Technologies with great potential like 3D-Printing advance slowly and only ever developed at a rate that profit will permit.

Government have only ever been the ones to lead big social changes of this magnitude, and leadership here is something that you must vote for as well.

Housing KPIs (Performance Measures)

Key Performance Indicators – KPIs, are mentioned throughout this book again and again. It's important that we have shelter for children and parents; it is important to accommodate other needs as well; and just as important are needs of setting expectation well and meeting promises consistently.

If we need another home; it must be made available within "x" months but "y" months is too long; we must have a chance to preview a few ("x") options and we need not less than three months' notice of confirmation of a change. When automated housing software systems break down, we need a manual system to work in its place very temporarily. Planning KPI-driven Risk-managed housing systems takes the stress out of life – as is the case with most good planning.

Automated Home maintenance, home construction, and even one-day home renovation and demolition, need sophisticated management and planning as well.

Good Planning with solid KPI & Exception Reporting alongside release-managed process improvement are the ingredients of the best self-correcting processes that you are ever going to work with.

Good Execution – I often say that the best programmers are those whose code cannot be broken easily by the next dozen changes.

Operational Performance of housing systems can be imperfect either through poor training, overload, or flubbed changes from time to time, so good Quality Assurance rigor and contingency planning go a long way to maintaining a stress-free work life and productivity that meet everyone's needs for Housing.

Chapter 15

-

Immigration & Refugee Policy

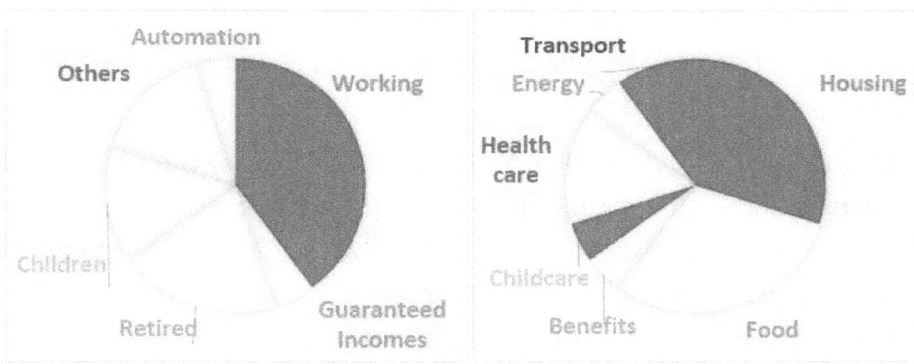

With just 20% of the planet living a Good Life, there is much work to do to correct a major problem without distractions like war, corruption, violence, and displaced communities and families getting in the way and slowing forward progress.

The difference between a productive society versus unproductive, comes down to planning for community, executing thought-leading policy and process, monitoring progress, and making optimizations that drive high rankings in wealth creation and wealth distribution in comparison to other countries.

Internationally, the U.N. have set initial goals for International progress in its Global Goals, but these are a start and work in progress. What they do not offer is planning of any sort. No step-by-step instructions are suggested on how to build sustainable solutions.

The difficulty created by having no planning, is that there can no training; with no training there can be no coordinated pulling - and as any coxswain (rowing team captain) can tell you, uncoordinated pulling in all directions turns you in circles, or worse, as often as not.

We see the result of slow and embarrassing progress in society today. Democracies have many thousands of voices, and each voice is quite certain that things are not working as they should today, but 99%+ all are trying to guess at which changes are needed. This is a recipe for year after year stagnation unfortunately – and not a desirable approach.

CSQ Research is a Canadian Think-tank that studies the policies of every country - over time – and compares the track record of policies to country's GDP track records. CSQ's CMI – Country Management Index and RAI – Renewable Automation Index explained above, measure the performance of each management team in every country by assigning a performance and maturity rating to each. Intuitively you might agree that this is what a pragmatic approach probably more closely looks like.

If our voted policies continue to lead us toward social collapse, as has happened to many civilizations in history, we see progressively increasing social problems. Symptoms of collapse start with increasing unemployment, divorce and lower fertility rates; usury and dual income traps begin; incarceration rates grow alongside homelessness, problems begin to include religious extremism, racism, gender inequality, substance abuse, incarceration rates increase, terrorism and then finally revolutions and war emerge as collapse takes hold fully.

Refugees

Refugees are individuals and families left without homes and supports in their own countries. Most often, they are displaced through no fault of their own whatsoever; sometimes as a result of voting poorly. Most refugees are regular citizens like you or I, going about their work and raising families, until they were driven out of their homes and communities by war or tyranny. Often refugees face starvation or death should they try to return to their homes and past lives.

The reasons for instability within a refugee's society can originate from purely internal conflicts and wars between competing local communities; sometimes the instabilities result from foreign influences. When foreign countries have intervened, very often the same countries who had a hand in creating the conflict – are next asked to assist by taking in and providing financial aid for the Refugees that they have also displaced.

The United States interceded in Iraq in 2003 and then left no strong leadership and authority as they pulled out in 2011. At that same time, in 2011, NATO allies – including Canada and the European Union, insisted on sanctions against President Bashir al-Assad of Syria, Iraq's neighbor.

Before extensive droughts beginning in 2004, Syria was one of the most beautiful countries in the Middle East; and was a place where women walked down the street safely at night. The political and security vacuum created by a civil war beginning in 2011, permitted mercenaries to descend from the north of Iraq into Syria and this began a well-entrenched war between many groups with many agendas; Arab Spring, Syrian Army, Kurds, Turks, Hammas Palestinians, IS Islamic State Muslim Extremists from Iraq, Hezbollah from Lebanon, Israelis, and many other groups, displaced 13 million of 22 million Syrian citizens (Wikipedia, 2016).

4.4 million Refugees were displaced outside of the country and fully 3.3 million are currently in Turkish Refugee Camps. Turkey has spent $8 billion in support of Syrian Refugees; the U.S. $4.7 billion. Details of aid spending are surprisingly well documented at Wikipedia at…
https://en.wikipedia.org/wiki/Refugees_of_the_Syrian_Civil_War
("Refugees of the Syrian Civil War," n.d.)

Millions of ordinary people in Syria lost everything and had to flee to find a safe place to live. The E.U. absorbed perhaps 200,000 refugees with 50,000 making their way to Greece, and Canada was the ninth largest aid supporter agreeing to also take 25,000 refugees and commit $1 billion.

Democracy is important, not because it works perfectly – democracy must constantly reform and improve. Democracy is important, because democratic countries do not continue wars with other democratic nations. Our governments undermine their value to humanity quite a bit, however, when our actions create and then leave political vacuums in parts of the world where education levels and longstanding rivalries require a strong policing presence.

Was a Canadian, American, or E.U. citizen consulted when NATO pulled supports for Syria's President Assad after arming ISIS forces throughout the IRAQ war? Absolutely not.

As a voting citizen I would want to ask; what are the alternatives? What are the long-term Costs and Benefits – in both human suffering and real dollar costs? It would have been a penny spent to save a million pounds.

The cost of Coalition and NATO interference in Iraq and Syria - in human suffering and refugee support dollars spent - have been staggering. Why was there no social plan presented, and no business plan that considered long-term costs?

Engineers and doctors pledge an oath to do no harm to society; and I think most voters agree we have a moral imperative to defend peace and security where we can while we work toward improving global human rights pragmatically. There are 11 million people displaced from their homes in Syria – a country of 22 million where women in 2010 could walk down the street at night safely.

I heard a Texas Republican Governor tell a story to a Fox newswoman last month - about How the Cow eats the Cabbage. The joke's point is to not make incorrect conclusions due to shortsightedness; it turns out that the cow in the joke is an escaped baby elephant and the elderly woman calling the police can't quite see that it's not a cow shoving cabbages up its butt.

The State of Texas' Governor doesn't understand the joke so he explains proudly that "In the South", his constituents know how the cow will get cabbages pushed at them – when it comes to U.S. foreign policy abroad. Ironic, and embarrassing, shortsightedness costs lives so cast your vote for an engineer next time.

There have been benevolent Dictators; and there have also been Leaders who strongly controlled the peace based on accurate analysis of credible threat and acceptable losses within their own countries. Saddam Hussein was no picnic, and the 100,000 Kurds that he is reported to have killed in order to keep the peace in Iraq is outrageous. However, from a well-intentioned place of moral high-ground, the Coalition countries removed Saddam from control at a cost of 500,000 Iraqi deaths from 2003 to 2011.

Today, Iraq's 33 million citizens endure one of the highest per capita murder rates in the world in excess of 9,000 per year. The U.S. has 12,000 murders per year but for a much larger population of 360 million. None of these numbers should be considered normal; Japan had two murders last year – "2" – and that is not a misprint.

And of course, events to date are hardly the end of the opportunity for tragedy because Russia was no longer prepared to stand by and watch their former ally Syria be torn to bits either. In 2015, they sent in ground troops and withdrew to support Syria with air strikes in March of 2016. On Sept 16th, The New York Times reported that "Russia Probably Attacked United Nations Humanity Convoy".

Fear sells newspapers and to add to this publishing pressure, the Times' new web-based newspaper format must provoke readers into reading the full article after paying a subscription charge as well. Quite honestly, an article has to be pretty provocative and exclusive for a web-reader to not prefer any number of free alternative web-based news sources.

So, now we have the world's two great nuclear super-powers (with 15,000 warheads between them) in close combat proximity with the United Nations crying "War Crimes" in a major U.S. newspaper while Donald Trump is President-elect.

That is a lot of pretty fantastic dominos really; as if Russia made a point of bombing an aid convoy. My own reaction was "What a load of nonsense"; but by all means decide for yourself.

None of these events described here were ever the doing of Syrian nor Iraqi citizens – and yet they are Refugees nonetheless. It is a fate you would not wish on your worst enemy.

Tensions are too high; awareness, education and leadership in what to do next to restart our played-out Economy are not understood; and not communicated. And much worse, emotions - and not logic, rule the day today as they did in 1930 Germany.

Our academics and experts have failed us too often now – and citizens are heated and open to listening to almost any message of perceived leadership now.

It may take a book like this one - to explain what is needed to diffuse a World War III sized powder-keg; and it definitely takes a democratic electorate that casts their votes in such a way that builds a Good Life and not a bomb shelter.

Bernie Sanders would have beaten Donald Trump – so take another look at Bernie's policies and consider how his policies aligned to policy discussed here in this book as well.

For country performance leaders, look to the management teams of The Netherlands, Germany, Norway, Sweden, Finland, China, Switzerland, and Russia as a strong start.

Abundance - is the cure for most petty conflicts over religion, gender, and race. In this next year, plan to build abundance by rolling out Livingry Projects and not Weaponry Projects: Projects like #WPProjects - that support food and shelter sustainably. Without these strategic renewable automation infrastructures, there will forever be the humanitarian need to care for displaced people and Refugees.

Immigration

What topics must the discussion of immigration touch on to assist a positive economic change new economic cycle?

Let us take a more detailed look at the benefits perceived to result from Immigration as follows:
- Foreign Investment
    - Real Estate
    - Business
- Population Increases vs Fertility Rates
- Humanitarian Outreach
- Skilled Labor

Canada boasts the G8's largest Immigration percentage increase – adding one-fifth, or six-million immigrants, to its population since 1990. The next G8s were Germany, Spain, and the U.S. at 14%.

The strategy of boosting new immigration has a historic track record of improving economies. New immigration was observed to relieve great depressions in 1883 and in 1779, however today's offshore banking and online trade networks seem to be negating a positive economic benefit as business and employee benefits are not shared within Canadian communities when this happens.

With no immigration controls, nor monitoring of settlement location, nor investment within country by its immigrants once in-country, the financial benefit and cultural impacts of immigration here have been arguably negative to Canada's own culture alongside disappointing observable economic performance in the same time period.

Consider ...

Country	# of Immigrants	% World	% Country	G8 or G20	Collapse or Advancing
Saudi Arabia	9,060,433	3.9	31.4	20	Advance
Australia	6,763,663	2.8	27.7	20	Collapse
Canada	7,284,069	3.1	20.7	8	Collapse
Germany	12,005,690	4.9	14.9	8	Advance
U.S.A.	46,627,102	19.8	14.3	8	Collapse
Spain	5,852,953	2.8	14	8	Collapse
France	7,784,418	3.1	11.1	8	Collapse
Italy	5,788,875	2	8	8	Advance
Russia	11,643,276	4.8	7.7	8	Advance
Turkey	4,580,678	2.1	5.81	20	Collapse
South Africa	2,399,238	1	4.6	20	Collapse
Argentina	1,885,678	0.8	4.6	20	Advance
South Korea	1,230,000	0.5	2.9	20	Advance
Japan	2,437,169	1.1	1.9	8	Advance
Brazil	1,847,274	0.8	0.9	20	Advance
Mexico	1,103,460	0.5	0.9	20	Collapse
India	5,338,486	2.3	0.4	20	Collapse
China	848,511	0.4	0.1	20	Advance
Indonesia	295,433	0.2	0.1	20	Advance

Immigration is not proven to improve Economic Growth in Canada.

According to Canada's GDP stats of exports; Canada's exports are down 50% since 2000, imports are up 50% since 1990's "250,000 Annual New Immigrant" Policy began. Record high trade deficits hit just last month at $3 billion after annual trade deficits every year since 2008. Canada's track-record in affordable housing is one of runaway housing bubbles, poor infrastructure improvement, and its

GINI is increasing throughout this time period. GINI is a measure of Inequity that indicates increasing wealth of richer individuals; this is generally seen to have a negative impact on Export per Capita and the economy at large.

Worse off is Australia who is in a worse situation in all areas of its economy, with a similar number of immigrants but a lower over-all country population which makes this immigrant percentage higher than Canada's.

Across the G20 chart above, High Immigration countries show negative economic track records, while low immigration countries are largely among the strongest economic improvers. If I draw a line at 10% Immigration rates for the G20 nations above, 75% of G20 countries (with higher than 10% of Immigrants) are in Collapse while 33% are in Collapse Trending with Low Immigration. Having lived through this time in Canada's history, I – like many – can attest to the dilution of the Canadian's standard of living throughout this period and a very notable period of culture shock particularly in major urban centers where Indian and Chinese communities settled closely together to comprise 80% of their communities.

With Canada's unemployment rates at 7% - and unreported unemployment at twice that, Canada's labor force struggles to find placement into jobs and incomes for its citizens today. Housing in major hiring centers is at thirteen-times inflation since 1987 due to an absence of responsible management controls as well. Usury here is rife and desperate homebuyers are forced into purchasing loans that they will seldom be able to repay.

"Usury" is the practice of extending loans that can never be repaid; the practice is illegal in most countries - and most social leaders would agree that these are immoral practices as well. Our dictionaries have altered Usury's definition to focus on unreasonably high interest rates only, but when essential housing costs within bubbles are thirteen-times the rate of inflation and inventories (supply) appear to be kept scarce artificially, Usury can happen at interest rates of just 2%.

The Canadian Mortgage Insurance people at CMHC have very recently started to realize this problem and just this week raised requirements to ensure that new owner can endure a percentage point or two in interest rate increases. This also means that many, many first time home owners and young families are not able to buy homes that they need.

Inviting immigrants to settle in these areas - as they have preferred, can have the negative effect of exaggerating these scarcities and bubbles.

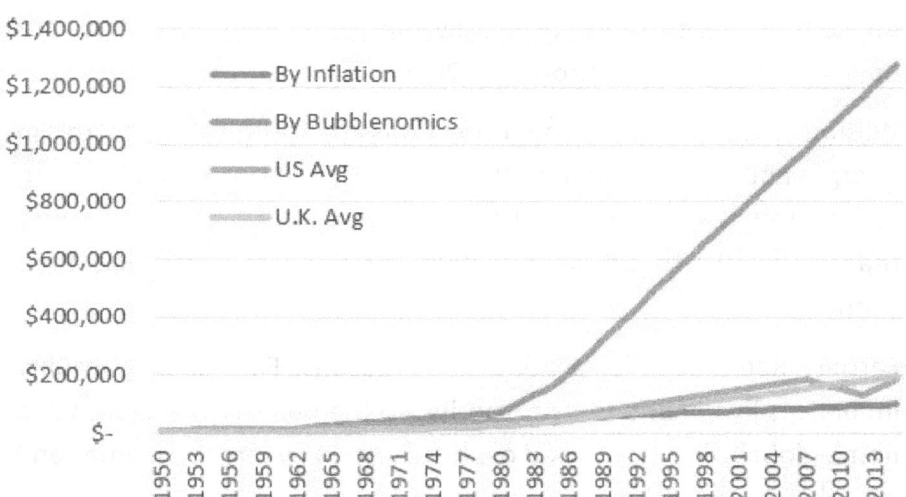

In the chart above, the Toronto Real-Estate bubble in Red is compared to the housing prices in non-bubble markets and the Inflation line over the same 65-year period (over the last economic

K-Wave cycle).

At #100 on The CMI Index, Canada is a country on a trajectory to Collapse – and not success – based on its poorly researched management decisions in energy, immigration, wealth distribution and due to its general declines in citizen spending-power which have resulted from a long list of lax monitoring and poor government control.

This hard evidence reinforces that there can be no business case for Immigration in many countries now, other than that of normal family unification best-practices. Increasing Immigration rates at this point would, therefore, amount to compounding "problem policy" at a time when this country can hardly afford another burden to infrastructure and to its automating and offshoring job market.

Despite this information, third-party groups like the Conference Board of Canada and Canada's Immigration Minister continue to call for 25% increased rates for immigration – no longer 250,000, but now 407,000 annually through to 2030.

Without Guaranteed Income protections and responsible controls in energy, housing, and many other areas, Canada could Collapse no different than Spain, Greece, England, Australia or any other country that is unable to devise effective solutions to restarting their economic cycles.

Fertility Rates vary for a number of reasons. First among fertility influences in all nations is prosperity; so the number of children in a home globally has decreased over the last 200 years as incomes and amenities have improved to families.

Women who live in countries with GDP per Capita at an average of $8,000 annually, tend to have fewer children on average internationally as the next chart depicts.

Population Increase and Fertility Rates

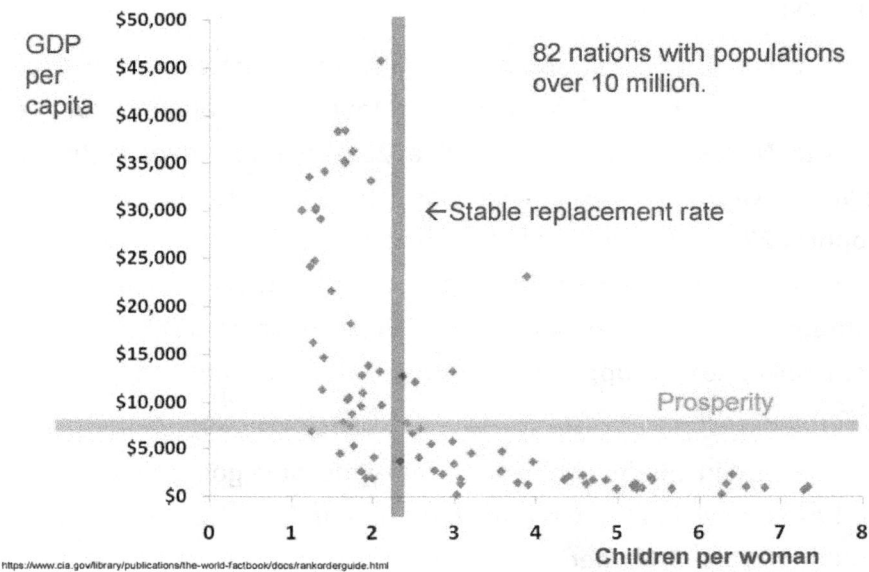

BIRTHRATES
Canada, Germany, Netherlands, U.K., U.S.

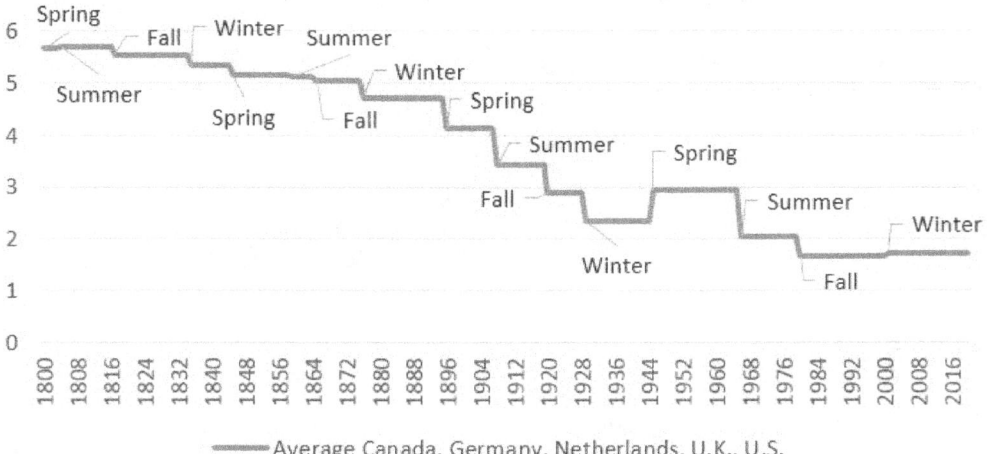

The second influence is based on Economic Cycle Phases. In this next chart of average Birthrates per Economic Phase, we averaged birthrates in North America and Europe. Here we see that birthrates are always higher in Spring and Summer Phases; and these are times when living is easier as well.

I also asked the question: Are fertility rates increased by Free Universal Day Care and Free University Programs as found in Quebec and the Nordic States? I did find a 20% increase over births in Germany. Germany does have a subsidized Day Care Program but it supports 220,000 fewer spots than are needed. Beginning in 2014, Germany made all university programs free. Russia's birthrate fell dramatically to German levels after Perestroika in 1986. Prior to Perestroika, Russia supported free University, Housing and Day-care in its major cities.

Free daycare in Quebec did lead to more mothers going to work but this has fact has led the German government to look closely at what should the role of women be in society.

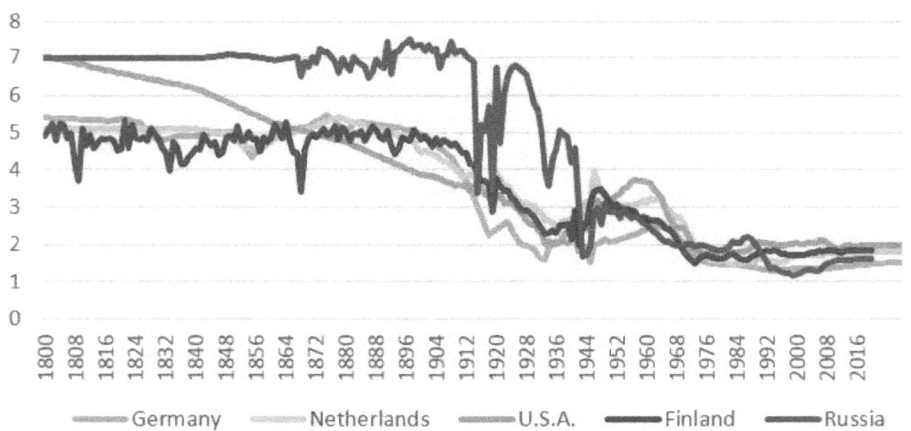

Gender Equality

Gender Equality discussions enter into daycare discussion as they have in Germany. Most will agree that Gender Inequality becomes a big problem whenever these policies are misused to:

- Shame women away from raising their own children at home should they wish
- Risk family pensions of $1.2 million to $1.8 million as 20-year working-dads are replaced in socially-irresponsible and even serpentine efforts by major businesses to by-pass pensions by hiring women; or
- Force families into a dual-income trap. With Canadian families at now 76% Dual Income Families, the realities of a dual income trap cannot be ignored and adversely impact birthrates as well.

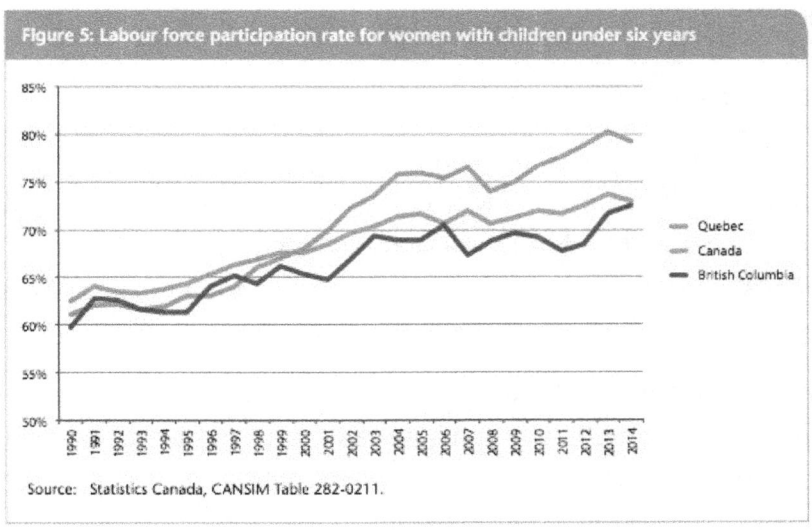

Source: Statistics Canada, CANSIM Table 282-0211.

Improving Fertility Rates by providing a Good Life

In the end, the biggest increases in fertility resulted from a Good Life in a Spring and Summer Economy; an Economic Phase that easily afforded the things a family needed with a single family income.

Immigration for Humanitarian Reasons

Immigration Author and Journalist Roy Beck put together a colorful presentation using Gumballs to represent Immigration Data in 2010. View this video yourself on YouTube at https://www.youtube.com/watch?v=LPjzfGChGlE (Beck, 2010).

Using statistics from the World Bank and U.S. Census Bureau, Mr. Beck proves with certainty that our first priority has to be to help impoverished people of the world in their own countries. Immigration for Humanitarian Purposes is an ineffective plan that steals away the best and brightest of countries that need agents of change at home who can move their communities forward with priority.

Immigration for Skilled Labor

Immigration for Skilled Labor is essentially the socially irresponsible practice of offshoring engineering. Often the imported skilled workers are invited due to lower salary expectations and then they will offshore work to remote teams in his or her homeland where he can funnel jobs and take a percentage as well.

When engineers graduate from advanced computing programs in Canada, they immediately head abroad realizing that the local skilled job marketplace is saturated with Offshore Engineering created by a complete lack of offshoring controls.

The social costs of immigration for skilled labor is tremendous.

Immigration for Unskilled Labor

This is a business practice that routinely externalizes its social costs. Whether for field workers or for nannies applying for families to join them, the social costs can be tremendous for what is largely an illegal immigration practice. If ever there was an easy business case to make, the automation of sustainable local food manufacturing and distribution would surely cost just a fraction of the social costs realized by managing the many and divisive social problems created by the immigration of unskilled labor.

Protecting Culture

Steel yourself for immigration policy discussions that protect culture because these discussions include topics such as intermarriage, immigrant percentage maximums in communities, and topics that would make a staunch liberal squeamish. The alternative to having these frank conversations, however, is to squander, blend, or diminish your culture. This makes these discussions very important to have openly and honestly.

Culture is a very important component of every country. Economies are influenced by a broad number of discussions as well. Transition Economics applies both scientific method and statistics to correcting the problems in our cyclic economies so that we make the correct policy decisions at the appropriate time. If there is no case for Immigration as a tool of Economic Growth by Scientific Method, Policy makers should be resistant to Immigration and focus on strengthening culture instead.

Chapter 16

Energy Policy

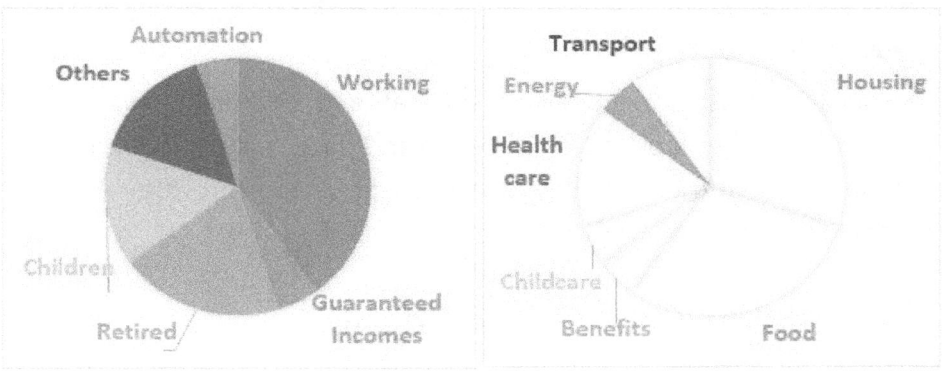

Few discussions will have a more positive impact on any society than the projects that create clean and **abundant** energy.

- Prosperity Depends on Energy
- Prosperity stabilizes population
- Therefore, Energy can stabilize Population worldwide too (Hargraves, 2016) (Slides 5 & 6)

Note that I use the word "Abundant" and not "Conservation" here. Energy Conservation does stop consumption growth and we do not want prosperity to be scarce either. Energy creates Clean Water and Food, Energy drives Prosperity, and Energy is the cornerstone to building a Good Life for everyone.

Fortunately, technologies exist to give us the safe, clean, inexpensive, full-time energy that we need in perpetuity today – contrary to the messages that are more often communicated to us in the media.

It is fundamentally important, therefore, to endorse only the science that makes inexpensive, abundant energy available to us. All other sources energy should always take a distant back seat – this is especially important in a K-Wave Winter as we have things today.

And so what of the Global Warming and Carbon Tax debacles that rage on globally?

Environmentalists have been guessing at, and Engineers have been working on, the question of what are the most sustainable energy technologies and trends for society - since long before the nuclear reactor era began in the 1950s.

CO^2 is the Foundation of Life on Earth

CO^2 (Carbon Dioxide) is the foundation of life on this planet; plants need CO^2 to live and globally we are at the lowest levels of CO^2 in our planet's long history as well. Contrary to Al Gore's message in 2006's "An Inconvenient Truth", CO^2 does not drive global warming - rather it's warming that drives CO^2; the other way around - and the varying cyclic tilts of the earth in relation to the sun have more to do with global warming than does Combustion.

CO^2, therefore, is far from the nemesis that it is made out to be. What we don't need, however, are the toxics that fossil fuels also set into the air during combustion. Clean CO^2 is just fine and - according to the science, there may well come a day, perhaps a million years from now, when we will have to generate Carbon in our air artificially in order to continue to live on this planet. See https://youtu.be/5Smhn1gL6Xg (Moore, 2016) for more.

New Energy Poverty and Legal Recourses

Energy Poverty is commonly discussed as a major problem in developing nations where electricity service is scarce or unavailable. The correlation between Energy and Prosperity is well understood and well documented, yet in the G20 and other developed nations, a New Energy Poverty is emerging alongside growing unemployment, poor safety-nets and rising energy cost.

During the past 60-years, scientists and engineers have routinely been forced to take a back seat to sponsors of Wind, Solar, Fossil Fuels, Uranium Nuclear Power Plants, and other finance-driven energy sponsors whose solutions hardly qualified as our strategic best next-steps in energy.

As a direct consequence, many G7 countries live in the shadow of a New Energy Poverty created by five-year-term politicians authorizing many 25-year financial procurement contracts totaling billions of dollars in inappropriate part-time energy spending.

Examples of New Energy Poverty are found in the U.K. where energy poverty kills 24,000 people every winter now; Spain reports 4,200 deaths each year. People turn their heat down to low because they can't afford it and they die in the night; highest at risk groups include rural citizens, children, the elderly and the poor.

Germany and Ontario, Canada, where Wind and Solar spending has created 100% increases in electricity costs in the last ten-years, experience Energy Poverty now as well (Bourbeau, 2016). Fully 800,000 Germans have had their power cut off because they can no longer afford it. (Clemente, 2014)(HUTZLER, 2014)

The case for legal accountability in politically-driven or financially-motivated decisions that have already been made; like decisions to invest billions in 25-year part-time energy infrastructure contracts, is just beginning. A small handful of benefactors won lucrative lending contracts and generation contracts at the very great expense of society - but defenders of energy poverty are certain to be out in full-force as well. (Kerr, 2016)

Carbon taxes too, will make power generation less profitable for many power generators. This meant that the Alberta Government in Canada had to move in 2016 to change PPAs (Power Purchase Agreements) to ensure that its power continued in the face of shrinking financial rewards now. By the present rules, power generators have the option to terminate Alberta's power if profitability drops. Alberta had two choices – to make this change, or to pay the Federal Government's New Carbon Tax on behalf of its power generators.

Similar to Tax Avoidance clean-up discussions in Chapter 18, the streamlining of legal processes needed to correct the Energy Contracts that led to Energy Poverty, is an important first step in ensuring that your country can reset and realize renewed spending power once again.

Full-Time Power Generation

The Future of Energy is Thorium 6th TEA Conference Attendees

So, let's take a look at what are the more promising, sustainable sources of energy that can carry us all most easily into the next cycle of clean, inexpensive, abundant and sustainable power.

Our power generation options can be categorized by efficiency, cost, safety, and by full-time vs part-time availability. Obviously, the aim here is to identify and adopt the most reliable, inexpensive, and safest full-time energy sources so as to ensure energy abundance and avoid Energy Poverty.

Geo-Thermal Electricity
Low-Emissions, Usually cheapest, Renewable, Concentrated

Whenever you can dig down into the earth to heat a sufficient amount of water to a sufficient temperature, you can run a city on the energy created. How is this possible? I will take you back to grade One Geography class: You might recall that our planet is a naturally-occurring Thorium Nuclear Reactor with a molten core, and so the deeper you drill, the hotter it gets.

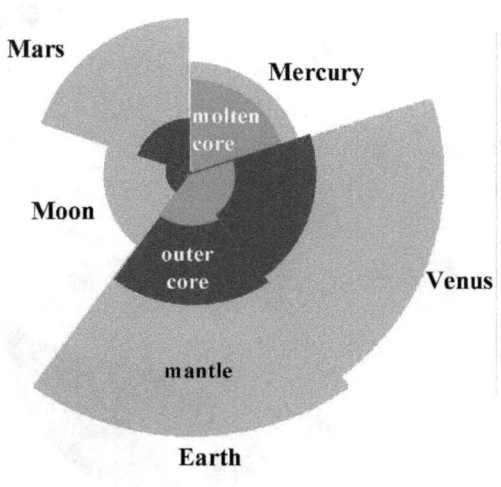

The Nuclear Reactions below our planet's surface create both tremendous heat, and the strong electro-magnetic fields that prevent our planet's atmosphere from being blown away as they have on Mars. Like our moon, Mars has no molten core and, therefore, it has a much less powerful magnetosphere.

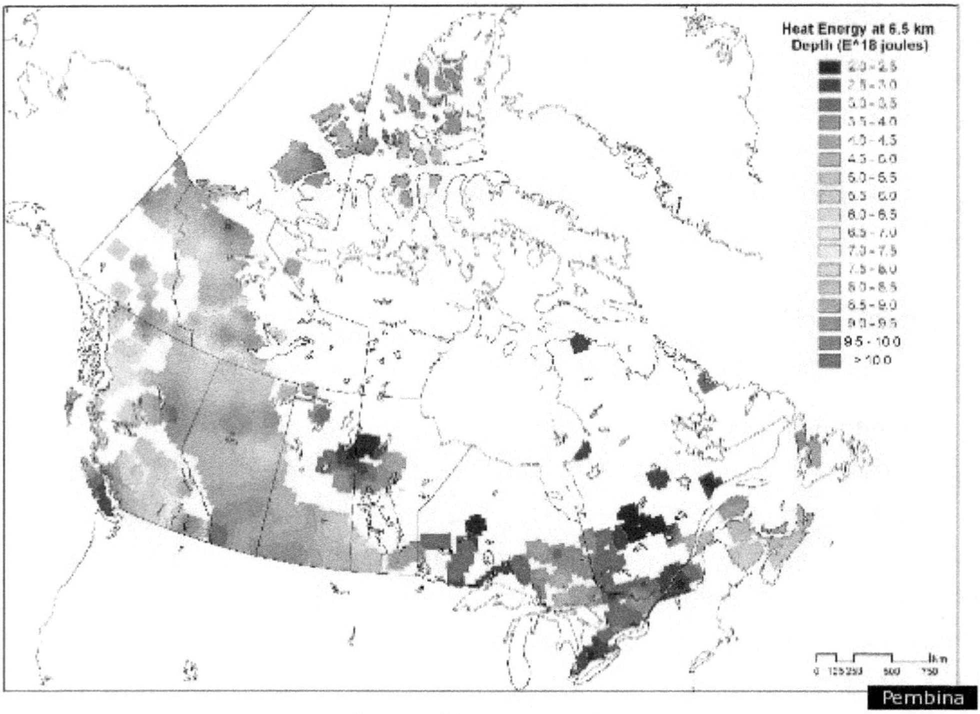

(Lopoukhine, 2014)

Geothermal Energy is abundant, clean, renewable and can be generated almost anywhere. The map above shows the heat energy of Canada at 6.5 kms below surface.

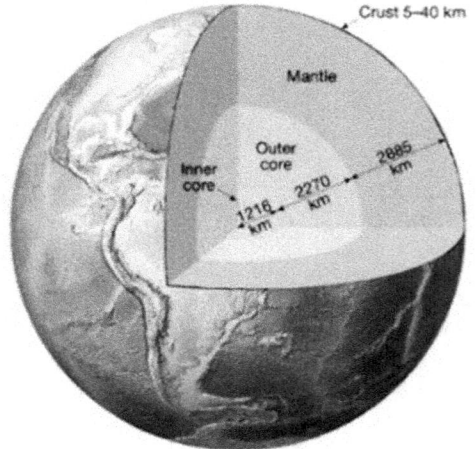

The deepest bore-hole in the world is in Kola, Russia at 12 kms (7.5 miles) deep. The Earth's center is 6,400 kms (4,000 miles) so this barely scratches the surface and probably does not extend through half of the distance to the earth's mantle. Temperatures at the bottom of Kola are 180 degrees Celsius (356°F) (Hamilton, n.d.).

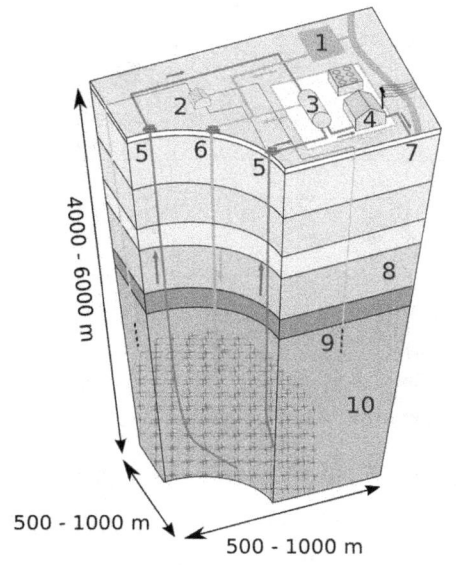

To get more heat, simply dig deeper. Commercial 6-km (18,000 ft) "fracking" wells cost $8 - $12 million to dig, so count on a cost of roughly $20 million to drill a feed and return hole for a geo-thermal plant.

Compare this cost to roughly $2 billion for a Rapid Breeder Uranium Reactor - which heats water to 300°C; or a Thorium Fluoride Salt Reactor – which heats water to 700°C for around $300 million.

With Geo-Thermal, engineers dig holes/bores and then pump heated water from the holes. The geothermally heated water drives a power plant (Wiki, 2016).

In 2015, there were 18,500 Geo-Thermal Power Plants Worldwide, almost double the number from 2010. Canada has no Geo-Thermal Plants in 2016 despite several local companies building and maintaining geo-thermal plants for other countries.

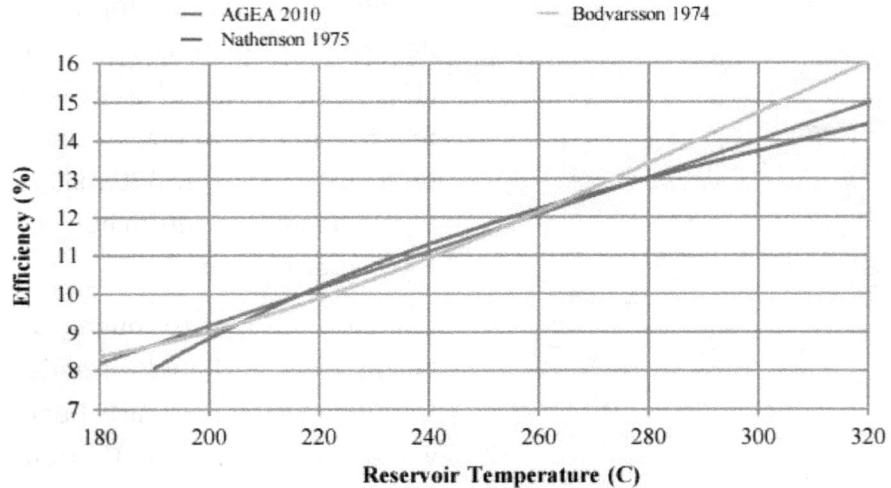

The chart above shows that the efficiency of Geo-Thermal plants are widely dependent on the heat of the water extracted. If water temperature is low, efficiency can be low as well. If water temperature is higher, efficiencies of 20% and more are possible. The Unit Cost of Geothermal in New Zealand is 20% shown below in Green with boxes lower than High-CO_2 alternatives of Coal and Natural Gas (CCGT).

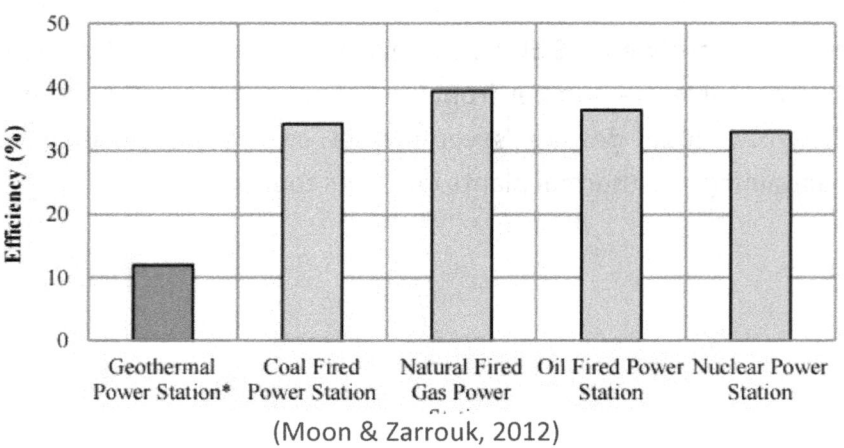

(Moon & Zarrouk, 2012)

Unit Costs Of Electricity Generation 1989-2005

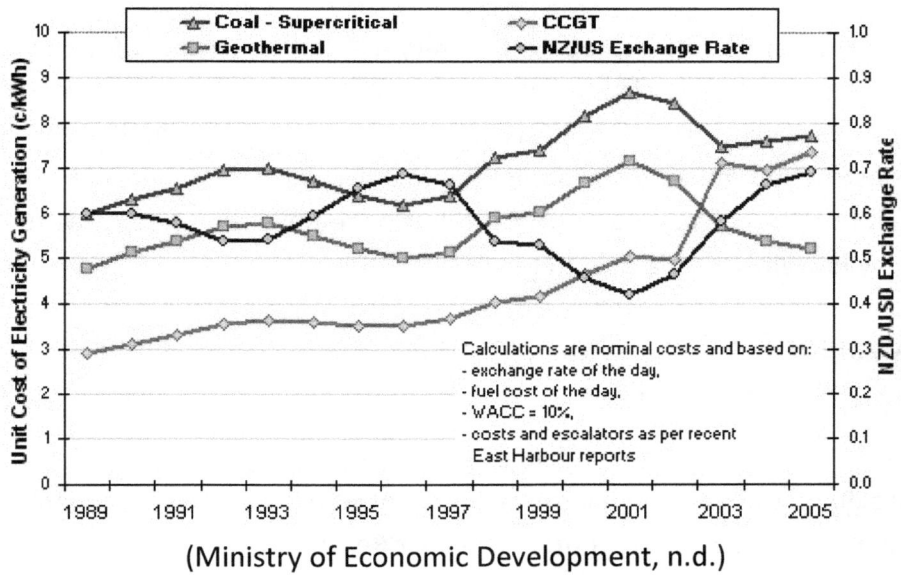

(Ministry of Economic Development, n.d.)

In countries where Natural Gas is abundant and cheap, often a Carbon Tax makes the difference between Geothermal being profitable and very profitable.

Water and Steam are most often used to generate electricity in turbine-driven power plants because steam expands very rapidly to one-thousand-times the volume of water. Pressurized Water at 300 degrees takes a very large turbine (perhaps the size of a high-school classroom) and a relatively large volume of water to generate. Water heated to 700 degrees under pressure however, takes far less water and a much, much smaller turbine to extract more electrical energy. Lava and molten rock reaches 700 to 1200 degrees Celsius (1,292 to 2,192 degrees Fahrenheit) and so stable but active volcano ranges like the one in Hawaii, create highly economic geo-thermal power plants – but most other locations can furnish heat with the right plant.

Hydro Electric
Low-Emissions, Very High Efficiency, Concentrated, Renewable

Hydro (Water) Turbines operate at very high efficiencies of 85% and can work to create clean electricity for decades. Hydro can require very expensive generating station startup costs – including the construction of dams and sometime massive reservoirs. Installation will tend to consume a lot of CO2, but once built will operate with very low emissions and with few interruptions.

Nuclear Fission - Thorium Reactors
Low-Emissions, Non-renewable, Concentrated Energy output

When you want clean reliable energy and you want it in close proximity to large populations where geothermal is marginal, cheap, plentiful, 30% Efficient Thorium Nuclear Reactors fit the bill.

Unlike our basic training, there are many different possible types of nuclear reactors; almost as many as there are models of cars today. Thorium Reactors were designed at the same time and place as our far more expensive Rapid Breeder Uranium Reactors, in the Oak Ridge National Laboratories near Nashville, Tennessee, U.S.A. in the mid-1950s and 1960s. A Thorium Molten Salt Reactor (fed with Uranium oddly, but designed for Thorium) ran for five-years alongside a Rapid Breeder Uranium Reactor. The Director of the U.S. Nuclear Power Research Program stated very clearly that Thorium was the better choice for civilian power needs; Thorium was better for reasons of safety, economy, reliable power production, and somewhat more responsible radioactive waste management.

Energy Generation Comparison

*Each ounce of thorium can produce $14,000 - $24,000 of electricity (at $0.04-0.07/kW*hr)

230 train cars (25,000 MT) of bituminous coal or,
600 train cars (66,000 MT) of brown coal,
(Source: World Coal Institute)

6 kg of thorium metal in a liquid-fluoride reactor has the energy equivalent (66,000 MW*hr electrical*)

or, 440 million cubic feet of natural gas (15% of a 125,000 cubic meter LNG tanker),

- ✓ **Low CO2 Impact**
- ✓ **Consumes Plutonium & Radio Active Waste**
- ✓ **Reduced quantity and shorter duration for storage of hazardous waste**

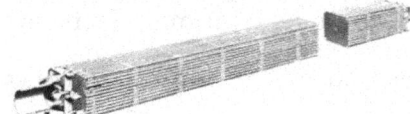

or, 300 kg of enriched (3%) uranium in a pressurized water reactor.

("Thorium Energy Generation," n.d.)

As the slide above explains, a 6 kg nodule of Thorium in a liquid-fluoride reactor has the energy of:

- 230 train cars of Bituminous Coal
- 600 train cars of Brown Coal
- 440 cubic feet of natural gas (that's 15% of a 125,000 cubic meter LNG tanker)
- 300 kg of enriched (3%) Uranium in a Pressurized Water Reactor

For reasons of reliability (Rapid Breeders didn't stop – which becomes a safety concern) and weaponized plutonium production (important through the cold-war nuclear build up years), U.S. President Richard Nixon funded the adoption of Rapid Breeder Uranium Reactors - and Thorium Reactor Research was halted.

Search in the bibliography document for "Excusable mistake" to read an explanation for why the Thorium Reactor program was halted (Moir & Teller, 2004).

To understand why today's Nuclear Industry defends its 470 rapid breeder uranium reactors vigorously - with little interest in Thorium, consider the investment and revenue that reactor manufacturers, security services, and weapons manufacturers all earn from this status quo.

A GE (General Electric) or Phillips reactor must be fed a specific blended ultra-high-profit fuel pellet from the manufacturer for the life of the Reactor; this is not a requirement nor revenue stream for Thorium Reactor manufacturers.

Like an ink-jet printer, Reactors are built as a loss leader to secure lucrative long term fueling contracts. I imagine that an upstart employee might be risking their position by making mention of considering a shift away from Uranium Reactors.

China, India, France and the U.S., have begun to design and build Thorium Reactors with an estimate of 2030 for large-scale electricity production.

India's Advanced Heavy Water Reactor (AHWR) Designs are based on improvements to Thorium designs from the 1960s – and, with India sitting on the world's largest deposits of Thorium, they strongly prefer this option to replace their country's inefficient and air polluting Coal Power Plant Infrastructure (IANS, 2016).

Once successful, the worry becomes that we in the West may very shortly have to buy, or license under-patent, our own reactor technology. This sounds like a considerable opportunity and wake up call for both Government and the Nuclear Industry.

Construction costs for Liquid Fluoride Thorium Reactors are much lower – approximately $200 million, than for Rapid Breeder Uranium Reactors that can run into the several billions of dollars. Spent thorium fuel is less voluminous and has a much shorter storage and radio-active half-life than Uranium.

Thorium Reactions require constant "feeding" of fuel and all reactions stop immediately as soon as power fails. Uranium Reactors must have cooling pumps operational in order to avoid melting down - as was seen in Fukushima, Japan in 2011.

Fusion - Cold and Hot
Low-Emissions, Inexpensive Cold, Expensive Hot, Concentrated

Clean, safe energy forever. Cold Fusion's name has changed to LENR (Low-Energy Nuclear Reactions) recently; I suspect the reason, to be brutally honest, is to ease the scientific peer-reviewing community's embarrassment at having irresponsibly ignored and even snubbed important development and research into Cold Fusion since Doctors Pons and Fleischmann first announced its discovery in 1989.

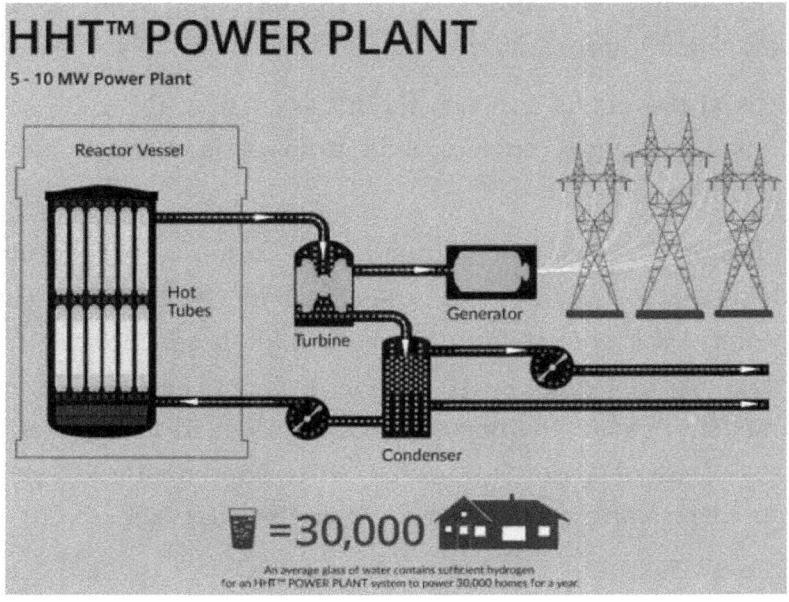

This slide from Brillouin Energy explains that there is enough energy in the hydrogen of a glass of water to power 30,000 homes. Real world measurements on how concentrated are Cold Fusion reactions have yet to be publicly announced but clearly there is fantastic potential. The reason for the excitement is that Cold Fusion appears to work as a power amplifier, taking one unit of power and returning six to ten just like it – and we are still in early days.

Nuclear Fusion does not create radioactive waste, as does Nuclear Fission. Of the two, Nuclear Fission has been far easier to make work reliably than has Fusion.

If there was ever a case to say that money is a very bad thing; or that academia's peer-review protocols are failed as well, surely Cold Fusion's bungled reputation, legal, patent and financial encumbrances surrounding the development and rapid rollout of safe Cold Fusion Power Plants showcase both.

With too many accredited scientific voices, governments, and major companies pouring money into LENR to ignore in 2016, 2017 promises to be a disruptive year for the status quo power industry. (Acland, 2016) (Brooks, 2016)

LENR is in the public domain and, by any name, this new energy technology promises no less than simple, clean, abundant and sustainable energy.

Hot Fusion too is right around the corner. Cold Fusion is exponentially simpler and less expensive than "Hot" Nuclear Fusion reactions – which are still to be proven in full-production trials. The expectation of scientists is that Hot Fusion should be available within the next ten years. Germany recently succeeded in completing a successful test of its Hot Fusion plant when it momentarily created a successful plasma stream in a trial within this past year.

Plasma, the fourth state of matter, streams out of a Hot Fusion reactor at temperatures in the billions of degrees Celsius; a temperature far too hot to be contained by anything other than very strong magnetic fields.

Combustion
High-Emissions; Reliable, Concentrated

Combustion is one of the least efficient means of extracting energy from matter. Our total life-time energy needs would require us to combust enough firewood to fill a gymnasium. In comparison, the fission of Thorium, could supply that same amount of energy very safely with a Billiard-ball-sized amount of readily available rare earth.

- **Gasoline** combusts with 15% Efficiency
- **Diesel** combusts with 30% efficiency – this is the highest efficiency of any combustible fuel.
- **Natural Gas** – 5% to 10% efficient
- **Fuel Oil** – 5% to 20%
- **Coal** – 15% to 60%
- **Clean Coal** – a research-only fuel alternative that is **not deemed practical for production use** anywhere in the world today.
- **Clean Fuels** – 30% Efficient (see Clean Fuels below)

("Combustion Efficiency and Excess Air," n.d.)

Combustible Fuels can be detonated in Generators to generate electricity, or can be burned to convert water to steam for collection by turbines.

The Catalytic Converter was added to gasoline cars as an emissions necessity in the 1970s. Its function is to re-burn the gasoline that is missed during combustion. Modern Diesel engines run lean and at much higher fuel injection pressures until they do not have to re-burn missed fuel. Instead of a catalytic converter, diesel cars have a filter that addresses the NOX emissions of fossil-fuel. So, not only is combustion inefficient, gasoline vehicles are inefficient at combusting gasoline as well.

Incineration and Plasma – Energy from Waste
Medium to Low Emissions; Reliable, Concentrated

The largest nuclear warships in the world, the USS Nimitz Class Aircraft Carriers were designed in 1972 and are due to be replaced by a new Gerald Ford Class in 2017. These ships are small cities that desalinate water, cook, run heavy equipment and hydraulics, hi-tech systems, and propel this five-football-field-sized watercraft 35-knots (55 km/hr) in sustained operation for months at sea with a crew of 6,000 via just two nuclear reactors. The ship's reactors need core replacements only every 25 years – so any notion that we have an energy crisis is bollocks – as the Brits say.

Technology that is deemed worthy of being on one of these marvels of technology can be counted among the best in the world. Waste from these super-ships could never be stored and so instead, it is converted to plasma and then to recyclable glass.

Plasma is the fourth state of matter; matter begins as a solid, then a liquid, then a gas, and then finally, at three-thousand to nine-trillion degrees Fahrenheit, all matter turns into ionized gas or "Plasma".

Plasma's temperatures can exceed the heat of even nuclear reactions; hotter than the sun itself. Measuring these temperatures in Fahrenheit is like measuring the galaxy in feet. Even "cold plasma" creates a lava waste byproduct that is so hot that it is mechanically explosive in the presence of water. So, instead, aircraft carriers convert their waste to recyclable glass via a Cold Plasma technology – and so should we too.

Plasma and other waste incineration technologies take our garbage, and landfills, and convert waste into heat and power with 70% to 80% efficiency and very low pollution and emissions. Sweden, Denmark and many other nations use this process with the proviso that the balance between waste-burning and waste generation is managed well.

Plasma and conventional incineration are a good energy generation and waste management pairing that promise to life-cycle-manage a majority of produced material turned waste as well.

Solar Thermal Tower
Low-Emissions, Efficient, Concentrated, Renewable

Suitable for high-sun regions, concentrated, reflected sunlight is used to superheat water or molten salts to temperatures of 550 degrees Celsius.

$5.27 cents per Kwh

The molten salts method retains heat for power generation when the sun is not shining but it also requires a morning startup procedure that gets the plant up to operating temperature using alternate fuel sources. In this configuration, the molten salts heat water into steam that drives Steam Turbines.

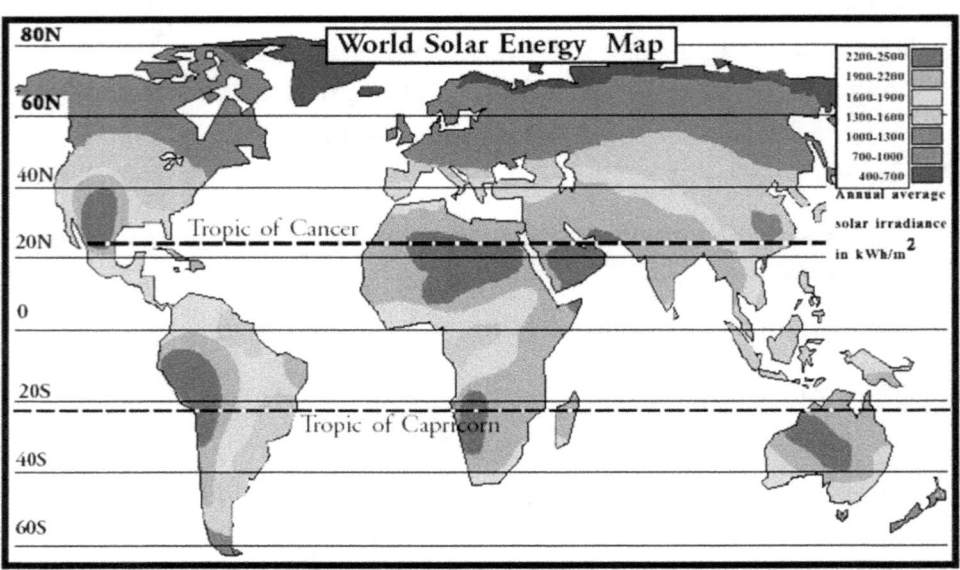

http://www.inforse.org/europe/dieret/Solar/solar.html

The design does unfortunately, kill bird-life as the air at the tower is superheated and birds flying into the pond-like mirrors, quite literally burst into flame at a rate of one every two minutes at times. ("Solar Thermal Tower," n.d.)

Nuclear Fission - Rapid Breeder Uranium
Low-Emissions, Reliable, Least Safe, Expensive, Concentrated

Very expensive to build and operate; not appropriate in close proximity to very large populations; security of facilities and spent fuel is also very expensive and the risk of melt-down and radioactive contamination exists although on only three occasions.

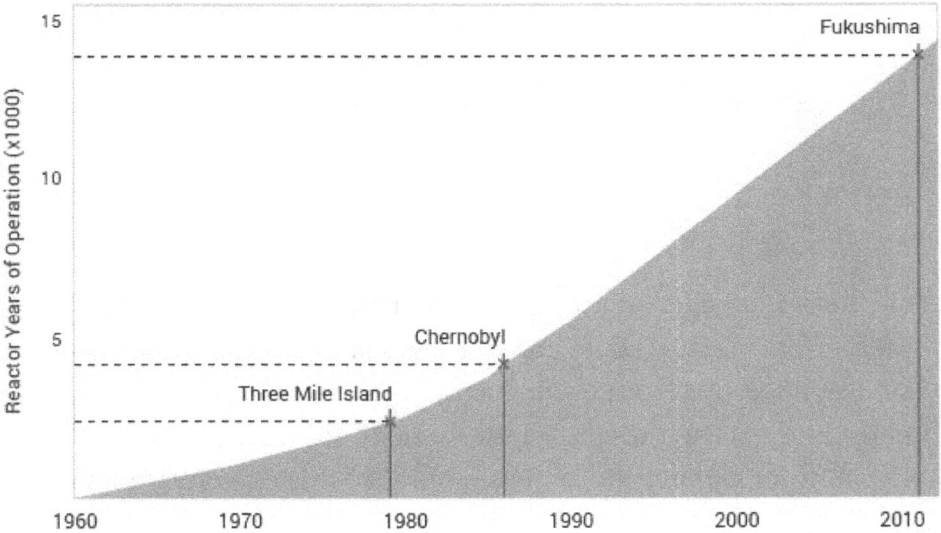

("Safety of Nuclear Reactors - World Nuclear Association," 2016)

Nuclear fission remains a heavy-lifter in clean power generation throughout the world. There are 470 of this type of Nuclear Power Plants in operation. Fukushima's accident was the first meltdown in 25 years – and Uranium reactors can never explode like an atomic bomb either. Explosives require much high levels of enrichment than the 5% fuel used in reactors.

Russia's brilliant new floating nuclear fission reactor ships are another mobile power-generating option based on a proven 50-year icebreaker design. This solution is designed to pull up beside major cities, in China and elsewhere, and supply mobile power on demand (Diggs, 2015) (OKBM, n.d.)

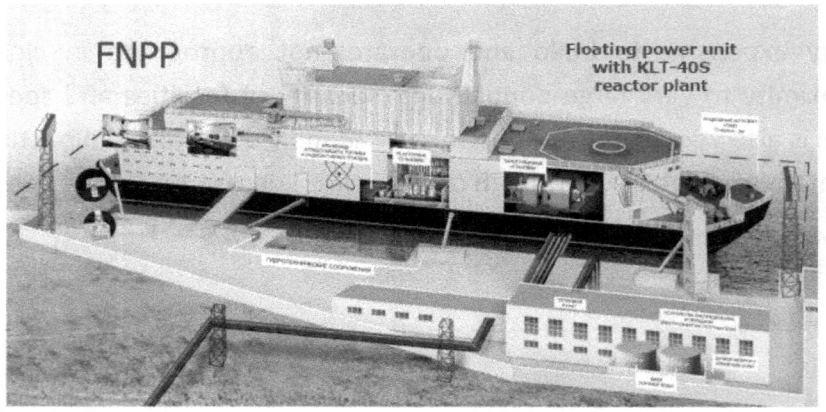

ThermoElectric
Low-Emissions; 8% efficient, Clean, Dilute

Uses Heat-sources, anytime of the day or night, to create electricity directly from the flow of electrons across semi-conductors (using the Seebeck effect). Once semiconductors are attached or exposed to heat sources like steam pipes, wood stoves, or even the temperatures within your car in summertime, heat is converted into electricity.

Replacing the alternator in a car with a thermoelectric exhaust pipe lining, is one example application. TECTEG Manufacturing, is working with McMaster University to produce high amperage cells for high-temperature environments. Its devices are engineered to deliver 100-200 amperes (enough electricity to meet the peak needs of a modern home). (Klein, 2014)

See https://www.youtube.com/watch?v=YhynSkFIJOs .

Part-time Energy Production

Part-time renewable energy sources are often dilute and too weak to warrant heavy investment so energy advisory committees that recommend these should be discounted heavily.

In the Energy Collectors section below, we discusses battery and other storage collectors that may one day make part-time energy of use, but currently there are no cost effective energy storage systems that can make part-time energy storage a consideration.

Part-time energy technologies include:

Solar Energy Cells

Low-Emissions, Renewable, Dilute, Unreliable, Expensive

Photovoltaics continue to mature. The drawback with Solar is that the sun is a weak energy source, unreliable and can only generate energy during the day - and then an energy-storage battery grid is needed. The most efficient photovoltaic energy conversion panels can still only convert 46% of the sun's energy - with affordable commercial panels at 15%.

The other main problem with Solar is the sun is a relatively weak, dilute, energy source.

Germany leads the world in investment in Solar and Wind and this fact has forced them to also increase their dependency on Coal. Electricity rates have had to climb so high as to lead many citizens into Energy Poverty.

Wind Power

Low-Emissions, Expensive, Dilute, Unreliable, Renewable

In addition to being one of the most expensive energy sources, wind is a weak and unreliable energy source as well. Wind power generators operate at efficiencies of 40% but it takes thousands of multi-million dollar fans to generate a significant amount unpredictable energy. Wind systems consume quite a lot of CO^2 in their manufacture and installation, but then run with no emissions thereafter. Maintenance is an ongoing expense and energy may not be available to the power grid when demand requires it.

One very concerning worry in Canada has been the fact that surplus power generated in off-peak times (times without local demand) by wind-farms has had to be sold to other neighboring governments at a lower cost than its production cost. With Hydro (Water) Turbines and other generators, power output can be "feathered" or steamed-off (adjusted up or down) as needed to make power available as needed at all times and not more at undesirable times.

Wave Power
Low-Emissions, Expensive, Dilute, Unreliable, Renewable

Although promising to be sure - due to the weight of water, wave farms are unproven as a source of cost-effective, reliable power at the time of this writing. According to Wikipedia, most investments in wave farms have stopped within just months of initial operation. Look for updates to this report on our website at csq1.org.

Energy Conversion

Energy converters include steam and gas turbines primarily:

Steam Turbine

Steam Turbine is used for 90% of the Energy Generation today - Water is heated under pressure to permit Steam Turbine blades to capture steam as it expands and turn that energy into electricity. Steam expands to one-thousand-times the volume of water. 300

degree Celsius steam needs a very large turbine but 700 degree Celsius needs much smaller turbines and converts the energy more efficiently as well.

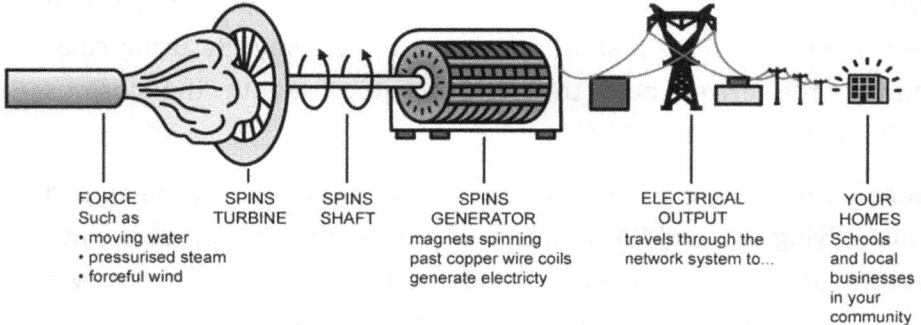

FORCE	SPINS	SPINS	SPINS	ELECTRICAL	YOUR
Such as	TURBINE	SHAFT	GENERATOR	OUTPUT	HOMES
• moving water			magnets spinning	travels through the	Schools
• pressurised steam			past copper wire coils	network system to...	and local
• forceful wind			generate electricty		businesses in your community

Gas Turbines

Air is used instead of Water in a Gas Turbine. "Air flows through a compressor that brings it to higher pressure. Energy is then added by spraying fuel into the air and igniting it so the combustion generates a high-temperature flow. This high-temperature high-pressure gas enters a turbine, where it expands down to the exhaust pressure, producing a shaft work output in the process. Gas turbines are used to power aircraft, trains, ships, electrical generators, and tanks " ("Gas Turbines," n.d.).

Engines - on Earth and in Space

Engines and generators/alternators convert fuels, by burning or reaction, to electrical or mechanical energy here within earth's atmosphere.

In Space, NASA has confirmed this fall that a Radio Frequency Resonant ElectroMagnetic Cavity "EmDrive", actually does appear to create thrust from microwave photons and quantum vacuum particle fluctuations; thrust from energy alone - without fuel.

Thrust in a vacuum with no fuel propellant is what Star Trek called an Impulse Drive; these were the smaller engines on the back of the saucer – and not the long tube-like warp drives. If EmDrive works - it would reduce the 414 day trip to Mars down to about 70 days and the moon would be a short four-hour drive away. By using solar power, the drive could theoretically motor about the cosmos indefinitely. (Knapton, 2015)

Superconducting EmDrives, the next generation, promise cheap and viable flying cars and this is pretty amazing research that we are not getting to spend the time and resources as needed now because we do not have our act straight here on planet earth.

An EmDrive does not expel anything. As this is contrary to Newton's third law, our scientific community want to research pragmatically before publishing wild claims. Once an energy-based propulsion system is working and proven, it will clearly have considerable impact on travel and exploration in the future.

Instead of investing in weaponry and unsustainable monetary policies, investing in Livingry – investing in automation projects like #WPProjects – permits our best and brightest engineers to automate our needs, build sustainable Good Lives easily, and frees us to advance incredible research projects like these.

Energy Collectors

Rapid Charge Battery Systems

Today's best electric cars, the Tesla is an example, require the installation of a special charging bay in your garage and then it can take up to nine-and-a-half hours of charge time to give your vehicle a 245 mile (394 km) range of travel. The Tesla's 'S' model has a 300-mile range but often 150 miles (241 km) is the max range if you do not want to be careful to drive it for optimal battery length.

Tesla fast-refilling stations – called Superchargers - can recharge up to 50% of the car within twenty minutes and are designed to move you along from a gas station during a long trip. On a 240 volt system (North America runs on a 120v standard), it takes one hour to charge for each 30 miles – therefore 9.5 hours for a full 300-mile charge; and on a standard 110v system, one hour of charge is required for every five miles or fifty-two hours to charge fully.

These battery charging overheads keep electric cars constrained to daily city and light highway use primarily, and then gas and diesel vehicles meet our long-haul transportation needs.

Battery powered cars are multiples more expensive than entry-level gas and diesel cars too; today's Tesla are an $80,000 to $120,000 CAN purchase, and this does not include the additional cost of installing a non-standard 240v charging station in your garage. Lithium-Ion Batteries too, have a lifespan of just six years and an environmental cost in manufacture and dis. The cost of a new Tesla battery will be between $12,000 and $29,000 U.S. to replace.

Now, to the bigger problem with battery cars; at present, battery powered cars do not save emission pollutions. See https://www.youtube.com/watch?v=17xh_VRrnMU for a full explanation. (PragerU, 2016)

Some reports have explained that battery cars create more CO_2 than gasoline cars due to their primary reliance on Coal Plants for 13+ hours of charging on a regular basis. If you are running a hybrid car less than 50kms per day, the smaller battery permits solar recharging and creates no CO_2, but much larger batteries, like the ones in the all-battery cars must be plugged into the power grid.

As soon as cost-effective, longer lifespan, faster charge-time batteries can replace current technology, then and only then, will battery-powered car become a superior alternative to gas and perhaps even diesel vehicles too.

Promising Battery Technologies to look forward to, include the Carbon-Polymer direct-charge batteries, Vanadium Redox Flow batteries (G1 VRB) or perhaps Graphene Nanosheets. Direct-charge systems permit direct charging to the atoms of the carbon polymer array instantly. Today, atoms within battery cells must pass charge to neighboring atoms in sequence – requiring many hours to permeate a large pool of battery atoms such as the designs found in a larger battery grid on a battery car today. A direct-charge system promises to drop charge times down to perhaps 15 minutes; or something comparable to a refill of fuel at a refilling station. I had heard that these batteries might be available in 2016, but so far there have been no announcement.

Flywheel Kinetic Energy Management Systems

Based on an idea as old as a potter's wheels, modern industrial flywheels provide data centers and industrial lines with uninterruptable power supplies based on only the momentum of a turning weight. Using mechanical or magnetic bearings (to reduce friction), and perhaps one day superconducting bearings, flywheels provide an environmentally friendly power backup that can last for decades almost maintenance-free with efficiencies as high as 90%.

Super Capacitors and Ultra Capacitors

Supercapacitors seem poised to shortly make life a whole lot more interesting. A cell phone that charges in seconds, or a battery-powered car that recharges in minutes as opposed to 30 hours – and supercapacitors don't wear out so this is really big news whenever it becomes available.

Before there were batteries, there were capacitors; quick charging and able to cycle for 10-years without degrading, these static-charge devices only hold small charges for short periods – not long enough to compete with batteries certainly.

Today's super capacitors can hold hundreds of times the energy that the old capacitor could until Super and Ultracapacitors now promise to outperform batteries - but they are more expensive as well. Li-Ion batteries improve by 10% annually and supercapacitors are still playing catchup albeit in leaps and bounds.

This makes supercapacitors very well purposed to recovering brake energy on vehicles and making that energy available for use on board a bus, for one example. Super Capacitors do not, however, appear to be able to cost-effectively turn part-time energy, into cost effective energy grids in the near future unfortunately. In time however, it actually seems inevitable.

Nuclear Diamond Batteries

Now here is a really fun-fact: Our nuclear reactors discard a uranium fuel cell contained within a carbon shell that collects most of its radioactivity at its surface. By applying heat to spent carbon 14 fuel cells, researchers in Britain are harvesting the surface layer of radioactive carbon and turning it into industrial diamonds using low pressure and high heat. These radioactive diamonds are then sealed in non-radioactive diamond until the resulting battery has the radioactivity of a banana and a charge that will only be half-spent in 5700 years.

Perfect for places where batteries can never be replaced, such as in space or in pacemakers, researchers are actually looking for your contributions and ideas for how to best use these batteries at #diamondbattery on twitter.

The invention of nuclear batteries promises to turn the long-term problem of nuclear waste into a nuclear-powered long-term energy supply. Now just add a cold-fusion 10x "boost", and we have something important and interesting indeed. There are no moving parts in these batteries; simply placing them close to a radioactive source is sufficient to create a charge indefinitely.

Fuels

Fuels are transportable energy that can be used to provide energy for our vehicles and homes. Gases (Natural Gas, Propane, Hydrogen), fluids (gasoline, aviation fuels, kerosene, diesel, etc.), and solids (coal, wood, charcoal, peat, pellets - made from wheat, corn, and rye and other grains). Finally there is uranium, thorium, and even solid-rocket fuels made of aluminum and other components.

Fuels are either combusted or energy is extracted from nuclear reaction - fission or fusion process.

Early on, wood and coal were combusted to boil water and create steam-piston propelled trains and even cars. With the invention of the carburetor in 1876, liquid fuel could be used to combust in large engines directly – and we have used either gaseous (propane or natural gas) or liquid fuels in our cars ever since.

As an aside, an inventor named John Weston is running a 1992 GEO Storm GSI 469 mpg (miles per gallon) on gas fumes directly - with or without a carburetor (Weston, 2016). A little on-line investigation shows that a handful of others seem to keep an Air & Vapor Flow System working pretty well. Similar news of a Pogue Vapor Carburetor that was suppressed in the 1930s by big investors' concern for lost oil profits, has been an urban legend since the 1940s. I will let the reader be the judge but clearly the catalytic converter's role to reburn missed fuel shows a potential for Improvement.

Zero-polluting alternatives to combustible fossil-fuels have existed since the Fischer-Tropshe process was first developed to create Paraffin Oil in 1925.

A viable alternative to fossil fuels is far from new technology, and it cannot come soon enough as fossil-fuels are far and away the dirtiest form of fuel that we can combust.

Clean Fuel & 100-MPG Diesel-Hybrids
Clean Fuel Puzzle

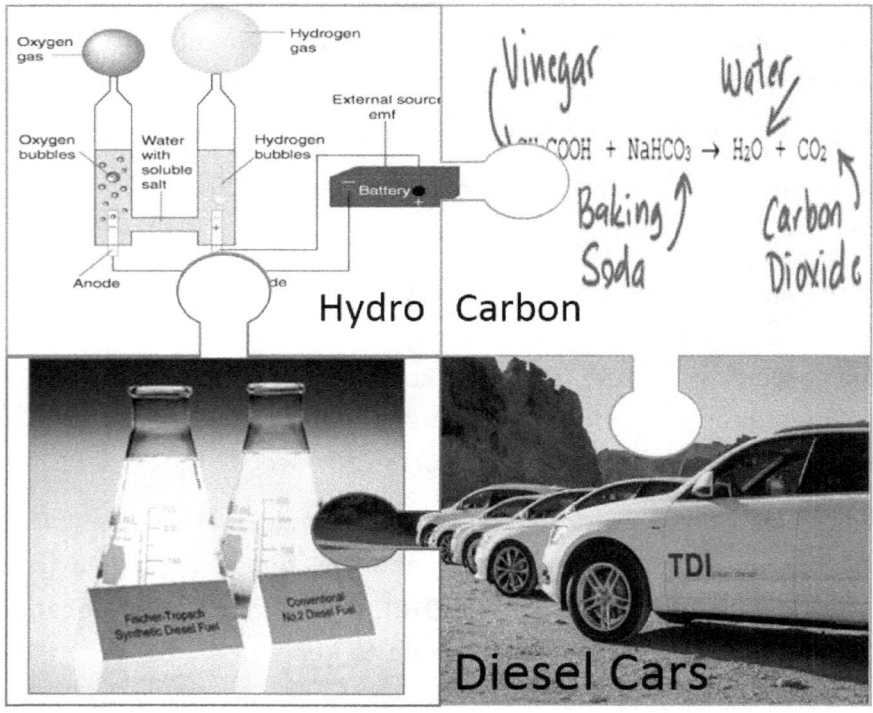

Today, Audi Automotive and parent company Volkswagen, are building cars of the future - as you might expect. You might not also realize that they are manufacturing fuel oils of the future too.

Audi makes crude oil from electrolyzed water (H^2O) and recovered carbon dioxide (CO^2) in a 70% efficient process that creates an ultra-low emission Blue Crude™. (Gray, 2015)

Audi's clean hydrocarbon crude uses the same Fischer-Tropsche process that has been around since the 1920s (Davis, 2015). Its zero-carbon-footprint process makes use of wind energy. Carbon Dioxide sources include simple, safe home recipes like baking soda and vinegar (Calkins, n.d.), CO^2 Air Recapturing, Natural Gas and other common sources.

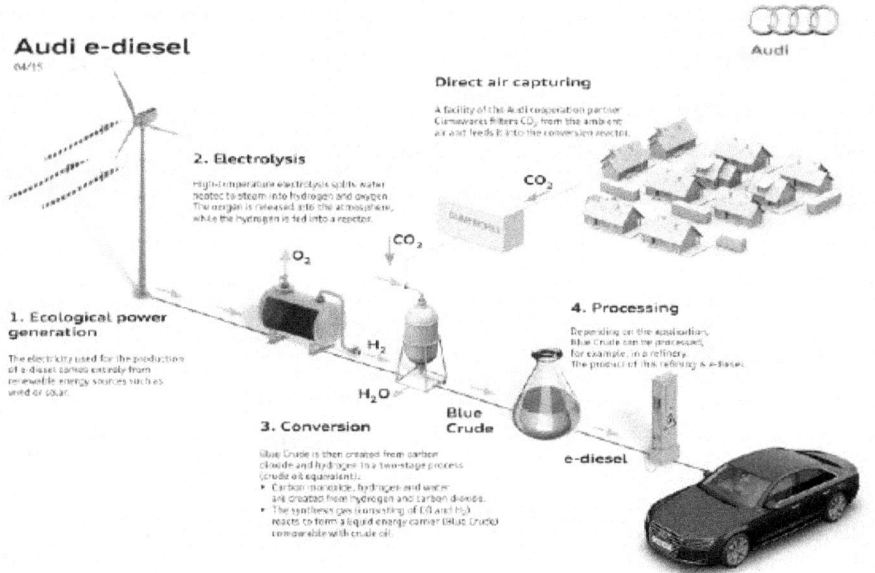

This Clean Crude needs only to be refined to create component diesel fuels, gasoline, kerosene, and aviation fuel as needed, just like a fossil-fuel based crude oil would. You could choose to refine gasoline from this Blue Crude, but the most efficient combusting fuel and engine combination is a diesel-battery hybrid configuration.

Diesel fuel takes less energy to refine from the crude, it has the highest energy recovery of any other combustible fuel source, and even without a readily available 100-mpg (miles per gallon – not a mis-print) hybrid configuration, is almost twice as efficient as a gasoline vehicle at highway speeds.

Audi's President runs this fuel in his A8 and he reports that this fuel makes a car run quieter and with more power too.

The reasons to adopt Blue Crude are compelling. The combustion power of Audi's e-Diesel fuel is greater than that of fossil-fuel diesel, it makes cars run quieter as well, and it is expected to be available to consumers for approximately the same price per liter at retail pumps – equal in cost, or less than, fossil-fuel-based diesel. Blue Crude could be used in our current fuel distribution system easily as well, without expensive modifications – and no pipelines are required as Blue Crude can be manufactured local to demand.

The only waste by-product from manufacturing Blue Crude is oxygen – which might lead to bigger insects and smarter people after much time - but the problem of what to do about all that clean air is a problem for another book.

Assuming that clean fuel additives can be found to guard against solidification in cold temperatures, and other practical storage considerations, I imagine that it might even be possible to create a food-grade version of this product – although, why would you choose to drink it?

Cost is of little consequence when a combination geothermal reactor and nearby Blue Crude refinery could provide a limitless supply of clean burning mobile fuels in the same way that the USS Nimitz Aircraft Carriers desalinate water through electrolysis for a crew of 6,000 every day for the past forty years.

Volkswagen, Audi's parent company, is one of the few companies to bring an affordable diesel car to North America, which is surprising considering Europe's predominant preference for more-efficient Diesel vehicles.

Diesel is Very Important

Diesel fuel, and diesel vehicles, are important because:

1) Diesel fuels made from water and Carbon Dioxide can be fabricated cost effectively in Zero-Carbon-Footprint processes, and burns with Near-Zero Emissions.
2) A Diesel-Hybrid configuration would bring Diesel Vehicles to 100 mpg almost immediately.
3) Gasoline-based cars prevent us from developing cleaner, cost-effective alternatives to fossil-based Crude Oil.
4) Diesel was originally developed to burn Paraffin Oil made from coal and natural gas. This hydrocarbon burns with 50% fewer emissions and Crude Oil was a dirtier alternative that Oil Companies made to work in Diesel engines.
5) Diesel takes less energy to refine, and its higher combustion efficiency takes the same car almost twice as far on the highway over gasoline.
6) Diesel does not dissolve in water making spills and environmental cleanups easier.
7) Diesel is a lubricant that ensures long engine life – where gasoline is "a corrosive" that wears out engines more quickly.
8) Diesel cars last longer, have fewer maintainable parts, lower running costs and set the high-bar for reliability, often continuing to operate for 500,000 to 1,000,000 kilometers and beyond during their service lives (double, and more, than gasoline engines).
9) Diesel fuel detonates through high compression only and is not flammable.
10) One can run a diesel passenger car for 10 hours without stopping as a tank of fuel will often sustain almost 1000 km of highway driving.

11) Replacing all cars with Diesel equivalents would reduce total energy needs by 15% and more overall (depending upon the country).

Defending Diesel Vehicles is Very Important Too

In the early autumn of 2015, Volkswagen was centered out for adjusting their in-car programming to turn off emission controls on their diesel passenger cars. EPA officials claimed that these changes resulted in diesel cars emitting nitrogen as high as ten to forty normal gasoline cars in operation.

A simple reprogramming changed these settings so that emissions were corrected. The EPA's testing of Diesel Vehicle Emissions does not consider the vehicle's greatly improved power and efficiency either. As such, the EPA does not compare apples and apples as it should.

I am assuming that the EPA is credible in their original assertions here too, despite a track record that has come under criticism in numerous cases in past years in regards of technology that promised to detract from fossil-fuels exclusively. I am referring to California's removal of 1997 GM EV1 electric cars in 2001 - upon the advice and direction of EPA Committee Hearings that were filled with Big-Oil-backed panel members. (EPA, 2001)

The failure of North American Governments to protect Volkswagen's diesel vehicles has compelled the company, and Renault in Europe as well, **to pull Diesel vehicles from our roads altogether.** This is a setback for Diesel that I hope every reader will urgently complain to his or her government to correct.

A more efficient, low-CO2 vehicle will not be available until the automotive Thorium Reactor is developed. A car with a Thorium energy source could run a car for 100 Years on a piece of abundant, inexpensive Rare Earth the size of a pea.

Hydrogen Fuels & Vehicles

Hydrogen is burned by fuel cell vehicles like buses and cars. The great thing about Hydrogen is that it can be fabricated right at the pump and a refill

Fossil Fuel is not needed

In 2012, researchers at Princeton University (Elia, Baliban, & Floudas, 2012) confirmed via an extensive research study that a combination of coal, natural gas, and non-food crops, could replace all of America's fossil-based crude oil needs altogether - with synthetic paraffin oil based fuels manufactured using the Fischer-Tropsch Method mentioned above as well. This fuel would reduce emissions by 50% immediately and do away with the need for expensive pipelines as fuels can be synthesized close to distribution centers.

Avoid Alcohol Fuels that dissolve in water

Hydro-Carbons can also be combined to create alcohols which can burn in today's gasoline automobiles as well. Ethanol in a 3% to 40% mix is the only form of alcohol that is consumable by humans, but I think that all other forms of alcohol are deadly poisons. Methanol - is so poisonous that just a thimble-full can cause blindness in humans and animals.

What makes Methanol especially unsafe for humans is that it dissolves in water, which means that spills or pipeline leaks - especially those pipelines that extend under water, are a very great environmental concern. Biodiesels contain a certain percentage of Methanol and Glycerines that dissolve in water as well.

Fossil Fuel Oils, diesel, gasoline, kerosene, aviation fuel, and others, do not dissolve in water; and Audi's Clean Diesel is created by a Fischer-Tropsch Method and does not dissolve in water.

Alcohol Fuels draw from corn and other food stocks that can also make food more expensive.

Pipelines versus producing fuels locally

Pipelines carry fuels to distant markets easily and can be important whenever we are forced to move Fossil Fuels like Crude Oil from source to destination. But pipelines create as many and more problems as they solve when spending on pipelines prevents spending on localized clean fuel production. As pipelines typically only carry one type of material, crude oil or natural gas are the most common pipelines; Crude can then be refined into its ten component fuels at destination.

How important are these expensive, disruptive investments when we can create fuel exactly where it is needed and as demand requires it? One-third of all of our energy cost goes to transporting food & energy so producing fuel locally is always preferable – until cheap and abundant energy is widely available.

Alternatives to Pipelines

Pipelines are not always cheaper. A Business Case is important when making the decision to move oil by pipeline versus train because barrels (# of rail cars) to remote destinations (like the gulf coast, east and west coast), need to be understood in order to support a decision. In the end, fossil fuel is polluting – so pollution-free clean fuels that are produced locally save transportation costs cannot be ignored (fully one-third of all of our energy is used to transport food and energy). For moving Oil and liquids, alternatives to pipelines discussed above included:

1) Driverless-trains reduce rail costs, permit refining in needy communities at any point between Oil Fields and Markets, and railways can be used for multi-purposes and financial benefit.
2) Locally manufactured clean Fischer-Tropsch Crude Oil – this option is available and done today in a Germany by Audi
3) Hydrogen - requires new vehicles North America-wide – but hydrogen can be manufactured right at the gas station.
4) Battery Cars – not yet ready but hopefully within the next ten years.

PROs and CONs of Oil Pipelines

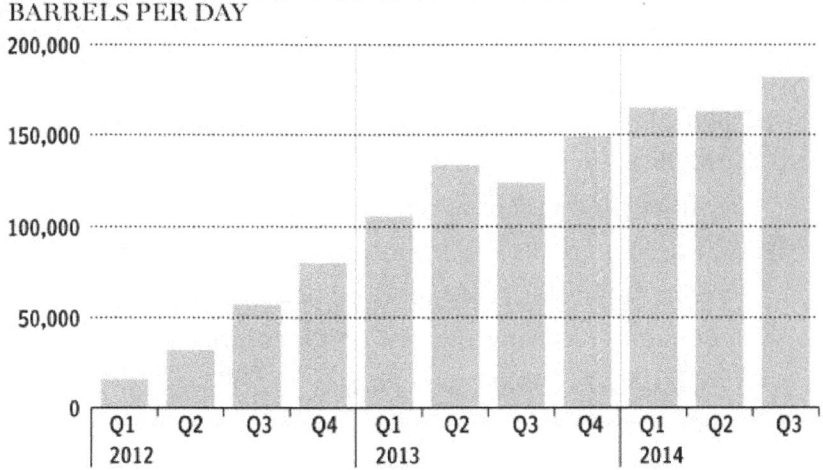

CANADIAN CRUDE OIL EXPORTS BY RAIL
BARRELS PER DAY

COST OF TRANSPORTING A BARREL OF OIL FROM HARDISTY TO MARKETS

	Pipeline	Rail-Manifest	Rail-Unit Train
To Gulf Coast	$7-11	$17-21	$12
To East Coast	N/A	$16-20	$13-16
To Canadian West Coast	$3	$10-14	$8-11
To U.S. West Coast	$5-6	$16-20	$13-16

(Hussain, 2015)

For Pipelines - PROs:
1) Shipping costs - $3 to $11 per barrel pipeline; $8 to $21 per barrel rail - for transport of fossil fuels

Against Pipelines - CONs:
1) Pipelines are expensive to build and environmentally disruptive; railways can be built robotically now too. See http://www.popularmechanics.com/technology/infrastructure/a22018/robot-railroad-track/
2) Job mobility forces Income Guarantee programs; when jobs are permitted to move, they can move to clean-fuel companies too, which is a PRO in several ways. Recall our Guaranteed Income Business Case in Chapter in 11.
3) Low-profit – pipelines carry unprocessed, raw material to remote markets where jobs and high-profits await refiners there.
4) High-profit – Truck or train hauling of locally refined fuels (gasoline, diesel, kerosene, etc.) creates good jobs, higher profit refined fuel products, locally.
5) Self-driving trucks and trains promise to reduce costs further leaving refineries profitable and able to employ easily.
6) Pipeline ties our investment and focus into status-quo fossil fuel businesses and technology
7) Rail permits us to build smart transportation networks that integrate to Connect Smart Factories in an overall Automation Strategy.

Rail vs Pipeline, the Environment, and Safety

Pipeline spills dwarf rail spills with the largest rail spill ever - equaling just eight cars in 2013. In the following graph we see that pipelines spilled 211 Rail Cars, or 148,235 barrels, of crude from 2010 to 2016 in Canada.

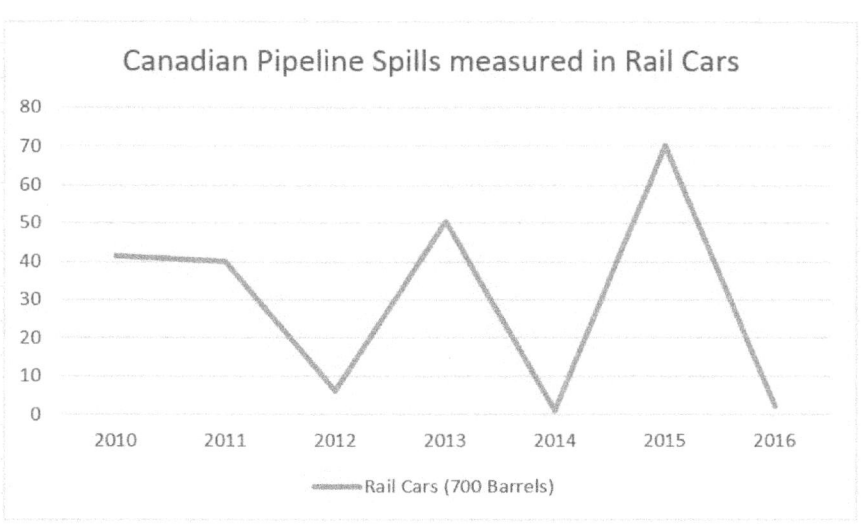

Moving Natural Gas

Natural Gas pipelines are typically buried and spills do not present expensive nor environmental harmful cleanup problems. When integrated into serviced subdivisions, natural gas is an expensive infrastructure initially, but it does make use of available inexpensive natural resources.

Fuels Summary

In an inexpensive, abundant, electrical-energy setting, use of electric boilers and similar building heating systems – alongside vehicles powered by either locally-manufactured clean fuel, or next-generation batteries, is preferred.

Investing in pipelines and other infrastructures to move fossil fuels long distances should be viewed as tactical planning - and not strategic planning.

Chapter 17

Reshoring Production & Engineering

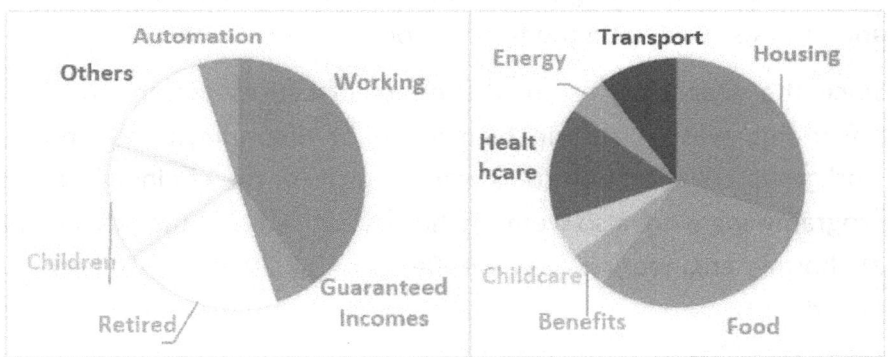

For 100 years or more, toward the end of the industrial revolution, offshoring production to countries where products could be built more inexpensively became a normal practice of business in North America. Pollution controls were less onerous abroad, and the damage to the environment was not felt here at home either.

Governments permitted or ignored this practice in countries where jobs were thought to be readily available in other industries or by retraining workers. Politicians believed that healthy businesses that made healthy profits would make a healthy and wealthy country as well.

This trickle-down was the model that worked throughout the early part of the 1920s when Henry Ford rebuffed the expressed opinions of peers, and insisted that his factory laborers receive high wages by the standard of the day. Mr. Ford realized that good wages and employment built good communities and that if he could be smart in his production, the highly incented workers would also ensure high quality and reliability of his products for a lifetime.

The strategy worked very well for Ford as every worker bought his cars and then generations of children did too. Truly, the interests of business were aligned with the interests of the country. The Great Depression and World War II trained a generation to understand very well that building strong societies was the only goal that mattered – and business was to be the tool for society's construction.

Since the year 1995 or so, the effect of causes automation and offshoring, was to sustain high levels of unemployment, and as workgroup collaboration tools were improved, the engineering and programming work also went offshore. I noticed that the practice of offshoring engineering became flagrant by 2014 or so here in Canada.

The Netherlands had none of these problems. Today the GDP in one of the smallest nations in the G20 is roughly the same as both Canada and Russia, and their technology industry is world renowned and thriving.

How did the Netherlands achieve this? They made offshoring their engineering illegal twenty years ago, and only permitted companies access to this market of 30 million when those companies produced good and jobs in the country.

The Netherlands was too small to sustain the job losses caused by offshoring early on and became an early adopter of reshoring twenty years ago.

Recently, a New York Times article that interviewed Maurice Taylor, the CEO of Titan International tire (Parussini, 2013). He had just returned from a visit to a plant in France that he was considering purchasing an unprofitable GoodYear plant in France. He announced to the reporter of the article "How stupid do you think we are?" Mr. Taylor went on to explain that he had watched workers labor four hours a day and then sit unproductively for the remainder. Competitor Michelin is 20 times larger and 35 times more profitable with a long history and one would assume future too, in France.

What the Netherlands did to defend themselves against offshore thinking of this sort, was to refuse access by a GoodYear - or other, to sell their products here if not manufactured in the Netherlands; and with ownership by Dutch citizens as well.

Starbucks Coffee Shops here are not owned by the U.S. Company for one example. The Starbucks in airports and other centers are local companies and local owners who license the name only. The Netherlands might be one of the few countries in the world that receive corporate taxes from Starbucks because of that company's famously aggressive multi-national corporate tax avoidance practices - in every country that they reside in.

The CEO of GoodYear Tires would remain CEO for about a month if France denied his company access to sell tires to 66-million French citizens – and with trade-ally support, the damage to GoodYear could be much greater. This is the power of on-shoring and responsible controls to eradicated manipulation by multinational business.

A country's bargaining power with any multi-national is its access to markets. Any corporation that wants to offer growth to its stockholders will abide by the law of the land.

Multinational businesses will externalize social costs and play a game of benefit and profit to their advantage until governments collaborate and take back their markets. Since the Bush administration, the U.S. has played Mexico and Canada off of one another in this way very successfully; pulling jobs from one country to give to the other country - unless each country contributes sizable ransoms to sustain jobs.

Creating international trade agreements that permit this behavior of trade extortion, and tax avoidance, diminishes all three countries.

Some of the first moves of U.S. President Elect Donald Trump were to reign in offshoring – and this is a strong TE-Maturity policy too. Trade is important and you will want to maintain healthy Export revenues, but do not offshore engineering and important self-sustaining manufacturing in the balance.

In short, a country needs to manage its imports and exports carefully.

Chapter 18

Business, GDP & Taxation

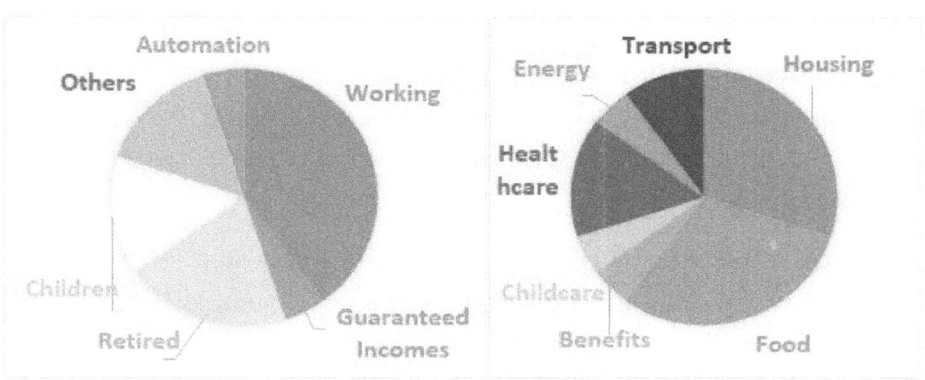

Absent on our Transition Economics Charts so far, are the contributions from commerce between businesses (B2B) and business-to-consumer (B2C).

An initial Transition Economics introduction could easily fill a much larger two or three volume book-set by simply explaining example throttles and Key Performance Indicators in every chapter. A book on Transition Economics for Business is in the works to do some of this.

Transition Economics Throttles

For example, if a mine operator wants to open in a foreign country but local governments refuse the use of excavator equipment to build roads in favor of local laborers with shovels because this creates local jobs, what Transition Economics throttles can calculate the compensation of local economies for the jobs-lost to road automation equipment? Recall that at some point, automated road builders will do away with these construction jobs altogether and so the guaranteed incomes of workers switching income sources must be considered before access is provided to this marketplace; and to the resources that the mining business wishes to harvest.

To keep Transition Economics simple and easy to incorporate, I preferred to keep first releases out of the weeds by presenting example throttles superficially only. A few dozen specific throttling algorithms and ratios are suggested in the Transition Economics' Reference Guide but a Business Case and Project Management Approach is provided to discuss these costs transparently – see Chapter 25.

An explanation of why I feel this has to be a two-step introduction might best be presented with an economics example. I generally disregard Keynesian Economic Theories; this is because historical observation has confirmed that these are the unsustainable practices that led to a global social collapse and war in the 1930s – and then they again permitted today's Winter Phase to continue on to extreme levels of inequity without responsible inequity controls.

Realizing that Keynesian Theories are policies that help a handful of special interest groups at society's expense, why would we care to learn these policies more deeply? As if to wonder if there is a missing complexification that will somehow overcome the underlying unsustainability and make them work; why would I commit to memory, or labor to research further, practices that are proven invalid and unsustainable by observation? Why would I choose to teach practices that are invalidated by Scientific Method?

This reality has in no way slowed down well-sponsored Economists like Milton Friedman (the "Capitalism invented everything" guy), Ann

Rand ("Greed is Good") and Allan Greenspan ("Trickle-down Economics", "Low Interest Rates", and "Low Tax"); household names that were not only incorrect in their directions, but research proved them socially irresponsible as well.

Transition Economics is none of these things; it is Scientific and Socially Responsible from inception, but readers will have to make up their own minds about the research presented here before diving deeper. This is what I would do; this is how I would do it as a reader. For this reason I will introduce throttle algorithms in two steps.

GDP Quality

The measurement of overall GDP is a summary aggregate of all transactions registered throughout the country. This number is only useful in comparison to other countries when ranking relative size from one country's economy to the next - as I can determine. The value of a country's GDP will broadly allow us to compare how large is your reporting of commerce compared to others but little useful information can be gleaned simply by itself.

Drilling down into the GDP, however, reveals important information about the efficiency and performance of your economy. Answers to Questions like: Are you importing more than exporting? Wealth is created by taking revenue from exporting your productions, so monetizing these productions are of essential importance to creating wealth.

Diverse Exports of high quality & high profit manufactured goods, like cars, pharmaceuticals, and technology, are preferred to commodity exports like coal, iron ore, and similar, which sell for pennies per ton on a highly competitive fluctuating world market.

High GDP Imports indicate that your citizens are unable to be self-sufficient and prefer instead to pay other countries so that those other countries can monetize their economies and build what is needed.

Maintaining a trade deficit; having more wealth leave the country than enters in - over time, diminishes the country just like it would any household. Many consecutive years of trade deficits can lead to real weakening as it did for the Soviet Union in 1986.

Incomes were always very low in the Eastern-European countries so I suspect that the U.S.S.R. did not collapse, as much as they more-likely preferred to align with the successful financial best-practices of their G8 trading partners who were successful in monetizing their economies through the 1950s, 60s, and 70s.

China remains the unprecedented champion of planning policies which successfully monetized their economy; China advanced more than any other nation for 30-years. This job of economy building was a mammoth effort for China because much of its one-billion population was just emerging from the stone-age 30-years ago.

GDP Export

I have always maintained that one of the best indicators of success for any country is their GDP Export per Capita. High GDP Export per Capita usually indicates high productivity across labor forces including retirement age people, and it is usually related to high quality exports as well.

The GINI Index is a good indicator of wealth distribution and the relative comfort of all citizens in low to high income brackets. More often than not, Socialistic Policy nations score best on the GINI Index and, more often than not, those same countries are among the highest GDP Export per Capita nations in the world as well.

These statistics are readily available online – just google the Wikipedia list. The GINI Index is above and on wiki as well. The CMI at CSQ Research combines this information to speak to each country's Management Team Performance as well.

Tax Revenue & Tax Increases

Taxes generated from citizens goes into treasuries large and small. The policies that these funds pay for determine will your society succeed or collapse entirely – as discussed above.

Conservatives are individuals who want to manage spending more carefully – just in case something goes pear-shaped and emergency funds are needed. These are the folks who will want to insist on a Business Case every time government spending is suggested.

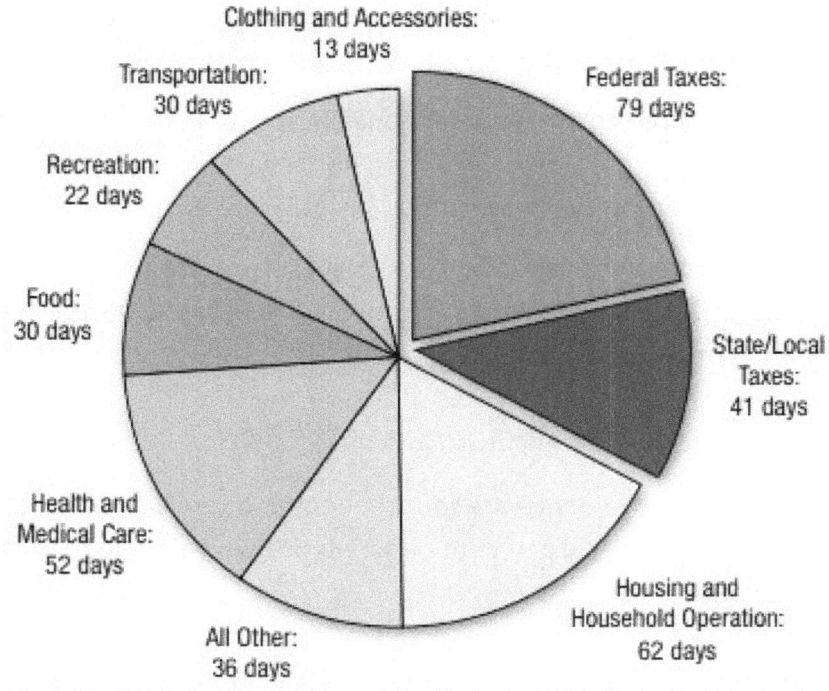

There are Conservatives in socialistic nations and Conservatives in capitalistic nations just the same – although their training on what is a Conservative spending policy might be very different.

Business Cases are very strong for Socialistic Policy based on GDP Export per Capita stats that I mentioned above.

A new Carbon Tax might have an excellent Return on Investment or it might offer no social benefit whatsoever depending on what this new income is used to fund. A Carbon Tax is probably not a great tax when it stimulates Part-time Renewable Energy Projects like Wind Farms for example.

Based on GDP Export returns, a country would take more benefit from taxes that spend on Guaranteed Incomes, DayCare, Free Education, Retirement Cost of Living Guarantees, and Renewable Automation. These are Income generation programs that will keep the economy strong at the same time.

Tax rates are not the problem; responsible spending that stimulates the economy, guarantees incomes for everyone, and returns spending power are the conservative tax programs to prefer.

But are tax increases needed at all? It might surprise you to learn that the answer to that question is "Probably not." based on the next discussion on Tax Laws and Tax Evasion.

Tax Laws and Tax Avoidance

Examples of tax avoidance are too frequent and too large to ignore. Tax evasion – the illegal payment of tax – is probably dwarfed by legal tax avoidance arguments.

In Canada, Revenue Agencies target individuals and small business because from experience, they realize that the teams of up to 100 lawyers at major businesses and even Canada's own Banks - are far too sophisticated to be collected from. Major Canadian Banks like CIBC, ScotiaBank, and Royal Bank's presence in the Cayman Islands gave that Tax Haven the early credibility it needed to attract 75% of the World's Hedge Funds as well.

Often, when Canadian Revenue Agents do finally find a way to collect on an illegal corporate tax dodge, the Supreme Court has sided with Business so that those tax avoidance cases have been permitted legally. Loopholes are set up in tax law with the intention to benefit local companies, but these options are exploited and then no-one ever goes back to confirm that the loopholes are in fact benefitting Canada as well.

This leaves frustrated Revenue Authorities with few other options than to come to pursue private citizens aggressively to pay for social programs.

"The Great Canadian Tax Dodge" ... http://tvo.org/video/documentaries/the-great-canadian-tax-dodge, is one of many documentaries which explain that Business Exceptions (right-offs), complicated tax avoidance mechanisms, and offshore tax havens enabled very well-paid tax specialists to avoid incredible amounts of tax – and this story is true in the U.K., U.S. and really everywhere else globally now.

Revenue Canada estimates that $100 billion to $170 billion dollars leaves Canada untaxed every year - to tax havens around the world, costing that country up to $80 billion in tax revenue that would otherwise go to pay for social programs. Often monies sit offshore in zero and negative return accounts doing nothing despite arguments that some of the money makes it back to its host countries where it creates jobs and pays tax. Tax Justice Experts assure that these claims are nonsense.

Statistics Canada reports that $100 billion reside in just three islands

– Barbados, Bermuda, and Cayman Islands which hold close to $2 trillion in contributions from all countries. Canada's debt is $636 billion - for comparison to your country – growing at a rate of $80 million per day. (TaxPayer.com, 2016)

Tax Fairness movements in Canada, the U.S., and elsewhere actively examine the issue of tax avoidance, and the exposing of sophisticated corporate strategies and tax loopholes commonly used to legally avoid tax. (Mirza, 2015)

Industry tax specialist Junaid Mirza cautions that "Simply turning off the tap on tax avoidance may not return a $100 billion increase in tax revenues for the Canadian government. "While revenues are likely to go up in the short-term, there is much academic research that suggests a decrease in investments would follow an increase in tax rates (or effective tax rates given inability to take advantages of tax planning). So that $100 billion, over time, is likely to be fairly close to zero."

Mr. Mirza's points are very valid, but upon reading, one realizes that there would be no negative impact in turning off the Tax Avoidance tap overnight, only benefit; and that with global financial regulatory controls in place, we would also not see other unregulated Tax Haven's absorb avoided tax in their place.

Tax Consultants, legal firms, accounting firms, tax havens, and handfuls of special interest Financial Services individuals benefit at the expense of every other member of society in these structures, so really I should not have to suggest that these structures are unsustainable, and nor should they.

I raised five kids and I find myself looking on these cases as a parent would look upon my children behaving in a socially unacceptable way in polite company. Society needs this now too; to reign in irresponsible behavior firmly again. No-one likes to feel reigned-in nor controlled - and for this reason, voluntary, pro-active social responsibility is always a preferable, albeit a sadly unreliable first option.

Chapter 19

CSR & Sustainable Business

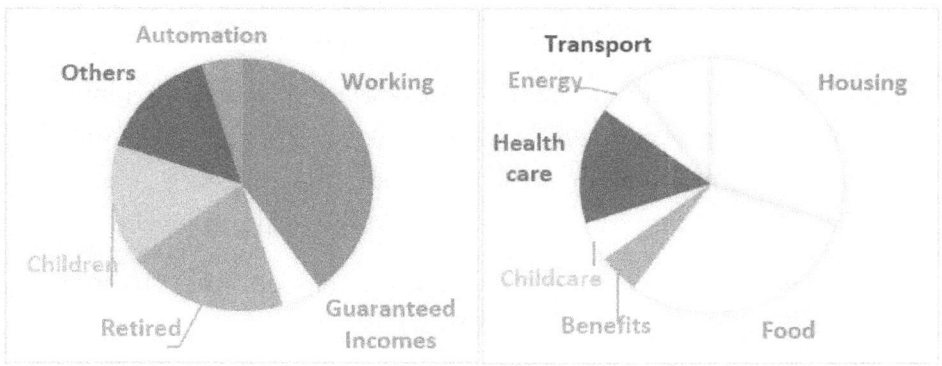

In the 2013 Oxford University Press publication "Firm Commitment", Colin Mayer explains in great detail why the corporation is failing us. Professor Mayor states that the corporation has created more prosperity and misery than ever imagined and that the balance is moving increasingly to the latter direction as it now threatens to consume us. These are failings that we now need to address as a matter of urgency.

Alignment and Accountability to Corporate Social Responsibility – CSR, in major corporations is among the most pressing issues in many societies today. CEOs, CFOs, Crown and State Government Procurement Departments, Hedge Fund managers, and most every business school grad today - is taught, and rewarded based upon business ethics that externalize social costs. What are social costs?

Taxes that pay for road networks and other systems essential to the success of the business, healthcare and pension costs, education, security, and other social systems that permit a business to generate profit.

The problem is recognized internationally and push-backs by lawmakers, although increasingly punitive, have done little in the past to correct a primary contributor to social collapse near the end of a capitalist cycle.

In 2015, Monsanto was brought before the World Court in The Hague under charge of Ecocide and Crimes against humanity.

Major Lending, Investment, and Risk organizations are just beginning to implement CSR Leads and Corporate Social Responsibility Policy that are inserting new considerations into Due Diligence approval workflows for lending and support of socially irresponsible clients.

High-Social-Cost behaviors - such as eradicating pensions, offshoring (also called globalization and offshoring), subsistence starvation-level minimum wages, tax and benefits dodges, and even mass eviction – have all become a norm in our largest corporations. Still, many of these socially irresponsible practices will get you bonuses or promoted at most any financially motivated companies today. Arguments that sound like "we won't be able to compete" have run 71% of all countries and half of G8 and G20 countries into a collapsing trend at this point.

Reconciling CSR and Sustainability Metrics

35 years ago, lucky investors who saw the first wave of personal computing as the future and who then invested heavily in fledgling companies like IBM, Microsoft, Oracle and similar, enjoyed a career of winning investment gains. The next wave of winning companies

and investment will come from companies that lead in renewable automations that create year-over-year efficiency and profitability.

High Sustainability countries are widely considered the better investment choice today. (UNRUH et al., 2016)

CSQ Research's RAI Company Index would call out Google as a technology company that has already set out to bridge this renewable automation and sustainability puzzle - beginning with the introduction of its driverless car business units.

Government Controls

Canada and the United Kingdom are in worse shape economically than others in recent years because they permit the wholesale offshoring of engineering - and other Collapse Policies. China was the recipient of much of their lost manufacturing revenue and then it invested heavily in automation and sustainable self-sufficiency. Needless to say, China does not offshore its Engineering.

The Offshoring of Engineering is a practice that the Netherlands outlawed twenty years ago and a process that America, Germany, and other nations, have started to correct very recently.

The Dutch legislated social responsibility in all aspects of their businesses 20-years ago and the reward was to give a country the size of Lake Ontario, an export GDP 20% larger than Canada and Russia.

When engineers and doctors harm society, they lose their license and can't practice: when business harms society by externalizing social costs, they get a bonus.

When politicians permit these behaviors, we vote for them and give them another mandate to do harm.

We are accountable as voters too of course; so voters need to be voting for engineers and not salespeople too. By electing business leads and career politicians that exacerbate these unproductive behaviors in many G7 countries, we establish a trend in which society will likely continue to struggle.

Controls are not always popular; TE Maturity's proven business-case-driven policies are important for sustainability just the same. An engineer will tell you what you need - and not what you want - from time to time.

Good Process Never Takes Longer

Democracy is an underpinning to sustainable World Peace and yet some democracies fair better than others. In the G7, a case could be made to say that more than half of elected Government Legislatures "wasted" 45 years eliminating a Good Life for the near-majority of their electorate. In those same years, in Denmark, Sweden, Netherlands, and Norway, 38 Million democratic electing voters preserved their Good Life. So, what was different between the G8 and these socialistic nations?

People of the rugged north, like people of the desert, realize that when they fail to feed a traveler or shelter him in a storm, that that person is being left to die as a certainty. Communities refused this outcome realizing that the next time it happens, it might be them or their children, who need help. These values were handed down from father to son, which embedded these thinking into their nation's basic values. With populations of 5 to 20 million, these were smaller democracies that could recognize and vote to correct bad policy much more easily than could a 360 million citizen and larger democracy.

These countries defended a Good Life - and their socialistic policies ensured support of each citizen's pension, healthcare, education, and childcare needs as a basic human right. This was hard work, with many detractors, costs, and attacks – but they defended their fundamental values and then they profited from it as well; they never lost the American Dream because they protected their values.

As a member of executive teams, I have seen good leadership and process in the boardroom. I have also seen meetings with the exact same people descend into chaos in the absence of a good process leader to direct them as well.

Anyone who has sat through a government or committee meeting has seen this too. When filibusters, emotional outbursts, over speaking, and other tools of delay and persuasion are thought needed and important, you are simply experiencing a situation in which good problem-solving process is absent.

As elected officials and assigned leaders, your duty is, therefore, to adjourn emotional meeting discussions and work to regain a professional and productive momentum again. Seek the advice of strong engineering leads when efforts to gain a productive momentum fail.

Politicians, who fail to do so, abuse the public trust and the business mandate that grants them permission to lead.

Revisit Law and Policy Regularly

Policies are meant to be reviewed on a regular basis and so too should the laws that support them. If laws are not monitored and updated when needed, they may not be accomplishing their intended purpose. I will cite the tax law and tax avoidance laws discussion above as an example.

If the law is protecting tax evasion and harming society, revisit it annually and if all is well, revisit it every four or five years to permit any anew information. Insufficient social supports drive 50 Canadian men a week to suicide, so social supports are not policies nor laws that can remain unvisited year after year.

This is the purpose of forced revision control protocols within the SUSTAIN Project Management Method explained here in the book. Initial laws and policies are v1.0s, version one; and then there will be a version 2.0, 3.0, 3.1 and so on. When the economy is doing well, the rate of revisit and update might be lower, and in winter economies where failing social problems are killing people, there will need to be more frequent requirement reviews.

Requirements change relatively more often than designs and monitored operational changes - and so scheduling the next revision of a law, permits stakeholders to prepare statistics and is a sign of a healthy, active, and transparent legal and policy system. In the end, all projects, laws and policies should be accountable to contribute to an improving society; failing this is grounds to revisit the project.

Designing Accountability

"Blame" is a very important legal term used when assessing financial and criminal accountabilities in a court of law. Blame looks to the past and assesses whether financial and criminal penalties should be levied or awarded to persons involved in unfortunate events that unfolded because of accident or intent.

For the most part, discussion of "blame" is best left in the courtroom as little more than lessons-learned can be gleaned by visiting events of the past in project work. Progress for the World Peace Agenda is expressed in status meetings and providing status reports on KPI targets as these are the best measure of performance.

If pension obligations appear to be shrinking year after year within our major businesses, where do those social obligations fall next? They shift to Pension Plans of that citizen's home country – and yet we hear nothing of these problems in the news. Present Conservatives and Republicans seem adamant to support business with no regard for social accountability whatsoever.

Once businesses, and business leaders, meet KPIs that include social accountability in quarterly and annual reporting, we are probably on the right track toward making businesses socially accountable.

Imagine what would be the impact if G8 countries agreed together to ban companies from their markets who did not meet minimum obligations for socially responsible business practices. I imagine that it would take just the smallest level of enforcement to turn the corporation back into the society-building asset that it once was. If the biggest markets on the planet all pulled products from the shelves of, no CEO could hope to keep his position.

The requirement of CSR should be a cornerstone of Business Ethics and KPI monitoring ensure that both profitability and social accountability are delivered reliably.

Business Accountability

Recalling the work of Dr. Mayer of Oxford University in the first paragraphs of this chapter.

Failure rates at major engineering universities are 20% to 30% despite the highest screening of any programs; I have never heard of an eMBA that did not graduate and yet MBAs are often thrust into roles that manage Technology or Engineering even within technology and engineering organizations, major airports, and similar.

An inverse correlation exists between society's forward progress and crowded executive administrator pools until finally, we begin to see major corporations pulled into The Hague under charge of Ecocide and Crimes against Humanity in 2015. Major Lending, Investment, and Risk organizations are just now beginning to implement CSR

Leads – heads of Corporate Social Responsibility Policy - that embed new Accountability Policies into Due Diligence approval workflows.

As long as the trend of CSR accountability can persist, there is every chance of a turn-around in investor-driven change for the better.

Consider also a typical corporation operating executive team – say a pension fund, or major airport, which might include a CEO, CFO, CAO/HR, COO, CIO, SVP Sales, and SVP Marketing. There are one or two engineers to as many as five or more admins and yet all have an equal vote at the boardroom table. Human resources, finance, and C-level administration stewards have accelerated hiring and bonuses to their ranks based on their boardroom voting numbers as well.

If engineering, or social-leaning voices are strong, they risk being marginalized or not permitted at the table; to be replaced by Non-SME generalists like MBAs, by the majority votes of other executive administrators.

From our discussion of Accountability and social responsibility above, this organizational design gives the strongest voice to those who are trained in Business Ethics classes - and not prevented by licensing - to externalize social costs with indifference to society's needs. Boards of Directors too, are often structured with far heavier administrative and financial votes.

Solutions to this accountability problem are implemented in Germany already. Here, workers vote for their executive team members. This means that Executives who have poor track records for socially irresponsible behavior, cannot be elected into the boardroom. Other controls might include the licensing of business leads in the same way that we license engineers and doctors today.

Whichever solution you choose, a choice must be made now. Business Accountability begins by revamping the Business Ethics programs within our biggest and richest business schools and in boardrooms everywhere.

Corruption

Corruption happens in every system, the dishonest or fraudulent conduct or bribery of those in power.

Monarchy was thought to be a protection from corruption, as these families were exempt from financial burden in perpetuity and history judged harsh abuses of their vows of service to the realm's greater good. Democracies, in contrast, could be persuaded relatively easily in comparison, as elected officials had to rely upon their incomes to provide for their family's needs.

How can this housing system keep corruption to a minimum and to the exception? There should be a reporting process. There should be a timely appeals process. Can complainants request changes to assigned committee leads? Ask for an answer to all of these questions in the Requirements and Design phases on your Project.

Mitigating Multinational Business Extortion

Extortion is a strong word, especially at a time when it is in the interests of both business and consumers to share economic benefit until a redistribution of wealth can sustain strong capitalist momentum again in a new K-Wave Spring.

No politician wants jobs lost within their electoral boundaries, and so governments have often made generous payments to multinational companies to keep jobs from being moved away in a brand of extortion that could have benefited society elsewhere. An example of this happened with GM in Oshawa, Ontario, Canada in early 2015. Lexus was given a generous subsidy immediately following this move without even asking, to pre-empt the possibility of an announcement that they too could leave.

To mitigate extortion – a problem that costs both Canada and Mexico money and jobs lost back and forth over time, all that these two NAFTA Trading Partners have to do is to work collaboratively to ensure that companies cannot operate in socially irresponsible ways. GM in this example might be required to set up production in both countries – or face penalties that limit their market access in both or all three countries. A win-win-win for Mexico, Canada, and the United States as the car maker continues to have access to sales markets and skilled labor in all three countries.

If all agree that the Netherlands' advice and fiscal GDP track record holds merit, a production plant would be set up in the United States as well.

Transition Economic for Business

Transition Economics for Business covers a broad range of important subjects from Corporate Social Responsibility education and strategy, to weathering, contributing, leading and profiting from the transition ahead, to leveraging and building solutions in Renewable Automation. Look for the book Transition Economics for Business - coming soon.

Chapter 20

—

Government Thought-Leadership

"Transition Economics" discusses social policies and their track-records in 180 countries; and it explains that 72% of all countries internationally are in a Collapsing trend right now. In 600 pages, this book lays out a plan to turn around the 72% countries using the lessons-learned from the 28% that are growing - and it explains that governments must plan and lead the way.

What are the next steps for civil servants charged with forwarding policies that correct their country's current situations?

Government must lead Technology

From our discussions above, Government must lead major advances in technology by leveraging its own Research Councils, independent think-tanks, academia and then finally business (as a secondary and supplier). This is true in history and it is even truer today in our finance-laden and litigious business landscape.

For government directors, this means that they have to get very good at recognizing, supporting and leveraging thought-leadership. Those who are good at it need promotion and those who are not good at it need to sit in admin capacity or millions of people will suffer. Take a look around and ask are there multi-billion dollar technology companies being created. If the answer is no and long-standing administrators have corrected shortcomings, replace these program decision-makers with engineers immediately.

Thought-leadership is not IQ; it is definitely not EQ, I call personal thought improvement CSQ in one of my books - but what Thought-Leadership really is, is a system of planning that has the highest possible probability of a positive outcome for society. Aristotle called this planning a "Right Plan" and think-tanks like CSQ Research support the building of Right Plans - as should we all.

At this time in our economic cycle, governments want to license the financial rewards of Renewable Automation to Business; ensuring that automated services are available for all, and ensuring that we can recover our investments in R&D, guaranteed incomes and Engineering Safety Nets. Perhaps governments should look to own or part-own all renewable automation smart factory patents in law too.

Consider in all of these discussions that anything less works against a sustainable society, leaves us with the unworkable Cancer industry model discussed in Chapter 10, and therefore has to be considered poor sustainability planning that is in no-one's best interest.

Fund Automation in a Focused and Planned Way

Automation will feed us, manufacture medicines, it will build housing and energy plants, it will pave and then drive our roads; Automation will also make money for us at the same time that it makes money problems quite a bit less important. Automation, therefore, is our greatest risk mitigation to international financial collapse and so we have to plan for it and we have to fund it generously.

WHAT DOES IT TAKE?
TO BUILD A RIGHT PLAN

Allocating $800 million of a $120 billion infrastructure budget (4%) is not "funding generously". Think big and not of mom-and-pop businesses levels initially; small grant programs are well and good but will ever return investment intermittently and usually in unsustainable technology only. Instead, make big commitments to solve specific big problems, for example:

In Infrastructure spending: Building a road without building a "robotic road-builder" at the same time; or in Housing: building a home without a home-building robot; means that next year the roads and houses will not simply build nor repair themselves, and without these robots the need for massive infrastructure spending will continue without end.

Public Transit investment makes little sense except in only the largest urban settings as driverless cars will make point-to-point transit dramatically less expensive than today's inconvenient and expensive buses and drivers.

A robotic road builder, home builder, point-to-point driverless transit etc. will take one to two years to design and build a first v1.0 Pilot. We would use these solutions ourselves and then we could resell it internationally as well.

Russia failed to sell its cars and watches where China and German succeeded; the difference between monetizing and not monetizing is in the attention to features and finish quality – so incent workers to build great robots. China has been 3D-Printing six-story buildings since 2013 and its cars have begun to rival German cars in just ten short years.

Citizens want their country to be a World Leader.

A country cannot usually do it all, so focus becomes key to success.

Canada can be a World Leader and make a positive impact very quickly, by supporting and promoting #WPProjects as a Canadian Plan – and so can your country. China has one-billion people and is rich from great planning too. One or two countries in the world can go head-to-head for technology leadership against China in everything at this time.

To become a World Leader, a country has to focus based on a long-term plan. South Korea focused on electronics; Japan on electronics, scientific equipment and cars; Hong Kong – cars; Germany – transportation and manufacturing equipment, and so on.

The #WPProjects' global approach assigns 250 automation projects to 200 countries so that everything that every country can be a leader at the same time that all of society's automation needs can be built in a quick and coordinated way. WP Projects assigned the following sustainable renewable automations to Canada for example:

In Tier 1 - Food, mining, farming, lumber, raw resources: Satellite Water Divining, Collection, and Packaging & Distribution

Tier 2 - Manufacturing, Baking, Food Prep, etc.: Drone Jets & Air Transport / Logistics

Tertiary Supporting industries - Energy: Clean Energy - Cold Fusion

Build an Engineering Safety Net

Income supports and funded education for individuals and small startup companies that want to build Sustainable Renewable Automation and Local IP (Intellectual Property) are essential.

Traditional Businesses, and especially startups, have to afford expensive finance and tax avoidance people to make their way. 50% of Waterloo Engineering grads leave the country immediately after graduation because engineering careers are not supported locally.

Governments can create "safe zones" for uninterrupted development – and they absolutely need to do this as well.

Engineers just want to build - and that is not always possible in many job settings.

Even large world-class engineering organizations have realized this problem and had to make this shift. NASA is a good. We have thousands of retired and out of work engineers in every country right now - let's put them to work.

Being a success just takes support. Salesforce is a mult-billion-dollar company that was started by Larry Ellison of Oracle when he signed a cheque for $30 million to one of his in-house VPs over in the lobby of their Mississauga Matheson offices. Multi-billion-dollar companies take support and engineering leadership to build. The VP assigned to CEO Salesforce was a weak engineering lead so it took the company many years to prosper, but support was consistent and so are the results.

Canada has not focused on its support of startups, they offer very small accelerator and $10k, $100k contest gifts but investment capital is scarce and decision-makers are uninvested finance leads - and as a result they have no skypes, no Airbnbs, no Microsofts; MARs and Innovatech are local Hi-tech Incubators that have really been wasted investments for the Governments of Canada as a result.

I brought an AirBnb ($25 billion market-cap in 2015) "Killer" company called TekRealtor/TheHomeDeal to Innovatech and MARs in 2009. I sat in large halls full of other startup companies, and comment after comment from the group was that none could find the sales funding that they needed.

Engineers must Lead

I heard this message loudly and clearly at a recent CEO Workshop that I attended with the Canadian Federal Innovation, Sciences and Economic Development Ministry. Progress is too often held back by finance and administrator generalists who are either not invested in moving society forward or simply do not know how. I talked about this historically confirmable phenomenon in my last book as well.

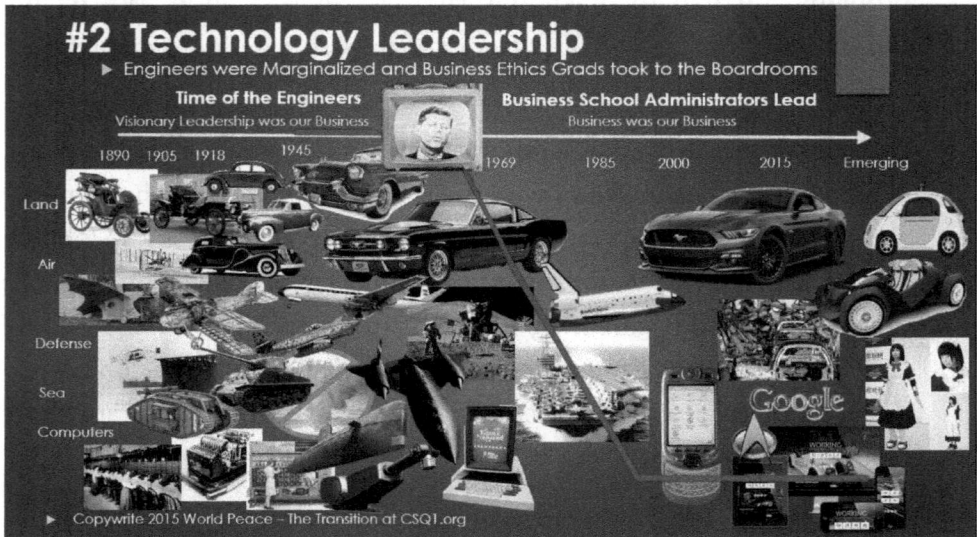

Engineers are not necessarily just tin ring holders, by using the term "engineers" I am also referring to career big-project builders and startup leads. People who understand a bit of everything from programing, to business cases, to leading 200 project staff and who have a mastery of SUSTAIN Project Management Method as well.

I am a career hi-tech lead and engineer; I can assure that Canada like every country, have tremendous, bright engineering minds. The weak link for many countries is in failing to find this engineering and entrepreneurial mindset in Government administrators and elected officials.

When thought-leadership is not revered; when it is not supported, the country will have suffered in the same way that academia has suffered from its ultraconservative and inward-looking peer-review processes - and the end product observation of its very poor result. Canada - as evidenced in its place among collapsing economies; and academia in its supplying of the economists, lawyers and business grads that have created a world economy with a 72% collapsing rate.

Life's messy, Clean it up

Business Accountability laws, tax evasion corrections, housing and anti-eviction controls, foreign ownership limits, engineering safety-nets and protections from offshoring, legal system acknowledgement of social obligation and freedoms, to name just a few policies that governments need on top of. Here is a hint: The Netherlands did it and so should you.

Chapter 21

-

Democratic Reform

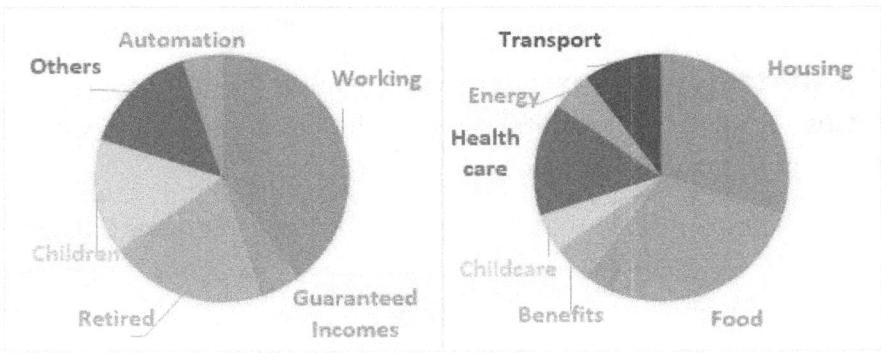

The improvement of democracy is a ongoing necessity that we must recognize and all stand in support of over time. An important part of part of democracy's success will be the ability to make changes based on expert direction too. With time, any system — regardless of its merits - can be corrupted. Corrupted, and systems turned counter to the tenants of democracy and the definitions of the first written Constitution — the Mayflower Compact, which succinctly stated:

"***We** ... covenant and **combine ourselves together into a civil body** politic; **for our better** ordering, and preservation and **furtherance of** the ends aforesaid; and by virtue hereof to enact, constitute, and frame, such **just and equal laws**, ordinances, acts, constitutions, and offices, from time to time, **as shall be thought most meet and convenient for the general good of the colony**; unto which we promise all due submission and obedience.*"

Abridged   November 11th, 1620

You might as well have laughed as cried over having to vote for the best-of-the-worst in North America this year, and most other G20 nations have similarly upset citizenry grasping to demand "Change".

This was the setting in the last K-Wave Winter - during the very early 1930s. European electorate chose Hitler, Mussolini; and elected fringe parties to high positions similar to today.

Anyone who suggests that Democratic Reform is undemocratic - is clearly protecting either a special interest or poor judgment. Whenever the needs of the democracy are overlooked to the point of protest votes such as these, Democratic Reform is in fact, an imperative.

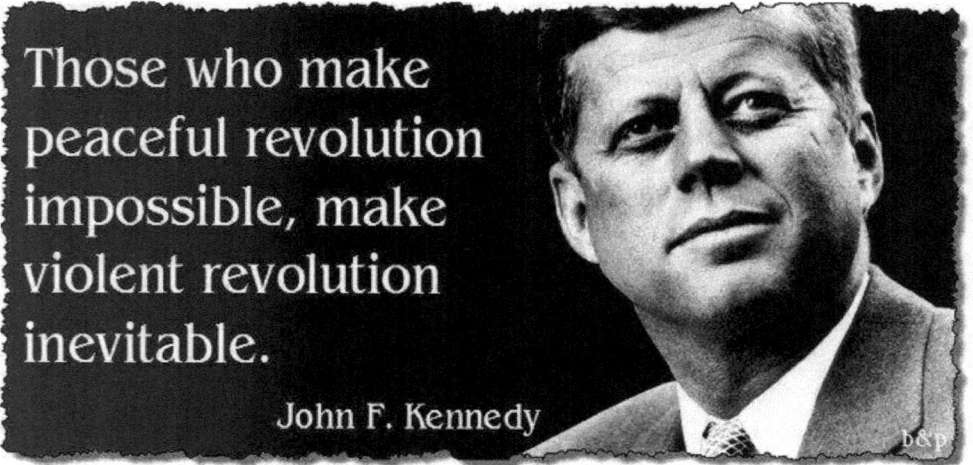

The coming years will really have to be spent reforming democracy in order to give voters the technology and training to let them vote for policy directly. The election of an individual to speak for voters was a limitation forced on us by practical considerations that don't exist any longer.

Benjamin Franklin said that "When the people find that they can vote themselves money, that will herald the end of the Republic", he was right of course, and the wealthiest 1% certainly have that now as well.

Whenever money can influence both elected officials and policy creation, you have the essentials of corruption and the mandate to design corrections that mitigate the problem.

In the U.S., a golden opportunity was missed with Bernie Sanders - who would have also soundly defeated Donald Trump. The U.S. loses $500 billion annually to Inequity; the cost of leaving 160 million fellow citizens with nothing - without the ability to start businesses that generate GDP Export Wealth and prosperity for the country.

Franklin Roosevelt's terrific quote is:

Democracy cannot succeed unless those who express their choice are prepared to choose wisely. The real safeguard of democracy, therefore, is education."

But understanding that by "education", one does not need an Ivy League education in Economics is important too. Obviously if Ivy School Economics PhDs were going to save global economies, that result would have already come to pass. Rather, the education that we need must be in a high-school Civics class that teaches us how to examine the world through the eyes of both a Business Case and also as a Parent who would want only good things for their children.

I wrote CSQ Common Sense 101 to be that course - and the learning that I took away by writing it, took six another six books to explain.

Education – can - be that powerful.

Education is like the computer and democracy; they are an invaluable tool, and they are what we make them. Either can lead us to, or away, from a sustainable Good Life as a society - depending entirely upon what we do with it.

Separating Wheat from Chaff

Superficial or unfounded messages of transparency, gender equality and accountability are tossed around with no intention of tracking progress, following up on, nor improving routinely today. It seems like wherever it is possible to appear inclusive but not to not be inclusive at the same time, which is the direction most politicians and their party leads seem to prefer to take.

Managing thousands of voices is impossible without terrific processes and most countries are in a varying state of maturity with their systems to manage this. Transition Economics and TE Maturity Models address this problem directly by establishing rules and approaches for looking for the best possible Policy for your country and communities – but these are new sciences not yet communicated to our societies.

The role of Government in Economic Policy is straightforward – keep the economy's wealth distributed and growing. Unfortunately, this responsibility of governments both left and right, is not well understood by democratically elected politicians, nor voters, who need to make correct course corrections at specific turning points in a Capitalist K-Wave cycle.

Capitalism troughs every 60 years due to compounding Interest, the year-over-year expectation of higher profits; the rich begin earning day and night; after enough time passes there are only rich and poor

– just like any game of Monopoly that you will ever play. These cycles have repeated within our capitalist civilizations for at least 4000 years - as mentioned, and so we can only hope to change this inherent instability of Capitalism when we manage wealth distribution proactively.

The start of a new economic cycle, the one right after World War II for one example, is a time in which the distribution of wealth within a society is relatively even. Everyone has what they need, a single family income provides all the basics, and a good life is available to everyone in society. This beginning is referred to by economists as the Spring of a Capitalist K-Wave Cycle.

Spring carries on like a monopoly game would - players buy houses easily, begin to collect preferred, high earning property and businesses and then start generating revenue by renting them out and earning income from these investments. Incomes were distributed across society somewhat evenly – similar to this pie-chart below where there are rich people, but that those top 20% of high-income earners control 35% of the wealth; the next 20% had about 25%, and the Lowest had 11 % of the wealth.

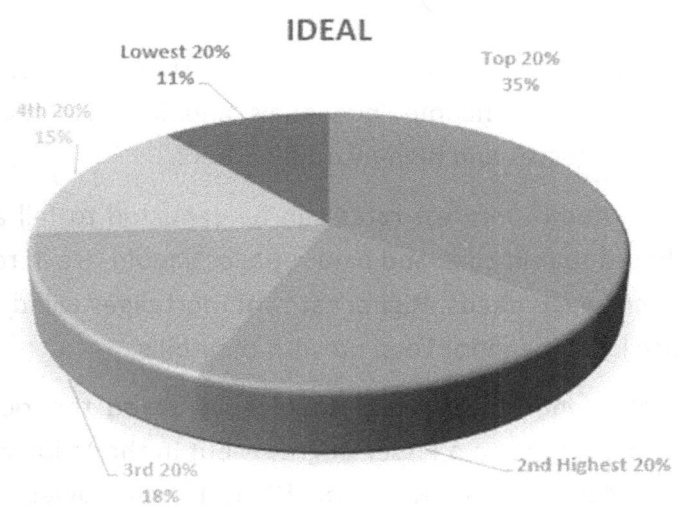

Michael I. Norton and Dan Ariely suggested the following arbitrary targets in their report "Building a better America – One Wealth Quintile at a time" (Norton & Ariely, 2011). The actual values assigned to each quintile are less important; the important task here is to create targets and manage wealth distribution to those targets.

In K-Wave Summer, some business owners start to make investment money available – initially at a higher interest rate. There are relatively few takers but still a few members of society start amassing wealth. Speculating and rental investment continues until all houses are gone and competition for homes drives up prices quickly. In the Toronto suburbs in 1982, a home could be bought for $30,000 at 22% interest annually. By 1986, four years later, the same house cost $90,000, and rates were 10%. By 2012, the house could be worth $500,000 with an interest rate at 3%. The notion of reality left real estate prices somewhere within this window of time.

As K-Wave summer ends, the Good Life too is ending now for many, and will be available for fewer and fewer families going forward now - until young adults do not have the same easy start in life that their parents did. Many families feel they need two salaries to afford a living at this time.

The end of a summer K-Wave is the time, in economic terms, to begin reducing tax to low-income individuals and increase the tax to successful businesses and high-income earners.

In K-Wave Autumn, interest rates can be expected to fall and fall, houses should soar in cost, and bankruptcies should rise in response to higher mortgage needs. Higher rates of mortgages will default as people lose jobs or cannot keep up with their bills.

The correct economic controls would have taxed the rich more heavily, and the poor to a lesser degree – but in the following chart "Historical Marginal Tax Rate for Highest and Lowest Income

Earners", the opposite happened throughout the 1980s.

Tax rates of 91% and more were levied on High-income earners in the 1940s through 1960s. By 1985, high-income tax rates were reduced to 28% and 35%. In 2012, the highest tax rate was lifted to 40%.

Taxes on the lowest income level hovered around 15% throughout the boom years of the spring and summer K-Wave, until the tax rate was reduced to zero for the poor in 1977. In the late 1980s, the tax rate for the lowest income earners returned to 15% and then has remained at 10% since 2003. (Blodget, 2011)

You have seen the Federal Reserve Pie Chart in Chapter 5, and below, that describes 2010's income distributions. In this chart, the bottom 40% of American's share 0.3% of the wealth, and the top 20%, share more wealth than all of the GDP of the G20 combined.

The point here is, that we all should have been able to see inequity of this magnitude coming - and then our government and voters should have prevented it from becoming as extreme as this was obviously going to become as well.

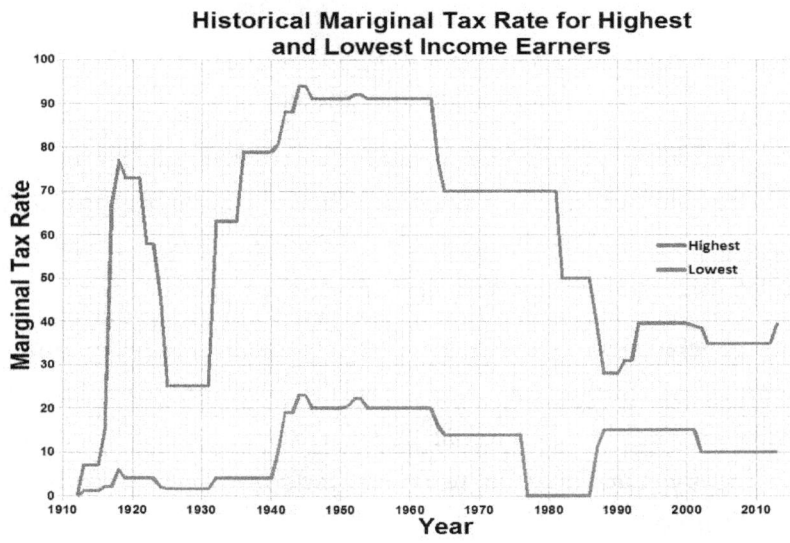

Today our income distributions are extreme for two groups; the rich, who should have stood up to insist on doing the right thing by society; and second, to every other one of us who voted for low taxes in every election since the 1970s.

The Pitfalls of Managing Proactively

What if our country had a President, Prime Minister, or Monarch who knew enough about Capitalist Economies and K-Waves to realize that a sixty-year cycle of wealth inequity was headed our way? As a good and responsible leader, he or she would have decided to prevent a calamitous outcome by implementing appropriate economic controls when wealth was still quite distributed in the Spring or early Summer - back in the 1950s through 1970s.

Finding a leader with a good grasp of K-Wave Economic Controls would have been a tall order. Although documented in 1925 - and in many economic thesis since, my five High School and University economics courses made no mention of it.

John F Kennedy acknowledged the need to manage society's revolutions proactively in 1962 with his famous quote:

"Those who make peaceful revolution impossible will make violent revolution inevitable."

Without fail, every politician that ran for election in the United States with a message of the importance of economic controls that tax the rich and proactively ensure wealth distribution – was voted down and never had a chance of making it into office.

At this crucial time, Americans voted instead for a wonderful, charming, untrained leader with a heart of gold - in Ronald Reagan. Reaganomics was an economic policy that embraced the Trickle-Down Theory and next it was also adopted into the U.K. as Thatchernomics.

Trickle-down said that "What was good for the rich and good for business, was good for society." Reaganomics gave money to the rich, and the rich would administer its trickling down into society with virtually no monitoring of the policy's success or failure by the government after that.

The campaign message of "Low Taxes" got Reagan nominated; "Low Taxes" got him voted President in 1981, and it reelected him again in 1985 – echoing a too long period of previous campaigns promising "low taxes" at a time when roads and highways were crumbling. Citizens began to abandon Major city centers due to neglect and security concerns. I can remember that administrators decided to close sidewalks in Buffalo rather than to repair collapsing buildings in their city center.

To not campaign based on "Low Taxes" was not to get elected in the United States and soon "Low Taxes" encouraged irresponsible administration too.

Outside the G8, Norway enacted strong economic controls proactively 25 years ago. Today they have very low unemployment (3%), universal healthcare, a $20 minimum wage, the seventh best income equity in the world, and the highest GDP exports per capita (wealth generation) annually for the past 20 years. Anyone looking for clues as to where the "American Dream" went, can look to Norway to find it protected and thriving here.

Norway's economy looks like a very smart Government Management Team's Performance Report. I suspect that it is no mere coincidence that the Nobel Peace Prize, and the Nobel Prize for Economics in neighboring Sweden, were founded here within Norway's very sustainable society.

Economic Controls - Right and Left

When wealth distributions can become this extreme, with all the negative social problems and embarrassment associated, neither Right nor Left parties are enforcing responsible economic controls.

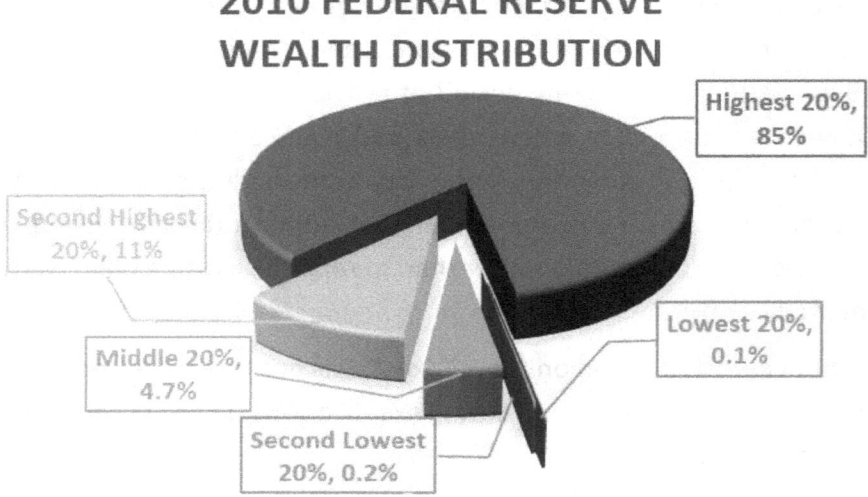

Essential services like hospitals must remain open, the ambulance must come when called, school children have to take a good education within secure communities – and we must avoid trough wars that gain support from destitute citizens in every economic depression.

For the first time, our technology is within just twenty years of ending our reliance on money altogether as well. Now is finally the time to stop voting for "Low Taxes" and look at our Wealth Distribution challenge as one that just needs resolving now.

The government's "Right" tend to be the more conservative managers between the two sides. The Left will support more social and communal services at higher cost and risk to the government – but both sides have the mandate to present an affordable suite of policy offerings to put to the decision-making hands of their voters.

For either Right or Left parties to ignore its responsibility to Economic Control is not Left nor Right behavior specifically – rather it is poor management, as permitted by poor voter education.

In 1980 America, and in other G7 countries, voters followed poor policy as political campaigns exploited the public's low education level to win election and further personal business interests.

Rather than to educate the public in how to judge what responsible financial controls for society are, political campaigning appealed to our emotions – and not to logic, because they could. Voters were told that if they didn't support "Low Tax", they were "a socialist" or "Un-American" - basically. The American Dream ended for most of the poor minority whose voting strength was smaller than the richer majority during these years. The cost? The U.S. loses $500 billion annually due to 160 million citizens (40%) who have nothing and have no vote either because they are not 51%.

Democracy is an important building block of a Good Life, so sound Financial Controls are important to a Good Life as well. Every democratic voter must be educated well enough to stand on guard against this, or Democracy itself becomes unsustainable over time.

The responsibility of the right and left should always extend to the "greater good" as a minimum precept, general rule, and guiding principle. If there are not enough resources to move everyone forward, then work on revenue growth until there is enough wealth – but once there is enough wealth, as is the case for the G20, keep it distributed by graduating tax.

Policy Creation and Policy Committee Reform

Political Party Policies are selected based on a variety of approaches. The constitutions of many political parties, offer a documented process to forward policy by democratic election – and this is a concern.

Policy Committees are not necessarily Subject Matter Experts - SMEs, and they are not screened for conflicts of interest in many cases. All policy reviewers should fully disclose conflicts that can include employment incomes from other members of committee - first. Second, you should be elected a Subject Matter Expert before being invited to vote on policy as well.

Ideally, SMEs come to agree based on expertise earned through a career and higher education in the subject area discussed. A 25-year career is considered PhD equivalent in that area of employment and experts both academic and practical only should be participating in policy creation.

When a career Engineer, Doctor, Lawyer, or Economist votes on Policy in which they are an SME, that vote cannot be weighed equally against a sprinkler repair technician who is voting as he feels his father might have voted when he was alive (or some other emotion-based voting).

Even within professional fields, there are experts and generalists; a cancer specialist needs to weigh in more heavily on Policy specific to Cancer, than would a GP General Practitioner - for example. As you drill down within a community of Cancer physicians, opinions are often divided here as well.

When SMEs are not valued above other voices, genius and best-and-brightest get tucked into a corner and democracy languishes. If you don't do this - Einstein, for just one example, was made to "sit out" by academic rivals for two decades so they could figure out his thinking; Alan Turing was abandoned by peers and dead at 41, Pons and Fleishman were disgraced for 25 years for discovering Cold Fusion – we are just finding that their discovery was valid finally this year.

A long time association and volunteering record with your party is terrific, but it does not however, justify your cancelling out the vote of an expert in a policy field. Invariably, there are far fewer experts in this world than not – so do not be offended if you are declined the vote in one subject area.

If, however, you believe you are an expert and have been denied your right to participate as an SME, an appeal process should be available to you.

Each policy typically makes its way from city riding offices throughout the country to a regional review. When policies are ratified at a regional level, the policy next moves forward to a vote at a national convention.

Poland is the world's longest running democracy; it was a Super-Power in 1600 and six-times the size that it was at the start of WWII. World War II almost killed 20% of its population in large part due to 400 years of democratically elected compromise and weakening. Point is, in a democratic system, once we create well-vetted policy, we have to protect it, we have to control or permit revision by brilliant authors carefully, and then we have to communicate it well too.

Democracy is very important - and history teaches us that Democracies dumb-down and weakens itself if we don't stand on guard in this way.

Left & Right Must Support Important Policy

If a marketing survey shows low voter support for an Important Policy or Economic Control, that policy's Business Case must be communicated and then implemented by parties both left and right to voters trained to expect a professional Business Case and argument for acceptance.

In our current system, the election marketing teams on both Left and Right, feel they must discard important policy in order to win elections - and will bring forward a platform of policies that they believe will win power in an election. In this way, Society's sustainability is discarded by political teams that simply want to win elections.

Voters must be able to vote their values. When a political party supports middle-class-only policy, they do so forsaking important low-income productivity that is proven to turn economies around. An educated voter will vote for these low-income supports, but others may vote selfishly - not realizing nor caring that their society will pay a steep opportunity cost that may even lead to social collapse.

Reagan's Policies of Low Tax and Trickle-Down, with no monitoring by small government, were popular policies because voters were never made aware that their kids would suffer Economic Recession and Depression as a direct result today.

Reagan won because no credible objection was raised within his party; today however, Reagan is regarded as the Salesman of today's Economic Collapses and is a shining example of what not to do.

Believing in a Party Policy Process that is failed by design – amounts to not understanding that the results of that process can never work for any country. Now that you understanding and acknowledge the problem - is the first step to resolving it. Ensure that you work to resolve this problem within your party with priority.

This list is a summary of all of the TE-Mature Policies discussed throughout this book.

	Transition Economics Mature Policy 5% to 10% in Collapse	**Collapse Policy** 72% of All Countries are in Collapse
Working Families & Individuals	Graduated Tax, Big-Business Tax Avoidance Crackdown, Inequity targets, Local Business Ownership, Local Govmt Business Ownership	Low Tax, Trickle-down, Middle-Class Focus, Diversity, Cheap Imports, Immigration, Small Business w/o support
Unemployed	Guaranteed Cost of Living Incomes, Business Automation Revenue Sharing	No benefits for underemployed nor all unemployed
Retirement	Employee & Pension Fund Protections, Cost of Living minimums, CSR & Business Accountability	Offshoring, Misuse of female diversity rules, ignoring pensions
Children	Free Mastery-based Education & Transition Economics Voter Education	Failure to support 20-year-olds starting families, High Divorce Rates
Others	Cost of Living Benefits for Disabled	Insufficient Support, High Debt Servicing Costs
Automation	Engineering Safety Nets, #WPProjects & Renewable Automation Support, Multi-Party Long Term Strategic Planning	Innovation programs that fail to support Renewable Automations and Trade & Selling Needs

SPENDING POWER RETURNS	Transition Economics Mature Policy 5% to 10% in Collapse	Collapse Policy 72% of All Countries are in Collapse
Healthcare & Benefits	Universal Healthcare, Employee Benefit Plans to Revenue Neutral Business Case targets	Private Plans, Patents that externalize Government R&D
Childcare	Universal Daycare & Free Education incl. University	Unaffordable Childcare
Housing	Public Housing (30%) Controlled to Inflation, Land Grants, Anti-Eviction, and Foreign Ownership Taxes	Energy Poverty, Housing Bubbles created by lax controls
Food & Goods	License Renewable Automation, Local Harvesting, Driverless Transport & Distribution, Local Self-Sufficiency & Abundance	Insufficient Farm Compensations, Failure to develop automation, Dollar & 99p Stores, Cheap Imports, Austerity Measures
Energy	Abundant Geo-Thermal, Hydro, Cold-Fusion, Thorium Nuclear, Zero-Pollution Fuels	Part-time Wind & Solar, Fossil Fuel Oil Pipelines, Energy Poverty
Transport	Driverless-cars & Automated Goods Delivery, Auto Road & Rail Construction	Infrastructure w/o Automation & Trickle-down Protection, Transit

Chapter 22

Cost of Divorce in Society

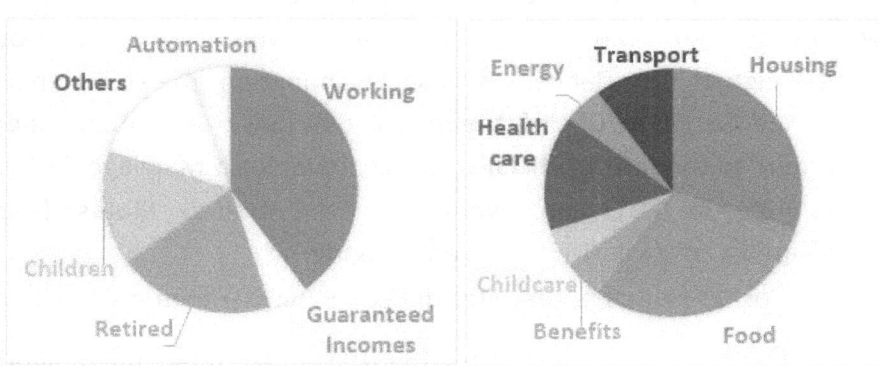

When marriages end, the finances of the couple split and the need for two homes replace a single shared home; separate retirement incomes and savings are now needed as well. The impacts of Divorce, to every facet of society, are not obvious until we begin to add up the cumulative costs.

Separations will mean that one or both of the spouses must spend more years in the work force. Because children are also born later in life today, many 50-year old parents are supporting University costs on top of alimony payments and retirement plans.

These changes often force people to need to work; to draw a workforce income, well into their late sixties; well beyond the point where retirement income structures would otherwise be providing for their needs.

With fewer jobs available, and more graduates needing jobs year over year as well, the chance that these 50 years olds will be able to stay in productive employment reduces and the need for support of these people by the state increases.

Effectively, the combination of high marriage failure, combined with economic downturn, much higher housing costs, automation-driven job losses, and later starting families, may make divorce a choice, and "Right", that our economy simply cannot afford.

The socio-economic impacts and cost of a 50% to 70% divorce rate when combined with a high male unemployment rate may not appear high at first glance. On closer examination, the costs when multiplied by 50%-70% of the population base, are staggering. According to the latest official statistics, Divorce to Marriage Ratios were 48% in 2011 on average in the United States (see en.wikipedia.org/wiki/Divorce_demography).

- Cost of sale of primary residence - $25,000+ commissions
- Purchase and move to other residences $36,000 in land transfer and fees
- Twice the Utilities, House Taxes, etc.
- Rental accommodations delay retirement savings - $100,000-$1,000,000 per pensioner
- $6,000 to $25,000++ divorce legal costs
- $2000 additional tax & accounting costs
- Purchase, maintenance and insurance for two cars - $6500 annually
- Additional Cell phones - $2000 to $6000 annually
- Jobs & support needed in society for two full-time workers - $100,000

- Retirements will be delayed to at least 65 or later.
- Double the clothes, computers, sundries for kids - $6,000
- School councilor costs increase as 50% of kids are now high-stress - $50,000 per school
- Help Line volumes increase as kids struggle with all aspects of change in family - $1 million annually per 100,000 population.
- If incomes are not steady, and jobs are scarce, all costs hit the social welfare and housing system - $40,000+ annually.

Actual numbers are very hard to guess because two divorces are never the same, divorces within housing bubbles are much more expensive than non-bubble divorces, and so on. Although I took two very different tacts to get to these estimates, the $12 trillion dollar cost came out just the same with these input costs. $12 trillion is 2/3rds of the U.S.'s total GDP and so I realize that these numbers have to be too high. The important thing to take away from this discussion is that social problems – from divorce, incarceration rates, and military spending and similar – probably accounts for very near half of the total GDP of the United States. If I add this cost to the opportunity costs lost by not supporting guaranteed income programs, universal healthcare, and similar, the United States is paying a very high cost to protect its inequity indeed.

Total Estimated additional cost of divorce per 100,000 population is between $6 and $7 billion first year, and half of that - $3 to $4.5 billion is needed annually thereafter, if you do not count an additional new salary requirement as a social burden. If I don't count additional income needs nor welfare costs, the cost of divorce for the population of Canada's 30 million people is $1.6 trillion best case; and trillions upon trillions for the U.S. See the detail chart for the worksheet that supports these cost estimates.

Cigarette Smoking kills 480,000 Americans annually; Smoking related illnesses cost more than $289 billion in a 45/55% split of medical costs and lost productivity. In 2012, 18.1% of the US's 350 million citizens were smokers.

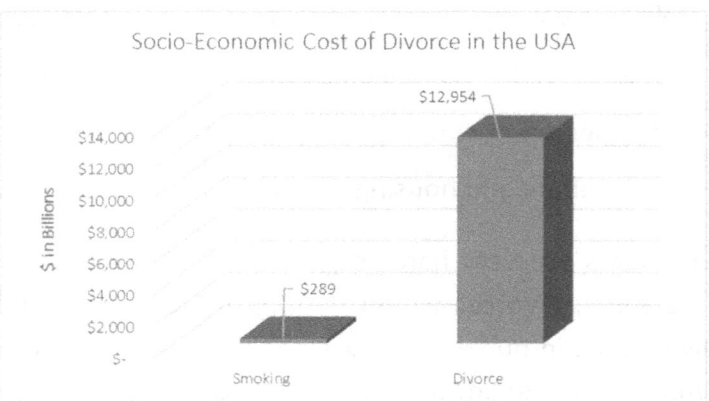

A comparison of costs shows that divorce dwarfs the cost of smoking in our society.

In the same way that we ban smoking because of its staggering health-care cost, we may find that our society has to control divorce rates in an effort to curb runaway social pensions as our citizens are unable to pay for their own retirements.

Socio-Economic Cost of Divorce (per Capita)

Costs Per Family	People Affected	Monthly Cost per	One Time	Annual per Family	Total One-time
Residence Sale	1		35000		35000
Purchase of New Homes	2		$18,000		36000
Rental or Utilities @ taxes & insurance	2	2300		55200	
Divorce Legal	2		3000		6000
Accounting	1			2000	
Extra Car	1			6500	
Insurance	1			1500	
Cell phones	3	110		3960	
Extra Full-time salary $60,000	1	5000			
Public Pensions	1			5000	
Extra Clothes	2			3000	
School Councellors	2			50	
Help Line	4	40000		1.6	
Social Housing	1	40000			
				$ 77,211.60	$ 77,000.00

Column1	Column2	Column3	Annual	One Time	Year One
People	30 Million		$ 2,316,348,000,000	$ 2,310,000,000,000	$ 4,626,348,000,000
Divorce Rate	x 70%	0.7	$ 1,621,443,600,000	$ 1,617,000,000,000	$ 3,238,443,600,000

* Assume either social housing or Rental Cost - but not both
* Rental Costs is assumed equivalent to carrying cost for a home
* Variables include Divorce Rate, Population
* Housing Costs assume $400k and 5% Mortgage

Chapter 23

Failing to Restart a Cycle

Revolutions and Wars result when Cycles are not restarted peacefully. What begins as a rise in social problems; as symptoms of scarcity like Race, Gender, or Religion Extremism and Terror, escalates to hostility more and more until attack finally becomes preferable to starvation or risk of violent aggression.

We realize the start of this process when we see shortfalls in accountability every day in finance and business unfortunately. "Its just business" is an expression that you may have heard before. This is an announcement of the failure to find a win-win outcome in a business deal. Every time that an opportunity to benefit society is by-passed, whenever costs are externalized to society; whenever communities are out-leveraged, double-dealt or subverted only to find that profits are internalized and offshored, you build a fine argument to justify removing the offending decision-makers from the next socially important discussion altogether.

Being shortsighted and uncaring of the condition of others is unsustainable as a model for any society; the Roman Empire's fall was a terrific example. Similar to Venezuela's collapse today, farmers outside the cities found insufficient compensation to fend to grow the food needed by the city. When food supplies stopped, societies collapse and civilizations scatter to other models.

The smaller that a society is, the more quickly will this outcome be realized; larger societies might take longer to feel the impacts of these behaviors, but no matter what size, all great societies in history have arrived at a point where their policies made them unsustainable.

Joseph Schumpeter was a famous economist and professor at Harvard University when he explained why he thought this is certainly true in his famous book "Capitalism, Socialism, and Democracy" in 1942. Schumpeter assumed that a more socialistic model was inevitable as Capitalism collapses for reasons discussed in his book.

Others conclude that dictatorships will surely follow collapsing democracies and of course there are examples in history to support these arguments too – Hitler, Mussolini, Roman Emperors and even the Emperor Napoleon, to name just a few of many examples. Google "Capitalism follows Dictatorship" and "Dictatorship follows Capitalism" to get a sense that there are more theories than you can shake a stick at.

There are many interesting and profoundly important parallel social discussions from history here. The definition of "Evil" from the 1945 Nuremburg Trials and the Golden Rule – are two important examples.

Dr. Gustav M. Gilbert summarized the atrocities reported during the Nuremburg trials of 1945 in Delft, Holland after World War II. Dr. Gilbert was the U.S. Army Psychologist assigned to the Nazi Generals put on trial after the war. In his book "Nuremberg Diary", published in 1946, Dr. Gilbert summarized "Evil is the endemic failing of finding empathy for the situations and suffering of others"; "Evil, I think, is the absence of empathy".

This statement meant to summarize the Nazi Government's atrocities in death camps to Jews, Russians, Poles, Ukrainians, of course, but it also spoke to the "It's just business" attitudes of uncaring wealthy Jewish, and other, business owners who employed slave-wage tactics widely in Germany at the start of the 1929 Great Depression.

History teaches much to those who listen well, and so one can hardly think it a coincidence that the Golden Rule has appeared in the text of every religion ever documented; even in religions of antiquity that are no longer practiced today. "Do unto others as you would have them do to you". You might not care for your neighbor's company; you don't need to love him or her, but you do have to ensure that his needs and those of his family are met – and vice-versa.

How does this problem look within our society; how does it reveal itself in discussions? My wife and kids and I were visiting friends at a multi-family get together close to the holidays years ago. My son took a compound fracture to his big toe while running around with the other kids later this evening - and so the night was memorable to be sure; I remember the evening more, however, due to a discussion between myself and our American hosts.

The hosting couple were both accountants with a very large, famously family-friendly American brand. They had been assigned to the company's Canadian office for a few years. Nicer people you are not going to meet anytime soon; fun and terrific company. When discussion rolled around to healthcare and dental coverage offered by our respective companies (he had been to the dentist that day), they mentioned that the company covered braces and other orthodontic procedures as well.

For whatever reason, I asked how the American system handle

healthcare for the uninsured. Their response was "The Church takes care of that". Hmmm – this was before Obama-Care programs and I was aware that charitable hospitals have to turn away many healthcare requests.

I did not want to turn a fun evening into a grilling of U.S. American Healthcare Policy and our lovely hosts were clearly satisfied with their response, so I did the polite thing and turned the discussion to talk about something else.

Not only was their answer incorrect but they also felt defensibly certain that their belief was correct – and that is was not polite conversation to continue on with the topic. Their belief was untrue; I mentioned above in Chapter 13 that poor Americans die an average of 13-years younger than insured Americans. If insured Americans are clearly taught that the strong will somehow prevail and that the weak need only work harder to make their way, you have now taught your children and community to ignore empathy and prefer to simply be ignorant of the true statistics that surround you.

As it turned out, I was no better; I grew up believing that Canada's safety nets were the envy of the world because I was told as much. I was at a house party last night and someone voiced how Canadians were very lucky to be covered in this way. If things are good in our lives, we find little reason to question and validate whether we are managing safety nets well in fact. The U.N. cited Canada for gross-shortcomings in its support of the homeless, housing and cost-of-living coverage in March 2016.

I was writing an article about Socialistic Policies in different countries in February 2016 when I picked up the phone to call the local homeless shelter. I asked how availability of rooming in the -20 Celsius temperatures was; they were full and turning people away. This prompted more investigation on my part ... it turns out that safety nets covered $370 per month in rent when the rents in the area are $1200; no coverages existed for storage of possessions for evicted families and there were no protections from Sheriff's eviction in -20 weather either.

I called the local housing authority to understand these shortcomings, only to find that administrators were adamant that they carefully follow provincial policy. No reconciliation of reality was permitted by their officers and clearly their own employment was on the line whenever they deviated from the rules as well.

I was very wrong about the state of lower income and unfortunate individuals in my own community in just the same way that my American friends were. I believed in Safety Nets that did not exist; food banks and charities that don't make a difference; and this revelation suddenly explained local suicides in the same way as reported in Spain where 100 evictions happen every week. Clearly, believing something that is easier doesn't make it true; and ignoring a serious problem is not saving lives forsaken by turning away our gaze.

The Golden Rule is not a platitude and not simply a nice sentiment; it is a time-tested sustainability model for every society – with a compelling business case.

In North America, we often refer to the generation that led in the years after World War II, as The Greatest Generation. This book will leave you with a lot of anecdotal explanations for why that was very true. World War II America was a productive dynamo in a Spring Economy. People did the right thing by one another and were rewarded for it with a Good Life in return.

That society is perhaps most sorely missed by our Populist voters in 2015 and 16's Canadian, Brexit and U.S. Presidential Elections - as our generation has seen first-hand the consequences of unsustainable financial policy.

To build a sustainable good life today, look to automation and also to Transition Economics Policy that ensure incomes, return spending power, and keep capitalist economies that benefit all members of the community.

Like solutions to most problems, changing the world for the better takes a series of simple adjustment – but they have to be right changes. The changes proposed must be empirically supportable and selected via a Scientific Method and sound Business Case.

Corporate Social Responsibility and Business Accountability, through professional licensing, education, and through governance, factor into the sustainable supports that build Good Lives as well. In the discussion of business accountability, business schools will require a long-overdue rewrite of our current Business Ethics courses, but once that is done – and governance controls are installed as they have been in Germany for decades, business grads can get started on the work of building sustainable societies immediately.

Chapter 24

-

Responsible Transition

Transition Economics is the first Theory in Economics to require a profound understanding of a very specific definition of sustainable Change and Project Management methodology.

The adoption of mature, well-proven, and scalable processes for change are fundamental to the success of any change large or small. For this reason, Transition Economics mandates a specific process to communicate, monitor and manage change well across a broad group of Government Policy changes for Business, Legal, Engineering, faculties, organizations, countries, and all other change.

Transition Projects are often large change programs containing dozens, and even hundreds, of social and engineering sub-projects. Having these all run under a common program reporting process ensures that all know next-steps at any point in a change.

Only SUSTAIN Project Management Method is suggested to manage these changes as only this methodology ensures that each project meets sustainability targets at appropriate points.

SUSTAIN PMM is the only certified Project Method certified as "Transition Economics Compliant" at this time - and is introduced in

Chapters 27 & 28.

Training in Project Process is the first place to start to ensure successfully making a change across many faculties and organizations with varying levels of expertise, experience, and even education, reliably.

Using SUSTAIN Project Management Method, all current and soon-to-be-affected organizations become empowered Project Owners and their Engineering Teams, Policy Management Teams, Legal, 3rd Party Consultants, Auditors, and Governance Team members become Steering Committee Stakeholders who are responsible to assign members of Working Teams. Programs are led by a Program Manager with one Project Manager assigned to at least one of each Project or Sub-Project.

All current processes: those of legal departments, governments, corporations and engineering teams are listed as "Inventory" and all are documented in the Requirements Document of an appropriate individual project or projects.

Program Charter Documents contain a list Stakeholders, Owners, Steering Team members, Projects, and other specific Program

I've worked in environments where 500 of these individual projects were running in a dozen large programs managing billions of dollars, so this process scales and executes reliably regardless of the number of stakeholders and complexity.

Individual Projects take on-average, six months to communicate and deliver with high quality, proper training and status reporting. Never advance a project past a sign-off milestone until all stakeholders sign to advance the project; you add risk to your successful outcome every time you do – and responsibility for delays becomes that of stakeholders alone.

It is always true to say that a **Great Process Never Takes Longer**.

TE Throttles and Throttle Rates

In Transition Economics, throttles are algorithms or ratios that suggest a safe rate of automation change. The rate that change can take place responsibly is referred to as the adjustable TE Throttle Rate.

For example, if automation can replace 50% of the world's five billion jobs (this assumes that approx. 70% of the world's population take incomes via a job; in the U.S. 63% have jobs) over the next 20 to 30 years, throttles must predict how to absorb 7 million lost working incomes per month globally over that time. 7 mil x $1,500 per month Cost of Living (CoL) means automation must offset $10.5 billion monthly or $126 billion annually.

That's a calculated cost of $17.5 million annually per every one million population; and it is also a cost that could easily be recovered through simply cleaning-up half of the tax avoidance estimated by major companies and financial institutions.

Calculation	Value
Global Population	7.2 Billion
% in Jobs	70%
Working	5.04 Billion
Targetted Job Automation	50%
Years to Automate Target	30
Months per Year	12
Jobs Automated per Month	7,000,000
Cost of Living Guarantee Income	$ 1,500
Monthly Cost of Automation	$10,500,000,000
Annual Cost of Automation	$126,000,000,000
Cost per 1,000,000 Population Annually	$17,500,000
Monthly Jobs Automated / 1 mill	972

Note Minimum guaranteed incomes differ based on Cost of Living (CoL) per country and also per municipality. For example min CoL for Toronto is $3000 CAD, London, New York, Chicago, Rome, etc. are all different.

With budgets in place and offset by tax or automation incomes, the acceptable Throttle for Jobs to switch to Guarantee Incomes - in Canada with its population of 36 million, would therefore be 972 monthly job automations multiplied by 36 (million) which is 35,000 jobs will be automated in Canada monthly. **If budgets cannot accept** these rates, throttle rates must calculate affordable compromises – both in spending and incomes.

The Goal of Transition Economics and adjustments in Throttle Rates is intended protect citizens in change while ensuring that every possible opportunity to avoid collapse with the economy has also been employed.

The goal is not - to compensate citizens undertaking a change automation change with the lowest standard of living possible over long stretches in time. For example, a $3,000 income in Toronto will not build a Good Life if all other costs remain unchanged or continue to increase. Whether Salaries increase or Cost of Living decreases, the better measure of any successful community is by the definition of a Good Life; one that can afford all of the things that we need.

Chapter 25

Business Cases

Transition Economics
BUSINESS PLAN PRESENTATION

Business Cases are summary documents that clarify the financial, social and other benefits and costs of a project in the short, mid and long term. These documents analyses and set targets for return on investment (ROI), time to return to profitability, time to return to positive cash flow, and similar important goals that an investment in time and money are anticipated to result in.

In social projects, one wants to prefer projects that build a good life at the same time as project teams are spending and implementing change. The calculation of ROI for Guaranteed Incomes above, is an example of an important Business Case discussion in support of a social Maturity Project.

Most large organizations keep templates for their business cases that ensure a minimum set of decision supporting metrics can be considered for each idea for a project. Here is a suggested minimum Business Case for decision makers and voters to want to see in support of Transition Economics Projects.

The Transition Economics Business Case

Business Cases are mentioned often in Transition Economics and even as a voter, you should be asking to see one before you you're your support for any policy. What is the track record of this policy in other countries? What is the targeted Return on Investment? Does this Policy Align with Transition Economics Maturity and Renewable Automation Goals? These are just a few of the questions that you will want answered before investing in a Policy and Project.

What to look for in a Business Case

Credibility of Business Cases is important. Basing targets on widely available GDP Exports, Imports, and similar statistics keeps strong focus on the ability of this program to advance economies; this is surely the way that the rest of the world will review your economic success. Consumer Surveys and non-standard are subjective and not relevant nor recommended to Transitioning your Economy from a collapsing trajectory.

Pros and Cons, Costs and Benefits – Optimistic/Pessimistic/Realistic and Long/Mid/Short Term, Return on Investment (ROI), Mean Time to Profitability, Track Record other Countries, and Contribution to RAI, TE Maturity; Is it Renewable; Is it Sustainable - are all Table of Content and Checklist items for a Transition Economics Business Case.

A Business Case and a Charter Document have a few things in common. Business Cases want to explain initial Stakeholders, Budget, Communications Plans, Timelines, Goals and Objectives.

A Business Case relies on estimates for cost that have to guess at some very broad design discussions. Consider that costs will differ depending on needs of redundancy, MTBF (Mean Time Between Failure), Percent of New vs Available Technology, new staff costs more than existing trained staff, size and cost of test equipment needed differs, land, technical complexity and so on.

According to SUSTAIN PPM, a general budgeting rule for Business Case estimates can often be +100% or -50% over/under; Requirements Docs can narrow those estimates down to +-25%, and Design Documents with Detail Implementation Plans completed - should be +-5% accurate.

You can make some general assumptions. Like a project will take six to 12 months to lead to a Pilot. 18 to 24 months to produce automations that integrate with other systems. These are pretty reliable guesses for a surprising percentage of most projects 12 and 24 months in duration.

Example starter Spreadsheet and PowerPoint templates are available on the CSQ Research site at http://csq1.org/forums/topic/transition-economics-business-case/ (Tilley, 2016)

Begin with a Dashboard Summary View

Spell out Financial Plan Cash Flow estimates - as expected first – and then also suggest Optimistic and Pessimistic estimates as well.

Elevator-pitch decks are used frequently in addition to Business Case Templates, so here are a few screens from the PowerPoint example template link above.

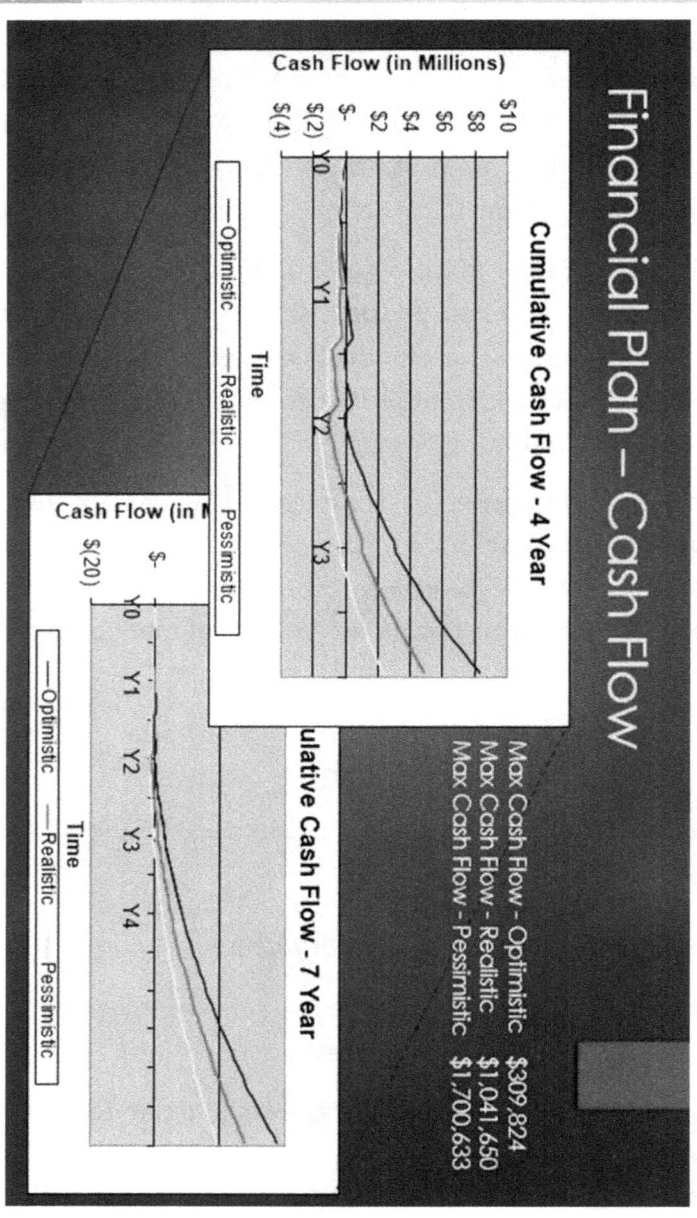

Inputs
- People, Processes, and Technology
- Stakeholder Staff & Organizations – Managers, Technical, Accounting, Legal, Advisory Committees, Think Tanks, Academics, Sales, Marketing, Operations, Trainers, QA, Governance.
- Business Driving KPIs - like Fleet Vehicles, Servers, software licenses per client; Average cost & profit per Sale
- SG&A – Sales, General and Admin, Advertising, Bank Fees, Credit Cards
- Rent, phones, automobiles, facilities, Insurance, Courier, Postage, office supplies, subscriptions
- Charitable Donations
- Professional Fees, Printing, Training
- Assets and Depreciation
- Tax
- Transition Economics Throttling Inputs – Jobs lost due to automation, offshore hiring and crews

Outputs
- Transition Economics Throttles; compensations and rates of change that afford guaranteed income programs from higher automation profits or efficiencies. See Chapter 18.
- Products and Cost per Product
- Sales Revenue & Profit Per Unit / Per Product
- Resource Assumptions - RACI it. Who does what? High-level only at this point of course.
- Risk Plans - Important risks should articulate a mitigation plan. List Probability/Impact.
- 7-year Cash Flow, Profit and Loss, Balance Sheet
- Short, Mid and Long Term Targets and Tracking
- Timelines and Summary

Goals and Objectives

- List five-year goals
- State specific, measurable objectives for achieving your five-year goals.
    - List market-share objectives.
    - List revenue/profitability objectives.

Policy Track Record

- The Netherlands - 1990 to present
    - GDP Export – Up   GDP Import - DOWN
- Germany – 2014 to present
    - GDP Export – Up   GDP Import - DOWN
- Aligns with Renewable Automation – RAI YES
- Improves Transition Economics Maturity – YES
- **Return on Investment – 230%**
- **Time to Profitability – 24 months**

The Team – for Discussion ...

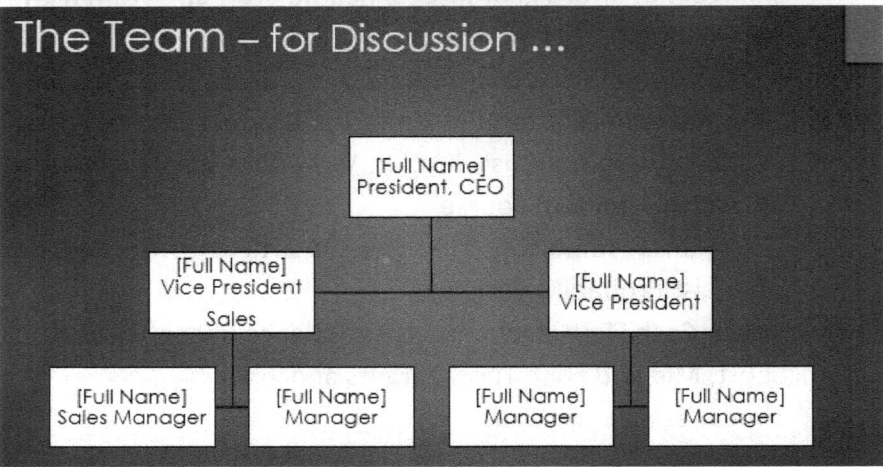

Risks and Rewards

- Summarize the risks of the proposed project and how they will be addressed.
- Estimate expected rewards, particularly if you are seeking funding.

P&L – for Planning Only

In thousands ...

	Y1 Realistic	Y2 Realistic	Y3 Realistic	Y4 Realistic	Y5 Realistic	Y6 Realistic	Y7 Realistic
Sales	$ 1,045	$ 3,347	$ 5,661	$ 7,942	$ 10,223	$ 11,375	$ 15,914
Cost of sales	$ 232	$ 1,011	$ 1,785	$ 1,860	$ 1,782	$ 1,440	$ 1,654
Gross margin	813	2,336	3,876	6,083	8,441	9,935	14,261
	77.7%	69.8%	68.5%	76.6%	82.6%	87.3%	89.6%
Operating expenses							
Compensation expenses	$ 460	$ 893	$ 1,083	$ 1,138	$ 1,195	$ 1,168	$ 1,342
	44.0%	26.7%	19.1%	14.3%	11.7%	10.3%	8.4%
Selling, general & administrative	$ 408.70	$ 754.81	$ 1,031.40	$ 1,321.57	$ 1,612.22	$ 1,734.04	$ 2,334.24
	39.1%	22.6%	18.2%	16.6%	15.8%	15.2%	14.7%
Depreciation	$ 10.17	$ 33.04	$ 46.77	$ 46.77	$ 46.77	$ 42.87	$ 47.61
	1.0%	1.0%	0.8%	0.6%	0.5%	0.4%	0.3%
Total	879	1,680	2,162	2,506	2,854	2,945	3,724
	84.0%	50.2%	38.2%	31.6%	27.9%	25.9%	23.4%
Operating income/(loss)	(65)	655	1,714	3,577	5,587	6,990	10,537
	-6.3%	19.6%	30.3%	45.0%	54.7%	61.5%	66.2%
Interest Expense	(31)	(47)	(20)	258	714	1,348	2,165
	-2.9%	-1.4%	-0.3%	3.2%	7.0%	11.8%	13.6%
Income before taxes	(96)	603	1,695	3,834	6,301	8,338	12,702
	-9.2%	18.2%	29.9%	48.3%	61.6%	73.3%	79.8%

Cash Flow Statement – for Planning Only

	Y1 Realistic	Y2 Realistic	Y3 Realistic	Y4 Realistic	Y5 Realistic	Y6 Realistic	Y7 Realistic
Net Income	(65,728)	655,331	1,714,470	3,576,636	5,587,282	7,733,203	9,793,924
Add back non cash items:	10,167	167,792	457,767	457,767	323,017	46,767	43,717
Cash flow from operations	(55,562)	823,122	2,172,237	4,034,403	5,910,299	7,779,969	9,837,640
Change in working capital	(136,346)	(162,426)	(163,461)	(165,899)	(165,859)	(165,817)	(168,286)
Cash flow used in investments	(115,900)	(1,318,400)	(18,300)	–	–	–	24,400
Cash flow provided by / used by financing	307,808	657,706	(1,990,476)	(3,868,504)	(5,744,440)	(7,614,152)	(9,693,755)
Due to parent company	307,808	965,513	(1,024,963)	(4,893,466)	(10,637,906)	(18,252,058)	(27,945,813)
Change in cash	–						
Beginning Cash	–						
Ending Cash	–						
Required Financing (before CF from Finance)	(307,808)	(657,706)	1,990,476	3,868,504	5,744,440	7,614,152	9,693,755
Required Financing - cumulative	(307,808)	(965,513)	1,024,963	4,893,466	10,637,906	18,252,058	27,945,813

Balance Sheet – for Planning Only   *In thousands ...*

	Y1 Realistic	Y2 Realistic	Y3 Realistic	Y4 Realistic	Y5 Realistic	Y6 Realistic	Y7 Realistic
Current Assets							
Cash	-	-	-	-	-	-	-
Accounts receivable	1,045	3,347	5,681	7,942	10,223	12,504	14,785
Long-term Assets							
Network equipment, net of amortization	-	0	4,365	10,508	5,576	1,130	-
Fixed Assets, net of depreciation	683	1,139	982	278	479	1,235	2,097
Net Fixed Assets	683	5,504	11,490	5,853	651	(1,235)	(2,097)
Total Assets	1,734	8,850	17,151	13,795	10,874	11,269	12,688
Liabilities							
Accounts payable/Accrued Liabilities	409	755	1,031	1,322	1,612	1,903	2,165
Due to (from) Parent Company	668	658	1,990	3,869	5,744	7,614	9,694
Total Liabilities	1,076	1,413	(959)	(2,547)	(4,132)	(5,711)	(7,529)
Shareholders' Equity and Deficit							
Income/(loss)	68	855	1,714	3,577	5,587	7,733	9,794
Retained earnings	68	855	1,714	3,577	5,587	7,733	9,794
Total Liabilities and Deficit	1,011	2,068	755	1,030	1,455	2,022	2,265
Liability less Deficit	723	6,782	16,396	12,766	9,419	9,247	10,423

Approvals to Proceed

With a clear understanding of what are the benefits targeted and timelines and budgets approved, a decision can be made on a course of action that begin as a project, or as a program of many projects - as needed.

Contribution, Acknowledgments and Recognition

Very important to the success of a sustainable, automated production society are the acknowledgments and recognition lauded upon the engineers of seemingly endless hours of hard thinking, work, and trial and error.

A TV Awards Program is in the works to acknowledge the efforts and progress of the "rock stars" of World Peace. Programming to parallel and rival the Oscars and the Super Bowl Pre-Game are also up for consideration. Nothing is too good; nothing is over the top.

Monitor performance of build and operations using Project and Service Management Summaries.

SUSTAIN Project Management Method

Running successful projects begins by filling in mature, proven project documentation templates. SUSTAIN Project Management Method is a book unto itself which explains in detail what each point in the summary below requires.

Look for detailed examples as well as important workshopping and quality control considerations there as well. This outline is high-level but is also comprehensive enough to get you started well.

Treat these summary document outlines as checklists for your project documentation deliverables.

Chapter 26

—

Voting Better

I have mentioned several times that the Game of Monopoly is a very close approximation of one life-cycle turn of a Capitalist Economy. "Capitalism" is the word used to describe most of the G20's systems of commerce and policies. Capitalistic Housing Policy, for example, asks that we should all purchase our own homes; Capitalistic Monetary Policy says that we should all work at a job, or buy and sell something (widgets), in order to generate a profit and create our incomes and pay workers.

Our children often take this basic policy training in Civics courses in school and they are usually well-trained in the current systems. It is not uncommon for educational systems to ignore, or even disparage, policies that are not presently at work in our current system.

This means that people living in America were rarely taught about the housing or monetary systems that were used in Russia or China, for example, and the opposite is true as well. This is a shortcoming in our education because most Policies have Pros and Cons, and a time when it is correct to utilize them; and a time to avoid them as well.

Both Capitalism and the Game of Monopoly, work in recognizable cycles. This is to say that they both have a start, a middle, an end, and even a Reset too. In Monopoly, at the end of a game, or cycle, all resources are grouped together at the bank and then they are redistributed back to players equally so that the game can begin playing again.

The same can be seen in Capitalism where Wealth Distribution policies must restart Capitalist Cycles just the same. The only obvious difference between the game and cycle, is that Capitalism's cycles take several decades to run through – where a game of Monopoly can be completed within just 60 or 90 minutes.

We call the end of a Capitalist cycle, a "Great Depression" or a "Panic" historically; this is the familiar "Hotels Phase" in a Monopoly Game. At this phase, one player emerges stronger than the rest and all others are bankrupt.

In real-world Capitalist societies, these Great Depressions are recorded in history to have happened approximately every sixty-years. The Code of Hammurabi records the first Economic Controls to manage Great Depressions, carved alongside the Law of Babylon in 1760 BCE on a massive stone which resides today in the Louvre Museum in Paris, France.

The Code of Hammurabi explained that "Jubilees" should redistribute wealth and forgive all debt every 50-years to pre-emptively restart the capitalist societies of Egypt. The average lifespan of humans at the time was probably 40-years at the time and so few individuals would easily recognize a Capitalist Cycle – and this Economic Control sustained Capitalism for perhaps a hundreds of years before it was "cast in stone" in 1760 BCE.

Science is defined by observation and calculation; and this economic cycling is a phenomenon not unlike other observed cycles – like geysers in geology.

Like many systems used worldwide and in history, few of us are likely to ever learn about cyclic economic controls in school. The answer to the question of why is policy that is not-strictly-Capitalistic also not taught to students in our schools, is simply that this is a failing of our educational systems. Civics courses in my own textbooks CSQ Common Sense and Teaching Doers – address this but only recently and these lessons are not in the hands of our economists nor politicians unfortunately.

Why are we struggling economically today? It's because the systems that work early in a capitalist cycle – do not work at the end of the cycle; you can't buy more hotels when you have neither wealth nor income; so the systems that we consider status-quo earlier in the game, have to change at the end.

For the past seven years, we kept interest rates low, but that doesn't put money into people's pockets unless business gains are passed down to a low-unemployment population through trickle-down. Trickle-down Economics is the notion that by not taxing the rich, they would have money needed to easily administer its trickling down to society. Trickle-down is a laughable failure since the 1990s, only to be followed by equally socially irresponsible policies like slow-hiring, high unemployment, underemployment, pension avoidance, and even gender equality worked to ensure that benefits to business were not seen by families – even more-so after 2008.

What we saw from low-interest rate policies was massive housing bubbles that grew up in urban centers fueled by need - people need shelter after all - and by foreign and public investors who realized that housing sales profits could out-perform stock markets quite easily.

I am going to talk about solutions later in this book because financial and housing pressures cause a great number of stresses in society and these pressures contribute directly to unhappiness, relationship and family instability.

Cycle Economists recognize these trends as normal and recommend economic controls and systems of housing and incomes that work according to the four phases of the capitalist cycle. Today's banks and governments, however - unfortunately, rely on systems that worked in earlier phases - with systems like Keynesian Economics.

Why we continue to use socially-irresponsible Keynesian Economics during Economic Depressions is an intrigue in itself, as this was the system developed in the 1930s that stalled important Wealth Distributions to the breaking point until Hitler in 1939 Germany found enough support to start a World War. By the end of that war, we surely did have wealth well distributed – but at terrible cost in lives and suffering.

Surely, the track-records of these systems are a mistake that we cannot want to repeat in a mature Nuclear Era where another World War could lead to an extinction-level event? Ironically, Keynes himself famously stated "And then we are all dead" when asked what about the consequences of his theories. He is also dead now and never would live to see the resulting Depression that had to result from his theories, and yet we see banks and economists wearing blinders to world events and continuing status-quo by these rules still in today's Great Depression.

The Economic Controls on the Code of Hammurabi were handed down from monarch-to-monarch (father-to-son), back when a Monarchy was the norm; today – most of us live within Democracies and so we all need to understand what are these controls so that we can vote knowledgeably and not be misled by special interests, short-sited, and socially irresponsible agenda. The code itself was used for a thousand years before it was recorded in stone. Its simple mechanisms averted misery and uprisings for the poor of Egypt for a millennia during that period in history.

In capitalist societies, wealth inequity is the natural effect caused by unequal earnings that are common near the end of a capitalist cycle. An individual who earns three million dollars a day for thirty years is not going to be caught-up-to by a man or woman taking a second and third job – so at some point inequities become too extreme for the poor to bear.

Most of the Revolutions of the past 300 years were fueled directly by the frustrations of the poor when asked to wait too long for wealth distribution. World War II can be considered in this category as well.

Revolutions can force rapid wealth distribution but they are imperfect vehicles of change. Revolutions do force wealth distribution in the short term, but they may not sustain wealth distributions over time - and, as I mentioned, in the absence of a trained Monarch, democratic voters have to understand and train their children on how to vote for economic controls that prevent the next sixty-year cycle of wealth consolidations proactively.

If we do not train our children in these lessons of how to manage wealth distribution, then no proactive distribution can occur until the suffering of the poor endures and deepens to a breaking point once again.

Democracy is a system that permits the majority of registered voters to decide which political leaders will set the direction of the nation for the next four or five years. Like any system, elections can be swayed, influenced, or simply perfect and simple, depending upon their design.

Hearing generalities from candidates that capitalism, socialism, or communism are good or bad; or, Left or Right policies - are good or bad; "Big Government" is Good or Bad; these are not usually very helpful summaries. Sometimes socialistic policies are best – perhaps in a healthcare discussion. Sometimes Communistic policies are best – in a discussion of public housing. Sometimes capitalistic policies are most appropriate – when discussing open and free market economies.

Human Rights and the pursuit of liberty, however, are always good considerations as they speak directly to the underpinnings of a Good Life. Democratic Process makes wars unsustainable – so that is a very good thing to make use of and add to a requirements list as well.

For everything else, we voters are asked to try to boil down a hundred considerations, based on imperfect definitions from others, until finally we vote for one party over another. I can tell you for a fact that a lot of vote election workers at the polling booth who they should vote for – and this is a real shame. Many of us appear to need a set of criteria and checklist to help us vote well.

Our father voted for the right; my ancestors were Democrats; or some voters have other little systems, for example – "if three candidates discuss two policies consistently, I will know which is the best leader and cast my vote in that way." Some voters elect what their union or even employer tells them; so on and so forth – there are many influencing considerations.

Most Democratic systems of government leave losers of elections without income support, so for many candidates – everything, is riding on winning. There is not another job to go back to, so saying and doing whatever it takes to get into office and get elected, becomes a somewhat desperate goal.

Having sat on an election campaign team, I can tell you that campaigns can bog down with twisted discussions of media and message. A politician has to give a great percentage of their time and effort to re-election and fund raising.

The process of campaigning is not getting society's work done either so for this reason it is always best to keep election campaigning confined to small windows of time – perhaps two or three months every four or five years.

Campaign spending limits are important; U.S. Elections spend $1 billion to win a Presidential election which means that fund raising is happening virtually every day of a five year term – which means that work is not being done for the electorate for fully half the term in office.

Discussions amongst supporters are not often practiced academic, point and counterpoint exchanges either. More often than not, untrained speakers use absolutes like "never" and "only"; they summarize better, best and worst imperfectly – and I am sure you can see yourself in this picture as can I see myself too. People draw emotions into these discussions, and there can be flashpoints among contrasting viewpoints.

We can get so deeply wrapped up in these details; discussions of the detail trees and blades of grass, that we can't easily step back to see the forest and big-picture issues and values anymore.

Can you remember why our founding fathers enacted democratic elections in the first place? What did they run away from in Europe, and what did they know was important to protect once they got here? How did they know what targets to work toward when building a new country that could sustain their children's happiness, liberty, good lives and happiness?

Did America's Puritan forefathers envision that their country could become one of the richest nations in the world back in 1620? Yes, they did - by the way. Did they envision that their land of milk and honey would be without healthcare and minimum support for the poor once it did? Decide for yourself after reading a little bit about them.

Think like a Founding Father

I will direct a paragraph here to an excellent essay - The Puritans and Money by Leland Ryken. Puritans were middle-to-wealthy merchant middle class for the most part. They believed in taking benefit from god's blessings, and they also believed that poverty was no crime; that it had benefit as it "starved lust" too; but that the goal of poverty had no merit either. Puritans were Protestants, and they differentiated themselves from Catholics in this way. Puritans were scholars and knew well that the previous thousand years of social stalemate was directly attributable to poverty. Catholics believed poverty was Godly and should be strived for based on the teachings of the Bible of Emperor Constantine in the fourth century when the official religion of the Roman Empire became Christianity.

These founding father Puritans taught that poor people required part of the riches of others to help and comfort them (Latimer, 1858). They acknowledged that, although it did not have to be this way that it was rare to find extremely wealthy individuals who behaved in ways considered Godly. "The acquisition of wealth also has a way of absorbing so much of a person's time and energy that it draws him or her away from religion and moral concern for others." Richard Mather (Ryken, 2015). Puritans were students of Aristotle and these writings echoed ancient Greek thinking too.

> *There is no man in all things prosperous,*
>
> *There is no man among us all is free,*
>
> *For all are slaves of money or of chance.*
>
> Aristotle, Politic 322 BCC

The Puritans laid the groundwork for Harvard University within two years after landing in Massachusetts, and implemented universal education at home or in classrooms for every settlement of 50 or more, from grade school, high school, and right up to university - within just their first seventeen years. Latin was the spoken language at Harvard in those early days. High School students read Greek and Latin works including Aesop's Fables, Cicero, Ovid, Justin, Isocrates, Homer, Virgil, Horace, Perseus, and the Greek Testament.

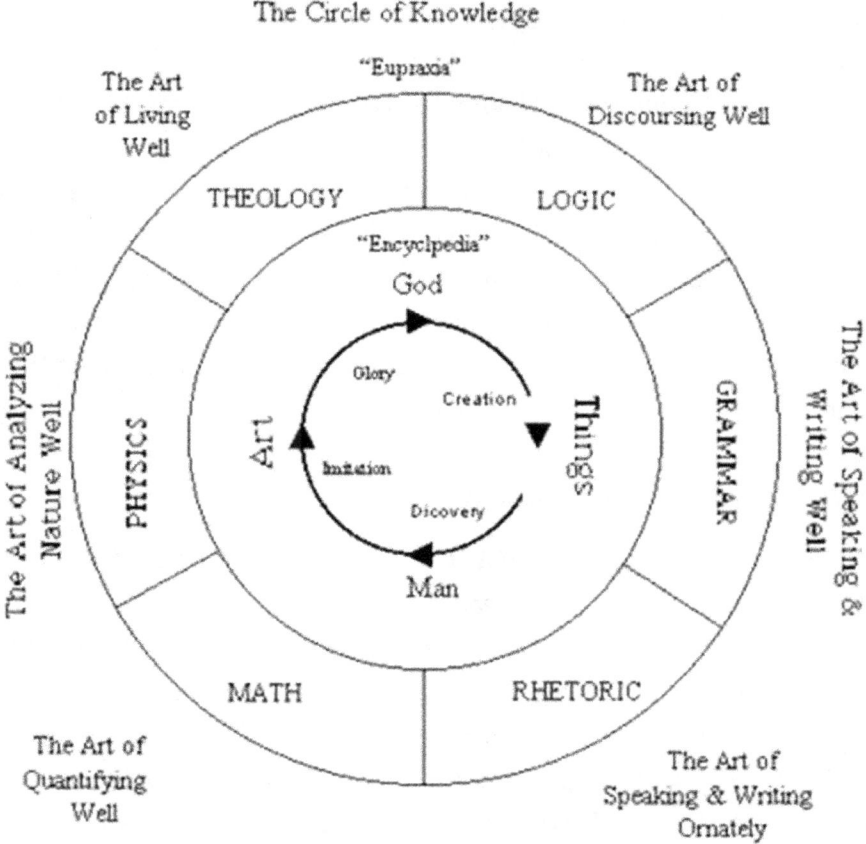

Harvard Studies were modeled after the Universities of Cambridge and Paris. A University's technique to creating a system of thought, logic, and philosophy – referred to in Latin as Techno-logia – is its curriculum. Not to be confused with the modern word "Technology".

Harvard was unique in that its *Technologia* included both metaphysics' cosmology, ontology (conceptualization), epistemology (philosophy), and anthropology; and it also integrated the three "books of truth" – Nature (Science by Aristotle), Scripture (The Bible), and Logic (Philosophy by Plato). Harvard's Seal became Veritas, or "Truth", signifying the Puritan passion for Truth.

Needless to say, the Puritans were no simple farmers. Much more than colonial leads from France, Spain or Holland, the British Puritans were country builders and lawmakers of the highest standard. When they arrived at a vast New World, their first act before disembarking ship even, was to build what would later be called the world's first written constitution, the Mayflower Compact. A legal guarantee of democratic vote and cooperation among settlers for the good of the colony first. My forefathers' brothers Edward and John Tilley, were among the 41 Pilgrims who committed the Compact to law with their signatures in November of 1620.

The Mayflower Compact

"IN THE NAME OF GOD, AMEN. We, whose names are underwritten, the Loyal Subjects of our dread Sovereign Lord King James, by the Grace of God, of Great Britain, France, and Ireland, King, Defender of the Faith, &c. Having undertaken for the Glory of God, and Advancement of the Christian Faith, and the Honour of our King and Country, a Voyage to plant the first Colony in the northern Parts of Virginia; Do by these Presents, solemnly and mutually, in the Presence of God and one another, covenant and combine ourselves together into a civil Body Politick, for our better Ordering and Preservation, and Furtherance of the Ends aforesaid: And by Virtue hereof do enact, constitute, and frame, such just and equal Laws,

Ordinances, Acts, Constitutions, and Officers, from time to time, as shall be thought most meet and convenient for the general Good of the Colony; unto which we promise all due Submission and Obedience. IN WITNESS whereof we have hereunto subscribed our names at Cape-Cod the eleventh of November, in the Reign of our Sovereign Lord King James, of England, France, and Ireland, the eighteenth, and of Scotland the fifty-fourth, Anno Domini; 1620."

John Milton is considered one of the greatest English writers of all time (Author of Paradise Lost, Paradise Refound, and others). He was a Puritan and a member of the Latin Office of the Cromwellian Protectorate in London when the Mayflower landed. Milton was just ten-years-old when William Shakespeare died in London, at age sixty-two in 1616. Shakespeare of course is globally accepted to be among the greatest playwrights of all time.

Puritans took a dim view of show business's 3,000 person crowds in an era with some of the best new theatre of all time. They took this view, not because of the plays; rather they began closing play houses widely by 1642 in the complaint of bear-baiting, gambling, cock and dog fights, prostitution and other immoral purposes at the Globe, Rose, and other theatres. Read more info in "The Puritans and Education" (Herring, 2003).

The Importance of Education in Democracy

To read the Mayflower's ship logs and excursion transcripts is to learn that many of these were men of impeccable education and elocution. Their diction was superior to most Advanced Degree Graduates today – although I suspect that the needs of our immature computer interfaces have taken a steep toll on this generation that will be restored as our automations mature.

In 1620, under a monarchy system of government, King James I managed economic controls, security spending, and taxation based on a lifetime of training and lessons provided in the proper management of the economy, capitalism, military, law, and so on.

Today, our voters hold this same power and so they too need lessons in how to build and run a country. We leave ourselves open to corruptions when we cannot judge impartially for ourselves. We humans are well-intentioned and smart enough, but we will often make decisions based on how we feel about a subject when we don't have a process and experience to fall back on in logic; based on our experiences and our technologia – our personal techniques in logic.

Campaign marketing advertisements that promoted "Low Tax" and Trickle-Down Economics, are a good example for discussion. During a K-Wave Spring and start of a Summer, you can get away with these long-term irresponsible economic controls that will tend to benefit a few. Trickle-down in K-Wave Autumn and Winter, however, leave the greater good at risk of desperate acts and even wars triggered during these Great Depressions.

Trickle-down only ever works when there is proper monitoring in place to keep tabs on its impact on Wealth Distribution. Without these economic controls set in place, the poorest 20% not only slipped to below 11% of total wealth (or a similar planning target) – it was allowed to slip to 0.1% in 2010. In the US, that means 80 million people struggled to share 0.1% of the wealth; worse, the next 20% shared just 0.2% while 60% shared 99.7%.

How could this happen? In an extreme democracy, the top 51% are ok so, the vote and call for help from the minority poor is not heard. It has taken 35 years from the start of this past K-Wave Autumn, for the poverty problem to grow to 49% and now their vote can finally be heard. As a voter, if you had been trained to manage wealth distribution back in high school, you would never have let it get this bad. Certainly a Monarch would have heard calls for revolution well before this level of income inequality.

King Hammurabi, for example, ruled a capitalist society by an economic control that forgave all debt every 50 years (Jubilee years) so that everyone was level-set before K-Wave Depressions could trigger rebellions and other social problems. Read more about debt forgiveness as long ago as 2400 BCE at http://www.globalresearch.ca/debt-cancellation-in-mesopotamia-and-egypt-from-3000-to-1000-bc/5303136 (Toussaint, 2012)

Reports by Berkeley economics professor Emmanuel Saezsay in his September 3, 2013, paper "Striking it Richer", documented that 95% of all new wealth from and after 2008 continued to go the top 1% directly without monitoring nor controls. So wealth distribution has not improved since 2010 reports at all. Clearly artificial low interest rates create housing bubbles (higher rents and housing prices) and make rich businesses and individuals richer, but it adds nothing or a negative impact, to the incomes and lives of citizens.

To showcase the need for nationwide education; at the same time that this "Low Tax" election dogma was widely used in the 80s, it is very true to say that less than 1% of North American voters were aware that Capitalist Societies trough every sixty years. So really, how could voters ever be expected to vote for good management in that aspect of our capitalist economy? Education in K-Wave economics in high school, therefore, is crucial.

In school, you might have learned that although Wealth Creation and Wealth Distribution (the American Dream) are both important to a healthy society; was it also made clear that of the two, only Wealth Distribution has a proven correlation to decreasing social problems?

During history class, we learned that by permitting wealth inequity to become extreme, the French and Russian Monarchs exposed their non-combatant families to revolution and death. It never dawns on us that by permitting history to repeat itself today, we expose our families to suffering and death through a possible World War III. World War II killed 60 million people and surviving one of these wars was no picnic either.

A code book instructed Hammurabi and the other Emperors of Mesopotamia and Egypt that they followed as laid down by Emperors of the past thousand years. The code commanded countrywide debt-forgiveness every fifty years – just like our 2008 bailouts and much more.

Anecdotally, the code and other similar texts in the Torah, and in the Bible, also ensured freedom from indentured servitude (slavery), every seven years as well.

Were you ever taught that building anything large, complex and worthwhile, takes strategic planning and consistent forward project management? Of course, you were - Yes. In the TED Talks slideshow above, we see forty-five years of back-to-back four-year election cycles resulting in our heading away from a good life for our society with no long term plan of any kind.

Are you aware of a long-term plan of any sort for society? The Transition Plan is, in fact, a fundamentally important document for every government to maintain.

There will be another Spring Economy in three to six years, but it will only come at the hands of a hotly opposed wealth distribution project – or at risk of nuclear war and human extinction.

We do not have all of these rules laid out by our fathers any longer – and so this education shortfall risks democracy and even humanity itself.

In the absence of country leadership lessons in school, we voters relied upon the most leader-like candidates to manage this well on our behalf. If you are over 60 years of age, you can remember a time when everything that you heard in the media and on television news was considered truthful, so many people believed these low-tax instructions as they would have accepted a formal classroom training.

What is the old expression – fool me once, shame on you. Fool me twice, shame on me.

Democracy is an important construct of a sustainable, happy home life, sustainable good life, and so we voters need to make intermittent adjustments that ensure it effectively manages our economy and detours us well clear of war and financial panics as well.

Voter Comparison Charts

Use a simple chart like the following to work with your Political Parties in non-election years and shape policies that permit sustainable democracy and economy. Once projects begin - and begin to help the economy thrive, so too should your communities prosper.

This chart is intended to be for example purposes only. Simply swap your own political parties and policies in as appropriate.

This is a great method for voters to help improve their country's Transition Economics Maturity.

#	A+ Priority Social Policy	Canada			
		Cons	Lib	NDP	Grn
1	Long Term Right Planning	No	No	No	Yes
2	Bench Strength of MPs for Project Execution	Maybe	No	No	No
Wealth Distribution					
3	Pension Controls				
4	Minimum Wage Targets	No	Maybe	Yes	Yes
5	Graduated Tax	No	No	No	Yes
6	Guaranteed Incomes	No	No	Yes	Yes
7	Housing & Usury Controls	No	No	No	No
8	End Tax Avoidance	No	No	No	No
9	Daycare, Healthcare, Higher Education	No	Maybe	Yes	No
10	Onshore Engineering	No	No	Yes	No
Wealth Creation					
11	Increase & Automate Quality Exports	No	No	No	No
12	Reduce Imports	No	Yes	Yes	Yes
13	Sellers Automate Manufacture Locally	No	No	Yes	Maybe
14	Local Profit becomes Investment & Tax Revs	No	No	Yes	Maybe
Transition Economics Maturity					
15	Engineering Project Safety Nets	No	No	No	Yes
16	Increase Spending Power & Opportunity	No	No	No	No
17	Renewable Automation #WPProjects	No	No	No	No
18	TE Maturity Model Goals	No	No	No	No
	If Yes=2, Maybe=1, No=0	3%	13%	47%	53%
	Leaning	Right	Left	Left	Left

Chapter 27

The #WPProjects Global Right Plan

The naming of the World Peace Transition Projects originated from a Common Sense 101 course exercise. All projects that were needed to provide a Good Life for students, were listed in non-chronological sequence from Global needs, to Country, to Community, to School, Family and then finally right down to Individual needs.

That list of projects was then sequenced chronologically to build a list called the CSQ 100 Year Plan. The 100-Year Plan list grew to 38 projects as needed to build a good life sustainably for our generation and for future generations as well.

By stepping back and cherry-picking from this 100-Year Plan, just those projects needed to deliver a Sustainable World Peace quickly today, just 19 Projects were needed to create a comprehensive solution - and that subset of projects became the World Peace Transition Projects, WPProjects for short - and a hashtag #WPProjects was added for social media discussions.

The book World Peace – The Transition explains these 19 social and technology projects in detail and it explains that two of the projects were particularly complex technology and economics tasks.

The first difficult project was the build of a Self-Powered Replicator, a device that could convert Light or Energy to Matter in any configuration required. The original theory for light to matter was suggested in 1936 and testing is being conducted by Physicists of London's Imperial College in 2016. These are the same groups whose work has been very distracted of late by quantum entanglement (used in China's newest satellite communications switches) and even teleportation of light.

The second complex project, was the development of the Science of Transition Economics – the explanation of changes and throttles (throttles describe responsible rates-of-change) needed to sustain unsustainable capitalism's repeating cycles. This book Transition Economics, with its broad solutions, was needed to explain in detail the specific policies, method, and rates of change for each policy that needed to change.

SUSTAIN Project Management Method was broken out to a fourth book as well, in order to permit detail examples and templates for that large breakout discussion.

#WPProjects became 250 projects - from its original 19, because of the need for hundreds of automation projects to mitigate an anticipated delay in Imperial College of London's Replicator science.

You have seen an example of #WPProjects depicted in the Hollywood movies Ironman and Tomorrowland; and you have seen similar assembly processes in car manufacturing plants.

Raw materials are either gathered automatically or by conventional mining, farming and so on; building materials are smelted or milled, and then an assembly line builds a mix of 3D-Printed and Machine Manufactured components according to computerized designed specs "automatically".

China 3D-prints six-story buildings and luxury homes for the past 4 years; Audi makes the world's highest-quality driverless cars without a human worker in the process, and the cost of LIDAR and robotics is falling dramatically. LIDAR, the vision-based driverless car computers, are being miniaturized onto a chip at MIT – reducing costs up to 1000 times per vehicle.

Robotic arm pricing is down to less than $5,000 for small units and 2,000 robotics companies presented to 120,000 attendants in the U.S.'s largest Manufacturing Technology show IMTS in Chicago in September.

As a society, we pay an Opportunity Cost for delays in failing to start, and then failing to monetize, our Renewable Automation Projects.

The Return on Investment – ROI, of an automated approach will always surpass our current manual production methods over time, so our governments have to ensure that approvals for financial support of these projects is generous and not misdirected to distracting gadgets and non-renewable technology projects.

This means that approval committee members at all levels of Government Innovation Programs must be engineers (career hi-tech builders) tasked with making the projects happen reliably.

Canada is an example of a G7 that had no automation technology on their innovation plan in 2016. Not surprisingly, they sit at an embarrassing #100 on the CSQ CMI Country Management Team performance ranking. The Netherlands are building automated robotic 3D-printed bridge building projects and a wide array of automated hi-tech – they sit at #5 on the CMI.

The World Peace Transition Projects (#WPProjects) are a Plan that suggests a combination of Renewable Automation Projects and Social Transition Economics Maturity Projects as needed to deliver a sustainable Good Life at home first - and then extend it globally. See csq1.org, Twitter and Google+ for #WPProjects. A detail explanation of the plan and the importance of building it, is laid out in the 475-page book World Peace – The Transition. #WPProjects assigns three Teams to a Four "Step" Plan of Social and Technology Projects that transitions us to an automated society responsibly.

The Three Teams are:

Team One – Voters and Policy Makers

Team Two – Engineers and Project Leads

Team Three is a central communications team; perhaps the United Nations at some point, but initially it begins with leadership teams at CSQ Research.

The Four Steps are:

Step 1 & 2 – Social and Technology Projects

What #WPProjects proposed in 2015 was that 180 countries should be assigned just one hi-tech automation project each. Some projects are advanced high-school-robotics-level projects, and others are sophisticated robotic automation builds.

Each Country is assigned a #WPProject

Countries with higher GDP were assigned more difficult projects - and were also asked to Sponsor smaller countries as well.

In order of ascending GDP, each country in the world is assigned the progressively more complex automation projects that build all of our basic needs.

The list of 250 projects leverage the top exports from every country so that if a country is a world leader in producing one of the products on the #WPProjects List below, then as much as possible, that country was assigned the task. Vietnam is the world's leading exporter of peppercorns, and so they were assigned Peppercorns; Hawaii leads Macadamia Nut production, and so on.

More complex tasks were given to countries with highest GDP and then the smallest GDP countries were paired with sponsor nations so that smallest and largest GDP countries can assist one another.

In this way, all countries can contribute to our generation's greatest accomplishment - an automated economy.

The creation of an automated economy heralds an end of a long era of slavery in civilization, and the start of a new era of universal human rights. High-schools, States, Companies too, engineer tinkerers, are all able to contribute.

The #WPProjects Project List begins as high-level release v1.0 list which recognizes that dozens of projects are likely missed initially. Many countries will be asked to add another project or two quickly as work rolls out and gaps are flushed out in design meetings.

How long does it take to build one of these projects? It takes 12 months for a v1.0 working release of each technology; 24 months for a 2.0 release with interoperability to all other systems. By v3.0, there will be at least three to ten versions available of each, which means that an automated house builder will be able to build three types of home – perhaps townhouse, bungalow, two-story-home; and then three styles of townhome and exponentially more with each release as well.

In the same way that our kids spend countless hours building new virtual worlds in MineCraft, Warcraft, Sims, and 3D Virtual Reality sites like NextLife, these kids can instead be designing real world living homes and neighborhoods. Design contests could kick off Worldville competitions worldwide beginning online at any time.

Each Country are Assigned #WPProjects

Country	GDP	#WPProjects
Belgium	524,806	Produce Transport, Chocolate
Brazil	2,243m	Auto Peacekeeping – Air, Confections Candies
Canada	1,838m	Satellite Water Divining, Collection & Distribution, Cold Fusion, Drone Jets & Air transport
Denmark	336,701	3D Printed or Assembled Buildings
Finland	267,329	Fishing fillet, package, freeze
France	2,806m	Auto Road Build/Repair, Cosmetics, Wine
Germany	3,730m	Auto Vehicle Delivery, Driverless Cars, Bavaria – Beer
Hong Kong	274,027	GPS Tractors, Holiday and Gift Wrapping
Indonesia	868,346	3D Food Printers
Israel	291,567	Auto Airplane design
Italy	2,149m	3D Cement Systems, Wine
Japan	4,898m	Household Robot, Grand & Upright Pianos
Mexico	1,259m	Pharma Diabetes - Lantus Solostar & related
Micronesia	333	Auto Steel Manufacture, Avocados, Mangos, Tequila
Monaco	6,559	Sponsor Japan
Netherlands	853,539	Auto Toilets and Installer Performance Management
Norway	522,349	Auto Oil Production, Diapers – All, Electronic Drum Sets
Pakistan	225,419	Conveyers – mining & farming
Philippines	272,067	Grocery Distribution & Delivery Technician robots

Country	GDP	#WPProjects
Poland	525,863	Tech Architects & QC Approvers, Interoperability Standards, Transportation Software
Russia	2,096m	Drone Peacekeeping – Ground, Auto Snow Removal
		Oil Alternatives - Paraffin Diesel and Blue Diesel Plants (perhaps using nuclear ship power), Vodka
Saudi Arabia	748,450	Rapid Charge Batteries - Robotics
South Africa	366,060	New Mining by Satellite
South Korea	1,304 m	Automated TV, & Monitor production
Spain	1,393m	Automatic Park Builder
Sweden	579,680	Marina Build System – up to 80 boats
Switzerland	685,434	Surgery – Knee, Hip, Elbow
Turkey	822,149	Satellite Driven Well & Irrigation Builder
United Arab Emirates	599,000	Fishing fillet, package, freeze
United Kingdom	2,678m	Energy to Matter Conversion Sanitation – Waste Treatment Scotch – Single Malt & Whiskey
United States	16,768 m	GPS Threshers Harvest Tricorder Med Console Hawaii – Auto Harvest Macadamia Nuts California – Blue Crude & e-Diesel Cheese & Cream Products

▼ Copywrite 2015 World Peace – The Transition at CSQ1.org ▼ **200 Countries with at least One Project**

372

To build this first #WPProjects list, we took the top 100 grocery items sold locally; then the top 25 Pharmaceuticals, then the top 50 household items, appliances, transportation, shelter, and energy and more.

Every region will have special requests, and #WPProjects simply asks that project teams contact the project lead for that technology so that your team can work on parallel or dependent projects simulaneously. These tech campuses are encouraged, as is swapping projects with other countries if this initial plan can be fine-tuned better. Simply request an update be made to the master WPA #WPProjects Plan with consent by the host country attached in our forums.

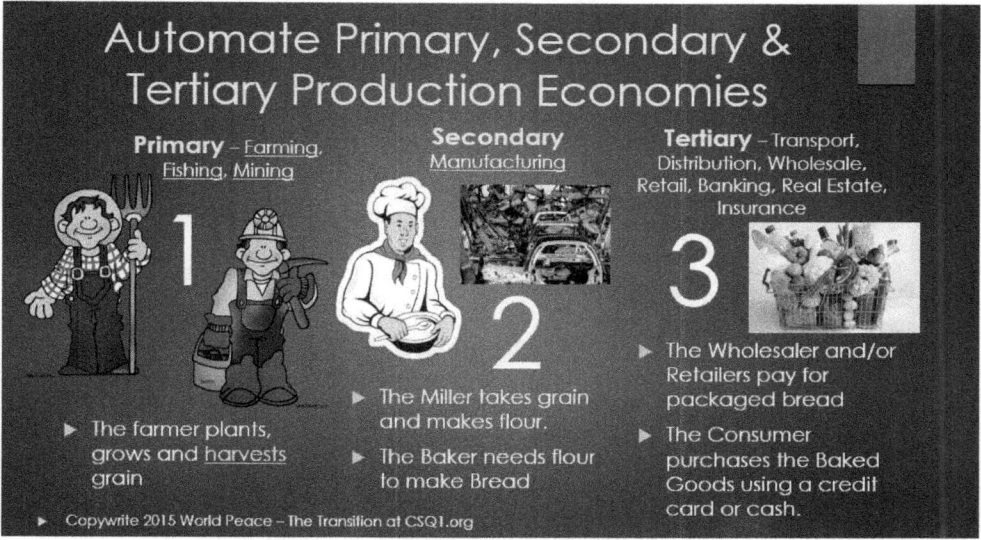

Automating Production Economies

Today we plant and pick our crops manually, or with manually driven tractors and transportation and processing equipment. Tomorrow we will automate Farming, Fishing, Mining, and the production of most other resource commodities. Where do we begin? We look at our country's GDP Exports today and also look at where you want it to be in 5 years, and then we automate the most important exports first. In this way, we grow both wealth creation and wealth distribution, at the same time.

Most people think to automate Secondary Manufacturing Production first, but begin to automate Primary Production of raw materials as well. Target Imports and seek to minimize dependency where any hardships that arise are manageable by your suppliers and customers.

Automated Wholesale, Retail, and Distribution are planned to implement at a rate that generate profits and rely upon Social Safety Nets less.

If you are concerned that your priorities and tasks are not well understood nor well executed, look to CSQ Certifications and CSQ CSR Training Worldwide designed to assure due diligence was exercised in the automation choices made first, so that social benefits and the greater good are served as best can.

Step 3 – Manage the Transition

Our Jobs are Automating. This is already happening, and it is important that these automations continue and even accelerate if we are to a reach a sustainable Good Life.

Automation has impacted Autoworkers, Warehouse workers, and many facets of manufacturing and distribution is next.

The largest employer in the U.S. is the trucking industry, and that industry will begin to lose jobs rapidly as automated self-driving cars and trucks begin to chip away at manual jobs in the inevitable countdown to 100% automation.

Create the field of Transition Economics, leveraging Transition Economy conventions and automation rate-of-change balancing. This book talks about these throttling and rate-of-change balances.

In the discussion of Safety Nets – we cover engineers first and then empower them to build automation with priority.

Then we automate Industry by Industry - in priority of profitable exports first – and coordinate with other nations so that Canada automates Mining, as Mexico takes on robotic food production; then the UK takes on landscaping and ground maintenance; and Japan leads household robot-maid production – and so on.

The Technology Projects will automate our production economy until we have a Technology-based Social Safety Net. #WPProjects Technology Projects target those projects that are required **to automate the production of the basics of life and a good society.**

Using the example from the opening chapter of World Peace - The Transition –

The knock on your door is a delight as you have been waiting for this day for a lifetime...

This person is living in a home with the basics of life; like potable water and sanitation. If this person's home already exists – as in an existing city, then there is little to build and maintenance bots will keep the building up to code throughout its useful service life.

If the home had to be built new, then a robotic building system would have to grade and service the land - according to a subdivision plan. A House Plan would then either 3D Print the house - or robotically assemble it from a bill of material of parts that arrived by automated transport just-in-time as needed.

The automated digging and pouring of the building's foundation was followed by framing, roofing, windows and doors, and then wiring and plumbing followed. Finishing drywall, flooring, and baseboards were installed and then painted, so that cabinets and finished fixtures could be plugged together. Final touches included lighting, furniture, and entertainment and computer equipment as necessary.

By adhering to conventions for rapid development, the building systems have taken about 18 months to develop and then another six months in integration testing designed to get the final bugs resolved. The finished house goes up in about a week and shows pretty well for a version 2.0.

Version 2.0 also includes the automated construction tools and processes needed to build this robotic tool so; now we can roll out both tools and homes automatically. All designs including how to improve the next release of the system are conveyed to the #WPProjects Charter as needed to let engineers get the remaining bugs out of the system by version 3.0. By version 2 or 3, there should also be at least three versions of the solution for the choosing. For the example project of a robotic house builder, there should be three styles such as a townhouse, bungalow, and two-story home; or perhaps a variety of townhouse designs to choose from in the same way that cars are built to order.

Assembling building materials takes place in a variety of automated cement plants and transports; forestry fabrication robots create wood; and automated mining and smelt solutions create metal framing. Window and door glass was created in a central plant in large sheets and then cut to size as needed in local distribution centers. Automatically manufactured door plastics and locking hardware transfer to the site just in time to install as needed. Adjustments to all plans for weather delays and material shortages were also factored into the project software and adjust lead-time plans automatically.

Food systems planted, cared for, harvested, cleaned and assembled vegetables, dairy, meats, canned goods and other grocery items into bags and delivered them automatically as orchestrated by ERP software once requested by members of each home. Groceries and other ordering takes place via a web-based grocery app on the homeowner's TV, smartphone and computer systems and is supported by the Help Desk as needed.

The "Worldville" Competitions

"Worldville" 1 & 2, whose final naming will be determined by a local competition, are the first Pilot Towns with an automated production economy towns.

Worldville One - is an existing town with new automation as needed to automate 90% of the production economy. With 100% automation worked toward within five years.

Worldville Two - is new construction with all systems tested to work together to deliver an automated town. This production economy can sustain 50 to 1000 residents in modern, comfortable, constantly improving, sustainable accommodation - complete with a park, school, marina, hospital, old age facilities, good jobs and a recreation center with growth plans as needed to ensure a terrific future for all members of the community.

Worldville towns and cities are no island communes nor amusement park attractions, Worldville is a plugged-in community and vital part of the planet's economy. A place where real people want to live.

By late in 2017, we could have a release 1.0 of many of these technologies, and hopefully enough of these systems should be under development to continue interoperability work as needed get these systems working together well enough to build one or two towns by 2018 - with 2019 as a rain date.

If that does not sound like an easy test, I do not know what does. Everything is up for discussion during design here so get working and stay tuned as the work continues.

All of this sounds straight-forward and it is, the very great obstacle is gaining awareness, acceptance, and consensus to move forward in a world that protects decision makers with a thick layer of insulation that makes sharing ideas very difficult and time consuming. How long this message will take to get out and to be accepted is yet to be seen.

Science Fiction is just a Technology Project

We have already made a lot of forward progress – as seen in the complete automation of car manufacturing at Audi, Tesla, and much of the auto industry, and in the Driverless Cars Program at Google. As it turns out, four of the projects identified in the plan are already completed this year as well – Communicators, Universal Translator, Performance Software and Clean Diesel.

Science Fiction is just a HiTech Project

Leonardo Da Vinci
1452 –1519

Helicopter realized 1947

Tanks, Robots, Planes Bicycles, and more.

Jules Verne
1828 – 1905

Nautilus realized 1940

Earth to the Moon 1969

Hanna & Barbera
1910-2001 1911-2006

Video Watches realized 2016

Robot Maids realized 2025

Gene Roddenbury
1921 - 1991

Communicators realized 2013
Universal Translator realized 2015
TriCorder XPrize 2016
HypoSpray 1960 perfected 2015
Replicators Today & 2032

Throughout time, visionary Engineers have imagined great works of technology that we come to accept as quite commonplace and not extraordinary at all today.

Leonardo da Vinci designed Helicopters, Airplanes, simple animatronic robots, bicycles, tanks and other technology that we accept as fact and commonplace today. It took 400 years for da Vinci's designs to take flight.

Jules Verne imagined sophisticated technology including Submarines, Time Machines and a Trip to the Moon. It would 100 years to build his Nautilus and Flight to the Moon.

More contemporary engineers employed contemporary mediums too. Hanna and Barbera's The Jetsons cartoon series envisioned Robot Maids, Video Watches, Anti-Gravity, and a broad array of social improvements, like two day work weeks, that would most probably need to be added to the fabric of society in the future as well.

Gene Roddenberry hasn't been gone long enough to be fully appreciated for the contributions that his visual creations gave us in support of space travel and a sustainable Good Life within his Star Trek TV episodes and movies. Mr. Roddenberry conceptualized replicators of food, air, clothing, vehicles and much of what we see today in our 3D Printing Industries.

Aristotle said that a Good Life is full of the things you need, and not necessarily the things you want. For this reason, products like Tobacco (which kill 20% of smokers), Marijuana, opium and illegal drugs and substances are excused from the list. Alcoholism too is a tragedy for individuals, families, and even whole communities but these products made it onto the list with the caveat that a world with everything provided cannot be a death sentence for the young and addicts. Addictive provisions will be monitored and restricted where public health and productivity concerns warrant it.

This list will be revision controlled, and Change Logged on the CSQ website as more projects are added.

Several countries have provinces or states that are the population and GDP of most countries – examples include Texas and California. Countries are assigned project leadership and may request or volunteer resources to or from other project teams.

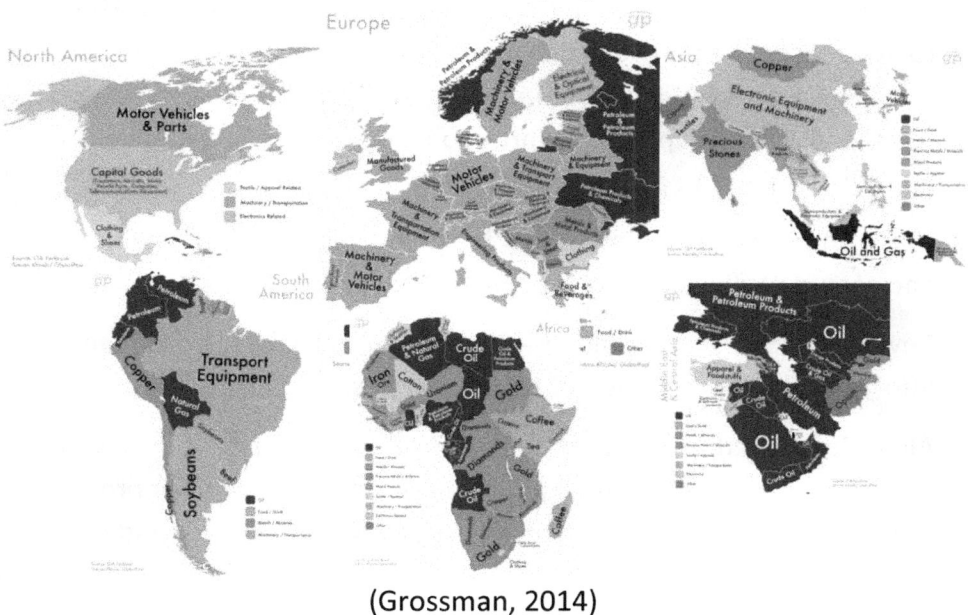

(Grossman, 2014)

Team Two – Automating our Production Economy

Adding World Peace Agenda Projects

This chart is a very high-level initial list that has missed dozens, and even hundreds of component projects. It might even be safe to count on at least one more project per country before the list completes.

These are complete automation projects, no human hands touch the products from raw materials to boxed product. Integrations should be well thought out so that housekeeping robots are able to spot and trash expired produce or meats in refrigerators. List dependent projects in Charter and communicate your needs to them in Requirements.

Never assign projects to Project Leads who do not know how to begin. You have handed it to the wrong resource and failure is imminent. The right project lead is the engineer who has run these projects a hundred times - and is someone who knows when and how to ask questions that guarantee immediate progress past roadblocks to a final successful v1.0, v2.0 and beyond. You have two years to release v2.0 with support for three to nine variances – so there is a busy two years ahead.

Liaise and seek sponsorship with leading companies and engineers and seek outside engineering help as needed.

Review the list above and use the forums at CSQ1.org or email info@csq1.org to suggest and track additions.

All projects need: assignment to a sponsoring country or business, a project manager with contact information, Charter and other project docs – both in-process or approved, budget and resources, and then the work can begin.

I have not tried to guess at what additional project teams, companies, and individuals will volunteer to take on component automation projects. I hope that the number is considerable and that a small army of engineers and master builders feel they are enabled and can take enough queues from these very basic sketches. I can tell you that the really capable engineers will find 80% of the directions they need here – and divine the rest during the build process.

Find the most recent version-controlled Master #WPProjects Project List at CSQ1.org.

If you are not assigned a project to begin with, seek funding, start with Maslow's Hierarchy of Needs, and build up from there. Water – Creation, Delivery Coordination, and Transport; Food, Clothing, Shelter, Sanitation, Security Communications, Transportation, Education, HealthCare, tablet computers, and so on.

Should TVs and video games be on the list? All of these questions need to be vetted so put them on your requirements list and build all deliverables in order of priority – whatever that priority might be.

Break down problems and then build up solutions. Wouldn't it be terrific to reach every High School Robotics team and have them collaborate with the coordinator of the technology that they decide they want to tackle first? Science Fairs, Exhibitions, Trade Shows, the sky is the limit, and I hope to see you and your project team results there.

Building Great Technology

When I was in Baccalaureate Math classes in High School, we had two members of the Canadian Space organization visit our class to talk about the importance of math in our future. I thought I had forgotten that 1979 – thirty-four-year-old memory entirely, but as I think back on lessons learned, I can recall their binary math demonstration in that class vividly.

The first instructor wrote down a sixty or eighty character string of 1's and 0's on the white board. The second instructor turned away as the first changed a dozen or more of the seemingly pattern-free binary, and then the second returned to the board and proceeded to correct all of the changes made easily and quickly. The instructors explained that the ability to correct errors in binary sequences was a critical part of any communication in space because of the low reliability and high loss rate of the transmissions received. More times than not, communications arrived scrambled and had to be corrected before they were useful.

The lesson here was always to embed a layer of self-correction into your work. I heard it echoed again years later while working with programming teams: a great programmer was someone who could create code that subsequent programming teams could not easily break during revision updates.

That was a great lesson.

The WPProjects List v1.0

Here is the initial per-country project assignments list. There are many missing projects, but this list covers a broad start. You could take an inventory of 100 top selling items at local grocery stores to get another list of projects, and popular staple products vary widely from country to country. A U.S. database of international trade information is available for query by the public online. (US-ITC, 2016). Just 15 of the top Pharmaceuticals are included on this list so unassigned countries can sponsor the following list (Drugs.com, 2014) and other important regional medicines must be added.

Most large countries are assigned Tier 1 Food, Mining, Raw materials; Tier 2 Manufacturing, Energy, and Tertiary Economy tasks like Transport and distribution projects – or should be. Volunteering for other projects is encouraged; we simply ask that you keep this central listing updated.

Country	GDP	#WPProjects Assignments v1.1
Afghanistan	21,618	Sponsor Uruguay Flower potting and shipping
Albania	12,904	Sponsor Lithuania Canning containers
Algeria	208 m	Automated Education Pre to K12
Andorra	3,249	Sponsor Pakistan LED Lights & Fixtures

Country	GDP	#WPProjects Assignments v1.1
Angola	121,692	Auto Harvest – Lettuce & Cabbage
Anguilla	284	Sponsor Brazil Coconut and Oils
Antigua and Barbuda	1,241	Sponsor Iran Medical Imaging – CAT Scan
Argentina	611,726	Auto Harvest – Wine Fresh Peppers Picking
Armenia	10,431	Sponsor Croatia Butter Production
Aruba	2,589	Clean Water Plants
Australia	1,531m	Rapid Charge Batteries Automotive
Austria	428,322	Ground Transportation Mgmt. Paint Systems Management
Azerbaijan	73,557	Hi-Rise Crane Operation Coffee Makers & Grills
Bahamas, The	8,420	Sponsor Sri Lanka Missing Supply Contingency Planning
Bahrain	32,898	Plastic Recycle
Bangladesh	153,505	Auto Harvest – Carrots & Potatoes
Barbados	4,228	Sponsor Iraq Garden Build, Plant, Sprinkler, Maintain
Belarus	71,710	Auto Dredger
Belgium	524,806	Produce Transport Chocolate
Belize	1,624	Sponsor Denmark Washer & Dryers
Benin	8,307	Sponsor Belarus Ice and Crushed Ice
Bermuda	5,574	Auto Ground Maintenance
Bhutan	1,781	Sponsor Malaysia Dish Washers
Bolivia	30,601	Auto Harvest - Corn
Bosnia and Herzegovina	17,852	Traffic Control Systems Boots - Rubber
Botswana	14,778	Sponsor Morocco Carpets & flooring covers
Brazil	2,243m	Auto Peacekeeping – Air Confections Candies
British Virgin Islands	916	Sponsor UAE Automated School Build

Country	GDP	#WPProjects Assignments v1.1
Brunei	16,111	3D Boat Building
Bulgaria	54,481	Farm Tires
Burkina Faso	12,547	Sponsor Ghana Table Honey
Burundi	2,549	Sponsor Finland Locomotives
Cambodia	15,250	Auto Food Distribution 30% of all emissions is food transport (ask for help from SAP & MS)
Cameroon	29,568	Auto Harvest Baby Foods
Canada	1,838m	Satellite Water Divining, Collection & Distribution Clean Energy - Cold Fusion Drone Jets & Air transport
Cape Verde	1,861	Sponsor Argentina Auto Defibrillator maker
Cayman Islands	3,474	Czech Republic Auto Fish Finders & Sonar
Central African Republic	1,585	Sponsor Uruguay Lamb Meat Processing
Chad	10,640	Sponsor South Africa Violins & Chelos
Chile	277,043	Beef Processing Leather - Beef
China	9,181m	Robotic humanoid hands & A.I. Trainer software Housewares, dishware, cooking utensils Clean Energy Thorium Reactors
Colombia	378,148	Auto Pharma - Pill/Package/Transport
Comoros	622	Sponsor Spain XG Guitar, hardware, and cables. Classical Guitars.
Congo	32,691	Satellite Resourcing & Mining exploration – Lithium, Gold, Diamond, etc.
Cook Islands	330	Sponsor Italy Cooking Tools - choice
Costa Rica	49,621	Fruit and Vegetable Distribution
Côte d'Ivoire	28,593	Assist France Dining Room Furniture
Croatia	57,869	Automated Dump trucks
Cuba	78,694	Surgery – Gall Bladder Removal

Country	GDP	#WPProjects Assignments v1.1
Curacao	3,148	Sponsor Portugal
		Automated Planting with Seed
Cyprus	24,057	Smelting Automation
Czech Republic	208,796	Robot-3D Printer handover
Denmark	336,701	3D Printed or Assembled Buildings
Djibouti	1,456	Sponsor Venezuela
		Shoes - Womens
Dominica	498	Sponsor Australia
		Motorcycle production
Dominican Republic	60,612	Auto Bathroom Tub and Shower Installation
Ecuador	94,473	Surgery – Eye
		Banana Picking and Processing
Egypt	255,199	Robotic Process - Poultry
El Salvador	24,259	Auto Harvest Onions & Mushrooms
Equatorial Guinea	18,532	Automated Forestry Harvesting & Milling
Eritrea	3,438	Sponsor Kazakhstan
		Aluminum Foil
Estonia	24,880	Stone Cutting & Transport
Ethiopia	46,017	Auto Harvest Carrots and Beets
Fiji	4,034	Sponsor Qatar
		Flex monitor screens & Active Glass Touch Monitors
Finland	267,329	Fishing fillet, package, freeze
France	2,806m	Auto Road Build/Repair
		Cosmetics
		Wine
French Polynesia	641	Sponsor France
		Shellfish and Clam Production
Gabon	16,970	Sponsor Luxemburg
		Diet Foods
Gambia, The	902	Sponsor Argentina
		Automated Seed Harvesting
Georgia	16,127	Auto Diesel Engines
Germany	3,730m	Auto Vehicle Delivery
		Driverless Cars
		Tricorder Med Console
		Bavaria – Beer
Ghana	47,830	Automated Marine Engine Mounts
Greece	242,230	Grocery Web Interface

Country	GDP	#WPProjects Assignments v1.1
Greenland	2,418	Sponsor Iran
		Organic House-cleaning products
Grenada	831	Sponsor Switzerland
		Medical Imaging – MRI
Guatemala	53,797	Construction Siding
		Coffee
Guinea	7,219	Sponsor Slovakia
		Synthesizers and Keyboards
Guinea-Bissau	1,036	Sponsor Poland
		Distribution Warehouse Makers
Guyana	2,990	Sponsor Ireland
		Hifi Music Microphones & Stands
Haiti	7,691	Sponsor Libya
		Shoes - Men
Honduras	18,569	Auto Grocery Bag Manufacture
Hong Kong	274,027	GPS Tractors
		Holiday and Gift Wrapping
Hungary	133,424	Auto Fence building
		Beer
Iceland	15,330	Pipelines – Oil & Gas
India	1,937m	Automated Community Build
Indonesia	868,346	3D Food Printers
Iran	492,783	3D Clothing, Tricorder
Iraq	195,517	Water/Waste Pipe Tunnelling
Ireland	232,077	Auto Ground Keeping
Israel	291,567	Auto Airplane design
Italy	2,149m	3D Cement Systems
		Wine
Jamaica	14,270	Travel Booking
Japan	4,898m	Household Robot
		Grand & Upright Pianos
		Pharma Diabetes - Lantus Solostar & related
Jordan	33,594	Blue Crude Plant Automation S/M/L
Kazakhstan	224,415	Automated Cement Mixers
Kenya	54,443	Construction Glass
Kiribati	175	Sponsor Germany
		Off road vehicles
Kosovo	6,837	Sponsor Morocco
		LED Stage Lighting, Scaffolds, control panels
Kuwait	175,831	Plastic Container - Water

Country	GDP	#WPProjects Assignments v1.1
Kyrgyzstan	7,226	Sponsor Ecuador
		Laundry – detergents & fabric softener
Laos	10,760	Sponsor Sudan
		Music Drum Sets
Latvia	30,886	Small Engine Marine
Lebanon	47,221	Construction Framing – Metal
Lesotho	2,230	Sponsor Hong Kong
		Zambonies & Ice Makers
Liberia	1,946	Sponsor Chile
		Ice Rinks
Libya	74,597	Auto Peacekeeping - Sea
Liechtenstein	5,647	Sponsor Angola
		Woodwind Instruments
Lithuania	46,403	Robotic Process – Rice
Luxembourg	60,131	Automated forklifts
Macau	51,753	Construction Brick
Macedonia	10,767	Sponsor Bulgaria
		Sport Canoes & Kayaks
Madagascar	10,612	Sponsor Uzbekistan
		X10 Home Controllers & Software
Malawi	5,146	Sponsor Kuwait
		Flower Seeds & Pots
Malaysia	312,434	Auto Kitchen Appliance Build
		Server Production
Maldives	2,836	Sponsor Greece
		Soccer Balls, Volleyballs, Baseballs, etc.
Mali	10,943	Sponsor Kenya
		Hockey Sticks & Raquets Tennis, RB & Squash
Malta	9,971	GPS Fishing Routes
Marshall Islands	189	Sponsor France
		Medical Imaging X-ray
Mauritania	5,516	Sponsor Bangladesh
Mauritius	11,938	Food Distribution Software
Mexico	1,259m	Auto Steel Manufacture
		Avacados, Mangos
		Tequila
Micronesia	333	Sponsor Japan
		Auto Toilets and Installer
Moldova	7,970	Sponsor Azerbaijan
		Music Drum Sets & Symbols
Monaco	6,559	Performance Management

Country	GDP	#WPProjects Assignments v1.1
Mongolia	11,516	Sponsor Macau Woodwind Instruments
Montenegro	4,417	Sponsor Romania Personal Hygene Grooming Products
Montserrat	59	Sponsor China Automated Rec Center & Gym, with Coffee Shop and Dance Hall
Morocco	103,836	Cold Fusion assisted Molten-Salt Solar
Mozambique	1,105	Sponsor Norway Feminine Hygiene Products
Myanmar	63,031	Safety - Human Detectors
Namibia	12,580	Sponsor Tunisia Music Sundry, Guitar Picks, Drum Sticks, Capos, Strings, stands
Nauru	153	Sponsor Japan Music Amps Solid State & Tubes
Nepal	18,179	Auto Wood Mouldings
Netherlands	853,539	Conveyers - mining & farming
New Caledonia	9,712	Sponsor Dominican Republic Bar Mix Bottles or Cans
New Zealand	189,025	Farming - herding
Nicaragua	11,256	Sponsor Guatemala Bass Violins
Niger	7,407	Sponsor Oman Violins, Chellos, etc.
Nigeria	514,965	Auto Med Supplies
North Korea	15,454	Auto Med Supplies
Norway	522,349	Auto Oil Production Diapers – All Electronic Drum Sets
Oman	79,656	3D or Auto Blankets
Pakistan	225,419	Grocery Distribution & Delivery
Palau	240	Sponsor UK Molusks Production
Panama	40,467	Auto Pier-Builder - Wood
Papua New Guinea	15,420	Auto Harvest Baby Powders
Paraguay	29,208	Automated Small Engine Manufacture - Marine
Peru	200,269	Robotic Sheering
Philippines	272,067	Technician robots

Country	GDP	#WPProjects Assignments v1.1
Poland	525,863	Tech Architects & QC Approvers
		Interoperability Standards
		Transportation Software
Portugal	227,324	Marina Management System
Puerto Rico	105,149	Construction Drywall – Manufacture & Auto Installation
Qatar	202,450	Automated Fish Net Harvest
Romania	192,094	Robotic Process - Fruit
Russia	2,096m	Drone Peacekeeping – Ground
		Auto Snow Removal
		Oil Alternatives - Paraffin Diesel and Blue Diesel Fuel Plants (perhaps using nuclear ship power)
		Vodka
Rwanda	7,601	Sponsor Cuba
		Automated Pest control
Saint Kitts and Nevis	743	Sponsor Turkey
		Pharma Remicade
Saint Lucia	1,336	Marina Management
Saint Maarten	1,021	Sponsor Sweden
		Pharma Enbrel
Saint Vincent and the Grenadines	709	Sponsor Netherlands
		Pharma Cymbalta
Samoa	691	Farming – Tropical Fruit
San Marino	1,802	Sponsor Singapore
		Pharma Neulasta
São Tomé and Príncipe	342	Sponsor India
		Cars for Wheelchair
Saudi Arabia	748,450	Rapid Charge Batteries - Robotics
Senegal	15,152	Sponsor Panama
		Pharma Humira
Serbia	45,520	Auto House Building
Seychelles	1,445	Prepared Meal delivery
Sierra Leone	4,929	Sponsor New Zealand
		Pharma Spiriva
Singapore	295,744	Robotic Mining System
Slovakia	97,713	Construction Framing Wood
		Bottling & Returns
Slovenia	47,990	Construction Plumbing
Solomon Islands	1,073	Sponsor Belgium
		Pharma Advair Diskus

Country	GDP	#WPProjects Assignments v1.1
Somalia	1,399	Sponsor Thailand Auto Fuel Station Clean Diesel, Gas
South Africa	366,060	New Mining by Satellite
South Korea	1,304 m	Automated TV, & Monitor production
South Sudan	11,804	Sponsor Lebanon Satellite phones
Spain	1,393m	Automatic Park Builder
Sri Lanka	67,203	Robotic Motor options Auto Tea
State of Palestine	12,579	Sponsor Costa Rica Pharma - Nexium
Sudan	54,595	Construction Tile
Suriname	5,299	Sponsor Vietnam Guitars
Swaziland	3,523	Sponsor Algeria Equestrian Equipment
Sweden	579,680	Marina Build System – up to 80 boats
Switzerland	685,434	Surgery – Knee, Hip, Elbow
Syria	35,164	Auto Harvest - Nuts
Tajikistan	8,506	Sponsor Myanmar Pharma Diabetes - Lantus Solostar
Tanzania	44,698	Auto Toilet Paper & Paper Towel
Thailand	420,167	Robotic & Drone Bulldozer
Timor-Leste	4,941	Sponsor Ukraine Pharma Copaxone Hockey Equipment
Togo	4,158	Sponsor Peru Pharma Rituxan & related Fishing equipment, tackle & boxes
Tonga	440	Sponsor Canada Pharma Abilify & related Hockey Sticks, Pucks, Goal Masks
Trinidad and Tobago	24,463	Tropical Fruit Pickers
Tunisia	46,883	Auto cabinet pre-fab, transport
Turkey	822,149	Satellite Driven Well & Irrigation Builder
Turkmenistan	41,851	Automated Kitchen cabinet installation
Turks and Caicos Islands	706	Sponsor Indonesia Medicine - Lyrica

Country	GDP	#WPProjects Assignments v1.1
Tuvalu	38	Sponsor United States Chronic Care Robots
Uganda	26,444	Auto Harvest Apples & Pears
Ukraine	188,350	Tunnel builders – Passenger
United Arab Emirates	599,000	Fishing fillet, package, freeze
United Kingdom	2,678m	Energy to Matter Conversion Sanitation – Waste Treatment Scotch – Single Malt & Whiskey
United States	16,768 m	GPS Threshers Harvest Hawaii - Auto Harvest Macadamia Nuts California – Blue Crude & e-Diesel Cheese & Cream Products Clean Energy – Geo Thermal
Uruguay	55,708	Construction Roofing
Uzbekistan	57,210	Construction Electrical
Vanuatu	800	Sponsor Saudi Arabia Power WheelChairs
Venezuela	371,339	Subway car builder
Vietnam	171,222	Rural Sanitation Black Peppercorns
Yemen	34,714	Auto Door Hardware Rock Cutting to Plan for Home and Harbour Foundation
Zambia	22,384	Auto Window Hardware
Zanzibar	1,161	Sponsor Nigeria Pharma Atripla
Zimbabwe	13,490	Sponsor Ethiopia Pharma Januvia

Chapter 28
—
Terror, Race, Gender, Religion or Empathy

The Business Case for Empathy

The Business Case for Empathy is compelling. And by empathy I am referring to socialistic policies including Anti-Eviction, Universal Healthcare, Anti-Bubble Housing Controls, Guaranteed Incomes, Engineering Safety Nets and similar. So much so in fact, that if you are arguing against Empathy, no matter the context, you are arguing on the wrong side. Let's discuss why this is true next.

After writing four books in Economics, and in years of research and fact finding, I have never been more convinced that reliable incomes and renewed spending power that manages inequity' creates abundance. Abundance in our basic needs of food, water, shelter, energy, education, healthcare, and security within family friendly communities. This Good Life was the basis of the American Dream of the 1950s and 60s throughout the G8 in the 1950s and 1960s.

Citizens that lived within that society had time to volunteer, to raise families, to invent, and they had the freedom to make decisions based on moral grounds without concern that they might do without something and feel forced to make socially irresponsible decisions. Citizens built the stable neighborhoods, schools, and the infrastructure needed to sustain commerce and a Good Life that would become the highest standard in the world.

There were concerns for race, gender equality, and religious persecution as in any society back then, but this period was the one that broke America out of racial segregation on buses and in schools too. It was not until wealth distribution began to become very unequal again in the 2000s that Race, Gender and Religion tempers began to flare once again.

Scarcity drives even the most passive creatures to both offensive and defensive violence. The Venus Project documented a terrific example of this in their video "Paradise or Oblivion" (available to view on YouTube): Picture two cows grazing in a late-spring pasture. With as much grass as they might want, the entire lifetimes of these two cows might be spent without a care nor conflict - and as much grazing as they might ever need sustainably. However, if you introduce a scarcity; if you offer one portion of carrot or honey to one of the two, they will kick, bite and violently fight the other for access to the new scarce resource.

I noticed that a number of popular Google+ forums had also become swamped, along with our news reports – with stories of Religion, Gender Issues, and Racial intolerance.

I found myself defending Socialistic Policy during a recent friendly lunch discussion – and that discussion sent me back to one of my articles and books, to assure the group that Socialistic Policies are very, very good for business at the same time that they are good for people too – as supported by the statistics shown below.

Are these two topics related? The widely published GDP statistics of every country did support that countries whose citizens have a Good Life; a life with strong Wealth Distribution and Wealth Equity (GINI), did also create more Wealth for their country and their social problems were lower as well.

Are concerns about Religion, Race and Gender problems, just symptoms of Wealth Distribution Inequities?

To answer the question, I will offer my conclusions below – but rather than convince the reader with my summary, I will give you the raw data to support your own analysis as well. I have assembled the statistics for countries that generate the most wealth per citizen (Export GDP per Capita) and compared these numbers for just a few example countries. You saw these stats in Chapter 11 as well.

Country	GDP Export per Capita	Multiplier to Dutch Export/Cap	GINI Wealth Equality	HDI	Leaning	American Dream?	Population (In Millions)	Export Quality
Netherlands	$33,652	100%	31	0.915	Socialistic	Yes	17	High
Norway	$28,807	117%	25	0.944	Socialistic	Yes	5	High
United States	$5,057	665%	45	0.914	Capitalistic	No	324	Very High
Sweden	$18,688	180%	23	0.911	Socialistic	Yes	10	Mid
Germany	$18,316	184%	27	0.911	Socialistic	Almost	80	Very High
Canada	$13,286	253%	32	0.902	Capitalistic	No	36	Low
United Kingdom	$7,378	456%	32	0.907	Capitalistic	No	65	Mid
Australia	$10,446	322%	30	0.935	Capitalistic	No	24	Low

GINI – is a statistic that measures country-wide wealth distribution pretty efficiently.

HDI – is the UN's less-than-perfect Human Development Index; I say less-than-perfect because 45% of Hong Kong's residents live in 8×8 apartments without a window – and still the country gets a quite-high HDI. Wealth Distribution is considered little in this calculation.

GDP Export Quality – is an assessment of export quality, and not necessarily quantity. The diversity of exports and the per-unit profitability of exports are important measures as well. For example, selling your mining resources at pennies a ton are low quality exports that put your country at much risk of commodity market fluctuation; far better to sell and ship manufactured pharmaceuticals, or engineered tunneling and automation equipment, at $1000 per box.

Compare the Exports and per Capita Exports of your Country to understand how much revenue that your country is failing to earn every year by not engaging every citizen in commerce. I have called this number "Opportunity Cost" in the chart below.

Country	GDP Export per Capita	Multiplier to Dutch Export/Cap	Export 2015 (in billions)	Opportunity Cost New Export (in billions)	Collapse or Advance Trending?
Netherlands	$33,652	100%	$477	$0	Advance
Norway	$28,807	117%	$103	$17	Advance
United States	$5,057	665%	$1,510	$8,538	Collapse
Sweden	$18,688	180%	$151	$121	Advance
Germany	$18,316	184%	$1,309	$1,096	Advance
Canada	$13,286	253%	$411	$630	Collapse
United Kingdom	$7,378	456%	$436	$1,553	Collapse
Australia	$10,446	322%	$188	$418	Collapse

Enabling the success of The Netherlands' citizens, are some of the strongest policies and economic controls in the world. Dutch Government controls protect spending power, employment, housing, and foreign investment and business ownership. Education at all levels is free, daycare, healthcare, guaranteed incomes and even retirements are all paid for through a graduated tax structure that permits all citizens to participate in businesses and other commercial work.

Taxes are higher here in Holland than in G7 countries presently, but these differences can be considered tax and revenue-neutral in that they cover healthcare, retirements, and other living costs that other countries do not call "taxes".

Conclusions

The Export per Capita statistics of Holland prove conclusively that citizens do take advantage of social benefits to improve both their productivity and the standard of living for their communities as well.

The last G8 country to support "The American Dream" was Russia when Perestroika ended support for a Good Life for all citizens in 1986. Once that universally sustained Good Life was lost, social problems began.

Incarceration Rates and divorce increased; longevity and birth rates decreased, and other stats confirmed too that social problems appear to simply be symptoms of economic inequity that are leading to social collapse.

Country	Incarceration Rate per 100,000	Longevity	Government System
United States	707	75	Pure Democracy Presidential Elections
UK	148	79	Parliamentary Monarchy Public Healthcare Democratic Elections Prime Minister by MP vote
Canada	118	81	Parliamentary Monarchy Public Healthcare Democratic Elections Prime Minister by MP vote
France	103	81	Socialist Parliamentary Republic Public Healthcare Presidential Elections
Italy	100	81	Parliamentary Monarchy Public Healthcare Democratic Elections Prime Minister by MP vote
Germany	78	80	Socialist Parliamentary Republic Public Healthcare Presidential Elections
Japan	49	82	Constitutional Monarchy

Lack of Empathy in History

The Nuremburg Diaries summarized Evil as the Absence of Empathy in 1946. This was a summary meant to highlight not only death camp atrocities to twelve-million Polish, Ukrainians, Russians, and European Jews in World War II, but it was also a commentary on the starvation-wage treatment of labor by business interests and governments putting World War I's Versailles Treaty compensations upon German's until it drove them to prefer a second war to untenable living conditions.

The Golden Rule is a Philosophy Lesson and Sustainability Model that is repeated in every religion; even the ones in antiquity that we know about and are no longer practiced. Ensure that your neighbor has what he needs; just as you have what you need. Remember, Philosophy — is not poetry nor verse, philosophy is the basis of all of our systems of education, school curriculums, and scientific method globally today.

Our secular education and government systems threw the baby out with the bathwater when we failed to recognize that flawed religious organizations should be separated from the infallible social sustainability lessons that fallible organizations, and even religious teachers, were originally charged to protect.

Chapter 29

Values and Sustainability

World Peace – The Transition is a book that invested two hundred pages of research to explain the important economic benefits for philosophy that asks us to build sustainable solutions in society. That work & effort seemed appropriate for a book titled "World Peace".

In Transition Economics, we want to understand that there is also a compelling business case for maintaining strong social values and building Right Plans.

Values and Philosophy that build sustainable economies that resist collapse – and sustain a higher level of Human Rights in a society of abundance - include:

The Golden Rule

The ultimate sustainability lesson as taught by every religion, philosopher, and playwright of note in history. Even religions of antiquity that are no longer practiced recognized that to respect and treat your neighbor as you would treat yourself and your family, was important to your own success as an individual and as a society.

The Golden Rule mandates win-win solutions in every business and personal transaction.

This chart of the Ten Things Great Leaders say to Highly Engaged Teams came to mind as I wrote this and thought to share it here.

Great Leaders say: Thank you! What do you need from me to make this a success? Do you have the capacity to do this now? How could we do this better? Sorry, my fault! I value your contribution! What do you think? You've done a great job! What did we learn from this that we can use next time? I have complete faith in you!

The Definition of Evil

Dr. Gustav M. Gilbert summarized the atrocities reported during the trials of 1945 in Nuremburg, Germany after World War II. Dr. Gilbert was the U.S. Army Psychologist assigned to study the thoughts and motivations of the Nazi Generals put on trial after the war. In his book

"Nuremberg Diary", published in 1946, Dr. Gilbert summarized "Evil as the endemic failing of finding empathy for the situations and suffering of others"; "Evil, I think, is the absence of empathy".

This statement meant to summarize the Nazi Government's atrocities in death camps to Jews, Russians, Poles, Ukrainians, of course, but it also spoke to the "It's just business" attitudes of uncaring wealthy Jewish, and other, business owners who employed slave-wage tactics widely in Germany at the start of the 1929 Great Depression.

CSR – Corporate Social Responsibility

BSR - Business Social Responsibility and CSR – Corporate Social Responsibility, go a long way toward assisting the efforts of Business and Governments to bolster a Good Life worldwide.

By not permitting investment nor lending to projects that would harm society and the earth as well, we prevent situations like Montana – where 100 year old tailing ponds from mining operations long retired, are bursting through decaying reservoir dams.

By directing investment toward sustainable automation, we spend once and realize benefit many times. In the example of tailing ponds, robotic dredgers could process contaminated soil with eco-friendly solvents separating component arsenic and other mining acids from soil. Unrecyclable chemicals can be converted to energy through a plasma-based waste elimination process and reusable chemicals can be transported to working mining installations. Once cleaned, the land can now be made-over to parkland by Spain's automated Park builder.

By monetizing while protecting the environment and society, we build strong, sustainable communities.

Sustainability Planning

When solving global social projects, consider the following definition of Sustainability:

1. Feed a man a fish - and he can eat for a day. This is the Top-Down example project. It works, but benefits are often unsustainable over time.
2. Teach a man to fish, and he will eat for a lifetime. This is a Bottom-Up plan that ensures self-sufficiency and food for a family for a lifetime.
3. Build automated tools that deliver fish automatically to everyone. This plan is a Sustainable Bottom-Up plan because he will have food and he will not be a "have" among neighbors who are "have-nots".

Inequity versus Diversity

Inequity is by far the most expensive social problem of the Winter Phase of any economic cycle. Although well-to-do individuals and organizations can often work diligently to divert attention from this reality, there is little business case for Diversity and only compelling business cases for Inequity; Chapter 15 above explained the business case for Gender Equality & Diversity while Chapters 11 & 28 discussed the Business Case for Inequity.

I mention these two topics together simply because a number of very large and important organizations are deflecting inequity discussions with diversity campaigns recently.

Diversity and Gender Equality Campaign examples include those sponsored by Harvard University, and the recent Canadian Government drive for equal numbers of each gender in Parliament.

Diversity campaigns sound like well-intended programs in support of resolving social problem effects/symptoms between genders and minorities, but these can never be used to divert attention from the cause/disease of far more important problem of inequity; Rich and Poor.

Merit & Reward

"Merit" is the useful product that our work results in; "Rewards" are our compensation for the work that we perform as well. Our work might feed others, we might build schools, teach university students to build the future; we might run businesses that provide good jobs, provide healthcare, build airplanes or build driverless automobiles, and so on. Ideally, our work's reward will increase while our merit to society but this is a difficult discussion in Capitalistic societies where Merit and Reward can even often have an upside-down relationship.

Revere Thought Leadership

The surest way to disincent someone who does ground-breaking, thought-leadership work with fantastic performance, is to not acknowledge, recognize their value, nor permit their contribution.

Alan Turing, founder of the Computer Science and one day perhaps even World Peace itself, was ostracized and chemically castrated with the result that he committed suicide at the age of forty-one. Over four years, from 1940 to 1943, he built and made work from concept, an electro-mechanical computer capable of deciphering Enigma - the most sophisticated mechanical encrypting computer ever built. Enigma was used to protect messages to German assault forces throughout World War II.

Alan's "Turing Machine" was an initial trial and pilot of the binary computer that all digital computers are based on today.

Mr. Turing's genius and contribution are estimated to have saved the lives of twelve million people and reduced World War II by two years. I recommend that everyone and young people especially, take some time out to watch the 2014 movie "The Imitation Game".

Albert Einstein (founder of the Theory of Relativity and Atomic Energy) was relegated to a patent clerk and ignored by academia for two decades; in 1989, Stanley Pons and Martin Fleischmann discovered Cold Fusion but academic peers condemned them to disgrace when they could not recreate their findings. It took twenty-five years to discover failings in the in the peer-review formulations of nickel and palladium nano-powders and then they did indeed create cold fusion reactions.

Years lost; promise squandered; contributions ignored, and a future of clean energy delayed.

Everyday examples of squandered experience and ability include resume-scanning heuristics software and Human Resource interviewers today. HR workers are not SMEs (Subject Matter Experts) and where middle-management has been eliminated in many companies, neither are their MBA leads. The result has been to consider highly-experienced hi-tech engineers poor candidates, and this makes experienced SMEs unhirable in a competitive job market.

Stereotypes of inflexibility, high cost, pension risk, non-relevant skills, distance of past training, ageism, racism, sexism, academic and other biases, and the dismissal of volunteerism, community leadership, and other life experience and measures - all work to increase a growing sense of arrogance within a greatly dumbed-down workplace.

The reality that experience and value are not always well considered is highly detrimental to a society because many of our best and most experienced engineers, sit at home without productive lives while business leaders call for the immigration of offshore experts and immigration. Both of these are among the most short-sighted policies that a government can endorse.

These are all problems that can be solved with an update to Business Ethics courses and governments must control this when required.

Thought Leadership

Building Thought-Leadership requires both strong individual contribution, and a strong process that consistently harvests contribution from new engineers, thinkers, and even random great ideas - on a regular basis. Too often, Administrators view their role as Chief Idea Creators when rather - a good administrator must instead nurture ideas from all of his or her resources – whether from within an organization or even an entire country. With good ideas in hand, he or she must next understand how to build an Expert Panel of SMEs and Engineers that can recommend the projects needed to realize those best-and-brightest ideas reliably.

It takes some character to not let one's ego confuse what is a leader's role in Thought Leadership.

Individual Contributors

> *"Sometimes it's the people that no one imagines anything of, who do the things that no one can imagine."*
>
> The Imitation Game 2014 - Andrew Hodges

We can never under-estimate people nor pre-judge another person's abilities. So often it is those who you might never expect to change the world that do - and the surest way to disincent someone from making important change is to not support nor permit their work, nor to acknowledge their contribution.

This is true for the very great majority of us, whose contributions and passions lead us to raise families and build tremendous communities too. Recognition is certainly as important for people among us who are different in that they do incredible, groundbreaking work with their fantastic contributions in science, technology, mathematics, medicine, and all other fields of study.

Gifted people and savants often struggle when interacting with the rest of us. "Gifts", are double-edged swords because even when a savant takes an active interest in communicating to the outside world, you can imagine that they might find that there are very few others who understand their interests with the same dexterity.

A man or woman who can play any song ever heard in any key or style on a piano, is not going to find very many interesting others in even a concert hall filled with other pianists. A man who can read a theatric play and hear the music just once before performing it perfectly - like my Anglican Minister and friend Ross Norton, will spend a lifetime waiting patiently for even the Mensa club members at his table to catch up. This can be frustrating - so when gifted people also feel bullied or ignored by less capable others, it can be a great challenge for them to take time for relatively unimportant social propriety.

As an aside, the ability to memorize a page and its contents on sight is an invaluable memory skill that I discuss can be developed by most of us in CSQ Common Sense 101. Like remembering names and developing good study habits, improving memory takes effort, a process, and a lot of practice for the rest of us - who are not gifted like Ross.

The surest way to disincent someone who does ground-breaking, thought-leadership work with fantastic performance, is to not acknowledge, recognize their value, nor permit their contribution.

Alan Turing, founder of Computer Science - and one day perhaps founder of World Peace too, was reclusive and permitted by his government to be chemically castrated by local authorities with the result that he committed suicide at the age of forty-one. Over the four years from 1940 to 1943, Mr. Turing built and made work from concept, an electro-mechanical computer capable of deciphering Enigma - the most sophisticated mechanical encrypting computer ever built — used to protect messages between German forces throughout World War II. By 1945, he had redesigned his Turing Machine with wholly digital components similar to the binary computers that we all use today.

Mr. Turing's genius and contribution are estimated to have saved the lives of twelve million people and reduced World War II by two years – as documented in the 2014 movie "The Imitation Game".

Albert Einstein (founder of the Theory of Relativity and Atomic Energy) was relegated to a patent clerk position and ignored by academia for two decades; in 1989, Stanley Pons and Martin Fleischmann announced their discovery of Cold Fusion but academic peers condemned them to disgrace when peer-reviewers could not repeat their findings. It took twenty-five years to rediscover formulations of nickel and palladium nano-powders that permitted cold fusion reactions. Years lost; reputations slighted; contributions ignored, and a future of clean energy delayed.

And those are just three of a dozen examples that come to mind.

Expert Panels:

Experts and Executive Advisory Boards can fill this need in many cases. However, when expert organizations are denied grants and supporting incomes, or when SMEs become unhirable in a competitive job market - as they are today; societies will probably continue the status-quo collapse trending that have led to revolution in 20% of Winter Economic Cycles; and unnecessary social problems in the other 80% of troughs historically.

Look to Expert Panels and Executive Board Advisors with wide consulting and building experiences to safeguard thought leadership impartially and objectively.

As a society, we cannot want dumbed-down business and government workplaces. We want instead, to encourage thought-leadership and lessons-learned in solutions that have turned around economies reliably.

Transition Economics implements Engineering Safety-Nets and Advisory Committees within Projects that ensure that we never have our best, brightest, and most experienced, sitting idle without productive output.

Thought-leadership is a complex but very solvable training challenge.

For Business, Government and Academia

Thought leadership is squandered routinely today in business, in government, and in academia. The importance of a well-thought out process to recognize, protect and encourage great ideas from all sources cannot be over-emphasized. A Chief Thought-Leadership Officer position is a very important addition to every organization and is an essential component of Strategic Planning certainly.

For Business: In the next few paragraphs, I am going to seem to very rude by calling out a number of shortcomings. These are not a shortcoming of you nor your teams – these are scenarios meant to open discussion up to the risks that need mitigating in the protection of thought leadership within your organization.

There are solutions to all of the problems that I am going to suggest; but the first step to solving any problem – is to recognize which problems exist. Here are a few sample problems to begin your own internal discussions.

1) In business, middle-management downsizing has replaced experienced line-managers with a top tier of business administration generalists and finance leads supported by junior Human Resources (HR) admins who are now made responsible for hiring. HR workers rely on interviews and immature key-word-driven heuristics software to fit skilled workers into important roles needed by the organization. Once hired, often these skilled employee hires will report to managers who have superficial knowledge of the business-unit and little experience in the ongoing roles which they lead in their departments.

2) This new business formulation has led to gross inefficiency. The first ERP system that I developed on a mainframe computer cost $250,000 and took a year to build; ERP systems implemented in major companies today can run up to a billion dollars and many take years to implement. The move to procurement and asset management team leadership in department-by-department cloud-managed SaaS applications in recent years, leaves gaps between end-to-end business workflow automations that would have never been an issue in end-to-end workflow solutions previously.

3) Experienced Engineering Leads are considered expensive in both their higher salaries and pension expectations, and so younger bosses, quotas for minorities, gender equality, and preferences for less expensive internal candidates too - all play a part in notably reducing-experience and capability within the organization.

This explains industry calls for offshore skills in recent years. The previous experienced managers would have simply shored up the skills gaps of local engineers; but today's resource managers do not have this ability.

Youth is no assurance of innovation nor capability either. Consider that most of the more experienced workers were given their great opportunities and elevated rank based on merit.

4) Lesser managers believe that they must be the only voice of good ideas from within their group, and worse, many in-house managers and even VPs, only hire people who they see could never replace them in their current executive or director role as well.

Be honest and analytical should you brave these difficult discussions because if I were to pose these scenarios to a dozen people at all levels of an organization, I would find varied answers to the question: "Do these structures exist in your organization - or government?" and "Are they creating a problem?".

These questions challenge ego, IQ, EQ, CSQ, and weaker individuals too, tend not to notice they have a difficult time seeing shortcomings as they are.

Leadership structures can prevent thought leadership by insulating leads from great ideas; structures like communications protocols, good manners, and even from well-intentioned junior staff who act as total information blockers many times. Even HR career-advancement rules and performance reviews can prohibit speaking our ideas or asking for our ideas to be forwarded up through management ranks.

Teams must be full of individuals who are capable of creating great ideas; people who feel free to contribute those great ideas; and then those ideas must make it to strategic planning discussions reliably. It takes a good process to see that thought-leadership happens consistently and that SMEs have a chance to review these ideas too.

Few people have the training to recognize when they are behaving in a way that is not well suited to their leadership roles – and there are many expensive Management Consultants and Business Schools that endorse socially destructive, thought-leadership stopping management structures too so be aware of this within your own organizations.

If societies were not collapsing around our feet worldwide, there would be no need to open up discussion of these structures for re-examination, but a great majority of economies are in a collapse trending today, so another point-of-view is essential in business.

Thought-averaging has extended into **Academia** too; some of today's Faculty Deans are very young and arguably less able to support or recognize what are mature, transparent processes to forward thought-leadership - from both traditional and non-traditional sources. Ideas good and bad come from many sources, such as think tanks, career problem-solvers, authors, futurists, philosophers and historians.

Group-thinking is almost inescapable here as Chair, Dean, and Tenure appointments are very often dependent on the vote of fellow department members and peer-reviewers. Popularity plays a role in academic appointments and the list of ignored genius here is long – as I mentioned above.

All research is of use, but was Oxford-Martin's outgoing banking lead making best use of his organization's extensive resources by showcasing Keynesian deep-dives into status quo banking papers this past spring? There is considerable evidence of these banking theories having contributed to collapse trending worldwide since the 1930s.

In other Universities, helpful research is happening too. I can call out Harvard's Anti-eviction and Princeton's calls to reverse inequity as two programs with terrific merit.

If you have great thought-leadership processes that you might like to share and collaborate on, I monitor contributions on our CSQ Research Google+ or CSQ1.org blogs and I would enjoy hearing your feedback.

In Government, politicians are relationship managers with little economic leadership training, who work with government administrators. "Lifers" (Career employees) are often wise to be mindful of pension or performance-impacting behaviors that affect their positions and salary. Thought-leadership from staff is not consistently encouraged nor rewarded and high-performance in thought-leadership is seldom a requirement of their advancement through their ranks.

In Politics: It took Brexit and Donald Trump to convince the entire world that leadership is often completely blind to what their performance really is; and frustrated populist voting does not ensure any more-correct next steps either.

For example: Bernie Sanders' strong character could have beaten Donald Trump in the 2016 election because, like Mr. Trump, he also stood for change. "Change" is an important theme in an economic cycle's Winter as Reset of the economy is critically important now for Collapse Trending nations. Not realizing this error, the Democratic Party asked Mr. Sanders after the election to defend his campaign because it had probably hurt Hillary Clinton's Status quo campaign.

Freedom

Worth repeating from above, **Freedom** - is a 20-year-old who can choose to start a family; one who can choose an education or work as he or she wishes; one whose children and children's children will live in family-friendly communities that promise lifetimes of interesting worthwhile projects, learning and exploration.

This Freedom is within our ability to build and it is also an imperative of responsible citizens worldwide to ensure.

Values

Why did some Nordic State countries reject the capitalist notions of "Greed is Good" and "Everyman for himself" that became synonymous in the movies with being American? There were a number of very good reasons.

First, the basic communal values of these countries taught them that helping neighbors ensured that their families could find help if ever needed too; often these families lived in a harsh climate with regular occurrences of severe scarcity. An unlucky fire or water damaged food store, could leave whole communities without provisions for winter – and so fathers taught sons to help others first and foremost as needed because, of course, the next natural disaster could as easily befall his own family.

Second, these countries were much smaller – smaller in size, resources and population - so when foreign businesses swooped in and ran off with profits, or polluted the land, or offshored engineering work, the economy felt the job losses of its educated citizens and lost incomes very quickly.

Third, these decisions were morally defendable and the Dutch, albeit progressive and not prudish, were ever-productive and pragmatic. From these values, a pervasively big-picture ethical society evolved dating back from well before the time of the 16th century Puritans.

It's ironic that Amsterdam, Holland's capital city, is also famous for legalized drug use and prostitution. Tourists are quite curious about

Amsterdam's Red Light District and yet the overwhelming majority of Dutch population makes more-worthwhile use of their time and personal lives.

What is the reason for the pervasive success of prostitution in a Puritan stronghold? Amsterdam is a major port city since the 1500s and the steady influx of hard-drinking men on shore-leaves resulted in rapes within the local population. It became obvious that prostitution, albeit "lowly", was also indispensable. By legalizing prostitution and centralizing it first outside city walls - and later into one area of the city, authorities actively protect minors, eliminate forced prostitution and combat the new phenomena of human trafficking. ("Prostitution in the Netherlands," n.d.)

In the Netherlands, guaranteed incomes ensure that its young women do not have to choose between sex work and destitution - as many young women now do in the U.S. where sex-workers are unregulated and growing rapidly. Approximately half of the 3000 Amsterdam women who choose a sex-worker role are battling drug or alcohol addiction. 80% of sex workers are foreign; those people who *are* running from destitution, are protected by this legalization. Sex workers in the U.S. are often students and low-wage workers battling against a $7 minimum wage and high education costs – conditions that do not permit them to make ends meet; this is the definition of destitution. The Dutch are pragmatic and responsible - and the U.S. is, arguably, enacting social governances in a much less responsible way.

Why am I choosing to compare the United States and Holland? I am comparing the two, because at a point their values were absolutely one and the same.

The Mayflower, the ship chartered by America's Puritan founding fathers, was a Dutch ship and America's British forefathers were cut from this Puritan cloth as well. No mere farmers, Puritans were Britain's scholars, lawmakers, great writers, and merchant-class who served as social architects to the British and European Royals.

When some of the Mayflower's passengers expressed their wish to settle with no order of law - and to live under "their owne Liberte", community leaders insisted that each of the ship's 41 settlers were required to sign an accord before off-boarding. That letter became the world's first written Democratic Constitution – the Mayflower Compact. (Foner & Garraty, n.d.)

The American Constitution was influenced by a collection of 150-year-wealthy landowners with influences from the French, Dutch, and Spanish Monarchies, and from private investors who made the eight-year war for American Independence possible.

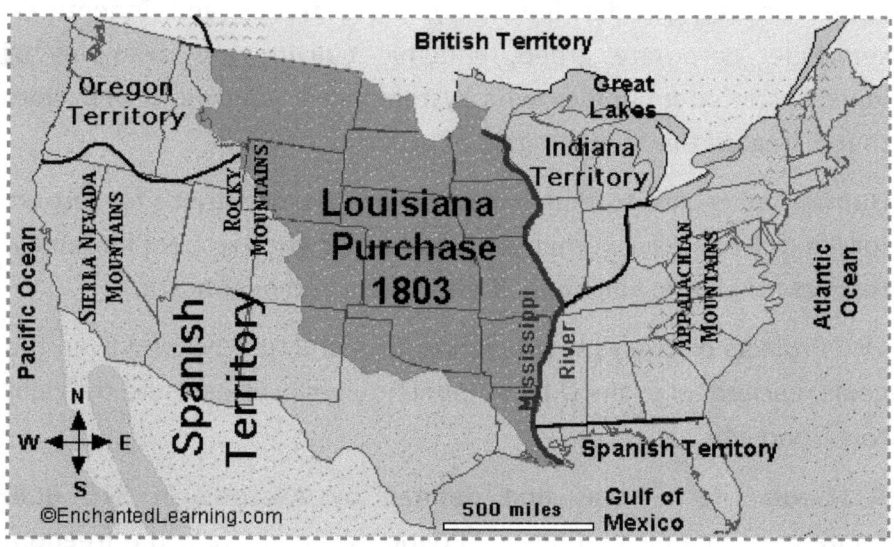

England became America's largest trade and debt partners immediately after the revolution, and the $1.3 billion Livres that France committed to this war bankrupt the country and set off the French Revolution. Spain invested $600 million Reales and both France and Spain assumed huge land grants in America for their support in armaments and military consulting.

Modern American governments might highlight the Constitution of 1776 as being the guiding values and viewpoints of America's first forefathers, but that is certainly not a claim supported in fact by history. (Smith, 2015)

Values are an important measure for any society to monitor carefully. Perhaps this was seen clearly in Populist election results in Canada, the U.S.A. and Great Britain in 2015 and 16.

Human Rights

The way that we set our "low-bar" for acceptable Human Rights as a society often dictates the future for our society as well.

Rape cultures, gender inequality, slave trades and indentured servitude, corporate greed, endemic bullying are examples of injustices in communities who systematically engage in behaviors that disregard the human rights of others.

Human Rights exist to explain our minimum expectations for respect for life, for equality, women and children's rights, respect for family, respect for elders, neighbors, free speech, and healthcare.

#WPProjects discusses that building infrastructure beyond even the goals reached for in the U.N.'s Global Goals, can also ensure the right to a Good Life.

A "Good Life" – was first defined by Aristotle in 325 BCE. Contemporizing his writings in "Politic", a Good Life is the freedom to start a family as a young adult - if you wish, in a family-friendly community, with shelter, food, higher education, transportation, healthcare and the ability to pursue worthwhile projects for a lifetime.

Respect for Life

No advanced society can exist where respect for the life of your neighbors does not exist. When you or members of your family can be killed with impunity, there is no security, there is no peace nor liberty, and there can be no humanity.

Violent passages that protect the right of murder, honor killing, and similar in society have often needed editing in keeping with history's generally increased education levels in society. The Nicaean Council's editing of the Christian Bible in 327 AD by Holy Roman Emperor Constantine is one example. A handful of violent passages remain in that text and in its Latin translation of 410 AD, but none are open-ended nor unconditional after that editing. Violent passages are shortcomings that have cost countless lives century-upon-century and it is my own hope that this century of unprecedented education can finally be the one to eradicate the exposure created by an editorial correction that should have been agree to take place centuries ago.

The United Nations maintains a Universal Declaration of Human Rights which lays out thirty Articles in pursuit of eight essential human needs. Examples of these needs include:
- Recognition of basic human dignity and equal rights are founded upon freedom, justice, and peace
- Where barbarous acts have outraged the conscience on mankind, human beings shall enjoy freedom of speech, belief and freedom from fear
- The right of last resort to rebel against tyranny and oppression and protection of law
- Friendly relations between nations with a common understanding of rights, social progress and better standards of life.

Respect for Equality

Under the U.K. Equality Act of 2010, nine pieces of primary legislation and 100 pieces of secondary legislation were simplified down into one piece of law. With it, people are not allowed to discriminate, harass, or victimize another person because they have any the protected characteristics. There is also protection against discrimination where someone is perceived to have one of the protected characteristics or where they are associated with someone who has a protected characteristic of:

Age
Disability
Gender Reassignment
Marriage and Civil Partnership
Pregnancy and Maternity
Race
Religion and belief
Gender
Sexual Orientation

- Discrimination means treating one person worse than another because of a protect characteristic
- Putting in place a rule or policy or way of doing things that has a worse impact on someone with a protected characteristic, when this cannot be objectively justified (indirect discrimination)
- Harassment includes unwanted conduct related to a protected characteristic that has the purpose of effect of violating someone's dignity or that creates a hostile, degrading, humiliating, or offensive environment for someone with a protected characteristic.
- Victimization is treating someone unfavorably because they have taken (or might be taking) action under the Equality Act or support someone who is.

Who is Responsible?
- Government departments
- Service providers
- Employers
- Education Providers (Schools, Colleges)
- Providers of public functions
- Associations and membership bodies
- Transport providers

Women's Rights

To take education, to have liberty, and to make choices that decide our destiny and happiness, are choices that not all women are permitted to have in our world. This needs correction.

Children's Rights

The right to be children without interference, to take a good and worthwhile education, to not be demanded to work, to have all basic needs of food, family, happiness, shelter, free from fear.

Respect for Family

Prosperity and equal rights have brought an alarming rise in divorce within the G20 countries.

In the 1950s and 1960s in Canada and the United States, it is widely believed that as many as 30% of married men hit their wives at some point in their marriage. For a short time, this embarrassing social problem was considered the responsibility of the wife and she was often asked to treat the repair of her marriage as she might treat her career at a time when a 5% divorce rate created a considerable negative stigma divorce.

Fast-forward sixty years and we see 50% to 70% divorce rates despite a very much smaller 6% wife abuse rate. Men who are weaned on lessons of integrity and honor of the family, marry women who are unwilling to continue in bad marriages in 80% of divorce cases in the United States. This means that 75% of society today are unwilling victims of a Divorce Culture as either children or adults. The cost of divorce to society is staggering because now, two homes are needed instead of one, and children must have double everything. Step-parents, family instability, poverty, anxiety, and a $6 trillion annual additional cost to society in the U.S. results.

Right to Healthcare

The issue of access to Healthcare is dwarfed in many developing nations by the simpler needs of clean water and nutritious food. Once these basic needs are met, efforts to build universal access to healthcare can begin.

In the G20, all countries have access to universal healthcare plans except the United States and India. In both of these countries, private insurance, and some local state funds are set aside for healthcare, but not in a way sufficient to be considered universally accessible at the time of this writing. Documented statistics reveal that poor members of society live twelve years less than the rich on average.

Free Speech

Many nations, the United States and China among them, struggle to ensure that human rights and free speech are consistently upheld whenever a good life is missing for a large percentage of their citizens.

In Capitalist nations it takes funding to get a message heard and in this way the rich have access to a free speech that the poor never could never afford. Authors too, compete not only with volumes of competing publications, but other Media (movies, television, video games) as well until our children prefer distraction to book learning.

An End to Terror

War - is not a Measured Response. The Iraq War killed one million mostly non-combatants, made a handful of oil companies and countries very modestly richer, and it also created ISIS by removing the policing infrastructure that managed militias within Iraq. In hindsight, it was a very poor investment with no recognizable business case as well.

The French attack on ISIS training centers and armaments in the days that followed France's Paris assault in 2015 and Nice Truck Attack in 2016 *was* a Measured Response.

ISIS is a militia of mercenaries, and relatively few in Syria, Iraq, and Somalia are Holy Warriors. Following the money - answers important questions about who are the parties responsible for paying these mercenary salaries and where armaments originate.

When ISIS took Syrian Oil fields, who bought the oil? Proceeds from captured Syrian Oil and support by a terrorized public pumped millions of dollars into a war chest that allowed them to buy weapons. Who sold them weapons? Looting yields little usually, so which are the bank accounts from which paychecks and cash originated?

Young men get on planes from the west to join this anarchic lifestyle because they do not feel they are important at home. At home, they cannot start lives, families, find a home, food, income and other basics of life; in extremist groups they are treated as important and valuable; they are fed and their basic needs are met.

These shortcomings at home, can be fixed sustainably by the strategic social and engineering projects described in Transition

Economics. For an end to terror to be sustained, those same support systems must be available to neighborhoods in high terror countries too.

First Steps are tactical; allow security forces to fix the top-down problem - as they are already working on through Measured Responses. Next, as a community, we need to get to work fixing the bottom-up projects that are detailed in chapters above. By automating our production economies through straight-forward social and technology projects, we solve these support shortcomings once and for all.

This Tactical and Strategic Right Planning is what good leadership looks like; no fear, nor intimidation and no confusion about what are the next steps.

Instead of saturating hearts and minds with media fear-mongering that pushes us closer to a World War III and the end of mankind, give our engineers and communities the support to start a Good Life by worthwhile projects - to "Jihad" (to strive forward) for a sustainable better life.

In Iraq, 9,900 are killed annually by terrorism; in America 12,000 are killed by terrorists with guns every year. Take away the underlying root cause of Terrorism by the providing a Good Life of importance and meaning, filled with worthwhile Top-down and Bottom-Up projects, and strong families and communities for all.

Freedom from Fear vs Global Crises in News

A wide variety of example crises fills our news reports, distract government planning, and keep young people from seeing a positive outlook and clear plan for a brighter future too. This section is from the CSQ 101 course "News vs. Reality".

Last year, the "Big" topic was Global Warming, a few years before that it was the stock markets crashing, next there was war in Iraq, and this year - the big stories are of the takeover in the Ukraine, Syria, Turkey and our Growing Global Populations.

Muslims, Mexicans, Russians – one crisis after another - as sure as you're doing just fine.

Every year seems to bring one or two new theme-stories that keep newspapers selling and the public in an emotional state of mind. First the reports appear in the news, and then they also pop up in our movie screens, television sets, and in popular reading too. At some point, the stories may well have an underpinning of truth to them, but the overwhelming majority lack credulity for the most part.

A Global Energy Crisis

Nonsense. Read the Energy discussions above to confirm this fact.

A Global Water Crisis

With sufficient energy, water can be extracted from seawater or air - and will eventually be synthesized directly from energy as well. The conservation of water is a short to mid-term issue for communities that have built settlements in arid regions where they lack the technology to transport or create fresh water in sufficient supply.

You don't hear about water shortages in Abu Dhabi nor Aruba – for example, as they simply extract clean water as needed from the sea.

Voicing Frustrations versus Solutions

So much for artificial crises; Life's messy, Clean it Up.

Problems are little more than opportunities for smart solutions/projects; all of these problems are straight-forward and solvable projects so simply apply the SUSTAIN Process to each project and work toward never get stuck in that quagmire again.

Let us take one example problem - Clean Water. Let's solve this global problem. How to start?

The problem can be defined as: Water quality is a serious concern for one-in-nine humans worldwide - with developing nations carrying the brunt of the 750 million people who lack access to clean water. There are 840,000 who die from water-borne diseases annually.

First, develop the automatable Geo-thermal energy robot (assigned to America on the #WPProjects list above) and then deploy one of its energy plants to a site in need. The energy plant would harvest energy from a Geo-thermal energy source or Cold Fusion-assisted molten-salt Solar Plant (Morocco) initially, and then electrolyze well or surface water, or collect water from the air with dehumidifying coil collectors (Canada), next.

Leverage these systems to setup energy and water assembly lines in your country. Next, from these assembly robots, deploy energy and water processing plants plus the transportation vehicles and distribution warehouse (Poland & Guinea-Bissau) needed to distribute clean water automatically (Kuwait and Pakistan) throughout the area that requires these household deliveries.

Daily, weekly, hourly (as needed) deliveries of water will be combined with other food and important goods as needed to provide for every household via efficient battery and clean-fuel driven robotic delivery vehicles sustainably.

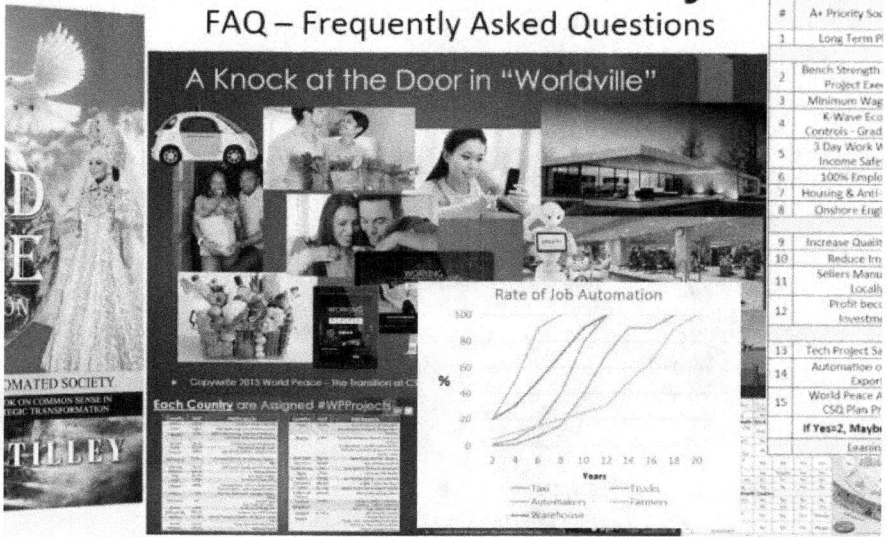

Almost all of these technologies are already developed; what remains incomplete is the integration of these automations only. Rather than read about it, get involved in the engineering projects to eradicate scarcity and build abundance.

Populism is Revolution

Revolution by any other name is still revolution. We simply call it Populism today. According to Wikipedia, Populism is:

"A political ideology that holds that virtuous citizens are mistreated by a small circle of elites, who can be overthrown if the people recognize the danger and work together. Populism depicts elites as trampling on the rights, values, and voice of the legitimate people."

Not surprisingly, this is also a very common attitude in collapsing countries as they make their way toward revolution. Populist is another polite word that avoid use of

Individuals, families, communities, and societies all have needs of food, clean water, shelter (homes), energy, security, healthcare, love, friendship, education, childcare, transportation, family-friendly neighborhoods, and equality of opportunity – to name just a few needs.

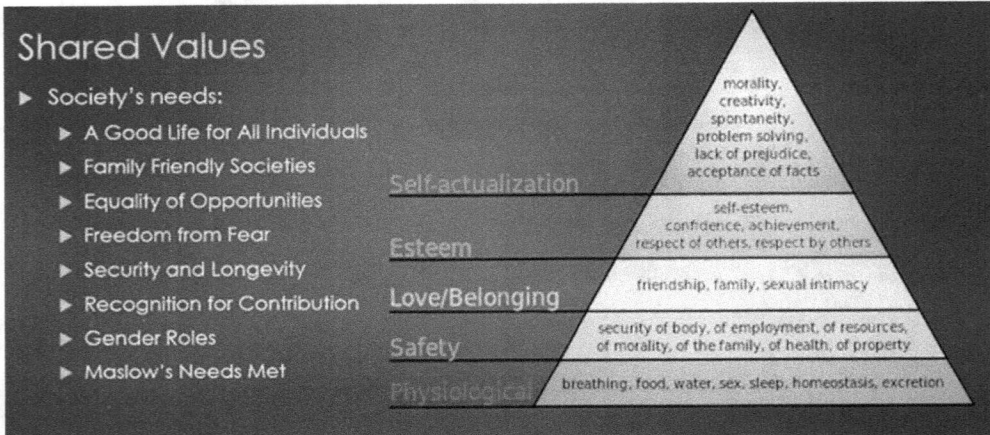

Within a strong family-friendly community, neighbors share values of human rights, gender roles, volunteerism, and freedoms as well.

I rely on Aristotle's summary of the importance of a Right Plan in building the worthwhile Projects that create a Good Life. Recall this definition from Chapter 9:

The Right Plan is the one whose ends, means, practical thinking and purposeful action result in a Good Life. A life full of things you need – and not necessarily a life full of everything you want. With a little luck, goods in body and soul, and by making a habit of good choices that reflect moral virtues of temperance, courage, and justice, a Good Life should be sought and found.

Abridged from Politics 322 BCE (Messerly, 2013)

The challenges that work against providing abundance for everyone are: resource scarcity, high cost, poor planning, poor leadership, inequity, corruption, and similar.

In any Capitalist system, the absence of reliable incomes creates a great difficulty for citizens. It really doesn't matter where incomes come from either. Incomes can come from employment, investment, inheritance, Guaranteed Income programs, Safety-nets, Pensions, and so on.

As long as a society's productivity and automations are of sufficient quality to profitably monetize its exports to other countries, that society will succeed by Capitalistic measures.

Whichever way we get income, incomes gives us the things we need to provide for our families and keep the economy working as it needs to sustain other pension and working incomes.

Societies won't always be reliant on incomes in this way; in an automated society where shelter, food, and other goods come to us robotically (read about #WPProjects below), incomes will likely have lesser importance. But until that work is completed, incomes that afford the costs of living are vitally important for an economy.

If we are lucky, we will find something we love to do in our work at the same time that we earn an income for our families. When we find ourselves in the service of society, our work can give us a strong purpose, identity, social utility, and allow us to build meaningful projects within our communities.

When we return home from work, we will all want to find a thriving, educated, well-supported community and secure families. Most people, but not all, will have children - and marriage is important for building and raising a stable family too.

We want our children to be able to graduate from an education that warrants incomes sufficient to be able to start families and buy homes on their own easily. Ideally, we also want our children to have the option to live in the town where they grew up as well - whenever they want this as well.

And most of us, want to leave this planet knowing that the society that we built and left behind has improved from the one that we came into; we want to understand how society will improve sustainably for future generations.

Which Governments manage which Policy?

In the charts above we have discussed how aspects of society change from phase to phase within Capitalist cycles - and then we reviewed how a number of key policies have to change through the cycles to restart the next capitalist cycle - again. We should also discuss what challenges will our Governments and voters have to navigate in order to realize all of these policy changes.

One challenge is found in that our Governments often split policies between different levels; federal, provincial or state, regional and municipal. Elections are often staggered so that they do not all happen in the same year as well and generally, around the world, four and five-year terms are the norm.

If I look at a Commonwealth country's Parliament System as an example, it does not vary much from a Republic's State-level House of Representatives and Senate Government assignment. Energy will often reside at the Provincial/State level; Immigration, will usually reside with the House of Commons or Congress Federally - as will Military, Trade and International Affairs. Housing will often be managed by Municipal or Regional levels of Government.

However your government splits responsibility of its important social policies, responsibility for a Good Life in every way is usually reliant upon multiple elections and multiple elected legislators and full-time government staff. This delegation makes sense as there is a tremendous amount of work required and citizens want to feel that issues close to home are handled by local people with which they can communicate and work with.

Overarching Governance of all levels usually falls to the Senate (called the House of Lords in Britain). It is important to understand the Senate's role is that of a governance committee that ensures that all important policies of a good life have been assigned to an appropriate level of lower government – at either federal, provincial, regional or municipal levels – and that nothing is falling between the cracks. The Senate is the house that ensures that important policies are not being missed nor run in an inadequate way.

In recent years, this important role has been misunderstood by Senates – certainly by the one in Canada at any rate - and so I want to take a minute here to remind that Senators and Lords are responsible first and foremost to ensure that all branches of government are working toward a sustainable reset of economies – as explained above. Although Housing Authorities will operate at local levels, the Senate should be ensuring continuity and quality controls across all levels of government in your country.

I set aside a letter to send to your Senate or Senator in the Case Studies section below, that is intended to remind them of this important responsibility – should you find as I did that they are not understanding or insisting that important changes are being made as they should.

Chapter 30

—

Case Studies

Case 1: Albert Einstein

> "I am convinced there is only *one* way to eliminate these grave evils, namely through the establishment of a socialist economy, accompanied by an educational system which would be oriented toward social goals. In such an economy, the means of production are owned by society itself and are utilized in a planned fashion. A planned economy, which adjusts production to the needs of the community, would distribute the work to be done among all those able to work and would guarantee a livelihood to every man, woman, and child."

EINSTEIN

"I am convinced there is only one way to eliminate these grave evils, namely through the establishment of a socialist economy, accompanied by an educational system which would be oriented toward social goals. In such an economy, the means of production are owned by society itself and are utilized in a planned fashion. A planned economy, which adjusts production to the needs of the community, would distribute the work to done among all those able to work and would guarantee a livelihood to every man, woman and child."

Apr 13, 2016

Einstein is so smart he figured our post scarcity economics is the only way. Sounds like a line from TVP or WPProjects.

I love and respect Einstein, but he wrote this before the collapse of the Soviet Union.

Soviet Union failed to monetize their production (they failed to sell their cars, watches, jets, etc.); China had the same system and yet it succeeded in monetizing their economy. Both countries had the same system; with two different outcomes. Capitalism too - falters every 60+- years predictably - just like clockwork - and then Wealth Distribution resets it like in a monopoly game. The approach robotically automates the 250 basic things that provide for a good life - like water, food, transport, shelter, etc. so that money becomes more of a nice-to-have than an essential.

+ I like that plan as it stands now money is the end all be all of every major decision.

+There are too many references from great thinkers and philosophers in history to count - on that exact point. Money is a very bad thing for anything above and beyond the basic bartering functions - and you have to actively keep it distributed with economic controls too. Read Aristotle, Shakespeare, the Bible, Q'uran, K-wave Theory on-and-on... 2008's debt forgiveness did not go far enough. If it had, we would all be in a 60-year boom right now.

+ I want to live in a steady state economy. I want off the capitalism rollercoaster ride.

That's is very doable with enforced Wealth Distribution targets. You can maintain capitalistic policy and sustain a K-Wave Spring indefinitely through high Minimum Wage, Guarantee Incomes, graduated tax, housing and democracy controls too ... removing the rollercoaster of Capitalism is only possible with responsible economic controls and socialistic policies - none of this "Low Tax", trickledown nonsense. The side benefit is that in this configuration, society allows all citizens to participate in wealth creation too - an average of 50% increase per American and 200% increase per Canadian, Australian and Britain (based on the Dutch GDP Exports per capita).

+ agreed I despise Allan Greenspan's notion of trickle down economics. Better he should call it what it is, table scraps economics – and only when the masters are feeling really generous of course. In fact I blame his mentor Ann Rand and all of her "Greed is good" disciples screw all those misguided fools.

Case 2: A Letter to Country Leads and Innovation Ministers

Here is a suggested Agenda for our upcoming meeting to discuss next steps in building a Country Innovation Strategy:
1. What is Innovation?
    - Investment in Renewable Automation
        - farms that produce 30,000 broccoli daily; mushrooms, bananas, kiwis - there are 100 grocery items; 35 pharma items; initially. Pick a couple...
        - highest exports and imports first - buys self-

sufficiency and ends trade deficit problems
2. What is not Innovation?
   - Social Networking Apps
   - Big-data that optimizes marketing effectiveness; most fintech, regtech, etc.
3. Thought-Leadership Strategies
   - Exec Advisory Committee & Fellows
   - Expert Councils - per Industry
4. Right Plans - Country Society Planning;
   - Not I4.0; but Connected Smart-Factories
   - Automation Transition Maturity & Throttle Rates
     - http://csq1.org/transition-economics-maturity-model/transition-economics-maturity-model-tm/
   - #WPProjects
     - http://csq1.org/world-peace-transition-projects-faq/Support Programs
   - Supports
     - Grants - Academic, Industry, 5% to 10% of Infrastructure Spending (on Livingry)
     - Engineering Safety-Nets - for Tinkerer Engineers and Engineers in Medical, Automation, etc.
5. Canada as a World Leader
   - #WPProject is a Global Right Plan - Canada could lead here easily.
   - Multi-billion dollar companies - this is similar to Britain's announcement this week.

These discussions could fill a few meetings - but as a high-level intro... it's a start.

Case 3: A Letter to your Senator

Sitting back and waiting for smart change to happen on its own is beyond wishful thinking; become a person of letters instead. This letter I sent to the Senate of Canada after a string of broadcast messages announced the group's Policy Work. Issues of superficial importance to society seemed to be the mainstay of this important body of legislators for more than a year before I sent the note around to each Senator individually.

The letter was a level-setting list of what are the important policy discussions in any Society.

Another approach might have been to send a Voter Evalutation Chart (above) with the statement – Here is what I am voting for this time around. You decide if you want my consideration - or not...
Dear Senator <?>:
Is it shocking how little we are all taught about which systems are available to us to provide the basics of a good life in Canada? Should we all be taught important Civics in topics of Freedom, Housing, Energy, Wealth Distribution, Innovation, Education and Democratic Process?

1. **Freedom and Quality of Life**:

    Question: What is a Good Life and Freedom? Is it...

    a. The example of a 1960s **Capitalist Housing Policy** anywhere in Canada or America:
        i. 18-year-olds could leave home for a job and afford to finance a home of their own; a University School dorm and courses cost what a summer job could afford
        ii. a bigger home could be bought when young couples married so that a family could begin...
        iii. Average age of new moms was 20;
        iv. a husband worked and wife could not easily attended a University and one language was the norm; this discouraged education in poorer families and created

an education gap. A cottage lot was available for $250 in 1960 when laborer incomes would have been $450 per month roughly. Cost of a new home was $5,000 to $10,000 - mortgage rate 8%?
   v. Divorce rate 10%; divorce was socially discouraged

America began to lose this good life in 1970s with recessions - they stopped supporting the American Dream for whoever could not find employment nor income.

  b. The example of a **Communist Housing Policy** from pre-perestroika (1986) Moscow:
     i. 18-year-olds could request a home of their own, or school dormitory (for free);
     ii. a bigger home was assigned when young couples married so that the family could begin...
     iii. husband and wife attended a free University (when marks and interests warranted it and these schools offered a better education than American Universities - often graduated kids in three languages), and a cottage was assigned to each family for summer vacations away from the city.
     iv. Average age of new moms was 20;
     v. - Divorce rate much less than 10% and divorce was socially discouraged too - right up to Perestroika in 1986
     vi. - Russia was pretty well the last G8 to support the American Dream for all of their kids.

Answer: They both were pretty darned good and a lot better than what our kids have today!

2. **Wealth Distribution**

Wealth Distribution - The Dutch citizen generates 200% higher

GDP Revenue (Wealth Generation per Capita) than a Canadian. Why? Because Holland Guarantees Incomes, protects local home ownership, encourages self-reliance and prevents the off-shoring of its engineering; it offers free Education, free Childcare, Healthcare, Minimum Wage of $20, and retirements with Nursing Home Care. Rather than encourage lazy people that sit idly, everyone can participate in production - and clearly, they do just that.

3. **Housing**
    a) In the USA, 70% of homes are mortgaged and the percentage still owing on those mortgages has increased year-over-year these past five years until it exceeds 50%. In fact, the ownership of homes vs loans has gotten to the point where a great majority of **these loans will never be repaid**. The illegal financial practice of extending loans that cannot be repaid is called Usury.
    b) A **Land Grant system** is needed now to permit mortgage holders to return their homes to Crown ownership - and continue living there at higher tax rates - rather than be evicted into the streets when interest rates are raised in defense of falling currencies. This Land Grant could be switched back to Capitalist Policy Ownership when the citizen cashes up again.
    c) **Housing Bubble** protections are required now to ensure that access by young families is available to housing in areas where there is employment opportunity; and that homes, work, schools, hospitals, etc. are close-by the schools where they grew up as well. To deny this protected option is to detonate a community of families; literally requiring them to dissolve and scatter - rather than to care for their young and elderly together easily.

4. **Energy:**
    a. **Geothermal Electricity** - whenever you can dig down into the earth and heat a sufficient amount of water to 300 degrees, you can run a city on the steam created. Why is this true? The earth is a natural Thorium Nuclear Reactor.
    b. **Cold Fusion** - clean, safe energy forever - it works; it is recently proven at an industrial scale; it is in the public domain. It works by amplifying power by up to 10 times.
    c. **Zero-Pollution alternatives to combustible fossil-fuel Crude Oil.** Princeton has said we can produce all we need where we live; no pipelines, no drilling; and incomes can be protected by guaranteed income programs so that we all come out ahead. Google search "Audi's Blue Crude" for more. Why are we not looking into these options?
    d. **Cheap, Plentiful Thorium Nuclear Reactors** - were designed at the same time as our far more Expensive & Rare Uranium Reactors - for reasons of profit only I think. China has now set out to build Thorium Reactors based on North American and European designs from the 1960s - so that we can buy back those designs from them?

    As a side note - a Thorium Reactor mounted in a car could run that car for 100 Years on a piece of Thorium the size of a Pea. As plans for such a reactor were penned in the 1960s and nothing done about them, why do we not look into these technologies too?
    e. **Pipelines** and part-time **Wind** & **Solar farms** equal Energy Poverty. Refine locally with our local manpower and then ship high-profit finished product by rail; it's a no-brainer.

5. **Innovation and Automation**
    a) 72% of 180 countries globally are in Collapse Trending - including ours. Capitalism has troughed every sixty years -

Google "K-Waves Financial Sense" to confirm and read more ... The Wealth Distribution strategies described above control these swings and sustain a Good Life all by themselves. This is why the socialistic-policy countries in Europe can be said to still enjoy "the American Dream" today. This is because they sustained their Economies with sustainable TE-Mature Policy.

   b) When our basic needs of life are produced automatically and robotically (food, clothes, shelter, energy, transportation, security, etc), money becomes unimportant - methodically and safely; evolving our society gradually for the better. Investing in, and leading these Transition Projects - #WPProjects at CSQ1.org - puts Canada in a Real* leadership seat for a change...

6. Social Supports

Our active working years amount to just 50% of our 80-plus-year lifespans, but our incomes need to keep the economy active all of our lives.

7. Education, Health Care, Day Care, Retirement Support

All supported by TE-Mature Policy, Business Cases, TE Throttle Rates, and SUSTAIN Project Method

8. Democratic Processes

   a) **Election of Candidates** - Democracy and Policies are important; Candidates are much less important - but we do not teach our kids that is this the case. We grew up voting for a candidate and assume there are no better options. At present time, we give voters no, or very little, access to vote on Policy directly.

When Policy is permitted to be influenced by financial gain - and elected MPs are unable or unwilling to challenge tainted policies, the Democratic process can be considered legitimately corrupt. When our young people do not - or even refuse to - vote, we can find this particular failure is often the cause of it.

b) **Election of Policy** - Today, we have the internet-based infrastructure needed to permit democratic voting by Policy. Our elected MPs can suggest pros and cons and then we can vote on each individually for the first time in History. When are the first Pilots to begin?

Case 6: Party Policy Reform Letter

Kick-start Policy Reform within your favorite Political Party with this letter:

Dear Conservative/Democratic Party President <insert name>….

The challenge with policy in any political organization is that there seems too much to discuss.

Last year, we came to a Recession Year Election with policy that "held the course", status-quo, which was inappropriate for these economic times.

This fact amounts to a failing within our internal party-constitutional processes; and this is a problem that we will want to correct to protect against repeating these election results again in future.

Our constitution has to target policy that ensures incomes and renews spending-power. At the same time we must protect our Policies from non-SME opinions, conflicts-of-interest, and special interest contributors – especially those moneys given specifically with expectation of financial return.

We also have to protect our Policy from the changes of party marketing leads that decide suddenly that they "can't win an election this way" and then make their own policy on the spot. Clearly they do not understand how a well-communicated, well-vetted plan can always win both electoral hearts **and** minds.

When a career Engineer, Doctor, Lawyer, or Economy Expert votes on Policy upon which they are an expert SME (Subject Matter Expert), that vote cannot be weighed equally against a sprinkler repair technician who is voting as he feels his father might have wanted.

Within professions there are experts and generalists too; a cancer specialist needs to weigh in more heavily on Policy specific to Cancer, than would a GP - for example. As you drill down within a community of Cancer physicians, opinions are often divided here as well.

Genius gets tucked into a corner, and democracy languishes if you don't do this - Einstein was made to "sit out" by academic rivals for two decades so that they could figure out his thinking; Turing was abandoned by peers and was dead by age 41, Pons and Fleishmann were disgraced for 25-years for discovering Cold Fusion.

Poland is the world's longest running democracy; it was a Super-Power, six times the size in 1600 that was at the start of WWII when its population was almost obliterated after 400 years of Democratically-elected compromise.

The point here is, that in a democratic system, once we create well-vetted policy - we have to protect it - we have to document it transparently, version control it, and then control or permit revision by brilliant authors carefully - and then communicate it well of course.

Democracy is very important - and history teaches us that Democracies dumb-down and weaken if we don't stand on guard in this way.

Current Party Policy Processes use a failed process - by design. Believing in this "policy of feelings" - equals not understanding that our organization can never meet the needs of any country that needs tough Economic Controls set in place from time to time.

The following list of Policy is proven to support Advancing Economies in all but 5% of adopting countries – which compares to 72% of economies that are currently collapsing under our status quo policy today.

INCOMES DISTRIBUTE	Transition Economics Mature Policy 5% to 10% in Collapse	Collapse Policy 72% of All Countries are in Collapse
Working Families & Individuals	Graduated Tax, Big-Business Tax Avoidance Crackdown, Inequity targets, Local Business Ownership, Local Govmt Business Ownership	Low Tax, Trickle-down, Middle-Class Focus, Diversity, Cheap Imports, Immigration, Small Business w/o support
Unemployed	Guaranteed Cost of Living Incomes, Business Automation Revenue Sharing	No benefits for underemployed nor all unemployed
Retirement	Employee & Pension Fund Protections, Cost of Living minimums, CSR & Business Accountability	Offshoring, Misuse of female diversity rules, ignoring pensions
Children	Free Mastery-based Education & Transition Economics Voter Education	Failure to support 20-year-olds starting families, High Divorce Rates
Others	Cost of Living Benefits for Disabled	Insufficient Support, High Debt Servicing Costs
Automation	Engineering Safety Nets, #WPProjects & Renewable Automation Support, Multi-Party Long Term Strategic Planning	Innovation programs that fail to support Renewable Automations and Trade & Selling Needs

	Transition Economics Mature Policy 5% to 10% in Collapse	**Collapse Policy** 72% of All Countries are in Collapse
Healthcare & Benefits	Universal Healthcare, Employee Benefit Plans to Revenue Neutral Business Case targets	Private Plans, Patents that externalize Government R&D
Childcare	Universal Daycare & Free Education incl. University	Unaffordable Childcare
Housing	Public Housing (30%) Controlled to Inflation, Land Grants, Anti-Eviction, and Foreign Ownership Taxes	Energy Poverty, Housing Bubbles created by lax controls
Food & Goods	License Renewable Automation, Local Harvesting, Driverless Transport & Distribution, Local Self-Sufficiency & Abundance	Insufficient Farm Compensations, Failure to develop automation, Dollar & 99p Stores, Cheap Imports, Austerity Measures
Energy	Abundant Geo-Thermal, Hydro, Cold-Fusion, Thorium Nuclear, Zero-Pollution Fuels	Part-time Wind & Solar, Fossil Fuel Oil Pipelines, Energy Poverty
Transport	Driverless-cars & Automated Goods Delivery, Auto Road & Rail Construction	Infrastructure w/o Automation & Trickle-down Protection, Transit

See Transition Economics and TE-Mature Policy at http://csq1.org/forums/topic/introducing-transition-economics/

Sincerely…

Chapter 31

-

Summary

Capitalism does work and it is sustainable, but not by itself. Without economic controls, managed targets for wealth distribution, or a proactive reset like "Jubilee", predictable 60-year Great Depressions have repeated consistently throughout our history. Great Depressions, therefore, are perfectly normal and will go on for longer or shorter lengths of time depending on how long it takes for us to reset these Economic Cycle and get incomes with spending power back into the hands of citizens.

Responsible economic controls look like those put in place by the Netherlands and Scandinavian countries twenty-five years ago. Citizens there continue to ensure that wealth stays somewhat distributed and that all citizens can benefit from universal healthcare, childcare, incomes, pensions, drug benefits, and so on.

Because Dutch citizens have the economic and personal freedom to engage in commerce, the average citizen here produces three times as much wealth (GDP Export) than a Canadian citizen – and 50% more than an American. That's another half-trillion dollars of new wealth lost to the U.S. economy annually; and $60 billion to Canada, the U.K. and Australia. That's is an incredibly large opportunity cost to lose in defense of inequity.

Recall that the social systems of capitalist G7 nations like America, Canada, Germany, France, etc. for systems like housing, debt, employment, insurance, pensions, bonus and reward, were all built on the notion that one-job-per-family would afford the family's retirement, education, and all other needs. When the one-job-per-lifetime job model stopped working over these past twenty years, these systems no longer sustain families who now have to resort to dual-incomes, poverty, homelessness, high divorce rates and other well-documented social problems.

This is the Education that our Last Generation need to take away now.

At the end of any Capitalist Cycle that has failed to manage inequity, we must ensure incomes and we have to reverse years of market bubbles, energy poverty, rampant inflation, and similar - so as to give families spending-powers again. One ubiquitous income per family must afford our basic needs again. Governments will have to devise walk away plans divorcing future generations from laws and unsustainable contracts that prevent this important change. Laws are intended to serve a society – and not the other way around.

Freedom and Opportunity must be restored – and then maintained sustainably in policy and economic controls thereafter.

Renewable Automations - ease the impact of future inequity and reduces the importance of money in society too. This also promises to return us to the value-based rewards systems that our Greatest Generation recognized too. Socially beneficial and moral decisions and action are possible once again once opportunity is restored.

Building communities that support families and Good Lives need a supporting infrastructure. People need guarantees of income, food, healthcare, education, in family friendly communities, in order to be able to think seriously about helping others.

Resetting an economy according to a Plan means that all policies must be driven by a compelling Business Case – so always ask for it before you vote.

I'll leave with a Leadership TODO list is:

1. Call every CEO to start hiring - free stimulus
2. Anti-eviction protections – put an end to homelessness.
3. Restore spending power - Day Care Affordability, Rental & Housing controls,
4. Look at foreign support spending - push for real sustainability in that spending and not an endless, increasing stream of outgoing cash.
5. Remove Tax Evasion's Legal protections
6. Restore Pensions
7. Target Wealth Distribution by introducing economic stimulus from new sources like the unemployed and retired through income programs.
8. Donald Trump is right - let's get our engineers working here again by putting an end to offshoring - like the Netherlands did 20 years ago; their hi-tech industry is thriving and engineers are in demand.
9. Automate of our basic needs - food, basic goods, roads, rail, housing, transport, energy. Invest in Livingry instead of Weaponry and endless infrastructure spending.

The social projects needed to reset the Economic Cycle have already started in Transition Economics "Mature" Countries and the renewable automation projects are just beginning.

Funding Local Renewable Automation Hi-Tech Companies will pay dividends to both countries and private investors the same. Governments who have lagged in the support of Renewable Automations should be focusing on these technologies directly for the far more promising investment returns – and future too.

The Transition Engineering Safety Net

Assuming governments adopt Transition Economics Mature Policy and Cycle-Managing Policy strategies, the work to automate our production economies will continue uninterrupted as jobs transition to new income safety-nets, and to an Engineering Safety Net, at a rate governed by GDP Export Targets, TE-Throttles and Responsible Throttle Rates, unemployment rates, and retraining program budgets as described in TE Throttles above.

Without engineering safety nets, our society risks having our most senior engineers unemployed due to their pension risk and then turned into underemployed or unproductive assets. With safety nets, our best and brightest engineers build a technology safety net that makes money irrelevant and a Good Life sustainable.

None of these automation projects are beyond our reach over just the next few years. We can ignore this disruptive automation - and it will happen painfully anyway, or we can plan for the change and implement it professionally and intelligently.

Rollout Worldwide

As countries around the world are fine tuning their TE-Mature Right Plans and new policies, Automation Projects continue to mature. New engineering teams come online to help the automation efforts, sustained by Transition Economics throttling algorithms that ensured resources were available after solutions were built locally.

Standardized status reports manage country budgets and other SUSTAIN Method Project KPIs. Administers coordinate status reports and World Wide Coordination rolls up to a #WPProjects countdown clock.

Within a surprisingly short time, our automated economy will begin to take on the heavy lifting and make a Good Life sustainable for us all.

I am very confident that this will be our last Last Lost Generation ever with your help.

For me, it is never enough to stop at explaining "<u>W</u>hat" the future holds, it is critical to explain "How" to achieve great things too. By explaining the how step-by-step, I think you will find it different from any other book in Economics that you have ever read.

This book just touched on the SUSTAIN Project Management Method but you are going to want to get the books and certify you company too.

Building sustainable policy is little different from building futuristic robots in that the way that we build plans for these projects happens in just the same way. TE-Mature Policy builds excellent lives all by itself – as mentioned; Renewable Automations make our societies easily sustainable too - and both programs require smart planning, good project process, brilliant engineers, hard work, strong leadership, and then with your support - anything is buildable.

We've tackled a trip to the moon, we already have robotically-built self-driving cars; ask yourself - What's Next? When will we have a robotically build home, a two-day work week, a Great Life in a robotically built family-friendly community?

So many books in Government Policy and Economics set out to discuss problems in and stop there. I hope that The Last Generation and Transition Economics, sorted out a lot of questions in real-world events for you; as it did for me.

The exercise of researching and writing this book, and then

summarizing all of my researches into easy to understand, buildable lists, allowed me to feel very confident that your country and our world have some very exciting times ahead.

Vote in support of – and become a project lead or team member for - a successful Transition Economics Policy and Project in your country.

Once you do – you can feel very confident that this effort can make your life's work meaningful and worthwhile too.

A successful economy and an automated society is our generation's Moon Launch mega-project – so let's get this Business Case approved and let's get started!

ABOUT THE AUTHOR

The process to transition our Last Generation to sustainable new economic cycles and automation heralds from learnings in economics, history, leadership, government, technology, engineering, business, physics and the social sciences. I hope that readers leverage my example and are inspired to keep their studies wide and goals important.

To give you some idea where these books come from; I have raised five terrific kids, built six high-tech startup companies, I learned something new every day of a 25 year high-tech engineering career after four years of post-secondary study.

I am a Lecturer, CEO; CIO, CTO and I have led 300+ complex projects in dozens of major programs with budgets up to $100+ million, 100,000 staff, and 200+ project team members in organizations that ran more than 500+ projects year after year. I have terrific coping skills that I exercise and practice often; I have worked with terrible bosses and terrific bosses.

Joseph Schumpeter had a famous line in the 1940s that I like - I know how to make a dance partner shine. I ran a full marathon a couple of years ago, I love mountain biking and hold my own sparing with a couple of different Marshall Arts belts; I read widely, travel, study languages, cultures, Religions, Academia, Business, Technology, Geography, and History.

I can say easily that I am a capable big-picture, process-minded and strategic thinker with a well-balanced resume for someone who thinks they know enough about building a Good Life - to be able to write an authoritative book that figures it all out too.

Family and society are important to me. My forefathers were Puritans and Founding Fathers, and so my history connects me to the importance of leveraging lessons from the past.

In community life, I founded one of the largest local Minor Football organization in Toronto, and that volunteer work gave me the chance to hire eight management teams annually and to get to know 800 young people and their parents every year as well. Volunteerism connected me to the next generation and to their hopes for a bright future.

Transition Economics is an important subject and book and I hope that I've provided a valuable foundation to begin from here. Writing it has changed the way that I look at politics and policies.

I choose to write books that are prodigious and to build projects that are worthwhile and can change the world for the better. I hope that your life is filled with successful worthwhile projects too.

Everything is Buildable - just keep working the problem.

Wishing you All the Best.

Edward Tilley

PS. Look for my new books Teaching Doers and Modern Love in 2017.

Bibliography

4 commit suicide in Spain over evictions as EU struggles with unemployment — RT News. (2013). Retrieved from https://www.rt.com/news/spain-eviction-suicide-homeless-184/

Acland, F. (2016). New Scientist: Cold Fusion is Back |. Retrieved from http://www.e-catworld.com/2016/09/16/new-scientist-cold-fusion-is-back/

Aldrick, P. (2015). Bubblenomics is back. Markets have become completely detached from economic reality – and it's going to get ugly – Telegraph Blogs. Retrieved November 23, 2015, from http://blogs.telegraph.co.uk/finance/philipaldrick/100024624/bubblenomics-is-back-markets-have-become-completely-detached-from-economic-reality-and-its-going-to-get-ugly/

American Press. (1995). A 120-Year Lease on Life Outlasts Apartment Heir - NYTimes.com. Retrieved November 23, 2015, from http://www.nytimes.com/1995/12/29/world/a-120-year-lease-on-life-outlasts-apartment-heir.html

Amnesty launches Spain anti-eviction campaign - The Local. (2015). Retrieved from https://www.thelocal.es/20150624/amnesty-launches-first-campaign-against-spanish-evictions

Babcock, J. (2015). Spain's Ruling Party punished in local elections. *The Telegraph*. Retrieved from http://www.telegraph.co.uk/news/worldnews/europe/spain/11627935/Spains-ruling-party-punished-in-local-elections.html

Bartz, G. (2005). The Code of Hammurabi. Retrieved from https://en.wikipedia.org/wiki/Code_of_Hammurabi

Beck, R. (2010). Immigration, World Poverty and Gumballs - NumbersUSA.com - YouTube. Retrieved from https://www.youtube.com/watch?v=LPjzfGChGlE

Blodget, H. (2011). TRUTH ABOUT TAXES: Are Today's Rates High? Retrieved November 8, 2015, from http://www.businessinsider.com/history-of-tax-rates

Bourbeau, J. (2016). Rural Ontarians left in the dark as electricity bills skyrocket | Globalnews.ca. Retrieved from http://globalnews.ca/news/2796958/rural-ontarians-left-in-the-dark-as-electricity-bills-skyrocket/

Brooks, M. (2016). Cold fusion: Science's most controversial technology is back | New Scientist. Retrieved from https://www.newscientist.com/article/mg23130910-300-cold-fusion-sciences-most-controversial-technology-is-back/

Calkins, D. (n.d.). How to make CO2 (Carbon Dioxide). Retrieved November 8, 2015, from https://www.youtube.com/watch?v=b_qdkKnftt8

CBC News. (2013). 30% of U.S. homeowners are mortgage-free - Business - CBC News. Retrieved from http://www.cbc.ca/news/business/30-of-u-s-homeowners-are-mortgage-free-1.1307957

Clemente, J. (2014). Americans Can't Afford Higher Electricity Prices. Retrieved from http://www.forbes.com/sites/judeclemente/2014/11/24/americans-cant-afford-higher-electricity-prices/#3066b5ec7261

Combustion Efficiency and Excess Air. (n.d.). Retrieved from http://www.engineeringtoolbox.com/boiler-combustion-efficiency-d_271.html

Davis, J. (2015). Diesel From Water And Carbon Dioxide | IFLScience. Retrieved November 8, 2015, from http://www.iflscience.com/chemistry/audi-make-diesel-water-and-carbon-dioxide

Delmendo, L. C. (2016). Property Prices in Netherlands | Dutch Real Estate Prices. *Global Property Guide*.

Diggs, C. (2015). Russian Floating Nuclear Power Plant. Retrieved November 8, 2015, from http://bellona.org/news/nuclear-issues/2015-05-new-documents-show-cost-russian-nuclear-power-plant-skyrockets

Drugs.com. (2014). Top 100 Drugs for Q4 2013 by Sales - U.S. Pharmaceutical Statistics. Retrieved November 18, 2015, from http://www.drugs.com/stats/top100/sales

Edward Tilley. (2015). World Peace 1.8.pptx - Google Slides. Retrieved from https://docs.google.com/presentation/d/1c-

7y2VknAT62acnBr42RF_FOAz_7SCYy2HmalbaeDU8/edit#slide=id.p4

Edward Tilley. (2016a). Topic: Socialistic Policies are Good for Business, Gender, Race, and Religion Issues | CSQ Research. Retrieved from http://csq1.org/forums/topic/socialistic-policies-are-good-for-business-gender-race-and-religion-issues/

Edward Tilley. (2016b). Topic: The Gender Inequality Problem in Canada | CSQ Research. Retrieved from http://csq1.org/forums/topic/the-gender-inequality-problem-in-canada/

Elia, J. A., Baliban, R. C., & Floudas, C. A. (2012). Nationwide energy supply chain analysis for hybrid feedstock processes with significant CO_2 emissions reduction. *AIChE Journal*, *58*(7), 2142–2154. http://doi.org/10.1002/aic.13842

EPA. (2001). AMENDMENTS TO THE CALIFORNIA ZERO EMISSION VEHICLE PROGRAM REGULATIONS: December 2001. Retrieved November 8, 2015, from http://www.arb.ca.gov/regact/zev2001/fsor.pdf

Erin Davis. (2015). Notable.ca | The Minimum Amount of Money Needed to Live in Toronto. Retrieved from http://notable.ca/breakdown-this-is-the-minimum-amount-of-money-a-young-professional-needs-to-live-in-toronto/

Exports per Capita. (n.d.). Retrieved from https://en.wikipedia.org/wiki/List_of_countries_by_exports_per_capita

Foner, E., & Garraty, J. A. (n.d.). Mayflower Compact - Facts & Summary - HISTORY.com. Retrieved from http://www.history.com/topics/mayflower-compact

For richer, for poorer | The Economist. (2012). Retrieved from http://www.economist.com/node/21564414?fsrc=rss%7Csp

Garrett, R. (2015). Inside An Eviction Party—For Two Anti-Eviction Groups | Hoodline. Retrieved from http://hoodline.com/2015/12/inside-an-eviction-party-for-anti-eviction-groups

Gas Turbines. (n.d.). Retrieved from https://en.wikipedia.org/wiki/Gas_turbine

Gordon, I. (2009). Fourth K-Wave Winter. *Longwave Group*.

Govan, F. (2016). Spain's suicide rate jumps to record high in economic crisis - The Local. Retrieved from http://www.thelocal.es/20160331/suicide-rate-in-spain-reaches-new-record

Gray, R. (2015). Audi creates DIESEL from air and water and its already powering a car | Daily Mail Online. Retrieved November 8, 2015, from http://www.dailymail.co.uk/sciencetech/article-3059025/Audi-creates-DIESEL-air-water-fuel-future-powering-car-driven-German-minister.html

Grossman, S. (2014). These Maps Show Every Country's Most Valuable Exports | TIME. Retrieved November 18, 2015, from http://time.com/106666/world-export-maps/

Hamilton, K. (n.d.). What's At The Bottom Of The Deepest Hole On Earth? | IFLScience. Retrieved from http://www.iflscience.com/environment/deepest-hole-world/

Hargraves, R. (2016). Thorium Energy Alliance. *Thorium Energy Alliance*.

Hatanaka, B., Keohane, J., Leech, J., & Nobrega, M. (2013). Pension shift puts decades of progress at risk - The Globe and Mail. Retrieved from http://www.theglobeandmail.com/opinion/pension-shift-puts-decades-of-progress-at-risk/article14966106/

Herring, D. (2003). *The Puritans and Education*.

Homeless in Russia: A visit with Valery Sokolov, by Jan Spence, Share International Archives. (1997). Retrieved from http://www.share-international.org/archives/homelessness/hl-jsrussia.htm

Hussain, Y. (2015). Oil-by-rail economics suffers amid narrowing spreads | Financial Post. Retrieved from http://business.financialpost.com/news/energy/oil-by-rail-economics-suffers-amid-narrowing-spreads?__lsa=240d-a4ea

HUTZLER, M. (2014). U.S. SECURITY IMPLICATIONS OF INTERNATIONAL ENERGY AND CLIMATE POLICIES AND ISSUES. *THE INSTITUTE FOR ENERGY RESEARCH*. Retrieved from http://www.foreign.senate.gov/imo/media/doc/Hutzler_Testimony.pdf

IANS. (2016). India doesn't lag in developing thorium-fuelled nuclear-reactor: MR Srinivasan, former AEC chairman - The Economic Times.

Retrieved from http://economictimes.indiatimes.com/news/science/india-doesnt-lag-in-developing-thorium-fuelled-nuclear-reactor-mr-srinivasan-former-aec-chairman/articleshow/52489649.cms

Investing in Dutch property. (2016). Retrieved from http://www.expatax.nl/investmentproperty.php

Jackson, A. (2011). Saving for Retirement | Canadian Centre for Policy Alternatives. Retrieved from https://www.policyalternatives.ca/publications/monitor/saving-retirement

Kerr, F. (2016). Kerr: Nenshi is right — NDP power lawsuit is "outrageous" | Calgary Herald. Retrieved from http://calgaryherald.com/opinion/columnists/kerr-nenshi-is-right-ndp-power-lawsuit-is-outrageous

Kevin Press. (n.d.). How do employee benefit plans work? | Sun Life Financial. Retrieved from https://www.sunlife.ca/ca/Learn+and+Plan/Money/Insuring+your+health/How+do+employee+benefit+plans+work?vgnLocale=en_CA

Klein, J. (2014). Can Thermoelectric Generators Compete Against Solar Photovoltaics? Retrieved October 26, 2016, from http://insights.globalspec.com/article/98/can-thermoelectric-generators-compete-against-solar-photovoltaics

Knapton, S. (2015). "Impossible" rocket drive works and could get to Moon in four hours - Telegraph. Retrieved from http://www.telegraph.co.uk/news/science/space/11769030/Impossible-rocket-drive-works-and-could-get-to-Moon-in-four-hours.html

Latimer, H. (1858). *The sermons and life of ... Hugh Latimer, some time bishop of Worcester, Volume 2*. Aylott. Retrieved from https://books.google.com/books?id=eJZQAAAAYAAJ&pgis=1

Leonhardt, D. (2016, December 8). The American Dream, Quantified at Last. *New York Times2*. Retrieved from http://www.nytimes.com/2016/12/08/opinion/the-american-dream-quantified-at-last.html

Lopoukhine, R. (2014). Top 5 Reasons Why Geothermal Power is Nowhere in Canada | DeSmog Canada. Retrieved from http://www.desmog.ca/2014/02/26/top-5-reasons-why-geothermal-power-nowhere-canada

Messerly, J. G. (2013). Aristotle on the Good Life | The Meaning of Life. Retrieved November 9, 2015, from http://reasonandmeaning.com/2013/12/19/aristotle-on-the-good-and-meaningful-life/

Ministry of Economic Development. (n.d.). Price - New Zealand Geothermal Association. Retrieved from http://www.nzgeothermal.org.nz/price.html

Mirza, J. (2015). The great Canadian tax dodge | Junaid Mirza | Pulse | LinkedIn. Retrieved from https://www.linkedin.com/pulse/great-canadian-tax-dodge-junaid-mirza

Moir, R. W., & Teller, E. (2004). THORIUM-FUELED UNDERGROUND POWER PLANT BASED ON MOLTEN SALT TECHNOLOGY. *Laurence Livermore National Laboratory*, *1*, 7. Retrieved from http://web.archive.org/web/20101005073843/http://www.geocities.com/rmoir2003/moir_teller.pdf

Moon, H., & Zarrouk, S. J. (2012). EFFICIENCY OF GEOTHERMAL POWER PLANTS: A WORLDWIDE REVIEW. *New Zealand Geothermal Workshop*, *19*.

Moore, P. (2016). The TRUTH about carbon dioxide (C02): Patrick Moore, Sensible Environmentalist - YouTube. Retrieved from https://www.youtube.com/watch?v=5Smhn1gL6Xg&feature=youtu.be

Neate, R. (2014). Scandal of Europe's 11m empty homes | Society | The Guardian. Retrieved from https://www.theguardian.com/society/2014/feb/23/europe-11m-empty-properties-enough-house-homeless-continent-twice

Noor, J. (2013). Detroit Anti-Eviction Campaign Keeping Families in Their Homes. Retrieved from http://therealnews.com/t2/index.php?option=com_content&task=view&id=31&Itemid=74&jumival=9738#newsletter1

Norton, M. I., & Ariely, D. (2011). Building a Better America--One Wealth Quintile at a Time. *Perspectives on Psychological Science*, *6*(1), 9–12. http://doi.org/10.1177/1745691610393524

OKBM. (n.d.). Reactor Plants. Retrieved November 9, 2015, from http://www.okbm.nnov.ru/english/npp

Parussini, G. (2013). U.S. CEO Blasts French Work Culture - WSJ. Retrieved from http://www.wsj.com/articles/SB10001424127887323549204578316101127838118

PragerU. (2016). Are Electric Cars Really Green? - YouTube. Retrieved from https://www.youtube.com/watch?v=17xh_VRrnMU

Press, K. (2015). How do employee pension plans work? | Sun Life Financial. Retrieved from https://www.sunlife.ca/ca/Learn+and+Plan/Money/Retirement+savings/How+do+employee+pension+plans+work?vgnLocale=en_CA

Prostitution in the Netherlands. (n.d.). Retrieved from https://en.wikipedia.org/wiki/Prostitution_in_the_Netherlands#History

Quigley, C. (2012). Kondratieff Waves and the Greater Depression of 2013 - 2020 | Christopher Quigley | FINANCIAL SENSE. Retrieved November 8, 2015, from http://www.financialsense.com/contributors/christopher-quigley/kondratieff-waves-and-the-greater-depression-of-2013-2020

Refugees of the Syrian Civil War. (n.d.). Retrieved from https://en.wikipedia.org/wiki/Refugees_of_the_Syrian_Civil_War

Ryken, L. (2015). A Puritan's Mind » That Which God Hath Lent Thee: The Puritans and Money. Retrieved December 10, 2015, from http://www.apuritansmind.com/stewardship/rykenlelandpuritansandmoney/

Safety of Nuclear Reactors - World Nuclear Association. (2016). Retrieved from http://www.world-nuclear.org/information-library/safety-and-security/safety-of-plants/safety-of-nuclear-power-reactors.aspx

Smith, J. L. (2015). How was the Revolutionary War paid for? - Journal of the American Revolution. Retrieved from https://allthingsliberty.com/2015/02/how-was-the-revolutionary-war-paid-for/

Snyder, M. (2014). If Economic Cycle Theorists Are Correct, 2015 To 2020 Will Be Pure Hell For The United States. Retrieved from http://theeconomiccollapseblog.com/archives/if-economic-cycle-theorists-are-correct-2015-to-2020-will-be-pure-hell-for-the-united-states

Solar Thermal Tower. (n.d.). *Wikipedia*. Retrieved from https://en.wikipedia.org/wiki/Solar_power_tower

TaxPayer.com. (2016). Canada's National Debt Clock: The Canadian Taxpayers Federation. Retrieved from http://www.debtclock.ca/

Tedesco, T., & Shecter, B. (2016). Inside the risky strategy that made Canada's biggest pension plans the new "masters of the universe" | Financial Post. Retrieved from http://business.financialpost.com/news/fp-street/inside-the-risky-strategy-that-made-canadas-biggest-pension-plans-the-new-masters-of-the-universe

Thorium Energy Generation. (n.d.). Retrieved from http://www.thoriumenergyalliance.com/downloads/thorium_Energy_Generation.ppt

Tilley, E. (2016). Topic: Transition Economics Business Case | CSQ Research. Retrieved from http://csq1.org/forums/topic/transition-economics-business-case/

Toussaint, E. (2012). Debt Cancellation in Mesopotamia and Egypt from 3000 to 1000 BC | Global Research - Centre for Research on Globalization. Retrieved November 8, 2015, from http://www.globalresearch.ca/debt-cancellation-in-mesopotamia-and-egypt-from-3000-to-1000-bc/5303136

UN critical of Canada's record on housing, homelessness - Business - CBC News. (2016). Retrieved from http://www.cbc.ca/news/business/un-housing-crisis-1.3480979

UNRUH, G., KIRON, D., KRUSCHWITZ, N., Reeves, M., Rubel, H., & ZUM FELDE, A. M. (2016). Investing For a Sustainable Future. Retrieved from http://sloanreview.mit.edu/projects/investing-for-a-sustainable-future/

US-ITC. (2016). USITC Interactive Tariff & Trade Data. Retrieved from https://dataweb.usitc.gov/scripts/user_set.asp

US Census Bureau, D. I. D. (2015). Income - US Census. *US Government*. Retrieved from http://www.census.gov/hhes/www/income/data/historical/household/

Weston, J. (2016). Car gets 400+ MPG – Fuel-Efficient-Vehicles.org. Retrieved from http://fuel-efficient-vehicles.org/energy-news/?page_id=968

Wiki. (2016). Geo-Thermal Energy. Retrieved from https://en.wikipedia.org/wiki/Geothermal_power

Wikipedia. (2016). Bashar al-Assad. Retrieved from https://en.wikipedia.org/wiki/Bashar_al-Assad

William Thompson | Department of Political Science | Indiana University Bloomington. (2016). Retrieved from http://polisci.indiana.edu/faculty/profiles/wthompso.shtml

Wolf, E. N. (2015). Wealth Inequity in the United States. Retrieved from https://en.wikipedia.org/wiki/Wealth_inequality_in_the_United_States#cite_note-levyinstitute.org-12

Index

#diamondbattery, 262
#WPProjects, 24, 53, 105, 125, 127, 138, 140, 144, 223, 259, 321, 364, 365, 368, 371, 384, 420, 428, 431, 443
100-MPG, 264
3D-printed bridge, 368
3D-Printed luxury home, 367
3D-printed six-story building, 367
3D-Printers, 212
5700 years, 262
99p, 92
Absence of Empathy, 401
abundance, 52, 141, 239, 396, 403, 429, 430
Abundance, 106, 111, 223
Advancing (A), 117
Aggregate Performance, 115
Aircraft Carriers, 250
Alcohol Fuels, 269
algorithms, 337
American Dream, 41, 47, 65, 82, 361, 396, 440, 443
Amnesty International, 193
Anti-austerity, 193
anti-eviction, 179
Anti-eviction, 451
Anti-Eviction, 193
anti-evictions, 91
Artificial Intelligence, 149
Assembly Lines, 141
assembly robots, 212

Audi, 264, 367
Audi Automotive, 141
Audi's Clean Diesel, 270
Automate, 451
Automated bricklaying, 212
automation, 46, 51, 58, 110, 173, 233, 334, 367, 370, 374, 378, 398, 429
Automation, 20, 23, 38, 105, 147, 148, 321, 442
Autumn, 47
avoid collapsing, 338
B2B, 279
B2C, 279
baking, 21
Banking, 22
bankruptcy, 91
bargaining power, 278
Battery Cars, 271
Benefits, 176
better imaging, 178
better medicines, 178
Bible, 362
Biodiesels, 269
birth rates, 400
Birthrates, 229
Blue Crude, 264
Bottom Tax Rate, 159
brilliant planning, 83
BSR, 405
Bubblenomics, 99, 185
Buckminster Fuller, 96
Bush, 84

Business, 279
Business Case, 280
Business Case for Empathy, 395
Business Cases, 339
Business Plan, 147
Calculus, 115
California Gold Rush, 31
Call every CEO, 451
Canada, 65, 194
Canada's Imports, 225
Canada's Exports, 225
Canadian Mortgage Insurance, 227
Cancer industry, 138, 300
Cancer Research, 137
Capitalism, 179
capitalistic, 32, 213, 284, 354, 437
Capitalistic, 42, 45, 58, 183, 206, 349, 351, 407
Capitalistic Policies, 82
carbon 14, 262
carbon polymer, 260
Carbon Tax, 236
Castro, 63
cerebral plasticity, 179
Charities, 137
Cherry picking, 80
childcare, 65
Cisco Networks, 95
Clean Coal, 249
Clean Fuels, 249
clean water, 138
Clean Water, 125
CMI, 65, 67, 83, 84, 148, 151, 218, 228, 368
CO^2, 236
Coal, 249
Coal Plants, 260
Code of Hammurabi, 350
CoL, 338
Cold Fusion, 247, 303, 318, 386, 390, 408, 428, 442, 445
cold-fusion, 262
, 225
Collapse Trending, 57, 207
Collapsing (C), 117
Collapsing G8 G20, 120
collapsing trend, 148
communal ownership, 136
Communications Plans, 341
commute, 87
Connected Smart Factories, 53, 125
Connected Smart Factory, 138
Conservative Investments, 146
Consumer Price Index, 99
Corrado Gini, 164
corruption, 59
Cost of Living, 338
Cost-of-Living, 170
Costs and Benefits, 340
Credit Cards, 22
Crude Oil, 270
CSR, 405
cubicles, 87
Culture, 233
Currency Devaluing, 32
Cycle Economics, 20, 21, 29, 31, 50, 71

Cyclic Economic, 75
cyclic economic controls, 351
Dacha, 82
Dachas, 206
DayCare, 451
debt, 63, 148, 149
Debt, 168
Debt forgiveness, 85
Debt is Forgivable, 50
debt load, 168
debt purchasing, 19
Debt to Asset Ratio, 168
debt to society, 94
Debt+Inflation=Prosperity, 32
debt-forgiveness, 50
Debt-Forgiveness, 95
delivery vans, 141
Democracy, 59
Democratic Reform, 308
Democratic Reforms, 67
Design competitions, 212
Diesel, 267
Direct Logic, 94
disabled, 178
distribution centers, 269
Distributive Justice, 32
diversity, 398
Diversity, 92
divorce, 400
Divorce, 56
Divorce rates, 47
Dollar Stores, 92
downstream, 87
driverless car, 139
driverless taxi, 139
drone cargo planes, 141

eating better, 179
Economic Controls, 350
Economic Cycle, 85
economic inequity, 400
Economic Sectors, 21
economic stimulus, 451
Education, 66
educational systems, 349
eight cylinder engine, 178
ElectroMagnetic, 257
electro-magnetic fields, 239
EmDrive, 257
emergency vehicles, 141
Emmanuel Saez, 50, 89
Empathy, 401
empty homes in Europe, 194
En Viager, 191
Energy Collectors, 259
energy poverty, 92, 237
Energy Poverty, 255
Energy Robots, 142
Engineering Nets, 96
Engineering Onshoring, 126
Engineering Safety Nets, 94, 136, 138, 300
engineering safety-net, 305
Engineering Safety-Net, 20
Engineering Safety-Nets, 179, 412
EV1, 268
Eviction Defense Collaborative, 192
Evil, 401, 405
Executive Advisory Boards, 411
Expert Panels, 411

Export per Capita, 76, 399
externalizing, 137
Extortion, 278
Facebook, 178
farming, 21
fintech, 80
first fully automated farm, 22
Fischer-Tropshe, 263, 270
fishing trawlers, 141
Flywheel, 261
foreign support spending, 451
Fossil Fuel, 269
Free University, 230
freedom, 82, 420
Freedom, 10, 46, 48, 58, 109, 416, 439
Fuel Oil, 249
fuel trucks, 141
Fuels, 263, 273
fulfilling, 180
Full-Time Power, 238
fun-fact, 262
Gas Turbines, 257
Gasoline, 267
GDP Export per Capita, 282
GDP Export Quality, 398
Gender Equality, 230
gender inequality, 53
Geodesic Dome, 96
Geothermal, 442
Geo-Thermal, 239
German economy, 63
Ghost Cities, 187
GINI, 226, 398
GINI Coefficient Index, 164
Global Goals, 128

Global Right Plan, 53
Global Transition, 128
Global Warming, 236
Glycerines, 269
Golden Rule, 402
Good Life, 47, 338
Government Hiring, 96
Governments, 137
governments want to, 137, 300
GPS-driven tractors, 141
graduated tax, 152, 159, 399
Graduated Tax, 127, 167
grants, 93
Graphene Nanosheets, 260
Great Depression, 27, 50, 192, 350, 405
Great Leaders, 404
Gross Domestic Product, 81
guaranteed income, 57, 325
Guaranteed Income, 153, 175, 228, 431
guaranteed incomes, 65, 97, 138, 159, 199, 300, 418
Guaranteed Incomes, 19, 76, 97, 104, 108, 122, 129, 136, 143, 147, 151, 155, 321, 339, 364
HDI, 398
healthcare, 65
Highly Engaged Teams, 404
Hitler, 63
hoarding, 178
Home Owners, 203
Home Ownership, 206
homeless, 178

homeless shelters, 91
Hot Fusion, 248
housing, 20, 31, 37, 38, 61, 65, 66, 83, 97, 101, 108, 152, 185, 201, 227, 297, 325, 399, 437, 450
Housing, 42, 46, 55, 58, 77, 104, 125, 185, 189, 191, 197, 198, 215, 226, 322, 349, 364, 432, 439, 441
housing bubbles, 351
Housing Bubbles, 186
housing controls, 97, 193
Housing controls, 451
Housing Controls, 198
Housing Policy, 206
human rights, 53, 128, 221, 371, 424
Human Rights, 201, 354, 420
Humanitarian, 232
Hydro (Water) Turbines, 256
hydrocarbon, 264
Hydrogen, 263, 269, 271
hydroponics, 22
hyper-competition, 90
hyperinflation, 99
Immature, 120
Immigration, 65, 126, 224
Imperial College of London, 367
importance of money, 450
incarcerated, 178
incarceration rate, 94
Incarceration Rates, 400
Incineration, 250
Indentured Servitude, 188

Inferno, 52
inflation, 99
Inflation-Driving, 32
Infrastructure Spending, 95
Insurance, 22
Intellectual Property, 146
intellectuals, 179
Interest Rates, 66
international trade agreements, 278
Isaac Newton, 115
Job Automation, 136
jobs lost monthly, 24
Joseph Schumpeter, 179
Jubilee, 31, 49, 85, 449
Keynesian, 22, 32, 87, 352
Keynesian Economic Theories, 280
Keynesian Theories, 280
King George, 61
Kola, 240
Kondratieff, 74
Kondratieff-Wave, 75
K-wave, 436
K-Wave, 28, 32, 56, 61, 75, 171, 198, 202, 204, 208, 228, 236, 311, 313, 443
K-Wave Autumn, 360
K-Wave Spring, 297, 360, 437
K-Wave Winter, 308
labor force, 178
Labour Pool, 153
Landlords, 204
Large-Sized Business, 90
Legal Recourses, 237
LENR, 247, 248

Level 1, 120
Liberte, 69, 419
license, 137, 300
Lithium-Ion, 260
living longer, 179
living wage, 167
Living Wage, 167, 170
livingry, 259
Livingry, 96, 223, 451
Logic Roundabouts, 93
Long/Mid/Short Term, 340
longevity, 400
major companies, 95
manufacturing, 21
mass unemployment, 193
Math, 118
Mature, 128
Mayflower Compact, 84, 182, 307, 358, 419
Mean Time to Profitability, 340
mental-health, 179
Methanol, 269
micro loans, 95
Mid-Size Business, 90
military, 178
Military Spending, 96
MineCraft, 212
minimum guaranteed incomes, 338
minimum wage, 167
Minimum Wage, 190
mining, 21, 280
mini-retirees, 179
Mini-retirements, 178, 179
mitigation, 22

monetary devaluation, 99
Monetary Policy, 32, 349
monetizable, 144
monetize, 44, 48, 60, 82, 158, 282, 367, 431, 436
monetizing their economy, 83
Money Lenders, 50
monopoly, 30, 31, 311, 436
Monopoly, 21, 27, 30, 42, 72, 104, 311, 349
Monopoly Game, 85
mortgage banking fraud, 193
MTBF, 341
Multinational, 278
Mussolini, 63
NASA, 139, 257
Natural Gas, 263, 273
Netherlands, 65, 83, 194, 277
New Economic Cycle, 136
New Energy Poverty, 237
Nordic, 46
Nordic Nations, 45, 48, 53
Nordic State, 417
Nordic States, 12, 18, 30, 58, 103, 230
Nuclear Diamond Batteries, 262
Nuclear fission, 253
nuclear reactors, 262
nuclear waste, 262
nuclear-powered long-term energy, 262
Nuremberg Diary, 405
Nuremburg, 404
Nuremburg Diaries, 401
Obama Care, 181

offshore, 178
one-stop-shop, 90
onshoring, 155
opportunity cost, 39, 80, 320, 325, 367, 449
, 154, 399
Optimistic/Pessimistic/Realistic, 340
overall GDP, 281
ownership by citizens, 277
ownership stakes, 19
packaging, 21
Panic, 350
paraffin oil, 269
Paraffin Oil, 263
Patent, 146
Paul Krugman, 50
pension avoidance, 351
pension incomes, 91
Pensions, 173
per capita export income, 65
Perestroika, 81, 230, 399
philanthropic organizations, 95
Philosophy, 402
Photovoltaics, 255
Pipeline spills, 272
pipelines, 269
Pipelines, 270
Plasma, 250
Podemos, 193
Populism, 12, 429
Populist, 63, 333, 420
post-cold-war, 22
prisoners, 94, 178
Procurement, 89

Project Management, 280
Propane, 263
Pros and Cons, 340
Protecting Culture, 233
public housing, 194
Puritan, 84
Quintile, 168
R&D, 137, 138, 300
Race, Gender and Religion, 396
racism, 53
Radio Frequency Resonant, 257
radioactive diamonds, 262
RAI, 79, 148, 150, 218, 340
RAI - Country Index, 149
RAI Company Index, 149, 291
RAI Country Index, 149
Rail vs Pipeline, 272
rate of automation, 337
ratios, 337
reactor ships, 254
Reagan, 82
Recognition, 346
regtech, 80
religious extremism, 54
Renewable, 135
Renewable Automated, 144
renewable automation, 19, 77, 291
Renewable Automation, 79, 80, 96, 127, 136, 138, 147, 177, 300, 321, 340, 364, 367, 368, 450
Renewable Automations, 111
renewed spending power, 11,

109, 238
Rental, 451
Renters, 204
Replicator, 141, 367
reset, 31
Resetting an economy, 451
responsible controls, 226
responsible management, 83
Restore spending power, 451
retirement, 20, 37, 41, 65, 83, 152, 159, 160, 173, 399
retrain, 87
Return on Investment, 340, 367
Revenue Neutral, 322
revenue-neutral, 124, 153, 399
revolutionary, 63
Revolutions, 353
Right Plan, 53, 120, 403
Right Plans, 129, 452
robot, 380, 382
robotic, 368
Robotic assembly lines, 142
robotic farms, 178
robotic house builder, 376
robotic tool, 376
robotically assemble, 376
robotics, 370
Robotics team, 383
robot-maid, 375
ROI, 340
Roosevelt, 84
Roundabout Logic, 93, 94
Safety-Nets, 126
Salaries, 89

Scarcity, 106
Scarcity of incomes, 53
Scientific Method, 280
Self-driving taxis, 141
Service Management, 346
Setting Targets, 167
shipbuilding robots, 142
Sideways logic, 93
Skilled Labor, 232
Slavery, 188
slow-hiring, 351
small business, 197, 284
small business owners, 91
small-businesses, 92
SME, 70
social collapse, 400
social interactions, 179
social problems, 53, 400
socially irresponsible, 143
Solar Thermal Tower, 251
Spain, 194
special interest groups, 280
spending power, 31, 70, 78, 85, 106, 120, 123, 152, 183, 284, 334, 399, 450
Spending Power, 104, 364
Spread Inc, 22, 52
spring, 313
Spring, 42, 311
Starbucks, 277
status-quo, 20, 39, 50, 63, 66, 201, 272, 351, 412, 444
Status-quo, 59, 93
stay connected with others, 179
staying in shape, 179

Steam Turbine, 256
Stimulus Spending, 95
suicide, 91, 179
Suicide, 193
summer, 313
Summer, 43
Super Capacitors, 261
Superconducting, 258
Sustain, 126
SUSTAIN Project Management Method, 143
sustainability, 403, 451
Sustainability, 406
Sustainability Model, 402
symptoms, 400
tax, 124, 153, 399
tax avoidance, 159, 278, 337
Tax Avoidance, 126, 127, 238
Tax Evasion, 451
tax haven, 178
tax-neutral, 151
TE Maturity, 118, 129
TE Throttles, 24
TE-Maturity, 115
TE-Maturity Level definitions, 120
terrorism, 54
Tertiary Economy, 22
the 1%, 93
The American Dream, 399
The Golden Rule, 404
The number one priority, 85
ThermoElectric, 254
thorium, 263
Thorium, 238, 241, 244, 245, 249, 268, 322, 386, 442

thought leadership, 128
Thought Leadership, 407, 409
Thought-Leadership, 438
throttle algorithms, 281
Throttle Rate, 24, 337
Throttles, 337
tinkerers, 144, 179, 371
Top Tax Rate, 159
Torah, 362
trains, 141
Transition Economics, 12
Transition Economics Throttles, 279
transportation, 22
Transportation, 125
TV, 179
TV Awards, 346
two-step introduction, 280
U.N., 193
U.S. Debt, 83
U.S. Government, 139
ultracapacitors, 261
underemployment, 351
unemployment, 68, 351
United Nations, 118, 128, 222, 368, 421
United States, 65
Universal Day Care, 230
universal healthcare, 166
Universal Healthcare, 173, 181
Unreported unemployment, 68
Unskilled Labor, 232
upstream, 87
uranium fuel cell, 262
Uranium Reactor, 241

usury, 218
Usury, 42, 46, 50, 58, 102, 127, 187, 202, 207, 226, 364, 441
variety, 142
Venus Project, 396
Volkswagen, 266
volunteerism, 408, 412, 430, 456
wage stagnation, 170
WarCraft, 212
Waste, 250
Wave, 34
Wealth Creation, 361
Wealth Distribution, 85, 350, 361
weaponry, 259
Weaponry, 96, 451
Winter, 49, 56, 360
Winter Phase, 85, 280
World Peace, 403
World Peace Transition Projects, 53
World War II, 353, 362
World War III, 362
World Wars, 63
Worldville, 212
worthwhile change, 179
worthwhile life, 180
worthwhile work, 179

www.ingramcontent.com/pod-product-compliance
Lightning Source LLC
Chambersburg PA
CBHW060447170426
43199CB00011B/1122